INSURANCE LAW IMPLICATIONS OF DELAY IN MARITIME TRANSPORT

CONTEMPORARY COMMERCIAL LAW

Causation in Insurance Contract Law
by
Meixian Song
(2014)

Insurance Law in China
by
Johanna Hjalmarsson and Dingjing Huang
(2015)

Maritime Law in China: Emerging Issues and Future Developments
by
Johanna Hjalmarsson and Jingbo Zhang
(2016)

Illegality in Marine Insurance Law
by
Feng Wang
(2016)

FIDIC Red Book: A Commentary
by
Ben Beaumont and Annette Anthony
(2018)

Insurance Law Implications of Delay in Maritime Transport
by
Ayşegül Buğra
(2018)

INSURANCE LAW IMPLICATIONS OF DELAY IN MARITIME TRANSPORT

AYŞEGÜL BUĞRA

informa law
from Routledge

First edition published 2018
by Informa Law from Routledge
2 Park Square, Milton Park, Abingdon, Oxon OX14 4RN

and by Informa Law from Routledge
711 Third Avenue, New York, NY 10017

Informa Law from Routledge is an imprint of the Taylor & Francis Group, an Informa business

© 2018 Ayşegül Buğra

The right of Ayşegül Buğra to be identified as author of this work has been asserted by her in accordance with sections 77 and 78 of the Copyright, Designs and Patents Act 1988.

All rights reserved. No part of this book may be reprinted or reproduced or utilised in any form or by any electronic, mechanical, or other means, now known or hereafter invented, including photocopying and recording, or in any information storage or retrieval system, without permission in writing from the publishers.

Whilst every effort has been made to ensure that the information contained in this book is correct, neither the author nor Informa Law can accept any responsibility for any errors or omissions or for any consequences arising therefrom.

Trademark notice: Product or corporate names may be trademarks or registered trademarks, and are used only for identification and explanation without intent to infringe.

British Library Cataloguing-in-Publication Data
A catalogue record for this book is available from the British Library

Library of Congress Cataloging-in-Publication Data
Names: Buğra, Ayşegül, author.
Title: Insurance law implications of delay in maritime transport/by Ayşegül Buğra
Description: First edition. | Abingdon, Oxon [UK] ; New York : Routledge, 2017. | Series: Contemporary commercial law | Includes index.
Identifiers: LCCN 2017006612 | ISBN 9781138683334 (hbk) | ISBN 9781315544564 (ebk)
Subjects: LCSH: Marine insurance – Law and legislation. | Marine insurance policies. | Marine insurance claims. | Liability for marine accidents. | Freight and freightage. | Contracts, Maritime.
Classification: LCC K1226 .B87 2017 | DDC 346/.0862 – dc23
LC record available at https://lccn.loc.gov/2017006612

ISBN: 978-1-138-68333-4 (hbk)
eISBN: 978-1-315-54456-4 (ebk)

Typeset in Times New Roman
by Apex CoVantage, LLC

CONTENTS

Foreword	xi
Preface	xiii
Table of Cases	xv
Table of Statutes and Other Instruments	xxv
Table of Legislation	xxix

CHAPTER 1 INTRODUCTION TO DELAY AS A RISK AND FORTUITY CONSIDERATIONS	1
Introduction	1
The use of the term 'delay' in the marine insurance law context	2
Definition of 'peril' and delay	3
General considerations on fortuity	4
Fortuity and existing policy language	6
Exclusion of delay	7
Naturally occurring losses, fortuity and ordinary delay	7
Ordinary delay	8
Fortuity: analogy of wilful conduct of the assured and delay within the control of the assured	11
Does delay or the peril causing delay have to be taken into account in assessing fortuity	12
Knowledge of the assured as to the certainty of loss	13

CHAPTER 2 CARGO INSURANCE AND DELAY: PHYSICAL LOSS TO THE SUBJECT-MATTER INSURED	14
Introduction	14
Delay and loss by deterioration	14
A general review of the pre-MIA authorities	15
'Last cause in time' rule	18
Delay as a proximate cause in deterioration cases	20
(a) General overview of proximate causation	20
(b) Proximate causation and delay following *Leyland*	21
(c) How to apply *Leyland* to delay cases	22
(d) The authorities of *Lanasa Fruit* and *Norwich Union*	23

v

CONTENTS

(e) Perils of the seas and delay	27
(f) Inherent vice and delay	28
(g) Deprivation perils and delay	29
Delay being a contributing factor or a cause other than the proximate cause	33
Delay and concurrent causation	36
(a) Limits to the rule in *Wayne Tank*: ordinary delay and delay beyond the control of the assured as uninsured perils	38
(b) Whether delay can be an independent cause of loss	39
Agreements altering the proximate cause rule and delay	40

CHAPTER 3 ISSUES ARISING FROM DELAY IN DELIVERY OF CARGO	43
Introduction	43
Meaning of delay in delivery	43
Marine Insurance Act 1906 and delay in delivery	45
Mere delay not resulting in loss of marine adventure and common law authorities	46
Loss of adventure and the MIA 1906	48
Marine adventure and 'due arrival of insured property' under the MIA 1906	51
(a) 'Due arrival of insurable property'	51
(b) Loss of profit, loss of market and loss of adventure by delay	53
Temporarily missing goods and delay	54
Duties of the assured subsequent to the delayed delivery of goods	57
Cargo policies and absence of physical loss of or damage to goods	58
Scope of loss of market and loss of market value caused by delay in delivery	61
Goods arriving late and undamaged	62
Damaged goods and loss of market value by delay	64
Whether loss of market value is a consequential loss in cargo policies	67
Loss of market value and directness under general contract law and carriage of goods by sea	67
Whether loss of market value is a consequential loss in cargo policies	69
Loss of use of cargo and resulting loss of sale contracts	70

CHAPTER 4 CARGO INSURANCE AND EXPENSES ARISING DURING THE PERIOD OF DELAY	72
Introduction	72
General average expenses	72
Loss of market caused by delay and general average	75
Sue and labour expenses	77
Forwarding and storage charges	79

CONTENTS

CHAPTER 5 MARINE DELAY IN START-UP INSURANCE	83
Introduction	83
'Insured' under the marine DSU cover	84
Site owners	84
Contractors	85
Lenders (banks)	85
Scope of cover and duration of risk	86
Measure of indemnity	88
Exclusions	88
The 'duty of insured' clause	89
Mitigation of losses and recoverability of mitigation expenses	90
Duty to act with reasonable dispatch	92

CHAPTER 6 FREIGHT INSURANCE AND THE LOSS OF TIME CLAUSE	94
Introduction	94
Early authorities on delay in earning freight	95
Introduction to the loss of time clause	97
Loss of freight, loss of adventure and the loss of time clause	98
Loss of marine adventure and delay	98
Can the loss of time clause be triggered where delay is not the cause of the loss of adventure	100
Actual and apprehended loss of time and the loss of time clause	102
'Consequent on loss of time' and causation	103
Time charters and the loss of time clause	104
Origins of the clause	104
Off-hire clauses and the loss of time clause	107
(a) Early cases on loss of hire and off-hire clauses	107
(b) Time charterparties, off-hire clauses and the meaning of 'loss of time'	108
(c) Whether loss of time a cause of loss or merely a measure of loss	109

CHAPTER 7 HULL AND MACHINERY INSURANCE AND DELAY CONSIDERATIONS	112
Introduction	112
Damage to the hull and delay: introduction	113
Deterioration of the hull by lengthy delays and ordinary wear and tear	113
Delay in carrying out repairs and increased cost of repairs	115
Expenses incurred during repairs	116
Are they losses proximately caused by delay?	116
Wages and maintenance expenses arising during repairs at port of refuge	117

vii

CONTENTS

(a) Under the common law	117
(b) Under the York-Antwerp Rules	119
Wages and maintenance expenses arising during repairs other than in general average	121
Fuel and stores and port charges occurring in general average	122
Fuel and stores and port charges occurring other than in general average	122
Loss of possession and use of the vessel, delay and constructive total loss	123
3/4th collision liability clause	124

CHAPTER 8	LOSS OF CHARTER HIRE INSURANCE AND LOSS OF TIME	126

Introduction	126
Events triggering the cover under the ABS forms	127
Loss of time in removing cargo and consequent loss of hire	129
'Expenses arising from delay'	130
Loss of hire arising during general average repairs – expense arising from delay?	130
(a) 'Loss of time is proportionate to the interests of the parties'	132
(b) 'Delay is not a direct consequence of general average act'	133
Aggregation of losses and delay	136
Mitigation of losses by the assured and loss of time	137

CHAPTER 9	IMPLIED CONDITION AS TO THE COMMENCEMENT OF RISK	140

Introduction	140
Delay before the risk attaches	141
Implied condition precedent to the attachment of risk	143
(a) Pre-contractual non-disclosure of circumstances which may result in delay	145
(I) Cases on delay and concealment	145
(II) Representations as to the time of sailing	147
(b) Delay within and beyond the control of the assured	147
(c) Institute Cargo Clauses and s 42	148
(I) Avoidance of delay clause and s 42	150
Other standard market terms and s 42	151
Negating the implied condition	151
(a) Waiver by the insurer	151
(b) Circumstances known to the insurer	153
(I) Usage of trade	155
Delay after the risk attaches, before the insured voyage commences	156
Alteration of risk by delay at the commencement of the voyage	157

viii

Types of alteration of risk	158
Delay has to be unreasonable	159
Unreasonable delay amounting to the abandonment of the voyage	161
Consequence of alteration and post-attachment delay	162
(I) Whether post-attachment delay is a breach of warranty and the Insurance Act 2015	165
(II) Whether post-attachment delay is breach of a condition subsequent or innominate term	165
Limits to the remedy of alteration: justifiable delays	166
The relation of justifiable and unreasonable delays	168
CHAPTER 10 DELAY IN VOYAGE	170
Introduction	170
Delay and deviation	170
Liberty clauses on deviation and their impact on delay	172
Time policies, mixed policies and s 48	173
The meaning of 'unreasonable delay'	175
Common law authorities and unreasonable delay: purpose and length	175
Excessive delay and the knowledge of the assured	178
Unreasonable delay under s 48 and the delay exclusion	178
Justifiable delays	178
(a) Unreasonableness under s 48 and excuses for delay	178
(b) Excuses for alteration of the risk and not for breach of warranty	180
(c) Excuses other than the ones enumerated in s 49	181
(I) Delay occurring in usage	181
Ordinary course of transit and interruption of the voyage	182
Delay which is not in the 'ordinary course of transit' discharges the insurers	182
(a) Interruption of transit brought about by the requirements of transport	183
(I) The moment cover ceases	184
(b) Storing pending payment for goods: whether storage in the ordinary course of transit	186
(c) Commercial convenience of the assured versus requirements of transport	189
'Delay beyond the control of the assured' and the transit clause	190
'Delay beyond the control of the assured' and justification for delay	193
Duty of the assured to act with reasonable despatch (avoidance of delay clause)	194
Scope of the clause	194

CONTENTS

(a) The transit clause and the avoidance of delay clause	195
(I) 'delay beyond the control of the assured' and avoidance of delay	195
(II) 'ordinary course of transit' and avoidance of delay	197
(b) Post-casualty situations and the avoidance of delay clause	198
Operation of the clause	199
(a) s 48 and the avoidance of delay clause	199
(b) Whether the clause operates as a warranty and burden of proof	201
(a) s 49 excuses and the avoidance of delay clause	203
Index	205

FOREWORD

The effect of delay is a recurring problem in maritime law. The Lloyd's SG policy in use for 200 years until 1983 for policies on hulls and cargo was construed as excluding loss resulting from delay, a principle codified in the Marine Insurance Act 1906 and now enshrined in the most recent versions of the Institute Clauses. In addition to constituting an excluded peril, at common law delay was regarded as a sub-class of deviation and operated to discharge the insurer under a voyage policy. So, delay is a pervasive issue, relating to the risk, to causation, to inherent vice and to fortuity.

Ayşegül Buğra's book is the first systematic study of the effect of delay on a marine policy. In successive chapters she examines delay in its various roles and manifestations in relation to cargo policies, hull and machinery policies and loss of hire policies. Each chapter takes the topic back to the earliest cases, showing how and why the law developed before the Marine Insurance Act 1906. Where Chalmers has failed to codify the pre-existing law accurately or fully, the matter is carefully analysed. Inconsistencies in the authorities are discussed in detail. The applicable principles are then applied to modern standard forms.

This is much more than a book on delay. Each chapter contains a wealth of learning on all aspects of marine insurance law, putting delay into its proper context. Analogies are drawn from the numerous authorities on charterparties and general average. Throughout, the analysis is minutely detailed, but the material is logically presented and the arguments are easy to follow. Ayşegül has produced a truly excellent book, which has succeeded in the difficult task of appealing both to practitioners seeking guidance on the impact of delay, and to scholars and students keen to learn more about the history and importance of the subject. This is one of those rare law books that is meticulously researched, packed with information and yet still a delight to read.

Professor Rob Merkin QC

PREFACE

This work began life seven years ago and an earlier version thereof was initially submitted in 2014 in partial fulfillment of the requirements for the Degree of Doctor of Philosophy in Law at the University of Southampton. It has further been developed into this book since 2016. The book aims at highlighting the insurance law implications of delay in maritime transport by providing a thorough analysis on the recoverability of losses arising from or during delay. Delay is an important and frequent phenomenon of maritime transport as it affects various parties and their interests under several types of insurance policies such as cargo, hull and machinery, freight, loss of hire and marine delay in start-up. The book addresses the losses and expenses that may arise from delay or loss of time in maritime transport, their recoverability under the enumerated types of policies and the impact of delay on voyage policies. It analyses the current law by tracing back the relevant common law authorities to the 18th century and examines the wordings used in practice from that time to today with a comprehensive and critical approach.

Although the text primarily aims at analysing the English law, efforts have been made to incorporate decisions from other common law jurisdictions such as Australia, Canada, Hong Kong, New Zealand, Singapore and the United States. It is hoped that the text will be of interest to legal practitioners, shipping professionals and academics alike.

I owe thanks to a number of individuals and organizations who have greatly contributed to this long-lasting project. The earlier version of this manuscript was examined by Professor Sarah Dromgoole and Professor Michael Tsimplis in 2014 who had given invaluable comments which helped me to develop some of the ideas in this book. During my postgraduate studies I was fortunate enough to receive the generous funding of the Max Planck Institute for Comparative and International Private Law to act as a visiting researcher, as well as to be awarded the generous scholarship of the University of Southampton Law School for my Ph.D studies. I am also indebted to the Institute of Maritime Law (IML) of the University of Southampton and to the Institute of Advanced Legal Studies (IALS) of the University of London for giving permissions to consult the wide range of material under their care. IML's support in this project has been particularly tremendous. Furthermore I owe a large debt of thanks to Koç University whose funding through the Visiting Scholar Program has secured the necessary research leave for preparing this work for publication.

Many thanks are due to Associate Professor Özlem Gürses and Associate Professor Johanna Hjalmarsson with whom I had the opportunity to have fruitful discussions on the topic throughout my studies and to Dr Meixian Song who read various chapters of this manuscript in draft form and from whose comments I benefited greatly.

Since the time this project first began, my supervisor Professor Robert Merkin QC has been an invaluable mentor whose guidance was absolutely crucial and priceless. I would like to take this opportunity to thank him for his continuous support and encouragement.

I would also like to thank the team at Informa Law from Routledge, particularly Caroline Church and Amy Jones, for their consistent support and for keeping this project on track so professionally.

Finally, I would like to express my deepest gratitude to my family and friends for their accustomed forbearance throughout this long journey.

All errors and omissions are entirely mine.

Ayşegül Buğra
February 2017

TABLE OF CASES

A. Tomlinson (Hauliers) Ltd v Hepburn [1964] 1 Lloyd's Rep. 416 ....3.23
Ace European Group Ltd v Chartis Insurance UK Ltd [2012]
    2 Lloyd's Rep 117; aff'd [2013] Lloyd's Rep I.R. 485 .... 5.5, 5.17
Admiral Shipping Co v Weidner (1916) 1 K.B. 429 .... 3.9, 3.9
Aktieselskabet Stavangeren v Hubard-Zemurray Shipping
    Co 250 F. 67, 162 C.C.A 239 (5th Cir.1918) 3.32
Allison v Bristol Marine Insurance Co (1876) 1 App. Cas. 209 ....3.7
Alstom Ltd v Liberty Mutual Insurance Co (No 2) [2013] FCA 116 ....5.5
American National Fire Insurance Co v Mirasco
    Inc 249 F.Supp.2d 303 (S.D.N.Y. 2003) 3.24
Andersen v Marten [1907] 2 K.B. 248 ....2.21
Anderson v Morice (1874-75) L.R. 10 C.P. 609 ....3.15
Anderson v Wallis (1813) 2 Maule and Selwyn 240 ....3.7, 3.8, 3.11, 6.4
Anglo-Argentine Live Stock Agency v Temperley
    Shipping Co [1899] 2 Q.B. 403 .... 4.8, 4.9, 7.13, 8.11, 8.13
Archer-Daniels-Midland Company v Phoenix Insurance
    Company of New York 975 F.Supp.1137 (1997) 2.14, 2.15, 2.21 2.35, 4.12
Assicurazioni Generali S.P.A. v Black & Veatch
    Corp 362 F.3d 1108, 2004 A.M.C. 773 .... 5.5, 5.16
Atlantic Maritime v Gibbon [1954] 1 Q.B. 88 .... 1.9, 6.14, 6.15, 6.20, 6.22
Atwood v Sellar (1880) 5 Q.B.D. 286 .... 7.11, 7.13
Austin Friars Steamship Co Ltd v Spillers &
    Bakers Ltd [1914] 1 K.B. 833 .... 4.8, 8.13
Australian Coastal Shipping Commission v Green
    [1971] 1 Q.B. 456 .... 4.7, 4.8, 8.13, 8.14
Avis v Hartford Fire Ins Co 283 N.C. 142, 195 S.E. 2d 545, 548 (1973) 1.7
Bah Lias Tobacco & Rubber Estates, Ltd v Volga Insurance
    Company Ltd (1920) 3 Lloyd's List Law Reports 155 .... 9.6, 9.21, 9.22, 9.42
Bain v Case (1829) 3 Car. & P. 496 .... 9.36, 10.16, 10.17, 10.19
Bamburi, The [1982] 1 Lloyd's Rep. 314 ....3.16
Bank Line Limited v Arthur Capel & Co [1919] A.C. 435 .... 1.15, 6.13, 6.19
Bank of Nova Scotia v Hellenic Mutual War Risks Association
    (Bermuda) Ltd (The Good Luck) [1991] 1 A.C. 233;
    [1990] 1 Q.B. 818 .... 9.5, 9.23
Barker v Blakes (1808) 9 East 283 .... 3.6, 3.8

TABLE OF CASES

Becker, Gray and Co v London Assurance Corpn [1918] A.C. 101............................2.34

Beckwith v Sydebotham (1807) 1 Campb. 118..9.11

Bedouin, The [1894] P 1.. 6.24, 6.31, 6.33, 6.34

Bensaude v Thames and Mersey Marine
Insurance Co [1897] A.C. 609...................................... 3.14, 4.17, 6.15, 6.21, 6.32

Benson v Chapman (1849) 2 HLC 496 ....5.17

Beresford v Royal Insurance Co Ltd [1938] A.C. 586...1.11

Blaine Richards & Co Inc v Marine Indemnity Insurance
Company of America and William H. McGee &
Co 635 F.2d 1051, 1981 A.M.C. 1, ...2.15, 2.21, 2.35, 3.23, 3.23, 3.29

Blankley v Central Manchester and Manchester Children's University
Hospitals NHS Trust [2014] EWHC 168 (QB); [2015] EWCA Civ 18.............6.13

Board of Trade v Hain Steamship Co Ltd [1929] A.C. 534 ....2.8

Bowden v Vaughan (1809) 10 East, 416..9.13

Boyd Motors Inc v Employers Ins of
Wausau 880 F.2d 270 (1989)...................................... 3.23, 3.23, 3.24, 3.27

Brandyce v United States Lloyds 207 A.D. 665,
203 N.Y.S.10, aff'd, 239 N.Y. 573, 147 N.E.201 (1924)......... 2.7, 2.10, 2.14, 2.17

British & Foreign Marine Ins. Co Ltd v Gaunt (No 2)
[1921] 2 A.C. 41 .... 1.7, 1.9

British & Foreign Marine Insurance Co Ltd v Samuel
Sanday & Co [1916] A.C. 650 ....3.8, 3.9, 3.11, 3.15

British-American Tobacco Company Ltd v H.G. Poland
(1921) 7 Ll. L.R. 108.. 10.16, 10.17, 10.20

CA Blackwell (Contracts) Ltd v Gerling General
Insurance Co [2008] Lloyd's Rep. IR 529.................... 1.9, 1.10, 1.12

Cantiere Navale Triestina v Handelsvertretung der Russe
Soviet Republik Naphtha Export (1925) 21 Ll. L.R. 204 ....7.21

CCR Fishing Ltd v Tomenson Inc (The La Pointe)
[1991] 1 Lloyd's Rep. 89.. 1.5, 1.6

Cepheus Shipping Corporation v Guardian Royal Exchange
(The Capricorn) [1995] 1 Lloyd's Rep. 622 ....8.5

Chitty v Selwyn and Martyn (1742) 2 ATK. 358.......................... 9.29, 9.39, 9.39, 9.40,
9.40, 9.41, 9.46, 9.47

Chubb Insurance Co of Canada v Cast Line Ltd 2001 CarswellQue 1616 ....2.15

Citta di Messina, The (1909) 169 F. 472 ....10.7

City Centre Cold Store Pty Ltd v Preservatrice Skandia
Insurance Ltd (1985) 3 NSWLR 739..2.29

Clark's Chick Hatchery Ltd v Commonwealth
Insurance Co 1982 CarswellNB 331 .... 2.24, 2.32, 3.4, 3.23

Clothing Management v Beazley Solutions [2012] Lloyd's Rep. IR. 329.................3.34

Collard v S.E. Ry (1861) 7 H. & N. 79..3.33

Columbian Insurance Co v Catlett (1827) 25 U.S. 383 .... 10.9, 10.21,
10.34, 10.35, 10.38

Commercial Union Assurance Co v The Niger
Co Ltd (1922) 13 Ll. L.R. 75.. 10.42, 10.42

Commercial Union Assurance Co v The Niger
Co Ltd [1922] 12 Ll. L. R 235..10.52

xvi

TABLE OF CASES

Compagnie des Bauxites de Guinée v Insurance Co of North America
554 F. Supp. 1080 (W.D. Pa) rev'd, 724 F.2d 369 (1983) 1.21

Company of African Merchants v British and Foreign Marine
Insurance Co (1873) L.R. 8 Ex 154 .... 9.29, 9.31, 9.46, 10.13,
10.16, 10.17, 10.22

Connect Shipping Inc v Sveriges Anfgartygs Assurans Forening
(The Swedish Club) ('The Renos') [2016] 2 Lloyd's Rep. 364 ....7.15

Continental Insurance Co v Almassa International Inc (2003)
46 C.C.L.I. 3d 206 .... 2.25, 2.32

Corporation of the Royal Exchange Assurance v M'Swiney (1849)
14 Queen's Bench Reports 646 ....3.26, 3.35, 3.36

Cory & Son v Burr (1883) 8 App. Cas. 393 ....2.21

Cory v Boylston Insurance Co 107 Mass 140, 9 Am.
Rep 14 (1871) 1.15, 2.17, 2.17

Coven SPA v Hong Kong Chinese Insurance Co [1999]
Lloyd's Rep. IR 565 ....3.22

Coxe v Employers' Liability Assurance Corp. Ltd [1916] 2 K.B. 629 .... 2.34, 2.35

Currie & Co v Bombay Native Insurance Co (1869) L.R. 3 PC 72 .... 5.17, 8.20

Czarnikow (C.) Ltd v Koufos [1969] 1 A.C. 350 ....8.14

Davis Contractors Ltd v Fareham U.D.C [1956] A.C. 696 .... 6.12, 6.13

De Vaux v Salvador (1836) 4 Adolphus and Ellis 420 ....7.15

De Wolf v Archangel Maritime (1874)
L.R. 9 Q.B. 451 .... 9.1, 9.2, 9.2, 9.5, 9.6, 9.7, 9.9,
9.14, 9.24, 9.29, 9.31, 9.32, 9.34,
9.35, 9.37, 9.39, 9.41, 9.43, 9.46

Doyle v Powell (1832) 4 B. & Ad. 267 ....9.35

Driscol v Passmore (1798) 1 B. & P. 202 ....9.6, 9.10, 9.33, 9.34, 9.46, 9.47

Duane Reade, Inc. v St. Paul Fire & Marine Ins. Co 279 F. Supp.
2d 235, 240, aff'd as modified, 411 F.3d 384 (2005) 3.31

Dudgeon v Pembroke (1877) 2 App. Cas. 284 .... 2.5, 2.31

ELAZ International Co v Hong Kong & Shanghai
Insurance Co Ltd [2006] HKEC 825 .... 10.39, 10.51

ENE Kos 1 Ltd v Petroleo Brasileiro SA (The Kos) [2012] UKSC 17 ....2.29

Everth v Smith (1814) 2 M. & S. 278 .... 6.4, 6.5, 6.6, 6.7, 6.8

Feasey v Sun Life Assurance Corporation of Canada [2003]
Lloyd's Rep. IR 637 .... 3.13, 3.15

Federation Insurance Company of Canada v Coret Accessories (1968)
2 Lloyd's Law Rep. 109 ....2.13, 3.3, 3.7, 3.17, 3.18, 3.19, 3.23, 3.24

Fedsure General Insurance Limited v Carefree Investments
(Proprietrary) Limited (477/99) [2001] ZASCA 88 .... 10.11, 10.37, 10.51

Fibrosa v Fairbairn [1943] A.C. 32 ....6.13

Field Steamship Co v Burr [1899] 1 Q.B. 579 .... 7.18, 7.19, 7.20, 8.6

Firemen's Fund Ins. Co v Trojan Powder Co (1918) 253 F.205 ....4.16

First Art Investments Ltd v Guardian Insurance Ltd (2002)
Unreported decision of Judge Hallgarten QC,
Central London C Ct 14 February 2002 .... 10.45, 10.46

Ford Motor Co of Canada Ltd v Prudential Assurance Co Ltd
14 DLR (2d) 7 (Ont, 1958), affirmed [1959] SCR 539 ....2.29

xvii

TABLE OF CASES

Forestal Land, Timber & Railways Company, Ltd v Rickards;
    Middows Ltd v Robertson and Others (1941) 70 Ll.L. Rep. 173 ....3.8
Friends Provident Life & Pensions Ltd v Sirius Intl
    Insurance [2005] 2 Lloyd's Rep. 517..10.74
Fudge v Charter Marine Insurance Co Ltd 1991, unreported,
    Newfoundland SC...8.20
Fuerst Day Lawson Ltd v Orion Insurance Co Ltd [1980]
    1 Lloyd's Rep. 656...3.22
Garvey v State Farm Fire and Casualty Co 770 P 2d 704 (1989)..........................2.28
Glencore International A.G. v Ryan (The Beursgracht (No 1))
    [2002] C.L.C. 547 ....9.45
Glencore International A.G. v Ryan (The Beursgracht (No 2))
    [2001] 2 Lloyd's Rep. 608..9.45
Glengate-KG Properties Ltd v Norwich Union Fire
    Insurance Society Ltd [1996] C.L.C. 676 ....3.15
Global Process Systems Inc v Syarikat Takaful Malaysia Berhad
    (The Cendor Mopu) [2009] 2 Lloyd's Rep. 71;
    [2010] 1 Lloyd's Rep. 243; [2011] 1 Lloyd's Rep. 560.....................................1.2
Global Process Systems Inc v Syarikat Takaful Malaysia Berhad
    (The Cendor Mopu) [2009] EWCH 637 (Comm) 1.9, 1.21
Global Process Systems Inc v Syarikat Takaful Malaysia Berhad
    (The Cendor Mopu) [2011] UKSC 5 .... 1.6, 1.11, 2.8, 2.8, 2.10, 2.11,
                                    2.16, 2.24, 2.29, 2.30, 2.31, 7.4
Goldman v Rhode Island (1951)100 F. Supp.196...2.17
Goodman v Fireman's Fund Insurance Co 600 F.2d 1040 (4th Circ. 1979)................1.9
Grant v King (1802) 4 Esp. 176........................ 9.29, 9.37, 9.39, 9.40, 9.40, 9.41, 9.42,
                                 9.46, 9.46, 9.47, 10.16, 10.17, 10.75
Grant v Parkinson (1781) 3 Doug. 16, 18 ....3.35
Grant, Smith and Co v Seattle Construction and Dry Dock Co [1920] A.C. 162........1.5
Gregson v Gilbert (1783) 3 Douglas 232..2.3
Groban v American Casualty Company (1972) 331 F.Supp. 883 .... 10.50, 10.52
Guaranty National Ins Co v North Rivers Ins Co 09 F 2d 132, 137 (1990) 2.29
Hadley v Baxendale (1854) 9 Ex. 341 .... 3.32, 3.33
Hallett v Wigram (1850) 9 C. B. 580 ....7.12
Hamilton v Pandorf (1887) 12 App. Cas 518..1.5
Hamilton v Sheddon (1837) 3 M. & W. 49 .... 9.29, 10.3, 10.16, 10.17
Handelsbanken Norwegian Branch of Svenska Handelsbanken AB
    (PUBL) v Dandridge (The Aliza Glacial) [2002]
    EWCA Vic 577, [2002] 2 Lloyd's Rep 421..2.34
Harris v Jacobs (1885) 15 Q.B.D 247 per Brett MR 7.21
Harrison Ltd v Shipping Controller (The Inkonka) [1921] 1 K.B. 122 ....2.23
Hartley v Buggin (1781) 3 Doug. K.B. 39 ....10.3, 10.17, 10.18
Helmville Ltd v Yorkshire Insurance Company Ltd
    (The Medina Princess) [1965] 1 Lloyd's Rep. 361 ....7.15
Heskell v Continental Express Ltd [1950] 1 All E.R. 1033, 1046 ....3.33
Hibernia Foods plc v McAuslin (The Joint Frost) [1998] 1 Lloyd's Rep. 310 ....3.15
Hick v Raymond [1893] A.C. 22 .... 9.36, 9.37

xviii

TABLE OF CASES

HIH Casualty & General Insurance Ltd v Waterwall Shipping Inc
(1998) 146 FLR 76 ....2.30
Holmes v Payne [1930] 2 K.B. 301, 310..3.16
Hong Kong Borneo Services Co Ltd v Anthony David Pilcher
[1992] 2 Lloyd's Law Rep. 293 ....8.3
Hongkong Fir Shipping Co Ltd v Kawasaki Kisen Kaisha Ltd
(The Hongkong Fir) [1961] 2 Lloyd's Rep. 478; [1962] 2 Q.B. 26..................10.74
Hore v Whitmore (1778) 2 Cowper 784...9.47
Horne v Midland Railway Company (1872-73) L.R. 8 C.P. 131 ....3.2
Houghton v Trafalgar Insurance Co Ltd [1954] 1 Q.B. 247....................................1.2
Howard Farrow v Ocean Accident & Guarantee Corpn (1940)
67 Ll. L. Rep. 27..2.21
Howard-Jones v Tate [2011] EWCA Civ 1330..9.45
Hull v Cooper (1811) 14 East 475 .... 9.6, 9.9, 9.25, 9.29, 9.34, 9.39, 9.41
Hyderabad (Deccan) Co v Willoughby [1899] 2 Q.B. 530.................10.6, 10.16, 10.17,
10.20, 10.26, 10.29,
10.43, 10.58, 10.75
Ikergi Compania Naviera SA v Palmer (The Wondrous)
[1991] 1 Lloyd's Rep. 400........................... 1.8, 1.19, 1.19, 1.20, 1.21, 6.2, 6.8, 8.4
Industrial Waxes Inc v Brown (1958) 258 F.2d 800 .... 10.48, 10.49
Inman SS Co v Bischoff (1882) 7 App. Cas. 670....................................2.23, 6.30, 6.34
Integrated Container Service Inc v British Traders
Insurance Co [1984] 1 Lloyd's Rep. 154.. 4.10, 5.17
Interpetrol Bermuda Ltd v Lloyd's Underwriters 1984 588
F. Supp 1199 (United States District Court, S.D New York)..............................3.30
Ionides v The Universal Marine Insurance Co (1863) 14 C.B. (NS) 259...................2.7
Irvin v Hine [1950] 1 K.B. 555..7.8
Jackson v The Union Marine Insurance (1874)
L.R. 10 C.P. 125... 3.3, 3.14, 6.12, 6.24, 6.25, 6.25, 6.26
Jamieson v Newcastle SS Freight Ins Assn, Re [1895]
2 Q.B. 90 ....3.3, 3.14, 6.10, 6.12, 6.26, 6.27
Jan de Nul v Axa Royal Belge SA (Formally NV Royale Belge)
[2001] EWCA Civ. 209...3.27
JJ Lloyd Instruments Ltd v Northern Star Insurance Co Ltd (The Miss Jay Jay)
[1987] 1 Lloyd's Rep. 32...2.8, 2.8, 2.10, 2.30, 2.31, 2.31
John Martin of London Ltd v Russell [1960] 1 Lloyd's
List Law Reports 554.. 10.66, 10.67
Kemble v Bowne (1803) 1 Caines, 75..9.2
Kidston v Empire Marine Insurance Co (1866) L.R. 1 C.P. 535..............................5.17
Kiriacoulis Lines SA v Compagnie d'Assurance Maritime
(The Demetra K) [2002] Lloyd's Rep. I.R. 795 ....2.2
Kiriacoulis Lines SA v Compagnie d'Assurance Maritime
(The Demetra K) [2002] Lloyd's Rep. IR 823 ....2.8
Koufos v C. Czarnikow Ltd (The Heron II) [1969]
1 A.C. 350.. 3.21, 3.32, 3.33, 3.33, 4.7
Kuwait Airways Corp v Kuwait Insurance Co SAK [1997]
2 Lloyd's Rep. 687..3.19

TABLE OF CASES

Lam Seng Hang Co Pte Ltd v The Insurance Corporation of
  Singapore Ltd [2001] SGHC 31 .... 1.18, 2.20, 10.54
Lambert v Liddard 1 Marsh. R. 149, (1814) 5 Taunt. 480 .... 9.2
Lanasa Fruit v Universal Ins. Co (1938) 302 U.S.556............. 2.7, 2.10, 2.12, 2.13, 2.13
Langhorn v Alnutt (1812) 4 Taunt. 511 .... 9.46, 10.17, 10.18
Lawrence v Aberdein (1821) 5 B. & Ald. 107 .... 2.4, 2.5
Leaders Shoes (Aust.) Pty Ltd v Liverpool and London and Globe
  Insurance Co Ltd [1968] 1 NSWR 279 .... 10.38
Lehmbackers Earth Moving and Excavators (Pty) Ltd.
  v Incorporated General Insurances Ltd (1984) (3) S.A. 513.................... 9.45
Leitrim, The [1902] P 256 .... 8.9, 8.11
Leon v Casey [1932] 2 K.B. 576 .... 9.15, 10.72
Lewis Emanuel & Son Ltd v Hepburn [1960]
  1 Lloyd's Rep. 304 .... 2.2, 3.3, 3.7, 3.21
Leyland Shipping Co v Norwich Union Fire
  Insurance Society Ltd [1918] A.C. 350 .... 2.7, 2.7, 2.8, 2.11, 2.13,
                                                    2.23, 2.24, 2.25, 2.27, 2.31
Liberian Insurance Agency Inc v Moussa [1977] 2 Lloyd's Rep. 560 .... 10.70
Lloyds TSB General Insurance Holdings v Lloyds Bank Group
  Insurance Co Ltd [2001] EWCA Civ. 1643, [2002] Lloyd's Rep IR 113 .... 2.34
London & Provincial Leather Processes Ltd v Hudson [1939] 2 K.B. 724 .... 1.7
Lucena v Craufurd (1806) 2 Bos. & Pul. (N.R.) 269 .... 3.15, 3.15, 3.35
M Almojil Establishment v Malayan Motor and General Underwriters
  (Private) Ltd (The Al-Jubail IV) [1982] 2 Ll. L. Rep. 637 .... 10.14
Magoun v New England Marine Insurance Company 1 Story 157,
  16 F.Cas. 483, C.C.Mass. (1840).. 7.4
Magoun v New England Marine Insurance Company Fed.
  Cas. No. 8,961, 1 Story 157 .... 2.24
Main, The [1894] P 320.. 6.7
Manning v Newnham (1792) 3 Douglas 130....................................... 3.7
Mardorf v Accident Insurance Co [1903] 1 K.B. 584............................ 2.24
Marina Offshore Pte Ltd v China Insurance Co
  (Singapore) Pte Ltd [2007] 1 Lloyd's Rep. 66 .... 10.12
Marine Insurance Co v China Trans-Pacific SS Co (1886) 11 App. Cas. 573............. 7.6
Martin v Fishing Ins. Co (1838) 20 Pick. 389 .... 9.2
Masefield AG v Amlin Corporate Member Ltd & Anor (The Bunga Melati Dua)
  [2011] EWCA Civ. 24, 2.19, 2.20; [2010] EWCH 280 (Comm)..................... 3.25
Maurice v Goldsbrough Mort & Co Ltd [1939] 64 Ll.L.Rep 1 .... 3.15
Mayban General Insurance Bhd v Alstom Power Plants Ltd [2004]
  2 Lloyd's Rep. 609.. 1.9
McAlpine Plc v BAI (Run Off) Ltd [1998] 2 Lloyd's Rep. 694;
  [2000] 1 Lloyd's Rep. 437 CA... 10.74, 10.74
M'Carthy, Corner and Henderson v Abel (1804) 5 East 388...................... 6.5
McCarthy v St Paul International Insurance Co Ltd [2007]
  FCAFC 28; (2007) 157 FCR 402.. 2.29
Mercantile v Tyser (1880-81) L.R. 7 Q.B.D 73 .... 6.34
Mersey Steamship Company Ltd v Thames and Mersey Marine
  Insurance Company Ltd (The Alps) [1893] P 109 .... 6.24, 6.31, 6.33, 6.34, 6.34

TABLE OF CASES

Minerva Navigation Inc v Oceana Shipping AG; Oceana Shipping AG v
Transatlantica Commodities SA (The M/V Athena)
[2013] EWCA Civ. 1723..6.32
Miruvor Ltd v National Insurance Co Ltd [2002] HKEC 1033 ....10.51
Miruvor Ltd v National Insurance Co Ltd [2003] HKEC 237 ....10.44, 10.45, 10.46
Mitsui & Co Ltd and Others v Beteiligungsgesellschaft LPG Tankerflotte
MBH & Co (The Longchamp) [2016] EWCA Civ. 708 ....4.4, 4.5, 4.6
Monarch Steamship Co Ltd v Karlshamns Olje-fabriker [1949] A.C. 196................2.31
Montrose Chemical Corp v Admiral Ins Co 42 Cal Rptr.2d 324 (1995)...................2.28
Morley v United Friendly Insurance plc [1993] 1 Lloyd's Rep. 490.........................2.28
Motteux v London Ass. Co 1 Atk. 545... 9.15, 9.49
Mount v Larkins (1831) 8 Bing 108....................... 9.3, 9.6, 9.14, 9.24, 9.28, 9.30, 9.31,
9.32, 9.39, 9.39, 9.46, 10.3, 10.72
Moussi H. Issa NV v Grand Union Insurance Co Ltd [1984] HKLR 137 ....10.74
National Carriers Ltd v Panalpina (Northern) Ltd [1981] A.C. 675................. 6.12, 6.12
Nationwide Brokers Inc v C & G Trucking Corp. No. 87-C-5770,
1988 WL 116827 (1988)..3.24
Naviera de Canarias SA v Nacional Hispanica Aseguradora SA
(The Playa de las Nieves) [1978] A.C. 853.....................................2.14, 2.24, 4.17,
6.11, 6.17, 6.18, 6.21, 6.23,
6.24, 6.32, 6.33, 6.34, 6.35
Nec Australia Pty Ltd v Gamif Pty Ltd; Neway Transport
Industries Pty Ltd; Australian Eagle Insurance Co Ltd;
Colonial Mutual General Insurance Company Ltd and
Webden Pty Ltd [1993] FCA 252..................................... 10.41, 10.42, 10.47, 10.51
New Market Investment Corp v Fireman's Fund 774 F.Supp. 909 (1991).................2.22
Ngo Chew Hong Edible Oil Pte v Knight [1988] 1 SLR 414....................................8.20
Niger Co Ltd v Guardian Assurance Co (1922) 13 Ll. L.R. 75.................. 10.16, 10.17
Nippon Yusen Kaisha Ltd v Scindia Steam Navigation Co
(The Jalagouri) [1998] CLC 1054 ....6.32
Northern Feather International Inc v Those Certain London
Underwriters Subscribing to Policy No JWP108 Through
Wigham Poland Ltd 714 F.Supp. 1352, 1989 AMC 1805 ....10.55
Norwich Union Fire Insurance v Wm.H. Price (1933) S.R.
(N.S.W.) 196.. 2.10, 2.12
Norwich Union Fire Insurance v Wm.H. Price (1934) A.C. 455 ....2.12
Notara v Henderson (1872) L.R. 7 Q.B. 225..5.17
Notting Hill, The (1884) 9 P.D. 105..3.33
Okanagan Prime Products Inc v Commercial Union Assurance Co of
Canada 1994 Carswell BC 874..2.25
Oliver v Maryland Insurance Company (1813) 11 U.S (7 Cranch 487) 10.35
Ontario Inc v Commonwealth Insurance Co 2005 CarswellOnt
2605 75 O.R. (3d) 653, 26 C.C.L.I. (4th) 225... 3.23, 3.35
Ostra Insurance Public Company Ltd v Kintex Shareholding
Company (M/V Szechuen) [2004] EWHC 357 (Comm) 5.19, 9.18, 10.74
Ougier v Jennings (1808) 1 Camp 505 .... 9.10, 9.27, 9.34, 9.46
Owners of the Steamship Gracie v Owners of the Steamship
Argentino (The Argentino) (1889) 14 App. Cas. 519..8.1

xxi

TABLE OF CASES

Owners of the Yero Carras v London & Scottish Assurance
    Corp Ltd (The Yero Carras) [1936] 1 K.B. 291 ....6.16
P. Samuel & Co Ltd v Dumas [1924] A.C. 431 ....1.9
Palmer v Fenning (1833) 9 Bing 460 ....9.34, 9.40, 9.40, 9.41, 9.46, 9.46
Palmer v Marshall (1832) 8 Bing 317 .... 9.29, 9.29, 9.33, 9.34, 9.39,
                                            9.39, 9.40, 9.41, 9.46, 9.46, 9.48
Parana, The (1877) 2 P.D. 118 .... 3.24, 3.32, 3.32, 4.7, 8.14
Parkinson v Mathews and Drysdale 1930 WLD 58 ....10.65
Pearson v Commercial Union (1876) 1 App. Cas. 498 .... 10.8, 10.11, 10.16,
                                                10.17, 10.34, 10.43
Perry v Cobb 49 L.R.A. 389, 88 Me. 435, 34 A. 278 (1896) 2.17, 2.17, 2.26
Petrinovic & Co Ltd v Mission Française des Transports Maritimes
    (1941) 71 Ll. L. Rep. 208 ....7.21
Phillips v Irving (1884) 7 Man. & G. 325 ....9.29, 10.9, 10.16,
                                                10.17, 10.19, 10.35
Phoenix Assurance Plc v Golden Imports Ltd 1989
    CarswellBC 555 .... 3.7, 3.17, 3.18, 3.19, 3.24
Phoenix Shipping Co v Apex Shipping Corp [1982] 2 Lloyd's Rep. 407 ....7.1
Pink v Fleming (1890) LR 25 Q.B.D. 396 ....1.16, 2.4, 2.5, 2.7, 2.7, 2.9,
                                            2.10, 2.13, 2.24, 2.31
Pioneer Shipping Ltd v B.T.P Tioxide Ltd (The Nema) [1982] A.C. 724 .... 6.12, 6.13
Pittegrew v Pringle (1832) 3 B. & Ad. 514 ....9.4
Pomeranian, The (1895) P 34 ....4.10
Puller v Glover (1810) 12 East 124 ....3.34
Puller v Staniforth (1809) 11 East 232 ....3.34
Quorum v Schramm [2002] 1 Lloyd's Rep. 249 .... 3.20, 3.27
Ranicar v Frigmobile Pty Ltd; Royal Insurance Pty Ltd BC8371124
    (Unreported Judgment by Green CJ, Supreme Court of Tasmania) 3.20
Rayner v Preston (1881), 18 Ch. D.1 ....3.7
Reed v Weldon (1869) Carswell NB 23 ....10.18
Reischer v Borwick (1874) 2 Q.B. 548 .... 2.11, 2.34
Renee Hyaffil, The T.L.R. vol 32, 660 (CA) 2.24
Rickards v Forestal Land Timber & Railways Co Ltd (The Minden)
    (1941) 70 Ll. L. Rep. 173 ....10.29
Rickards v Forestal Land, Timber and Railways Co
    (The Minden) [1942] A.C. 50 .... 3.8, 3.9
Robertson v Ewer (1786) 1 Term Rep. 127 ....7.15
Robertson v Petros Nomikos Ltd [1939] A.C. 371 .... 6.14, 6.17, 6.18, 6.21, 6.22
Rodocanachi v Elliott (1873) L.R. 9 C.P. 649 .... 3.8, 3.15
Roura & Forgas v Townend [1919] 1 K.B. 189 ....6.14
Roura v Forgas [1919] 1 K.B. 189 ....2.34
Roux v Salvador (1836) 3 Bing NC 266 .... 3.7, 3.12
Russian Bank for Foreign Trade v Excess Ins Co Ltd [1918]
    2 K.B. 123; [1919] 1 K.B. 39 .... 2.14, 2.14, 3.28, 4.16,
                                           4.17, 6.11, 6.14, 6.18, 6.23
Sadler Brothers Company v Meredith [1963] 2 Lloyd's Law Reporter 293 ....9.3
Safadi v Western Assurance Co (1933)
    46 Ll. L. Rep. 140 .... 1.19, 10.51, 10.53, 10.54

TABLE OF CASES

Safeco Ins. Co v Guyton 692 F.2d 551 (1982)..2.25
Samuel v Royal Exchange Assurance (1828) 8 B. & C. 119 .... 10.16, 10.17
SCA. (Freight) Ltd v Gibson [1974] 2 Lloyd's Rep. 533...10.38
Schloss Bros v Stevens [1906] 2 K.B. 665...................... 1.5, 1.15, 1.16, 2.20, 10.24
Schroder v Thompson (1817) 7 Taunt 462 .... 9.29, 10.16, 10.17, 10.75
Schulze v G.E. Ry (1887) 19 Q.B.D. 30 ....3.33
Scott v Copenhagen Reinsurance Co (UK) Ltd [2003] EWCA Civ. 688,
    [2003] Lloyd's Rep. IR 696..2.27
Scottish Navigation Co Ltd v W.A Souter & Co [1917] 1 K.B. 222 ....3.9
Scottish Shire Line, Limited and Others v London and Provincial
    Marine and General Insurance Company Limited [1912] 3 K.B. 51 ....6.28
Sealion Shipping v Valiant Insurance Co (The Toisa Pisces)
    [2013] 1 Lloyd's Rep. 108...8.2, 8.17, 8.18
Seamans v Loring (1816) 1 Mason, 128..9.2
Sellar v M'Vicar (1804) 1 Bosanquet and Puller 23 ....9.2
Shelbourne & Co v Law Investment and Insurance
    Corporation Ltd [1898] 2 Q.B. 626..3.34, 7.1, 8.1
Smit Tak Offshore Services Ltd v Youell (The Mare)
    [1992] 1 Lloyd's Rep. 154..2.28
Smith v Surridge (1801) 4 Esp. 25 ....9.3, 9.15, 9.34, 9.41, 9.41, 9.42,
    9.46, 9.46, 9.49, 10.16, 10.17, 10.75
Soya GmbH Kommanditgesellschaft v White [1980] 1 Lloyd's Rep. 491;
    [1982] 1 Lloyd's Rep. 136; [1983] 1 Lloyd's Rep. 122......................1.2, 1.9, 1.21,
    1.21, 1.21, 2.17
St. Margaret's Trust Ltd v Navigators and General Ins Co Ltd
    (1949) 82 Ll. L. Rep 752...7.5
Stanley v Onetta Boat Works, Inc 303 F.Supp. 99..3.30
State Farm Mutual Auto Ins Co v Partridge 10 Cal. 3d 102 (1973)................. 2.28, 2.28
State of Netherlands v Youell [1998] 1 Lloyd's Rep. 236 .... 5.17, 8.20
Strive Shipping Corporation v Hellenic Mutual War Risks Association
    (Bermuda) Ltd, The Grecia Express [2002] Lloyd's Rep. IR 669......................5.17
Svenska Handelsbanken AB v Dandridge (The Aliza Glacial) [2002]
    EWCA Civ. 577...2.27
Syers v Bridge (1790) 2 Dougl. 526 ....10.6
Synder v Atlantic Mutual Ins. Co (1884) 95 N.Y. 196 ....9.2
Talbot Underwriting Ltd v Nausch Hohan & Murray Inc (The Jascon 5)
    [2006] EWCA Civ. 889; [2005] EWHC 2359 (Comm) 7.9, 7.9
Tatem v Gamboa (1938) 61 Ll.L.Rep. 149..6.12
Tatham v Hodgson (1796) 6 TR 656 .... 2.4, 2.5, 2.13, 2.17
Taylor v Caldwell (1863) 3 B. & S 826 ....6.12
Taylor v Dunbar (1869) L.R. 4 C.P. 206 ....1.11, 2.4, 2.5, 2.5, 2.7, 2.9,
    2.13, 2.16, 2.17, 4.16
Technology Holdings Ltd v IAG New Zealand Ltd (2009)
    15 ANZ Insurance Cases 61-786...3.20
Tension Overhead Electric (Pty) Ltd v National Employers
    General Insurance Co Ltd [1990] 4 SA 190 .... 10.20, 10.43
Thames and Mersey Marine Insurance Co v Hamilton (1887)
    L.R. 12 App. Cas. 484 ....1.11

xxiii

TABLE OF CASES

Thomas Wilson Sons v The Owners of the Cargo per the Xantho
(The Xantho) (1887) LR 12 App. Cas. 503 .... 1.2, 1.13, 2.31
Thompson v Hopper (1856) 6 E & B 172 .... 2.5
TM Noten BV v Harding [1990] 2 Lloyd's Rep. 283 .... 1.9, 1.12
Trinder, Anderson & Co v Thames & Mersey Marine Co [1898] 2 Q.B. 114 .... 2.34
Triple Five Corp v Simcoe & Erie Group 1994 CarswellAlta 451 .... 3.35
Tudor v New England Marine Insurance Company 12 Cush. Mass. 554 .... 2.17
Turnbull, Martin & Co v Hull Underwriters' Association Ltd
[1900] Q.B. 402 .... 2.13, 6.7, 6.11, 6.18, 6.20
Union Castle Mail Steamship Co Ltd v United Kingdom
Mutual War Risks Association [1958] 1 All ER 431 .... 7.14, 10.4
Union Insurance Society of Canton v George Wills [1916] 1 A.C. 281 .... 9.45
Univeg Direct Fruit Marketing DFM GMBH v MSC Mediterranean
Shipping Company SA [2013] EWHC 2962 (Comm) 2.15
Usher v Noble (1810) 104 E.R. 249 .... 3.15
Vallance v Dewar (1808) 1 Camp 503 .... 9.10, 9.27, 9.34, 9.39, 9.39, 9.41, 9.46
Vana Trading Co, Inc v S.S. 'Mette Skou' 556 F.2d 100, 104 (1977) 2.17
Verna Trading Pty Ltd v New India Assurance
Co Ltd [1991] 1 VR 129 .... 5.19, 9.15, 9.16, 9.17, 10.1, 10.38,
10.38, 10.40, 10.43, 10.54, 10.60, 10.65,
10.68, 10.69, 10.70, 10.72, 10.73, 10.74
Versloot Dredging BV v HDI-Gerling Industrie Versicherung AG
(The DC Merwestone) [2013] 2 Lloyd's Rep. 131 .... 1.6
Wadsworth Lighterage and Cooling Co Ltd v Sea Insurance Co Ltd
(1929) 34 Ll. L. Rep. 285 .... 7.4
Wayne Tank & Pump Co Ltd v Employers' Liability Assurance Corp Ltd
[1974] Q.B. 57 .... 1.9, 2.8, 2.10, 2.27, 2.29, 2.30
Weissberg v Lamb [1950] 84 Ll. L. Rep. 509 .... 3.5, 4.11
Wetherall v The London Assurance [1931] 2 K.B. 448 .... 8.10, 8.13
Wiggins Teape Australia Pty Ltd v Baltica Insurance
Co Ltd [1970] 2 NSWR 77 .... 5.19, 5.21, 9.15, 9.18, 10.38, 10.40,
10.54, 10.60, 10.64, 10.65, 10.69, 10.74
Williams v Shee (1813) 3 Camp. 469 .... 9.29
Wilson Brothers Bobbin v Green [1917] 1 K.B. 860 .... 2.34, 4.16
Wilson v Lancashire and Yorkshire Railway Company (1861)
9 Common Bench Reports (New Series) 632 .... 3.2, 3.33
Witcher Construction Company v Saint Paul Fire and Marine
Insurance Company 1996 550 N.W. 2d 1 .... 4.12
Wong Wing Fai Co SA v Netherlands Insurance Co
(1945) [1980-81] 1 SLR 242 .... 3.16
Xenos v Fox (1868) L.R. 3 C.P. 630 .... 4.10
Yorkshire Dale Steamship Co Ltd v Minister of War Transport
(The Coxwold) [1942] A.C. 691 .... 2.23, 2.23
Yorkshire Water v Sun Alliance & London Insurance [1997]
2 Lloyd's Rep. 21 .... 5.17
Zeus Tradition Marine Ltd v Bell (The Zeus V) [2000] 2 Lloyd's Rep. 587 .... 1.3

xxiv

TABLE OF STATUTES AND OTHER INSTRUMENTS

Contains:

- Conventions
- Institute Clauses (International Underwriting Association of London)
- Loss of Charter Hire Insurance – Including War & Loss of Charter Hire Insurance – Excluding War ABS 1/10/83
- Regulations
- York-Antwerp Rules

York-Antwerp Rules

York-Antwerp Rules 4.2, 7.14, 8.13
    Rule A 8.16
    Rule C 7.14, 8.16
    Rule C § 1 .... 8.15
    Rule C § 3 ....4.9, 8.11,
                            8.14, 8.15
    Rule of Interpretation 7.14
    Rule X 7.14
    Rule XI (a) 8.16
York-Antwerp Rules 1890 ....4.7, 7.13,
                            8.9, 8.11
York-Antwerp Rules 1924 ....4.7, 8.14
    Rule C 4.7, 8.13
York-Antwerp Rules 1974 .... 8.15
    Rule A 4.4, 4.5, 4.6
    Rule A/1 .... 7.12
    Rule C 4.5, 4.6, 4.7, 4.9,
                      8.9, 8.10, 8.15
    Rule F 4.4, 4.5, 4.6
    Rule Paramount 4.4

    Rule Rule XI(b) 4.2, 7.16
    Rule X(a) 4.2, 7.14
    Rule XI(a) 4.2, 7.14
    Rule XI(b) 4.2, 7.14, 7.16
York-Antwerp Rules 1994
    Rule C 4.7, 4.9, 7.13, 8.9
    Rule C § 3 .... 8.10
York-Antwerp Rules 2004 .... 8.15
    Rule A/1 .... 7.12
    Rule C 4.6, 4.7, 4.9, 7.13, 8.9
    Rule C § 1 .... 8.13
    Rule C § 3 .... 8.10
    Rule X(a(ii)) 4.2, 7.14
    Rule XI(a) 4.2, 7.14
    Rule XI(c)(i) 4.2, 7.16
    Rule XI(c)(ii) 4.2, 7.16
York-Antwerp Rules 2016 .... 8.15
    Rule A/1 .... 7.12
    Rule C 4.6, 4.7, 4.9, 7.13, 7.17,
                   7.17, 8.9, 8.13, 8.13
    Rule C § 1 .... 8.13
    Rule C § 3 .... 8.10
    Rule X(a(ii)) 4.2, 7.14
    Rule XI(a) 4.2, 7.14
    Rule XI(b)(i) 4.2, 7.14, 7.16
    Rule XI(b)(ii) 4.2, 7.16
    Rule XI(b)(iii) 4.2, 7.16
    Rule XI(c)(ii) 7.16

Regulations

Carriage of Goods by Sea Regulations
  1998 of Australia
    art 4A(2)(b) 3.2

Conventions

Hague Rules (International Convention for the Unification of Certain Rules of Law relating to Bills of Lading 1924)......................3.2
Hague-Visby Rules (Protocol to Amend the International Convention for the Unification of Certain Rules of Law Relating to Bills of Lading 1968)......................3.2
Hamburg Rules (United Nations Convention on the Carriage of Goods by Sea 1978)..........................3.2
  Art 5(2) 3.2
  Art 5(3) 3.16
Rotterdam Rules (United Nations Convention on Contracts for the International Carriage of Goods Wholly or Partly by Sea 2008)..................................3.2, 3.16

Institute Clauses (International Underwriting Association of London)

Institute Bulk Oil Clauses 1983
  cl 4.4 ....2.2
Institute Cargo Clauses................1.9, 3.22, 5.20, 10.2,
Institute Cargo Clauses (Air) 1982
  cl 13.1 ....3.19
Institute Cargo Clauses (All Risks) 1951 ....10.63
Institute Cargo Clauses (All Risks) 1982 ....2.30
  cl 6.2 ....2.19
  cl 8.1.1 ....10.39
  cl 8.1.2 ....10.40
  cl 8.1.2.1 ....10.39
  cl 8.1.4 ....10.40
Institute Cargo Clauses (All Risks) 2009 ....3.11, 5.8
  cl 2 ....3.3
  cl 4.3 ....2.18
  cl 4.5 ....3.3, 4.14
  cl 6.2 ....2.19, 5.8

cl 8.1.2 ....10.44
cl 8.3 ....3.3, 10.3, 10.9
cl 16.1 ....3.19
Institute Cargo Clauses (Extended Cover) 1952 ....10.63, 10.66
Institute Cargo Clauses (Extended Cover) 1956
  cl 6 ....10.63
Institute Cargo Clauses (F.P.A) 1946.................................10.63
Institute Cargo Clauses (W.A.)..10.48
Institute Cargo Clauses (W.A) 1946 ....10.63
Institute Cargo Clauses (Wartime Extension) 1941.............10.63
Institute Cargo Clauses 1958 ....10.64
Institute Cargo Clauses A-B-C 1982 ....3.23
  cl 4.2 ....1.13
  cl 4.5 ....1.18, 2.2, 2.10, 2.25, 2.30, 2,34, 3.24
  cl 6.2 ....2.21
  cl 8.1.2 ....10.51
  cl 8.3 ....2.20, 10.51, 10.52
  cl 16.1 ....3.19
Institute Cargo Clauses A-B-C 2009................3.3, 3.23, 4.2, 4.11, 4.13, 10.31, 10.36, 10.62, 10.69
  cl 2 ....4.2
  cl 4 ....4.13
  cl 4.2 ....1.13
  cl 4.4 ....2.17
  cl 4.5 ....1.18, 2.10, 2.13, 2.17, 2.25, 2.30, 2.34, 3.24, 4.2, 4.14
  cl 5 ....4.13
  cl 6 ....4.13
  cl 7 ....4.13
  cl 8 ....4.14, 5.21
  cl 8.1 ....10.36, 10.65, 10.66
  cl 8.1.2 ....10.36, 10.37, 10.51
  cl 8.1.4 ....10.51
  cl 8.3 ....2.20, 10.31, 10.51, 10.52, 10.61, 10.71
  cl 9 ....10.52, 10.70
  cl 10 ....10.70

xxvi

TABLE OF STATUTES AND OTHER INSTRUMENTS

cl 12 ....4.13
cl 13 ....3.19
cl 16 .... 4.11, 8.20, 10.69
cl 16.1 ....3.19
cl 18 ....5.19, 7.7, 9.15, 9.18,
10.31, 10.40, 10.59, 10.67
Institute Clauses......................................1.2
Institute Commodity Trades Clauses
A-B-C 1983
cl 4.5 ....2.2
cl 12 ....4.13
Institute FOSFA Clauses A-B-C 1985
cl 4.5 ....2.2
Institute Frozen Food Clauses (Excluding
Frozen Meat) A-B-C 1986
cl 4.5 ....2.2
Institute Frozen Food Clauses (Excluding
Frozen Meat) (All Risks) 1986
cl 4.5 ....3.23
Institute Frozen Food Clauses
(Excluding Frozen Meat) 'Full
Conditions' 1968
cl 4 ....1.10, 2.2
Institute Frozen Meat Clauses (All
Risks) – 24 hours break – down 1986
cl 4.5 ....2.2
Institute Frozen Meat Clauses (All
Risks) 1986
cl 4.5 ....2.2
Institute Mortgagees Interest Clauses
(Hulls) 1986......................................2.34
Institute Natural Rubber Clauses 1984
cl 4.5 ....2.2
Institute Strikes Clauses (Cargo) 2009.....4.2
cl 2 ....4.2
cl 3.5 ....4.2
cl 3.8 ....3.35
Institute Strikes Clauses (Extended
Cover) 1956
Institute Timber Trade Federation
Clauses 1986
cl 4.5 ....2.2
Institute Time Clauses –
Freight..6.2, 6.22
Institute Time Clauses – Freight 1983
cl 14 .... 6.3, 6.10, 8.4
Institute Time Clauses – Freight 1995
cl 15 .... 6.3, 6.10, 6.24

Institute Time Clauses – Hulls – Port
Risks 1987
cl 9.2.1 ....7.17
cl 9.3.8 ....7.17
Institute Time Clauses –
Hulls 1983......................... 8.3, 8.6, 8.21
cl 6.1.2 ....7.2
cl 8 ....8.3
cl 8.1.2 ....7.21
cl 10.2 ....8.21
cl.10.3..8.21
cl 11 ....8.3
cl 12 ....8.3
cl 13 ....8.3, 8.20
cl 16 ....7.15
cl 18.1 ....7.7
cl 23 ....2.21
Institute Time Clauses – Hulls 1995
cl 16 ....7.15
cl 8.1.2 ....7.21
Institute Voyage Clauses – Freight 6.2
Institute Voyage Clauses – Freight 1983
cl 12 ....6.3, 6.10
Institute Voyage Clauses – Freight
1995
cl 11 ....6.24
cl 12 ....6.3, 6.10
cl 14.2 ....2.21
Institute Voyage Clauses –
Hulls 1983...................... 5.7, 5.13, 9.19
cl 6.1.2 ....7.21
cl 8.1.2 ....7.2
cl 14 ....7.15
Institute Voyage Clauses – Hulls 1995
cl 6.1.2 ....7.21
cl 14 ....7.15
Institute War Clauses 1955
cl 7 ....10.63
Institute War Clauses (Cargo) 1982
cl 1.2 ....2.21
Institute War Clauses (Cargo) 2009 ....5.8
cl 1.2 ....2.21
cl 3.7 ....3.11, 3.35
Institute War and Strikes Clauses
Freight – Time 1983
cl 3 ....3.16
cl 4.4 ....6.22

xxvii

Institute War and Strikes Clauses
  Freight – Time 1995
    cl 3 ....3.16
    cl 1.1.2 ....2.21
    cl 4.5 ....6.22
Institute War and Strikes Clauses
  Freight – Voyage 1983
    cl 4.4 ....6.22
Institute War and Strikes Clauses
  Freight – Voyage 1995
    cl 1.1.2 ....2.21
    cl 4.5 ....6.22
    cl 5 ....9.19
    cl 5.1 ....9.19
Institute War and Strikes Clauses
  Hulls – Time 1983.............................8.3
    cl 3 ....3.16
    cl 4.4 ....7.7
Institute War and Strikes Clauses
  Hulls – Time 1995
    cl 3 ....3.16
    cl 4.4 ....2.34
    cl 5.5 ....7.17
Institute War and Strikes Clauses
  Hulls – Voyage 1983................5.7, 5.13
    cl 3 ....3.16
    cl 4.4 ....7.7

cl 5 ....9.19
cl 6 ....9.19
Institute War and Strikes Clauses
  Hulls – Voyage 1995
    cl 3 ....3.16
    cl 5 ....9.19
    cl 5.5 ....7.17
    cl 6 ....9.19
International Hull Clauses 2003...........7.3,
        7.7, 7.15, 7.21, 8.21, 9.19

Loss of Charter Hire Insurance – Including War & Loss of Charter Hire Insurance – Excluding War ABS 1/10/83

Loss of Charter Hire Insurance
  (Excluding War) ABS 1/10/83 ....8.2,
        8.3, 8.5, 8.6, 8.8,
        8.17, 8.19, 8.20
Loss of Charter Hire Insurance
  (Including War) ABS 1/10/83 ....8.2,
        8.3, 8.5, 8.6, 8.7, 8.8, 8.15,
        8.17, 8.19, 8.20, 8.22

TABLE OF LEGISLATION

Application of English Law Act 1993
  (Singapore)
    Cap 7A, First Schedule,
    Part II, item 5 ....2.2
Insurance Act 2015............ 2.22, 3.34, 9.5,
    9.22, 9.25, 9.42, 9.44, 10.2, 10.32
    Pt 2...10.24
    s 3...3.34
    s 3(3)(c)...................................9.13
    s 3(4)...................................3.36, 9.25
    s 3(4)(a)...................................9.13
    s 3(5)..................3.34, 9.7, 9.25, 9.27
    s 3(5)(c)..................................10.24
    s 3(5)(d) 10.24
    s 10.................................9.12, 10.30
    s 10(1)...............................9.42, 10.76
    s 10(4)................................9.44, 9.44
    s 11...5.22
    s 11(1).......................................10.76
    s 11(3).......................................10.76
    Sch 1 Pt 1 ....10.24
Marine Insurance Act 1906...........2.4, 2.5,
    2.6, 2.13, 3.6, 3.8,
    3.12, 6.5, 7.18,
    8.13, 10.1, 10.20,
    10.22, 10.32
    s 2...9.16
    s 2(1)...10.72
    s 2(2)...............................9.15, 10.72
    s 3.....................1.4, 3.8, 3.12, 10.72
    s 3(2)..................1.4, 3.12, 9.2, 9.16
    s 3(2)(a)...................... 3.13, 9.2, 9.16
    s 3(5)..9.10
    s 3(b)...9.10
    s 5.......................................3.8, 3.12
    s 5(1)..3.13

s 5(2).................3.8, 3.13, 3.13, 3.13,
    3.15, 3.36, 5.4, 6.4
s 16(3)..3.15
s 17..9.7
s 18..9.7
s 18(1)...9.10
s 18(2)...9.25
s 25(1)...10.12
s 26(3)..3.7
s 33(3)..................... 9.4, 9.22, 9.42
s 34...10.32
s 34(2)...9.4
s 34(3)..................... 9.22, 9.23, 9.42
ss 34–41 ....9.42
ss 35–42 ....9.42
ss 36–41 ....9.42
s 40(2)..9.42
s 41...3.8, 9.42
s 42.......................... 1.3, 3.5, 3.8, 9.1,
    9.2, 9.3, 9.4, 9.5, 9.7, 9.8, 9.12,
    9.14, 9.15, 9.16, 9.17, 9.18, 9.19,
    9.20, 9.23, 9.35, 9.41, 9.42, 9.42,
    9.43, 9.46, 9.48, 10.72
s 42(1)............ 1.3, 9.1, 9.5, 9.9, 9.32
s 42(2).................... 1.1, 9.10, 9.20,
    9.21, 9.22, 9.24, 9.27,
    9.29, 9.34, 9.36, 9.37,
    9.38, 9.46, 10.77
s 43..9.40, 9.42
s 44..9.40, 9.42
s 46......................... 9.42, 10.3, 10.23
s 46(1)...10.28
s 48......................... 1.3, 3.5, 3.5, 3.8,
    8.19, 9.3, 9.4, 9.15,
    9.28, 9.29, 9.42, 9.43,
    9.47, 9.48, 10.2, 10.3,

10.9, 10.10, 10.12, 10.14,
10.15, 10.16, 10.22, 10.25,
10.26, 10.27, 10.29, 10.30,
10.31, 10.43, 10.59, 10.72,
10.73, 10.74, 10.75, 10.77
s 49.................9.32, 9.38, 9.40, 9.42,
9.46, 10.2, 10.23, 10.26,
10.27, 10.28, 10.29, 10.31,
10.32, 10.33, 10.54,
10.57, 10.77
s 49(1)(a)............. 10.29, 10.57, 10.77
s 49(1)(b) 10.30
s 49(1)(c).................................... 10.29
s 49(1)(d) 10.30, 10.57
s 49(1)(e)........................10.57, 10.77
s 49(1)(f).................................... 10.77
s 49(1)(g) 10.77
s 49(2)... 10.1
s 55... 1.9
s 55(1)... 2.8
s 55(1)(a)...................................... 2.34
s 55(2)(a)...................................... 1.19
s 55(2)(b) 1.1, 1.2, 1.3, 1.4,
1.9, 1.10, 1.11, 1.18,
2.1, 2.2, 2.5, 2.6, 2.7,
2.8, 2.10, 2.12, 2.13,
2.14, 2.25, 2.34, 3.25,
4.11, 4.16, 6.2, 6.10,
6.22, 6.23, 7.1, 7.3, 7.5,
7.6, 7.9, 8.1, 10.25, 10.54
s 55(2)(c).............. 1.13, 2.30, 7.3, 7.4
s 56(1)... 2.20
s 57.. 3.7
s 57(1)................................2.20, 3.17
s 60....................................... 3.7, 3.8
s 60(2)(i) 7.18
s 60(2)(i)(a)................................. 3.16
s 63(1)... 3.19
s 66... 8.13
s 66(1).. 4.7
s 66(2)... 7.12
s 7(2)... 3.5
s 71(1)... 2.20
s 71(3)... 2.20
s 78... 8.20
s 78(1)... 8.20
s 78(3)...................... 4.10, 4.11, 8.22

s 78(4)...................................5.17, 7.6
s 79(1).. 3.19
s 84... 9.7
s 88.....................................1.3, 9.36
s 90(2).. 3.12
s 91(2)........................ 2.6, 9.1, 10.10
Sch 1 r 17 .... 3.13
Sch 1 r 2 ....9.2, 9.4
Sch 1 r 3 .... 9.2
Sch 1 r 3(b) 9.2
Sch 1 r 4 ....9.16, 9.28
Sch 1 r 7 ....1.5, 1.6
Marine Insurance Act 1908, Public
Act 1908 No 112 (New Zealand)
s 55(2)(b) 2.2
Marine Insurance Act 1909
(Australia) 2.12, 10.31
s 48.......................................9.43, 10.31
s 54......................... 9.15, 9.43, 10.31,
10.72, 10.74
s 55... 10.1
s 56(2).. 10.1
s 61(2)(b) 2.2, 2.12
s 68.. 2.12
Marine Insurance Act 1993 c.22 (Canada)
s 53(2)(a).. 2.2
s 56(1).. 3.17
s 8(2)... 3.13
Marine Insurance Ordinance – Chapter
329 (Hong Kong)
s 55(2)(b) 2.2
Nordic Marine Insurance Plan of 2013
Version 2016
cl 12.6 .... 7.8
cl 12-12 .... 8.21
Chapter 16................................... 8.5
cl 16(2)(c) 8.6
cl 16-9.. 8.21
Sale of Goods Act 1893 ....9.27
s 55.. 9.27
Slave Trade Act 1790 (30 Geo. 3,
c. 33)
s 8...................................... 2.3, 2.4
Slave Trade Act 1794 (34 G. 3, c. 80)
s 10.....................................2.3, 2.4
Swedish Marine Insurance Plan of 1957
s 157(c) para.2 .... 2.6

CHAPTER 1

Introduction to delay as a risk and fortuity considerations

Introduction

1.1 The occurrence of delay or some loss of time is frequent in maritime transport. This emanates firstly from the fact that many incidents may result in delay, such as including but not limited to perils of the seas, strikes, collisions, detentions, port congestions or health condition of crew members. Secondly, modern speed of transport requires either timely prosecution of marine adventures where a specific time frame is agreed, or failing this, their prosecution in reasonable time. All these circumstances as well as a mere loss of time upon the voyage insured may result in various types of losses and expenses that may be incurred by several parties such as shipowners, voyage and time charterers, cargo interests and project owners whose projects depend upon the timely arrival of goods carried by sea. These losses may be recoverable from the parties who are liable for delay under individual contracts, or depending upon the terms of the contracts, may have to be borne by the parties themselves who incur the losses. The relevant interests of the parties which can be affected by these losses or expenses can also be insurable under several types of marine insurance policies such as cargo, hull and machinery, freight, loss of hire and marine delay in start-up insurance.

1.2 Losses arising from delay have traditionally been excluded under cargo, hull and machinery and freight policies under the Common law. The exclusion of delay losses in cargo policies was due to an analogy with inherent vice and naturally occurring losses. This approach was then embodied in s 55(2)(b) of the MIA 1906 in respect of cargo and hull and machinery policies which provides that:

> 'Unless the policy otherwise provides, the insurer on ship or goods is not liable for any loss proximately caused by delay, although the delay be caused by a peril insured against'.

The main reason behind the exclusion of inherent vice or naturally occurring losses rests upon the fact that the losses in these cases are not fortuitous. The doctrine of fortuity is an obscure area of law and this chapter looks into whether one of the motives behind the exclusion of delay losses can be based on the suggestion that some types of delay losses are not fortuitous.

A number of cases have discussed the requirement for a loss to be fortuitous so as to be recoverable and that insurers are not liable for inevitable losses.[1] It is not clear whether any of the decided cases have ever established the said rule beyond doubt[2] and even if so, very few cases have addressed the issue of whether delay losses are fortuitous or inevitable. Fortuity which may indeed operate as an 'unnamed exclusion'[3] may at first sight seem to have little to add to the discussion of delay as an excluded peril given the express exclusion found in s 55(2)(b) and the relevant Institute Clauses. Nevertheless those provisions and other delay exclusions almost never distinguish between the types of delay which may give rise to the argument that where they are construed *contra proferentem*,[4] some types of delay may be deemed to escape the application of the exclusion such as delay beyond the control of the assured and extraordinary delay. This chapter generally examines delay as a risk and within the context of naturally occurring losses. Particular focus shall also be placed on types of delays with the view of assessing them in the context of the generic delay exclusion and in light of the doctrine of fortuity.

The use of the term 'delay' in the marine insurance law context

1.3 The meaning of delay in legal parlance is 'the act of postponing or slowing'.[5] The MIA 1906 does not provide a clear definition of the term, however careful reading of the rules set out in ss 42, 48 and 55(2)(b) would shed light on its meaning. Section 42(1) provides the implied condition that:

'. . . the adventure shall be commenced within a *reasonable time*'[6]

which can in turn:

'be negatived by showing that the *delay* was caused by circumstances known to the insurer before the contract was concluded'.[7]

---

1 *The Xantho* (1887) 12 App Cas 503; *Soya GmbH Kommanditgesellschaft v White* [1980] 1 Lloyd's Rep 491; [1982] 1 Lloyd's Rep 136; [1983] 1 Lloyd's Rep 122; *Global Process Systems Inc v Syarikat Takaful Malaysia Berhad (The Cendor Mopu)* [2009] 2 Lloyd's Rep 71; [2010] 1 Lloyd's Rep 243; [2011] 1 Lloyd's Rep 560.

2 See the doubt cast in Jonathan Gilman, Robert Merkin, Claire Blanchard and Mark Templeman, *Arnould's Law of Marine Insurance* (18th edn, Sweet & Maxwell 2013), para 22–24.

3 See the article of Stephen A. Cozen and Richard C. Bennett, 'Fortuity: The Unnamed Exclusion' (1984–1985) 20 Forum 222.

4 See *Houghton v Trafalgar Insurance Co Ltd* [1954] 1 QB 247; *Zeus Tradition Marine Ltd v Bell (The Zeus V)* [2000] 2 Lloyd's Rep 587 for the application of the *contra proferentem* rule of construction to exclusions.

5 Bryan A. Gardner (ed.), *Black's Law Dictionary* (10th edn, Thomson Reuters 2014), 518.

6 Emphasis added.

7 s 42(2).

A similar provision is found in s 48 which states that:

> '. . .the adventure insured must be prosecuted throughout its course with *reasonable dispatch* and, if without lawful excuse it is not so prosecuted, the insurer is discharged from liability as from the time when the *delay* became unreasonable'.[8]

The term is therefore used in the MIA 1906 context to denote prolongation of voyage beyond a reasonable time, reasonableness being a question of fact which has to be decided on a case-by-case basis.[9]

Definition of 'peril' and delay

1.4 'Risk' and 'peril' are often used interchangeably, however 'risk' that is an equivalent term to 'peril' must be distinguished from 'risk' in the general sense of the term that insurers undertake which includes uncertainty about the occurrence of a loss.[10] 'Marine peril' is defined as 'the perils consequent on, or incidental to, the navigation of the sea'.[11] The MIA also provides examples of marine perils such as perils of the seas, fire, war perils, pirates, rovers, thieves, captures and seizures; however does not limit the perils to this group providing that 'any other perils, either of the like kind or which may be designated by the policy' may also be covered.[12] Albeit not expressly enumerated in this definition, delay is stipulated as a peril that is excluded under s 55(2)(b) of the MIA 1906. This being said, it is doubtful whether all types of delay could be caught by this definition, particularly where delay is within the control of the assured and is therefore consequent on the assured's act and not on the navigation of the sea.[13]

1.5 Rules for Construction scheduled to the MIA reads 'perils of the seas' as 'fortuitous accidents or casualties of the seas',[14] and 'peril' is qualified as the cause of the loss which must be fortuitous.[15] Under English law, defining 'marine risk' which is used interchangeably with 'marine peril' was approached reluctantly[16] however there were attempts to describe the term 'risk' as an accidental cause in a

---

8 Emphasis added.

9 s 88.

10 E.G. Vaughan and M. Vaughan, *Fundamentals of Risk and Insurance* (10th edn, John Wiley & Sons 2008), 2. See also A. Willett, *Economic Theory of Risk and Insurance* (New York: The Columbia University Press 1901), 29.

11 MIA 1906 s 3.

12 MIA 1906 s 3(2).

13 This issue is analysed in paras 1.18–1.19.

14 r 7.

15 Per Lord Halsbury *Hamilton v Pandorf* (1887) 12 App Cas 518 at 524; similarly McLachlin J, *CCR Fishing Inc v Tomenson* [1991] 1 Lloyd's Rep 89, at 91.

16 Lord Buckmaster in the Privy Council in *Grant, Smith and Co v Seattle Construction and Dry Dock Co* [1920] AC 162, 171–172 stated that: 'It is not desirable to attempt to define too exactly a "marine risk" or a "peril of the sea". . . but it can be said that it is some condition of sea or weather or accident of navigation producing a result which but for these conditions would not have occurred'.

commercial insurance policy where the loss was caused by abnormal delay arising from accidental circumstances.[17]

In *Schloss Brothers v Stevens*[18] the policy was in the printed form of an ordinary Lloyd's policy at the time and involved a clause covering 'all risks by land and by water'. The combination of disorganisation of the transport arrangements due to a revolution in the area of the port, the damp climate and storage conditions meant that a delay of two years had necessarily exposed goods to damp. The term 'all risks by land and by water' meant for Walter J all risks whatsoever, i.e. 'all losses by any accidental cause of any kind occurring during transit'.[19] He asked whether the damage was from some accidental cause and answered that:

'there was an abnormal delay in the transit arising from unusual and accidental causes, which necessarily involved an exposure of the goods to damp'.[20]

The loss was held to be the direct result of an accidental cause and was therefore recoverable. Delay in this case was a delay beyond the control of the assured and was due to abnormally disorganized transport arrangements arising from a revolution that was going on at the time. The loss, although caused by delay which was not expressly excluded under the policy, was therefore held to be accidental and within the wording 'all risks by land and water'.

General considerations on fortuity

1.6 English authorities do not seem consistent in deciding whether the loss or the cause of the loss must occur fortuitously. The lack of clarity in this respect could have been due to the fact that 'in insurance contract law, fortuity is a concept involving both the likelihood of loss and the cause of loss'.[21] In *The Cendor Mopu*[22] the Supreme Court recently interpreted fortuity in the context of perils of the seas, which are defined as 'fortuitous accidents or casualties of the seas' and which do not include 'ordinary action of winds and waves'.[23] The Court held that 'ordinary' qualified the 'action' of the winds and waves and not the winds and waves themselves. It followed accordingly that the result of the peril and not the peril itself was the subject of the assessment on fortuity. It is submitted however that the judgment in this case and generally in decisions on perils of the seas would inevitably turn upon the interpretation of the definition thereof and cannot be therefore authority for a general suggestion that the result of the perils and not

---

17 *Schloss Bros v Stevens* [1906] 2 KB 665. See also Howard Bennett, 'Fortuity in the law of Marine Insurance' *Lloyd's Maritime and Commercial Law Quarterly* 3 (Aug) 2007, 315–361, 316.

18 [1906] 2 KB 665.

19 At 673.

20 At 673.

21 Bennett, *Fortuity in the law of Marine Insurance*, 315.

22 *Global Process Systems Inc v Syarikat Takaful Malaysia Berhad (The Cendor Mopu)* [2011] UKSC 5.

23 r 7 of the Schedule to the MIA 1906.

the perils themselves must be taken into account in assessing fortuity. Shortly after *The Cendor Mopu*, in *The DC Merwestone*[24] which was decided also in the context of perils of the seas, Popplewell J cited the following part of the decision of the Supreme Court of Canada in *CCR Fishing Ltd v Tomenson Inc (The La Pointe)*:[25] 'In general the word "fortuitous", as interpreted by the cases, carries the connotation that the cause of the loss should not have been intentional or inevitable'.[26]

1.7 In the leading authority on fortuity *British v Gaunt*[27] it was stated that 'Damage . . . must be due to some fortuitous circumstance or casualty',[28] in other words fortuity was assessed by reference to the peril causing the loss. Lord Sumner enunciated that

> '"All risks" . . . includes the risk that when it happens to be raining the men who ought to use the tarpaulins to protect the wool may happen to be neglecting their duty. This concurrence is fortuitous; it is also the cause of loss by wetting'.[29]

Accordingly negligence was the cause of the loss and was fortuitous. In another like instance the meaning of 'accidental and fortuitous' was regarded as where the 'assured is deprived *by some unexpected acts* of his property in the goods or his possession in the goods'.[30] Judgments from other common law jurisdictions were also delivered which assessed fortuity with reference to the peril and not to the loss.[31]

1.8 Fortuity within the context of delay and losses arising therefrom have not been canvassed to a great extent by judicial authorities as yet except in *The Wondrous*[32] where the cause of the loss and not the loss itself was considered to be fortuitous in respect of losses arising from detention and delay. This discussion is necessary in distinguishing between ordinary and extraordinary delays that result in a loss. Where fortuity is assessed on the basis of the cause of the loss and not the loss itself, ordinary delays that are inevitably to occur would readily constitute non-fortuity and the resulting losses, damages or expenses would not be recoverable on such ground. A distinction between losses and expenses arising from this type of delay would lie in that it would be more likely for such a delay to cause an expense than to cause a loss of perishable goods. In the latter case, the issue would particularly turn upon whether the loss arose from causes such as insufficiency of packing, machinery breakdown or inherent vice, rather than ordinary delay.

---

24 *Versloot Dredging BV v HDI-Gerling Industrie Versicherung AG (The DC Merwestone)* [2013] 2 Lloyd's Rep 131.

25 [1991] 1 Lloyd's Rep 89.

26 At para 32.

27 *British & Foreign Marine Ins. Co Ltd v Gaunt (No 2)* [1921] 2 AC 41.

28 [1921] 2 AC 41, 47.

29 At 57.

30 *London & Provincial Leather Processes Ltd v Hudson* [1939] 2 KB 724, 730 per Goddard LJ (emphasis added).

31 In the US, a fortuitous loss was considered as a loss caused by a fortuitous event in *Avis v Hartford Fire Ins Co* 283 N.C. 142, 195 S.E. 2d 545, 548 (1973) as cited in Cozen and Bennett, *Fortuity: The Unnamed Exclusion*, 225.

32 In *Ikerigi Compania Naviera SA v Palmer (The Wondrous)* [1991] 1 Lloyd's Rep 400.

Fortuity and existing policy language

1.9 One of the main questions to be raised is what implications would fortuity have on existing policy language considering that most marine insurance policies in standard form such as the Institute Cargo Clauses contain the exclusion of delay clause which is an equivalent of s 55(2)(b) of the MIA 1906. Lord Sumner in *British v Gaunt*[33] approached fortuity as a fundamental rule whereby its requirement would arise from the nature of the risks insured under an all risks policy rather than the precise words of the policy. This approach had also found support later on in *Blackwell*[34] where the insurance cover was 'against all damage . . . of whatsoever nature'. The assured accordingly had to prove that the loss was caused by a fortuitous event and it was not inevitable. It was also stated in *Soya G.m.b.H. Kommanditgesellschaft v White*[35] that:

> 'inevitability of loss is not mentioned in s. 55 of the MIA, because it operates at a much more fundamental level than the rule that underwriters are only liable for losses proximately caused by perils insured against. Underwriters can rely upon inevitability of loss, because the whole concept of insurance is about risks, not certainty'.[36]

A loss can result from a fortuitous event, yet this would not necessarily connote that it would not fall within a contractual exclusion.[37] However, it is submitted that the contractual exclusion should give no room for doubt and shall not be ambiguous in order for the exclusion to apply notwithstanding the fact that the event causing the loss is fortuitous. In this case the unambiguous contract language would probably prevail and although losses are fortuitous, exclusions would avail insurers from liability under the policy. It was considered in *Wayne Tank*[38] that:

> '. . . The effect of an exception is to save the Insurer from liability for a loss which, but for the exception would be covered. The effect of the cover is not to impose on the Insurer liability for something which is within the exception'.[39]

---

33 *British & Foreign Marine Ins. Co Ltd v Gaunt (No 2)* [1921] 2 AC 41.

34 *CA Blackwell (Contracts) Ltd v Gerling General Insurance Co* [2008] Lloyd's Rep IR 529. This was later supported also in *Mayban General Insurance Bhd v Alstom Power Plants Ltd* [2004] 2 Lloyd's Rep 609 per Moore-Bick J at 686.

35 [1982] 1 Lloyd's Rep 136.

36 At 149 per Donaldson LJ.

37 This was made clear by Blair J in *Global Process Sytems Inc, Global Process Systems (Asia Pacific) Sdn Bhd v Syarikat Takaful Malaysia Berhad (The Cendor Mopu)* [2009] EWHC 637 (Comm), para 90 where he enunciated that damage may be caused by inherent vice without being inevitable by reference to *TM Noten BV v Harding* [1990] 2 Lloyd's Rep 283; he also added that not being factually inevitable did not mean that the loss was fortuitous. See also the American case *Goodman v Fireman's Fund Insurance Co*, 600 F.2d 1040 (4th Circ. 1979).

38 [1974] QB 57.

39 ibid per Cairns LJ at 69. This view was previously mentioned in *P. Samuel & Co Ltd v Dumas* [1924] AC 431, 467 and 468 per Lord Sumner; and in *Atlantic Maritime Co Inc. v Gibbon* [1954] 1 QB 88 which was a case on delay losses per Sir Raymond Evershed MR at pp 118, 119 and Morris LJ at p 138.

Exclusion of delay

1.10 It was suggested that delay cover may be provided by including the wording 'deterioration from any cause' against a higher premium or by certain standard form market clauses.[40] In all risks policies or in named perils policies where no specific exclusion clause is found the recovery is subject to the occurrence of losses caused by fortuitous events.[41] Where the policy insures against 'all damage of whatsoever nature' as was the case in *Blackwell* and does not contain a delay exclusion, the next question that would arise would be whether the exclusion in s 55(2)(b) could be implied and relieve insurers from liability where the loss is proximately caused by delay. The rule in s 55(2)(b) applies 'unless the policy otherwise provides' and it can be submitted that the wording 'all damage of whatsoever nature' is an instance where the policy merely requires that the loss is caused by a fortuity. The exclusion of delay would not automatically apply in this case and the issue would be what type of delay could be considered as a fortuity. It is submitted below that ordinary delays and delay within the control of the assured would arguably not constitute fortuitous delays.

Naturally occurring losses, fortuity and ordinary delay

1.11 Commonly, insurance contracts do not cover losses that are inevitably to occur in the ordinary course of events without the intervention of any external accidental factor. Fortuity is therefore a concept that was elaborated by courts mainly in the context of losses by inherent vice[42] and wilful conduct of the assured.[43] Prior to the enactment of the MIA, delay was enumerated in *Thames and Mersey v Hamilton*[44] along with ordinary wear and tear and wilful conduct of the assured to qualify that every accidental circumstance resulting not from the formers, incidental to navigation, happening in the course of the navigation of the ship and causing

---

40 Victor Dover, *A Handbook to Marine Insurance* (8th edn, London: Witherby 1975), 408. cl 4 of the Institute Frozen Food Clauses (Excluding Frozen Meat) 'Full Conditions' 01/04/68 provides:

> 'This insurance covers loss of, deterioration of or damage to the interest insured from *any cause* which shall arise during the currency of the insurance'. Emphasis added.
>
> According to UNCTAD Legal and Documentary Aspects of the Marine Insurance Contract's document TD/B/C.4/ ISL/27/ Rev.1 (1982), 35, a majority of the replies from developed market-economy countries to the questionnaire of the secretariat of the UNCTAD on cargo delay cover indicated that coverage for losses caused by delay is possible usually on ad hoc basis and usually in the form of coverage for physical loss or damage only. One of the responses from a developing country using British conditions indicated that due to the absence of a standard delay cover wording, the insurance companies stick to the terms and conditions stipulated by the Institute of London Underwriters which specifically exclude delay.

41 Suggestions were made as to the fact that the term 'all risks' is sufficient to exclude any liability for loss or damage due solely to delay and inherent vice, see R.J. Lambeth, *Templeman on Marine Insurance* (5th edn, Macdonald and Evans Ltd 1981), 151.

42 See for instance *Global Process Systems Inc v Syarikat Takaful Malaysia Berhad (The Cendor Mopu)* [2011] UKSC 5.

43 See for instance *Beresford v Royal Insurance Co Ltd* [1938] AC 586 which involved a policy on life insurance.

44 *Thames and Mersey Marine Insurance Co v Hamilton* (1887) LR 12 App Cas 484.

loss to the subject matter insured would be a peril of the sea.[45] It is submitted that this approach assumes that no accidental circumstance may result from delay, an approach which was also taken in *Taylor v Dunbar*,[46] one of the main authorities on delay constituting the background for the current s 55(2)(b) of the MIA 1906. It was stated in that decision that 'there are so many cargoes which are necessarily affected by the voyage being delayed' which was a ground for not allowing recovery for delay losses.[47] For Keating J, 'it would even be dangerous to establish a precedent to the contrary'.[48] Accordingly had the voyage been in the ordinary duration expected for that particular adventure, the goods would have arrived in good condition and no loss would have occurred; or at least the loss would not have been caused by delay.

1.12 The reason why delay is enumerated along with perils resulting in naturally occurring losses can rest upon the fact that delay, so far as perishables are concerned, is mostly part of the process of natural deterioration of goods, particularly where it is of extraordinary length.[49] However, it can be argued that the fallacy with relating delay losses to inevitable losses caused by perils such as inherent vice is twofold. Firstly, the doctrine of fortuity is based on the happening of accidental 'perils' and not of accidental 'losses'. In other words, the peril and not the loss must occur accidentally, or fortuitously. It would follow that in pure inherent vice cases[50] or ordinary wear and tear cases, questioning whether these perils were accidental may turn out without satisfying result; they merely 'exist' as happenings in consequence of which inevitable losses may occur. Delay is nevertheless distinct from inherent vice and ordinary wear and tear as a cause of loss as it may or may not be accidental. Where for instance a delay is of ordinary nature, meaning that a certain amount of loss of time is expected on every voyage and goods are packed accordingly, any loss that would ensue would either not be caused by delay, or if it is, the ordinary nature of such delay would not constitute fortuity because such delay is usually inevitable.

Ordinary delay

1.13 Usually ordinary incidents of the voyage such as ordinary wear and tear and ordinary leakage and breakage are excluded from policy cover.[51] *A contrario* meaning of the exclusion of 'ordinary leakage and breakage' may suggest that

---

45 per Lord Bramwell in *Thames and Mersey Marine Insurance Co v Hamilton* (1887) LR 12 App Cas 484, 492 although Lord Bramwell recognised 'the probability that severe criticism might detect some faults in this'.

46 (1869) LR 4 CP 206.

47 per Keating J at 210.

48 ibid.

49 In *CA Blackwell (Contracts) Ltd v Gerling General Insurance Co* [2008] Lloyd's Rep IR 529, HHJ Mackie QC held that as long as the loss was not the result of ordinary wear and tear or necessary deterioration but resulted from some sort of occurrence, the loss was fortuitous.

50 e.g. *Noten v Harding* [1990] 2 Lloyd's Rep 283.

51 s 55(2)(c); Institute Cargo Clauses A-B-C 1982 and 2009 cl 4.2. *A contrario* meaning of the exclusion of 'ordinary leakage and breakage' may suggest that extraordinary leakage and breakage is not excluded and an analogy may be drawn in this respect with 'ordinary delay'.

INTRODUCTION TO DELAY

extraordinary leakage and breakage is not excluded. An analogy may be drawn between ordinary leakage and breakage and ordinary delay.

The essential reason why losses caused by ordinary occurrences are excluded is given that

> 'so as to consider an incident as a "peril" there must be some casualty, something that "could not be foreseen as one of the necessary incidents of the voyage"'.[52]

The ordinary nature of the occurrences therefore would make the occurrences something else than a 'risk'. This reasoning gives rise to the question of whether an ordinary delay could be classified as a 'risk',[53] where delay is expected by the insurer and assured in the ordinary course of trade. Delay may be expected to occur at the time the insurance contract is made; by way of example during a voyage in winter season between ports where it is a known fact that ice causes port congestion, the resulting delay of a few hours can be classified as ordinary delay. Albeit such delay is highly likely to arise in that situation, whether a loss will result therefrom would not be certain.

1.14 Given that delay arises from perils preceding it (perils either insured, uninsured or excluded), assessment of fortuity would result in the questions of whether firstly one of the perils leading to delay is to occur, secondly whether a delay is to result inevitably from such peril and thirdly cause a loss. It would follow that although it is not certain that perils insured under the policy will occur, it can almost be inevitable at least for some perils (e.g. deprivation perils such as detention and seizure) that a certain delay which is expected both by the insurer and the assured would result therefrom, in particular if such delay occurs in the usual course of transit or trade and can be classified as ordinary. The foregoing discussion on whether delay or loss caused by delay must be fortuitous[54] shall accordingly be important in this respect. By way of example, in case of port congestion it is highly likely (or inevitable) that some delay will occur; however it may not be very likely that the goods will be damaged by an ordinary delay where the cargo is not perishable or even if perishable, where it is suitably packed and cared for to withstand the ordinary course of transit.

1.15 The above shall not strictly be read as suggesting that merely delays which are likely to occur in the ordinary course of transit are ordinary,[55] and the reasons are twofold. Firstly, although no decision was made on the point, it was suggested that even a delay of considerable length and of uncertain duration is an incident

---

52 *Thomas Wilson Sons v The Owners of the Cargo per the Xantho (The Xantho)* (1887) LR 12 App Cas 503, 509 per Lord Herschell.

53 Susan Hodges, *Cases and Materials on Marine Insurance Law* (London: Cavendish Publishing Ltd 1999), 435.

54 See para 1.8.

55 The length of delay may be of importance in aggravating the loss caused by necessary incidents or ordinary perils of the voyage. In the US case *Cory v Boylston Insurance Co* 107 Mass 140 (1871) the Supreme Judicial Court of Massachusetts held that the underwriters do not assume the risk of the ordinary perils incident to the course of the voyage, nor of ordinary dampness of the holds though aggravated by the length of delay.

of maritime adventure which is clearly within the contemplation of the parties and can be an ordinary delay which makes it something other than the cause of frustration.[56] Secondly, while deciding whether delay is ordinary or accidental, attention may be somewhat given to the circumstances causing delay and to their accidental nature. In *Schloss Brothers v Stevens*[57] the policy involved an all risks clause covering 'all losses by any accidental cause of any kind occurring during transit'.[58] The combination of disorganisation of the transport arrangements due to a revolution in the area of the port, the damp climate and storage conditions meant that a delay of two years arising from unusual and accidental causes necessarily involved exposure of goods to damp. The abnormal delay that resulted in damage of the cargo of bales was qualified as an accidental cause on the facts. The term 'all risks by land and by water' meant for Walter J all risks whatsoever, i.e. 'all losses by any accidental cause of any kind occurring during transit'. He asked 'was the damage from some accidental cause' and answered that:

> '. . . there was an abnormal delay in the transit arising from unusual and accidental causes, which necessarily involved an exposure of the goods to damp'.[59]

The delay in this case had many preceding events such as revolution, damp climate and storage conditions; it was considered that delay was aggravated by such events.[60] It may therefore be argued that a delay caused by unusual circumstances is not an ordinary delay and is fortuitous, hence within the wording 'all risks' and recoverable where the policy contains no express and unambiguous exclusion clause for delay losses.

1.16 According to the authority of *Schloss Brothers v Stevens*, it may be argued that loss caused by abnormal delay falls into a category of its own, and constitutes an all risks loss;[61] nevertheless a careful reading of the case would suggest that it may somewhat be authority that abnormal delay is an accidental cause 'if resulted by unusual and accidental circumstances'.[62] What made the delay abnormal in *Schloss Brothers v Stevens* was not merely its length yet also whether the circumstance resulting in delay is accidental and unforeseen.

---

56 Argued by Lord Sumner in *Bank Line v Capel* [1919] AC 435, 458–459. In this case, the dispute turned upon whether a lengthy delay frustrated the object of a charterparty.

57 [1906] 2 KB 665.

58 ibid at 673.

59 At 673.

60 At 668. It is noteworthy that the policy in this case was 'warranted free from capture, seizure and detention, and consequences thereof' however there was no defence set up under that clause although the delay resulted from the revolution in the area.

61 Dunt, *Marine Cargo Insurance* (2nd edn, Informa Law from Routledge 2015), 7.25, who argues that this seems doubtful as delay is by its nature unusual following the reference of *The Chambers Dictionary* (11th edn, 2008) which had, as cited, defined delay as 'the (amount of) time during which something is put off'.

62 See the passage in para 1.15 above. The case was distinguished from *Pink v Fleming* (1890) 25 QBD 396 on the basis that in that case the assured needed to prove that the damage resulted directly from collision whereas in this case it needs to prove that the loss is the direct result of 'some such accidental cause'.

INTRODUCTION TO DELAY

1.17 If the above reasoning is tenable, in 'all risks' policies not containing an express exclusion clause as to delay, losses arising from ordinary delays and not arising from abnormal delays should be excluded on the ground of fortuity. If the term 'all risks' inherently excludes non fortuitous events such as ordinary wear and tear or inherent vice, their express exclusion in the policies must mean something other than 'ordinary' wear and tear, for instance an extraordinary wear and tear.[63] The exclusion of delay in all risks policies makes no reference to ordinary or extraordinary delay, therefore would arguably exclude ordinary delay which would not be considered as fortuitous. Moreover, an ordinary delay, as an event foreseeable by both the insurer and assured at the time of the contract can be taken to be part of the definition of perils of the seas if it results therefrom; otherwise it can be part of the preceding peril resulting in delay. Whether losses arising from these events where delay is involved could be considered as caused by delay is another issue. Delay, if ordinary in nature, can arguably not be a separate cause and so long as the preceding peril is not an excluded peril, the loss would be caused by a fortuity and therefore would be recoverable. Alternatively, losses arising during an ordinary delay would likely to indicate that the proximate cause of the loss is a peril other than delay. In the case of perishables, therefore, the initial unsuitability of packing, inherent vice or uncargoworthiness of the vessel must be considered as potential causes of the loss.

Fortuity: analogy of wilful conduct of the assured and delay within the control of the assured

1.18 The general delay exclusion in s 55(2)(b) and in the Institute Cargo Clauses A-B-C 1982 and 2009 cl 4.5 do not specify whether losses caused by delay beyond the control of the assured are also excluded. Under most of the Institute Clauses delay beyond the control of the assured does not terminate the cover,[64] yet this shall not necessarily connote that losses caused by delay beyond the control of the assured shall be recoverable.[65] In effect such losses can be approached from the angle of fortuity. Losses caused by delay beyond the control of the assured are accidental; conversely losses caused by delay within the control of the assured where for instance the assured delays the voyage knowingly would be considered as a loss that is not accidental. This would raise the question of whether these losses are fortuitous the discussion of which would be crucial where the policy does not contain an unambiguous delay exclusion. It is submitted that the current exclusion clause in the Institute Cargo Clause is not of this type for no distinction is made within the clause in respect of delay within or beyond the control of the assured. This arguably gives rise to the argument that the exclusion clause is ambiguous

---

63 Cozen and Bennett, 250.

64 This issue is discussed in Chapter 10.

65 *Lam Seng Hang Co Pte Ltd v The Insurance Corporation of Singapore Ltd* [2001] SGHC 31. See also Dunt, *Marine Cargo Insurance*, 11.66.

11

and shall be interpreted *contra proferentem*, in which case a loss caused by a delay beyond the control of the assured can arguably be recoverable.[66]

1.19 An analogy may be drawn between losses caused by delay within the control of the assured and losses caused by wilful conduct of the assured which are excluded on the ground of want of fortuity.[67] It was stated in *The Wondrous*[68] that a policy should not be construed as covering the ordinary consequence of voluntary conduct of the assured arising out of ordinary incidents of trading, as this would not be a risk.[69] The test in *The Wondrous* required two stages, namely that the loss must be unexpected from the point of view of the assured and that it must not be within the control of the assured.[70] With respect to the latter, an assured may for instance cause loss of time by not paying the customs fees that can consequently result in the goods being damaged as in *Safadi v Western Assurance Co.*[71] In this case a cargo of bales of cotton was destroyed by fire during transit whilst they were delayed in the Customs House at Beirut. The goods had not been released by the Customs because nobody had paid for them. The insurers refused payment as they contended the delay was within the control of the assured and the court held in their favour. In such a case a delay within the control of the assured that causes the loss may be accepted as a non-fortuity as the loss occurs by the mere passage of time induced by the assured. It goes without saying that this case is of importance particularly with respect to deprivation perils such as detention and strikes which naturally contain an element of delay. Accordingly, where a deprivation peril is ensued by a delay within the control of the assured,[72] any loss resulting therefrom would have been caused (proximately or not) by the conduct of the assured and not by a fortuity. This would particularly apply to situations where the loss has an inevitable connection with loss of time, for instance in respect of loss of hire.

Does delay or the peril causing delay have to be taken into account in assessing fortuity

1.20 In *The Wondrous*[73] Hobhouse J dealt with interpreting 'loss of hire' under a freight policy. Owing to the fact that customs duties had not been paid which was characterised by Hobhouse J as the voluntary conduct of the assured, the vessel

---

66 See the discussion in para 2.20.

67 s 55(2)(a).

68 *Ikerigi Compania Naviera SA v Palmer (The Wondrous)* [1991] 1 Lloyd's Rep 400.

69 ibid, 416

70 For a more detailed analysis on this aspect, please see James Davey and John Coggon, 'Life Assurance and Consensual Death: Law Making for the Rationally Suicidal', *Cambridge Law Journal* 65(3) November 2006, 521–548, 530.

71 (1933) 46 Ll L Rep 140.

72 Where for example after the initially forced detention comes to an end, the vessel is detained for a longer time because the assured fails to provide necessary documents to satisfy customs authorities for the release of the vessel. In *Ikerigi Compania Naviera SA v Palmer (The Wondrous)* [1991] 1 Lloyd's Rep. 400 the loss of hire was caused by a detention given that the customs duties had not been paid by the assured.

73 *Ikergi Compania Naviera SA v Palmer (The Wondrous)* [1991] 1 Lloyd's Rep 400.

was detained by harbour authorities which caused a delay resulting in loss of hire. One of the questions raised was whether delay was fortuitous and Hobhouse J referred to the detention peril and not to delay in deciding whether it was foreseeable at the time when the contract was concluded. He noted that the consequence of a voluntary conduct of the assured which was the delay would not be described as fortuitous and that in the absence of any statement to the contrary no policy should be construed as 'covering the ordinary consequences of voluntary conduct of the assured arising out of the ordinary incidents of trading'.[74] This case may therefore stand as authority that the delay resulting from the wilful conduct of the assured could be qualified as a non-fortuitous event.

Knowledge of the assured as to the certainty of loss

1.21 The concept of uncertainty of loss which is required for fortuity in insurance law was considered in *Soya v White*[75] with the introduction of the knowledge of the assured by Donaldson LJ as a complementary requirement of uncertainty.[76] The knowledge of the assured must be approached cautiously as there is considerable view that it does not have a strict impact on deciding about fortuity. In *Global Process Systems Inc v Syarikat Takaful Malaysia Berhad (The Cendor Mopu)*[77] Blair J after holding that the loss was not inevitable did not go further to ask whether the claimants knew about the inevitability.[78] This view is also consistent with Waller LJ's approach in *Soya v White*[79] where he makes no distinction between known and unknown certainty of loss.[80] Although knowledge is not widely accepted as an essential criterion, it is important to set out at which time the knowledge is required to assess fortuity for losses caused by delay. The usual rule is that the knowledge of the assured is required at the conclusion of the contract,[81] moreover knowledge at the commencement of the voyage was also suggested.[82]

---

74 At 416. The decision was appealed on other grounds.

75 [1982] 1 Lloyd's Rep 136.

76 This introduction was made *obiter* by Donaldson LJ at 149. Also considered as 'conscious awareness of the certainty' in Abraham S. Kenneth, 'Peril and Fortuity in Property and Liability Insurance', *Tort & Insurance Law Journal*, 36(3) Spring 2001, 777–802, 792.

77 [2009] EWHC 637 (Comm).

78 See para 88.

79 [1982] 1 Lloyd's Rep 136.

80 ibid, 140.

81 *Ikerigi Compania Naviera SA v Palmer (The Wondrous)* [1991] 1 Lloyd's Rep 400, at 415–416. Furthermore it was stated that the knowledge could also have been assessed according to the time of making the charterparty (the decision was with respect to loss of hire under a loss of hire policy). It is submitted that the knowledge at the time of making the insurance contract shall be favoured on the ground that the extent of the knowledge of the assured may change between the date of the charterparty and the date of the insurance contract assuming that the latter is usually concluded after the charterparty is entered into. See also Bennett, *Fortuity* 358, this has also been stated in many leading American cases on fortuity such as *Compagnie des Bauxites de Guinée v Insurance Co of North America* 554 F. Supp. 1080 (W.D. Pa) rev'd, 724 F.2d 369 (3d Cir. 1983).

82 *Soya v White* [1980] 1 Lloyd's Rep 491, 504 per Lloyd J.

CHAPTER 2

Cargo insurance and delay: physical loss to the subject-matter insured

Introduction

2.1 The main interest covered by a cargo policy is physical loss of or damage to the cargo. This type of loss has been the subject of the earlier cases on delay through which the current exclusion of delay losses in s 55(2)(b) of the MIA and in the standard market conditions have been developed. The motives behind excluding these losses were mainly twofold: the first one rested upon an analogy to inherent vice as an excluded event and the second one related to the approach to proximate causation in the late 19th century which sought to exclude delay as the last cause in time. This chapter will analyse the origins of the delay exclusion from the scope of cargo policies and assess whether the earlier authorities can survive the changes in law as to the rule of proximate causation. It will also be speculated on how the new rules on causation can be applied to circumstances involving delay as a cause of loss.

Delay and loss by deterioration

2.2 In cargo insurance, delay cover may be provided in the British market on an *ad hoc* basis by express provision in the policy[1] by including the wording 'deterioration from any cause'[2] against a higher premium. Moreover, even after

---

1 *Lewis Emanuel & Son Ltd v Hepburn* [1960] 1 Lloyd's Rep 304.
2 cl 4 of the Institute Frozen Food Clauses (Excluding Frozen Meat) 'Full Conditions' 01/04/68 provides:

'This insurance covers loss of, deterioration of or damage to the interest insured from *any cause* which shall arise during the currency of the insurance' (emphasis added).

See also Dover, A Handbook to Marine Insurance (8th edn, Witherby 1975) 408. However this wording is not standardised and in other national markets using Institute Clauses where delay is strictly excluded, the assureds may be at a disadvantage in asserting that such cover is a legitimate concern of a marine insurance policy.

According to UNCTAD Legal and Documentary Aspects of the Marine Insurance Contract's document TD/B/C.4/ ISL/27/ Rev.1 (1982), p 35, a majority of the replies from developed market-economy countries to the questionnaire of the secretariat of the UNCTAD on cargo delay cover indicated that coverage for losses caused by delay is possible usually on ad hoc basis and usually in the form of coverage for physical loss or damage only. One of the responses from a developing country using British conditions indicated that due to the absence of a standard delay cover wording, the insurance companies stick to the terms and conditions stipulated by the Institute of London Underwriters which specifically exclude delay.

the conclusion of the insurance contract, the insurer may extend the cover to losses caused by delay by endorsement.[3] This being the case, losses caused by delay are customarily excluded in standard form cargo policies[4] which followed the delay exclusion in s 55(2)(b) of the MIA 1906. The common law background of this generic exclusion shall be scrutinised below. It is noteworthy that the analysis of the earlier common law authorities which were embodied in s 55(2)(b) would have an impact on several common law jurisdictions as their relevant legislations contain equivalent provisions.[5]

A general review of the pre-MIA authorities

2.3 Delay is an event which is capable of causing loss of or damage to perishable goods. Therefore most of the cases constituting the basis of the current law on delay as an excluded peril are on deterioration of perishables. Close examination of these early cases is required so as to determine in which context they assessed delay and whether they are currently still good law. One of the most influential decisions of the law on delay was *Gregson v Gilbert*.[6] The negligence of the captain in finding the destination of the vessel caused delay on the voyage and want of provisions, which consequently resulted in the natural death of the slaves which were at the time considered as cargo. The delay in this decision was not considered as an event that had to be excluded, it was merely stated as an event resulting in the natural death of the slaves if coupled by want of provisions and the negligence of the captain. Following this decision, the Slave Trade Act 1790 (30 Geo. 3, c. 33),[7] s 8, and the Slave Trade Act 1794 (34 G. 3, c. 80), s 10 had been passed prohibiting the insurance on slaves for losses caused by natural death or ill-treatment.

---

3 An analogy may be made in this respect to *Kiriacoulis Lines SA v Compagnie d'Assurance Maritime (The Demetra K)* [2002] Lloyd's Rep IR 795 where the insurer by endorsement extended the cover to war risks and malicious acts which were initially excluded.

4 e.g. Institute Cargo Clauses A-B-C 1982 cl 4.5.; Institute Frozen Food Clauses A-B-C 1986 cl 4.5.; Institute Commodity Trades Clauses A-B-C 1983 cl 4.5; Institute FOSFA Clauses A-B-C 1985 cl 4.5; Institute Frozen Meat Clauses A 1986 cl 4.5; Institute Frozen Meat Clauses A-24 hours breakdown 1986 cl 4.5; Institute Natural Rubber Clauses 1984 cl 4.5; Institute Bulk Oil Clauses 1983 cl 4.4; Institute Timber Trade Federation Clauses 1986 cl 4.5. In all these conditions the wording used for the exclusion was 'loss of or damage to goods proximately caused by delay'.
United Nations Cargo Insurance All Risks Cover 1987 provides in cl 3.8:

'loss, damage, liability or expense caused by delay, even though the delay is caused by a peril insured against, except liability or expense payable under clause 5 (the General Average and Salvage Clause)'.

5 MIA 1906 s 55(2)(b) is applicable in Singapore by virtue of the Application of English Law Act 1993, Cap 7A, First Schedule, Part II, item 5. The equivalent provisions in other common law jurisdictions are as follows: Marine Insurance Act 1909 (Australia) s 61(2)(b); Marine Insurance Act 1993, c.22 (Canada) s 53(2)(a); Marine Insurance Ordinance – Chapter 329 (Hong Kong) s 55(2)(b); Marine Insurance Act 1908, Public Act 1908 No 112 (New Zealand) s 55(2)(b).

6 *Gregson v Gilbert* (1783) 3 Douglas 232.

7 The title of the Act was 'An Act to amend and continue, for a limited Time, several Acts of Parliament for regulating the shipping and carrying Slaves in British Vessels from the Coast of Africa' in the preamble of which the Slave Trade Act 1788 was recited.

2.4 Following the enactment of the statutes on natural death of slaves, a similar issue was raised in *Tatham v Hodgson*[8] a few years later. Several slaves had perished for want of food owing to the prolongation of the voyage due to bad weather. The dispute arose as to whether the loss was by perils of the seas or by the natural death (mortality) which was statutorily excluded. The Statute 30 Geo. 3, c. 33, s 8 on which the policy was then based had enacted that it was not lawful for any owner of a vessel to insure any cargo of slaves against any loss or damage, except the perils of the sea, piracy, insurrection, or capture by the King's enemies, barratry by the master or crew, and destruction by fire. Moreover the Statute 34 Geo. 3, c. 80, s 10, which had recited the former Act, provided that no loss or damage was recoverable on account of the mortality of slaves by natural death or ill treatment, or against loss by throwing overboard of slaves on any account whatsoever. The ordinary course of the voyage was six to eight weeks yet the voyage had lasted for over six months, in other words the delay was unreasonably long for the specific voyage. It was argued that the length of the voyage arising from the perils of the seas was the genuine source of the death and that accordingly the loss was not natural, thus excluded.[9] Delay was not discussed as a cause of the loss which was not covered by the policy. It was merely an event causing death because of the want of provisions whereas the fundamental issue was whether the death was natural given the statutory exclusion.[10] Delay in this case was merely an event induced by the perils of the seas, causing the exhaustion of the provisions which resulted in the loss. Accordingly, the natural death would not have been caused but for the delay; nonetheless the relation of delay to the loss was merely incidental in that it would not have caused the loss had there been sufficient provisions. The Court decided that the loss was by mortality and not by perils of the sea by referring to the intention behind passing the Statute, namely to prevent situations where masters would knowingly equip the vessel with less provisions than required and claim against insurers for the loss of slaves.

Although in this case Lawrence J mentioned that delay could be the cause of the loss where the slaves had died of fevers occasioned by the length of the voyage,[11] that was merely due to the natural death exclusion of the Statute. Perhaps the only *ratio* that can be extracted from the judgment is that unreasonable delay in the voyage was considered distinct from the perils of the seas (whereas an ordinary delay could have been a natural result of the perils of the seas and not a distinct peril) and had occasioned want of provisions and consequently natural death which was an excluded peril according to the Statute. Given that the judgment was delivered upon consideration of the provisions of the Statute, it is not clear whether the authority of *Tatham v Hodgson* should have been an authority for the general suggestion that delay losses are excluded under English law which

---

8 *Tatham v Hodgson* (1796) 6 TR 656.

9 At 658.

10 i.e. the statutes 30 G. 3, c. 33, s 8, and 34 G. 3, c. 80, s 10.

11 At 659.

was later on enshrined in the MIA 1906. It is submitted that this argument can be supported by the view expressed by Abbott CJ in *Lawrence v Aberdein*[12] who considered[13] that underwriters would be liable where live animals perish for want of provisions as a result of the prolongation of the voyage by perils of the sea in the absence of an express exclusion of mortality or statutory prohibition. This background used to be the background against which the leading cases on the exclusion of delay, i.e. *Taylor v Dunbar*[14] and *Pink v Fleming*[15] were decided.

2.5 In *Taylor v Dunbar*[16] a cargo of meat had become putrid given that the vessel carrying the cargo had been delayed due to bad weather. The meat was in no way affected or injured by the sea water however had to be jettisoned because of the damage. It was held by the court that the reason why the goods deteriorated was delay on the grounds that it was not among 'other perils, losses and misfortunes' recoverable under the policy and that 'delay in the voyage has never been considered as covered'.[17] This principle was subsequently embodied in the Marine Insurance Act 1906[18] and has been thenceforth one of the few leading cases on delay. Two points require clarification in respect of the decision. Firstly, the judgment contained no particular reference to causation and delay as the last cause in time. Upon the facts of the case, there was more than one delay and albeit the first delay had occurred prior to the perils of the seas, the unexpectedly long delay had incidentally occurred last in time. It is submitted that considering the approach taken by courts to proximate causation in the nineteenth century,[19] it would nevertheless not be a fallacy to argue that the unreasonably long delay in the voyage was held not to be covered as it was the last cause in time although this was not expressly held in the decision.[20] The second point relies on the fact that the interpretation of *Tatham v Hodgson* lacked consideration of the statutory exclusion of mortality which was the main ground upon which the earlier judgments on delay were delivered, as well as the speech of Abbott CJ in *Lawrence v Aberdein*.[21] Even where it is assumed that *Taylor v Dunbar* was a correct interpretation of the early cases on delay, it may have nevertheless been interpreted when it was enacted in the MIA 1906 as to apply to all types of delay, both to ordinary and extraordinary delays. This is given that there were specific statements in the

---

12 *Lawrence v Aberdein* (1821) 5 B & Ald 107.

13 At 111.

14 *Taylor v Dunbar* (1869) LR 4 CP 206.

15 (1890) LR 25 QBD 396.

16 (1869) LR 4 CP 206.

17 per Montague Smith J at 211.

18 s 55(2)(b).

19 *Thompson v Hopper* (1856) 6 E & B 172, 937; *Dudgeon v Pembroke* (1877) 2 App Cas 284.

20 *Pink v Fleming* (1890) LR 25 QBD 396 is the leading case on delay applying the last-in-time causation rule. It is not very clear from the reference of *Pink v Fleming* to *Taylor v Dunbar* as to whether the reference was to the application of the last-in-time causation or whether losses caused by delay were never covered under English law. *Taylor v Dunbar* had not expressly applied the last-in-time causation rule and the ratio of the decision rested upon that merely losses caused by unreasonably long delays were not recoverable. The delay in *Pink v Fleming* was arguably not of such kind.

21 (1821) 5 B & Ald 107.

judgment as to the comparison between the ordinary duration of the voyage and the actual and unreasonable length of the voyage.[22] One of the reasons according to which an unexpected duration of the voyage can be held as a proximate cause or a cause of the loss can be because this type of delay may not be the natural result of a preceding peril (e.g. perils of the seas and ordinary delay resulting from it) and in this sense it may be a delay that could break the chain of causation between the initial peril and the loss.

2.6 It is well known that the MIA 1906 is an Act codifying the pre-MIA authorities and that the common law authorities continue to apply, save in so far as they are inconsistent with the express provisions of the Act.[23] The exclusion of delay in s 55(2)(b) is general and ambiguous as to whether it excludes both ordinary and extraordinary delay. It can therefore be argued that if *Taylor v Dunbar* is considered as good law – this work supports the opposite view – against the background of earlier decisions, s 55(2)(b) would apply to only extraordinary delays.[24] It is noteworthy that in some of the Scandinavian jurisdictions, the unusual length of delay was an essential element for the cover available for deterioration losses caused by delay.[25]

'Last cause in time' rule

2.7 According to the approach to the proximate causation rule prior to *Leyland Shipping Co Ltd v Norwich Union Fire Insurance Society Ltd,*[26] the cause must not have been too distant to the loss in time or in space.[27] The rule was applied in the leading case on deterioration and delay *Pink v Fleming*[28] where a cargo of fruit was insured under a marine policy against 'damage consequent on

---

22 It was stated in the decision that the ordinary voyage of the two vessels was normally fifty hours; whereas the delay of one of the vessels was a week and the other vessel had delayed for five days. The reference in the decision to *Tatham v Hodgson* (1796) 6 T.R. 656 where, according to the Court in *Taylor v Dunbar* the loss was 'occasioned by extraordinary delay in the voyage from bad weather' can also support this argument.

23 MIA 1906 s 91(2).

24 It can be argued that the word 'delay' alone is sufficient to describe a situation where the ordinary duration of the voyage is exceeded. Nevertheless, not every delay (in the sense where the ordinary duration of the voyage is exceeded) would be capable of causing cargo damage whereas every delay in that sense could cause loss of market. Cargoes are usually shipped adequately to overcome ordinary delays in the voyage, and most of the cargo damages usually occur where extraordinary delays are involved save in so far as there was inadequate packaging or inherent vice at the commencement of the voyage.

25 The Swedish Marine Insurance Plan of 1957 s 157(c) para.2: 'If the voyage, on account of an incident as mentioned in the 1st paragraph (stranding), has taken longer time than normally must be expected, the insurer is liable for damage to the goods caused by the delay, provided that there has been at least three months delay'.

26 *Leyland Shipping Co Ltd v Norwich Union Fire Insurance Society Ltd* [1918] AC 350.

27 *Ionides v The Universal Marine Insurance Co* (1863) 14 CB (NS) 259, 289 per Willes J.

28 (1890) L.R. 25 QBD 396.

collision'. The vessel carrying the cargo had sustained damage due to a collision in consequence of which she had to be repaired and the fruits be discharged and re-shipped during which they had perished. The dispute turned on whether the proximate cause of the loss was delay or collision, in which case the assured would have been able to recover. The speeches delivered as to the cause of the loss approached the matter from different angles. It was stated by Lindley and Bowen LJJ that the damage had been partly caused by delay and partly by the handling of the fruit which necessarily took place in the discharging and re-shipment for the purposes of the repairs;[29] whereas Lord Esher MR, delivering the leading speech, found that the handling was the proximate cause of the loss.[30] The Court had observed that delay was not within the wording 'consequent on collision' as it had not resulted naturally from the collision. The ground for this argument was that a collision might have occurred without either delay or handling of cargo. The concerns with such an argument are twofold; firstly that it has an inclination of adopting 'but for' causation which is no longer applicable following the proximate causation doctrine;[31] and secondly that some delay during the voyage is the natural consequence of collision even if handling is not, especially where repairs are necessary. The crucial point is whether the delay which ensues is unreasonably long compared to the expected duration of the voyage of the goods. Moreover, the reference of the Court to *Taylor v Dunbar*[32] as an authority supporting their view is controversial. A closer examination of the latter would suggest that the reference of *Pink v Fleming* was not plausible.

It is submitted that the authority of *Pink v Fleming* can no longer apply following *Leyland*[33] and losses caused by delay in circumstances where delay is the last cause in time can therefore no longer be excluded on this basis. The principles arising from the above cases, as conceived at the time of the enactment of the MIA 1906, were embodied in s 55(2)(b).

---

29 At 397–398.

30 Lord Esher's reasoning was as follows: Without collision the loss would not occur however the loss had not occurred from the collision alone. The collision had resulted in the vessel being repaired and the cargo had to be discharged. If there was no repairs and discharge of the cargo, *consequent delay* and handling of the fruit the loss would not have happened. Collision was an effective cause of putting into port and repairs. For the repairs it was necessary to remove the fruit and such removal caused damage to the cargo. Accordingly 'The agent. . .which proximately caused the damage to the fruit was the handling', at 397.

31 That is, subsequent to *Leyland Shipping Co Ltd v Norwich Union Fire Insurance Society Ltd* [1918] AC 350.

32 (1869) LR 4 CP 206.

33 The earlier approach of 'last cause in time' was abandoned with *Leyland Shipping Co Ltd v Norwich Union Fire Insurance Society Ltd* [1918] AC 350. Post-*Leyland* authorities on delay in the United States observed that the authority of *Pink v Fleming* (1890) LR 25 QBD 396 could not be reconciled with that of *Leyland. Lanasa Fruit v Universal Ins. Co* 302 U.S.556 per Chief Justice Hughes at 567; *Brandyce v United States Lloyds*, 207 A.D. 665, 203 N.Y.S. 10. For the discussion please see below.

Delay as a proximate cause in deterioration cases

(a) General overview of proximate causation

2.8 The problem of causation involves prioritising some causes over others or rejecting the idea that some are causes.[34] The device developed to achieve the finding of a proximate cause of loss was codified by the MIA in s 55(1) which is a default rule and operates unless the policy otherwise provides.[35] The delay exclusion set out in the MIA[36] and in many other standard form policies is subject to the proximate causation rule, hence a close scrutiny of the rule is required so as to have a better understanding of delay exclusions and their scope.

A strict reading of s 55(1) which expresses that an 'insurer is not liable for *any loss not proximately caused* by a peril insured against'[37] raises an important issue as to proximate causation. It may be read as suggesting that the insurers would not be liable where a proximate cause of the loss is not expressly covered. This line of interpretation could invite the conclusion that *The Miss Jay Jay*[38] was not correctly decided[39] where the Court of Appeal held that the assured could recover where the loss was proximately caused by both a peril insured against and an uninsured peril. Against this background, it is possible to reconcile *The Miss Jay Jay* and s 55(1) on the ground that s 55(1) refers solely to single proximate cause situations, i.e. where the other cause is not a proximate cause of the loss. This suggestion may be supported by the fact that before *Leyland*,[40] the proximate cause was accepted as the last cause in time, therefore a single proximate cause was mostly to be found among other causes. The approach of Courts in the pre-MIA decisions showed a determination to find a single cause and the possibility that there could have been two or more proximate causes was rarely acknowledged.[41]

---

34 John Lowry and Phillip Rawlings, 'Proximate Causation in Insurance Law', *Modern Law Review* 68(2) 310–319, (2005), 311.

35 s 55(1) provides: 'Subject to the provisions of this Act, and unless the policy otherwise provides'.

36 s 55(2)(b).

37 Emphasis added.

38 *JJ Lloyd Instruments Ltd v Northern Star Insurance Co Ltd (The Miss Jay Jay)* [1987] 1 Lloyd's Rep 32.

39 Lowry and Rawlings, 314.

40 *Leyland Shipping Co Ltd v Norwich Union Fire Insurance Society Ltd* [1918] AC 350.

41 *Leyland Shipping Co Ltd v Norwich Union Fire Insurance Society Ltd* [1918] AC 350, at 353, 371; *Board of Trade v Hain Steamship Co Ltd* [1929] AC 534, 541. Recently courts make attempts to find in favour of one cause rather than to content themselves with finding that there were concurrent causes, as was the approach in certain post-*Leyland* cases. For illustrations of recent cases decided in line of the former please see *Kiriacoulis Lines SA v Compagnie d'Assurance Maritime, Aeriennes et Terrestres (The Demetra K)* [2002] Lloyd's Rep IR 823 and *Global Process Systems Inc v Syarikat Takaful Malaysia Berhad (The Cendor Mopu)* [2011] UKSC 5.

For illustrations of cases decided with the latter approach, see *Wayne Tank & Pump Co Ltd v Employers' Liability Assurance Corp Ltd* [1974] QB 57, 69 per Cairns LJ who suggested that the judges 'should not strain to find a dominant cause'. Similarly please see *JJ Lloyd Instruments Ltd v Northern Star Insurance Co Ltd (The Miss Jay Jay)* [1987] 1 Lloyd's Rep 32. The Supreme Court in *Global Process Systems Inc v Syarikat Takaful Malaysia Berhad (The Cendor Mopu)* [2011] UKSC 5, para 79 criticised this case in relation to its approach to the definition of perils of the seas, however presumed that it was not suggesting that where there were two causes both playing a role in the loss, the court must always treat them as equal proximate causes.

It would follow that the ensuing s 55(2)(b) on delay arguably applies to circumstances where delay is the single proximate cause of the loss. The reluctance to find a single dominant cause and the importance given to concurrent causes gives insurers room to exclude liability where one of the proximate causes is excluded.[42] This approach is of essence for delay exclusions which are ambiguous as to the type of delays and do not distinguish between a delay beyond and within the control of the assured as separate perils. As a result of this approach, policies would not meet the reasonable expectations of the ordinary assureds who are unaware of this rule of causation[43] and who would expect to be covered in case of delay beyond their control, and yet may be left without cover.

(b) Proximate causation and delay following *Leyland*

2.9 The approach of *Pink v Fleming*[44] to proximate causation and delay has not yet been challenged by a higher court in England. Nonetheless, the 19th century cases on causation in relation to delay inevitably require careful consideration in the light of the abandonment of the last cause in time approach to proximate causation. Mainly two views exist as to the applicability of the earlier authorities on the recoverability of losses caused by delay: The first view rests upon the proposition that *Taylor v Dunbar* and *Pink v Fleming* were decided before the introduction of the new proximate causation doctrine established by *Leyland* and shall no longer apply in resolving disputes on causation where delay is involved as a peril.[45] The second view argues that although *Pink v Fleming* is no longer good law given the abandonment of the earlier rule, the authority of *Taylor v Dunbar* is not yet challenged in English courts and that the insurers could still exclude liability on facts similar to *Taylor v Dunbar*.[46] It is noteworthy that even though it can be submitted that *Taylor v Dunbar* where the last cause in time rule of causation was not

---

42 *Wayne Tank & Pump Co Ltd v Employers' Liability Assurance Corp Ltd* [1974] QB 57.

43 Lowry and Rawlings, 316. It is noteworthy that the interpretation of the policy according to the 'reasonable expectation of the assured doctrine' is not yet adopted under English law however is a device that courts refer to where there are ambiguities in the policies. Nevertheless the English Law Commission has proposed in its Consultation Paper no.182 on *Misrepresentation, Non-Disclosure and Breach of Warranty* that business contracts concluded on insurers' terms (standard market policies) should involve an element of reasonable expectation of the assured which would establish a fair balance between insurers and assureds (at 1.37). The Commission pointed out that the system would be adopted while protecting also the legitimate benefits of the insurers.

44 (1890) LR 25 QBD 396.

45 Bennett, *The Law of Marine Insurance*, 15–35. See also Gilman and Merkin, *Arnould's Law of Marine Insurance* (18th edn), para 22–34 which mentions this view and John Dunt and William Welbourne, 'Insuring Cargoes in the New Millenium: The Institute Cargo Clauses 2009', Chapter 6 in D.R. Thomas (ed.), *The Modern Law of Marine Insurance*, Volume 3, para 6.38 as to the view that post-*Leyland* rule of causation is likely to prevail.

46 The editors of the 18th edition of *Arnould* stated that both views were, according to them, of equal weight. The latter view was adopted by the editors of the earlier edition of this work, see Gilman and Merkin, *Arnould's Law of Marine Insurance and Average* (17th edn), 22–33. See also E.H. Coghill, 'Marine Insurance- Damage by Delay', *The Australian Law Journal*, Vol 12, 1939, 427–430, 429 supporting the view that *Taylor v Dunbar* is still good law.

expressly applied can be reconciled with *Leyland* and is still good law, the type of delay there excluded was merely extraordinary delay.

2.10 It is submitted that the former view is favoured for three reasons. Firstly the MIA had been enacted against the background of cases where courts were trying to find a single proximate cause of the loss; this approach was challenged by *Leyland* and was followed by lower courts in the following years.[47] Secondly, an analogy can be drawn from the inherent vice exclusion and the recent speech of Lord Mance in *The Cendor Mopu*,[48] where he enunciated:

> '. . . it might be thought relevant that the 1906 Act, crystallising statutorily the concepts of perils of the seas and inherent vice, was enacted against the background of the Victorian authorities, and before the definitive emergence of the modern conception of proximity'.[49]

This view can support the argument that the modern approach to proximate causation should be adopted in determining the dominant cause in lieu of the pre-*Leyland* authorities. Thirdly, post-*Leyland* key judgments on delay delivered in the United States[50] and Australia,[51] albeit not applying the authority of *Leyland*, held that it is impossible to reconcile the ratio of *Leyland* and the ruling of Lord Esher in *Pink v Fleming*[52] as to the fact that the last cause in time must be looked at. The consequence of suggesting that the last cause in time rule of causation no longer applies to construe the delay exclusion in s 55(2)(b) would also extend to the construction of the same exclusion found in the Institute Cargo Clauses.[53] The key judgments delivered in other jurisdictions shall be analysed in the below sections.

(c) How to apply *Leyland* to delay cases

2.11 In *Leyland Shipping Co Ltd v Norwich Union Fire Insurance Society Ltd*[54] the vessel was torpedoed by a submarine, following which some water had penetrated through the holes of the hull. Repeated groundings followed after the ship was requested to beach outside the harbour by the port authorities. The House of Lords held that the repeated grounding was not a *novus actus interveniens* and that the torpedoing was the proximate cause of loss.

---

47 *Wayne Tank & Pump Co Ltd v Employers' Liability Assurance Corp Ltd* [1974] QB 57, 69 per Cairns LJ who suggested that the judges 'should not strain to find a dominant cause'; *JJ Lloyd Instruments Ltd v Northern Star Insurance Co Ltd (The Miss Jay Jay)*.

48 *Global Process Systems Inc v Syarikat Takaful Malaysia Berhad (The Cendor Mopu)* [2011] UKSC 5.

49 At para 76.

50 *Lanasa Fruit v Universal Ins. Co* 302 U.S. 556, 567 per Chief Justice Hughes; *Brandyce v United States Lloyds*, 207 A.D. 665, 203 N.Y.S. 10.

51 *Norwich Union Fire Insurance v Wm.H. Price* (1933) S.R. (N.S.W.) 196.

52 (1890) LR 25 QBD 396.

53 The Institute Cargo Clauses A-B-C 1982 cl 4.5 contained the identical exclusion wording as s 55(2)(b), 'loss damage or expense *proximately caused* by delay'. In the Institute Cargo Clauses A-B-C 2009 cl 4.5 provides 'loss damage or expense *caused* by delay' (Emphasis added).

54 [1918] AC 350.

So as to be able to apply the decision of *Leyland* to cases involving delay, careful reading of *Leyland* is required to distinguish what this case brought about with respect to efficient causes. It was suggested that to find the efficient cause, 'the loss of the *kind* covered must be inevitable, but the *extent* of the loss need only be such as would have been within reasonable contemplation or not unlikely to occur.'[55] According to this test, a delay of one day or one month where goods are adequately refrigerated during carriage would not make them dissimilar as such delay would not inevitably lead to the perishing of goods. Where no refrigeration is in place, whereas a delay of two days may not render delay as the proximate cause of damage to goods, a delay of one month could render it *the* or *a* proximate cause as such delay would inevitably result in the loss of or damage to goods. This approach also draws a link to the earlier discussion with respect to excessive delay. In case of inadequate refrigeration and delay, unseaworthiness (or uncargoworthiness) of the vessel can also be considered as a proximate cause of the loss. By way of example, the lack of refrigeration for frozen goods would inevitably result in loss which would make unseaworthiness the proximate cause of loss and delay could be an event aggravating the loss.

Identifying the proximate cause of the loss rests upon identifying whether the loss is the inevitable consequence of a peril or whether the loss follows from that peril in the ordinary course of events.[56] It is therefore crucial to determine the circumstances where delay can be a *novus actus interveniens*, in other words, where delay can break the chain of causation. This issue will be discussed in the following parts of this work.

(d) The authorities of *Lanasa Fruit* and *Norwich Union*

2.12 The pre-MIA authorities on perishable goods and delay have not been tested after the enactment of the MIA in England. It is nevertheless possible to make speculations on the basis of recent and relevant case law from other jurisdictions and the technological developments in shipping and containerising.

---

55 Malcolm Clarke, 'Insurance: The Proximate Cause in English Law', *Cambridge Law Journal* 40(2), November 1981, 284–306, 288. The 'loss of the *kind* covered' referred to the loss by seawater and explosion. The '*extent* of the loss' was the sinking given the time of the year and wartime conditions.

Clarke further develops his view at 289 suggesting that the proximate cause is the event, which, 'in all the circumstances prevailing at the time of the event, led inevitably to the kind of loss in question.' and that 'If such loss was the inevitable result of a peril, its full extent will be recoverable, even though such extent was no more than not unlikely to occur at the time of the peril'. Arguably, the Supreme Court in *Global Process Systems Inc v Syarikat Takaful Malaysia Berhad (The Cendor Mopu)* [2011] UKSC 5 did not approach the perils of the sea on this basis; namely that a usual move of the waves would not inevitably result in loss by seawater (although a higher degree of them could do) although the extent of loss, i.e. breaking of the legs of the rig was not unlikely to occur. If the above interpretation was adopted by the Supreme Court the perils of the seas would not have been held to be the proximate cause.

56 Bennett, *The Law of Marine Insurance*, 9–35. In *Reischer v Borwick* [1894] 2 QB 548, a vessel insured against sustained a leak by collision. Temporary repairs were carried out, but while the vessel was being towed to port for permanent repairs, a motion of water (peril of the sea) re-opened the leak and the vessel ran aground. It was held per Davey LJ at 553 that the hole was 'a continuing source of risk and danger' and that the failure of the temporary repairs did not break the chain of causation.

Upon an appeal from the Supreme Court of New South Wales (Australia), the Privy Council in *Norwich Union Fire Insurance v Wm.H. Price*[57] went into determining whether perishable goods were lost by delay where they were undamaged by sea water in a collision and had to be sold because of ripening during repairs. The essential dispute between the parties in the appeal was with respect to the interpretation of s 68 of the Australian Marine Insurance Act 1909 on constructive total loss, therefore the issue on delay was touched upon with no more than a few words both in the judgment of the Supreme Court of New South Wales[58] where Street CJ had pronounced that 'the plaintiff was not liable for any loss caused by delay'; and of the Privy Council. It was stated in the Privy Council that:

> 'the sale was not the result of any sea damage or peril insured against affecting the lemons, but of their inherent vice or of delay: the sale, unless justifiable in consequence of perils insured against, gave no claim against the appellants: it could not on any view constitute a constructive total loss'.[59]

The judgment did in no way refer to the general delay exclusion in the Marine Insurance Act 1909 of Australia[60] and no analysis of the proximate cause of the loss was carried out by the Privy Council.

2.13 A few years later in the United States, the leading judgment *Lanasa Fruit Steamship v Universal Insurance*[61] was delivered in relation to damage to perishable goods and delay. In that case a cargo of bananas was insured against 'perils of the seas' and was totally lost following the stranding of the vessel upon which they were carried. The policy had not contained any specific exclusion of delay, therefore the main question was whether a general clause in a cargo policy covering the assured against perils of the seas would cover a loss where stranding so delays the voyage that the cargo becomes a total loss. The Court assumed that the goods were in sound condition when shipped and would have been merchantable at the end of the ordinary length of the voyage.[62] It is submitted that otherwise, inherent vice could have been a potential cause of loss, or that delay in the voyage could have merely been an event aggravating the initial deterioration which occurred before shipment. The Court found that delay was caused by stranding and the proximate cause of the deterioration was stranding which was a loss by perils of the seas, thus covered under the policy. The judgment contained several references to the earlier authorities on delay under English law[63] and suggested that the law in the United States was different from that of England in that the MIA 1906 restricted

---

57 (1934) AC 455.
58 *Norwich Union Fire Insurance v Wm.H. Price* (1933) S.R. (N.S.W.) 196, 202.
59 At 464–465 per Lord Wright.
60 The exclusions of delay in s 55(2)(b) of the MIA 1906 and s 61(2)(b) of the MIA 1909 are identical for these purposes.
61 *Lanasa Fruit v Universal Ins. Co* (1938) 302 U.S. 556 (Supreme Court of the United States).
62 *Lanasa Fruit v Universal Ins. Co* (1938) 302 U.S. 556, 559.
63 Such as *Tatham v Hodgson* (1796) 6 TR 656; *Taylor v Dunbar* (1783) 3 Douglas 232; *Pink v Fleming* (1890) 25 QBD 396. The Court rejected the approach of *Pink v Fleming* to proximate causation in light of *Leyland*.

CARGO INSURANCE AND DELAY

the doctrine of proximate cause by introducing to the s 55(2)(b) the expression 'although the delay be caused by a peril insured against'.[64] This wording clearly means that the delay exclusion shall apply even where delay is caused by a risk insured against.[65]

2.14 In *Brandyce v United States Lloyds*[66] which was decided prior to *Lanasa* where no express clause excluding delay was inserted in the policy, the Court decided that if the ship had not been damaged by reason of sea perils the potatoes would have arrived in sound condition. The proximate cause of the loss therefore was the sea peril because it was the efficient dominant cause which, although incidentally involving delay, placed the cargo in such a condition that because of inevitable deterioration or decay, it could not be reshipped and carried to its destination. In *Archer-Daniels-Midland Company v Phoenix Insurance Company of New York*[67] where the policy contained a delay exclusion including the expression 'whether caused by a peril insured against or otherwise' it was stated that:

> '. . .Delay Clause in the Policy at issue clearly states that losses arising from delay are excluded whether caused by a peril insured against or otherwise. . .Prior to the addition of this italicized language, cases such as *Brandyce* and *Lanasa Fruit* suggested that losses caused by delay are covered if the delay was caused by an insured peril. With the addition of this language, however, it is irrelevant whether the delay was caused by an insured peril'.[68]

The expression gave rise to discussions under English law where it was enunciated that it was a surplusage given that delay is always caused by an event, and mostly a peril insured against such as perils of the seas.[69] The House of Lords in *The Playa de las Nieves*[70] pronounced in the context of a freight policy that 'whether arising from a peril of the sea or otherwise' was there to make it plain that 'the clause is concerned with an intermediate event between the occurrence

---

64 At 567. The wording appears also in Time Charter Clauses in freight policies. The phrase is usually part of the exclusions of delay and has several equivalents, such as 'even though the delay be caused by a risk insured against' in the Institute Cargo Clauses 1982 and 2009 A-B-C cl.4.5 and in almost all the delay exclusions appearing in the Institute Clauses; 'whether caused by a peril insured against or otherwise' in *Turnbull, Martin & Co v Hull Underwriters Association, Ltd* [1900] QB 402 where it was stated that 'otherwise' meant 'other perils insured against' and this issue was not disputed. A similar wording was inserted in the policy discussed in *Federation Insurance Company of Canada v Coret Accessories Inc. & Hirch* [1968] 2 Lloyd's Rep 109.

65 In some foreign policies, losses caused by delay are excluded only where delay is not caused by an insured risk. *See* Cargo Insurance Policy of Antwerp 20 April 2004 (Goederenverzekeringspolis van Antwerpen 20 April 2004) art 11.2.4.

66 207 A.D. 665, 203 N.Y.S.10, aff'd, 239 N.Y. 573, 147 N.E.201 (1924).

67 975 F.Supp. 1137 (United States District Court S.D. Illinois, 1997).

68 At 1147.

69 In *Russian Bank for Foreign Trade v Excess Insurance Company Ltd* [1918] 2 KB 123, 127 with respect to a clause reading 'warranted free from any claim consequent on loss of time, whether arising from a peril of the sea or otherwise' Bailhache J stated *obiter* that the expression was a surplusage and that every claim upon a policy must arise from a peril insured against and that the expression was therefore obsolete.

70 *Naviera de Canarias S.A. v Nacional Hispanica Aseguradora S.A (The Playa de las Nieves)* [1978] AC 853, 882 per Lord Diplock.

of a peril insured against and the loss of freight of which the peril was, in insurance law, the proximate cause.'[71] The difference between this view expressed in the House of Lords and the expression found in s 55(2)(b) which applies merely to policies on ships and goods and not to freight policies is that whereas for triggering a loss of time clause it suffices that the loss of time is merely an intermediate event between the peril and the loss of freight; delay has to be the proximate cause of the loss for the exclusion of delay under s 55(2)(b).

2.15 The expression 'although the delay be caused by a peril insured against' requires a certain degree of causal link between delay and the insured peril however it is not clear whether the delay has to be proximately or otherwise caused by such a peril.[72] It is submitted that the exclusion would be likely to apply where delay is naturally consequent upon an insured peril; a refined causal link between the insured peril and delay is thus not required. In modern times, perishable goods are shipped in refrigerated containers or on board vessels equipped with refrigerated holds. It is therefore likely that nowadays disputes involving delay and perishable goods will rather turn on the connection between delay and other causes such as the initial unseaworthiness of the ship, the negligence of the carrier[73] or the soundness of the cargo when shipped on board.[74] In *Chubb Insurance Co of Canada v Cast Line Ltd*[75] the policy was an open ocean cargo policy on all risks of physical loss or damage from any external cause excluding loss due to delay or the deterioration of the merchandise caused by atmospheric conditions or the passage of time. The cargo was carried in containers and one of the containers had been delayed in reaching the destination for four weeks. During that delay the container was exposed to sun and heat, in consequence of which the cheese had deteriorated in value. The Court, suggesting that there was no need for expert evidence to determine that the cargo does not deteriorate in value by ageing,[76] held that the cause of the loss was not delay but the failure on the part of the carrier to ensure that the temperature inside the container remained at adequate levels so as not to spoil the quality of the cargo. In *Univeg Direct Fruit Marketing DFM GMBH v MSC Mediterranean Shipping Company SA*[77] a perishable type of cargo was carried in refrigerated containers on board a vessel and her arrival to the port of destination was delayed due to a strike at the port of loading. The cargo had started to deteriorate and was therefore sold for salvage at a considerably lower

---

71 Lord Diplock also rejected the *obiter dictum* of Bailhache J in *Russian Bank for Foreign Trade v Excess Insurance Company Ltd* [1918] 2 KB 123 that the expression was a mere surplusage.

72 *Archer-Daniels-Midland Company v Phoenix Insurance Company of New York* 975 F.Supp. 1137, 1147.

73 *Chubb Insurance Co of Canada v Cast Line Ltd* 2001 CarswellQue 1616 (Cour Supérieure du Québec).

74 *Univeg Direct Fruit Marketing DFM GMBH v MSC Mediterranean Shipping Company SA* [2013] EWHC 2962 (Comm).

75 2001 CarswellQue 1616 (Cour Supérieure du Québec).

76 At para 23.

77 *Univeg Direct Fruit Marketing DFM GMBH v MSC Mediterranean Shipping Company SA* [2013] EWHC 2962 (Comm).

figure than would have been realised had the cargo not started to deteriorate. The Court found that the ordinary course of the voyage would have taken between 14–18 days and a delay of five days was merely part of a gradual deterioration which had started earlier, during the transit to the port of loading. Therefore the claim for the difference in value of the goods failed. In terms of the standard of proof, the assured in such a case may have to prove that the damage occurred before the delay came into existence and thus is within the cover.[78]

(e) Perils of the seas and delay

2.16 In *Taylor v Dunbar*,[79] the court concluded that a loss caused by delay during sea transit is not a loss caused by perils of the sea. In this case delay during the voyage was an unexpectedly long delay, which can arguably be accepted as a separate cause on its own in the circumstances, not resulting naturally from perils of the seas. The case is also of interest as it involved a statement as to a policy consideration why delay losses are excluded. Montague Smith J expressed a view that if they were to allow the recovery of a loss by delay because it is caused by bad weather,[80] they would open a door for claims for losses which were never intended to be covered under an insurance policy. The court has nonetheless never made a distinction among the types of delays and therefore the policy consideration may not be taken to cover all sorts of delays.

In *The Cendor Mopu*,[81] 'fortuitous action of the winds and waves' which is in the definition of perils of the seas was interpreted by the Supreme Court to signify that the result of the winds and waves, and not the winds and waves themselves, must be fortuitous, accidental and unexpected. An ordinary and expected delay resulting from winds and waves can be considered as within the definition of perils of the seas and not as a separate cause of loss. How courts would approach a loss involving both perils of the seas and delay after the Supreme Court's approach to causation in *The Cendor Mopu* is hard to foresee. In this decision, inherent vice was not classified as an exception to cover, yet as a description of circumstances where there were no perils of the sea and it is not clear whether the same reasoning would apply in case of perils of the sea and delay. One may argue that insofar as the evidence points out perils of the seas, the loss would not have been caused by delay.[82] This suggestion and analogy with perils of the seas and inherent vice

---

78 In *Blaine Richards & Co v Marine Indemnity Insurance Co* 635 F.2d 1051 (2d Cir.1980) the damage of the perishable goods was caused by fumigation which was proved to have occurred prior to the delay, it was therefore held that that loss was covered by the policy.

79 (1869) LR 4 CP 206.

80 The court had taken bad weather as a peril of the sea; this view is no longer tenable as per *The Cendor Mopu.*

81 *Global Process Systems Inc v Syarikat Takaful Malaysia Berhad (The Cendor Mopu)* [2011] UKSC 5.

82 In *Global Process Systems Inc v Syarikat Takaful Malaysia Berhad (The Cendor Mopu)* [2011] UKSC 5, Lord Clarke stated at para 137 that if the question whether loss or damage has been proximately caused at least in part by perils of the seas '. . . is answered in the affirmative, it follows there was no inherent vice, thereby avoiding the causation issues that arise where there are multiple causes of loss, one of which is an insured risk and one of which is an uninsured or excluded risk'.

must nevertheless be approached cautiously: in *The Cendor Mopu* the cargo was directly affected by the perils of the sea as the leg breaking wave had hit the oil rig which was carrying the barge and caused the breaking of the barge's legs. In circumstances involving both delay and perils of the seas, unless perils of the seas damage the goods directly which is subsequently aggravated by delay, perils of the seas would likely be a remote cause if it merely affects the vessel which requires repairs resulting in delay and consequent loss of goods. Cases on delay such as *Taylor v Dunbar* may therefore have to be reconsidered in light of the new approach to perils of the seas as the proximate cause of a loss.

(f) Inherent vice and delay

2.17 The reason for excluding delay is often based on an analogy with 'inherent vice'; goods susceptible of being perished are likely to perish if they encounter delay and insurers would not wish to underwrite such a risk.[83] It may be very difficult to distinguish in which cases delay could be the proximate cause of the loss rather than inherent vice where both of these perils are in operation, the discussion of which would be rather theoretical as both of these perils are excluded under the MIA 1906[84] and standard market terms.[85] Raising the defence based on both of the exclusions would merely increase the possibility of succeeding in excluding the claim and decisions from the UK as well as the US do not usually discuss them separately.[86]

It was stated in *Soya v White*[87] that inherent vice would be the proximate cause of the loss if the goods were such 'that they could not withstand any normal voyage of that duration'.[88] According to this statement, one may argue that inherent vice would be the proximate cause if there is no abnormal delay: 'normal voyage of that duration' is likely to be the equivalent of the expected duration of a voyage for the carriage of a certain type of cargo at a specific time of the year. In case the duration exceeds the length expected for that particular voyage, there would be a delay and inherent vice would not be the only cause. In most of the

---

83 Such analogy was claimed to be ill-founded, see K.S. Selmer, 'Delay in Cargo Insurance' in K. Grönförs (ed.), *Cargo Insurance and Modern Transport* (Akademiförlaget 1970) 13.

84 s 55(2)(b) and (c).

85 Institute Cargo Clauses 2009 cl 4.4 and cl 4.5.

86 For the US examples, see *Goldman v Rhode Island* (1951)100 F. Supp.196 United States District Court Pennsylvania (the shoes carried had a delay of three months and deteriorated by molding). The court decided that the assured could not prove that the damage was caused by an insured risk without discussing whether the loss was caused by both inherent vice and delay. For more cases mentioning both but not discussing them separately please see *Cory v Boylston Insurance Company* 107 Mass. 140, 9 Am. Rep 14; *Perry v Cobb* 88 Me. 435, 34 A. 278, 49 L.R.A 389; *Tudor v New England Marine Insurance Company* 12 Cush. Mass. 554.

Under American law, the inherent vice definition involves an element of lapse of time or delay, see *Vana Trading Co, Inc v S.S. 'Mette Skou'* 556 F.2d 100, 104 (2d. Cir. 1977) where the definition of inherent vice was given along the lines of 'any existing defects, diseases, decay or the inherent nature of the commodity which will cause it to deteriorate with a lapse of time'.

87 *Soya G.M.b.H. v White* [1980] 1 Lloyd's Rep 491, 505 per Lloyd J.

88 ibid, 505. This decision was later on affirmed by the House of Lords.

US decisions involving inherent vice and delay, courts usually considered delay as an event aggravating the loss caused by inherent vice.[89] It is submitted that this intertwinement of delay and inherent vice is of no surprise as the Slave Trade Act 1794 had itself prohibited insurance on slaves against mortality by natural death which then gave rise to the decision of *Tatham v Hodgson*[90] followed in *Taylor v Dunbar*.[91] Natural death in that context was seen as a loss caused by the inherent qualities of human nature coupled by the length of an unusually protracted voyage. It is submitted that the interpretation of *Taylor v Dunbar* that *Tatham v Hodgson* is authority for the proposition that any loss arising from unusually long voyages is not covered lacks the point that *Tatham v Hodgson* was decided only on the basis of the statutory exclusion then in force. The statutory exclusion was no longer applicable when *Taylor v Dunbar* was decided as insurance transactions on slaves were abolished in Great Britain and its colonies long before 1869. The reference to *Tatham v Hodgson* in that case is therefore a curiosity. It is submitted that according to recent case law and approach to inherent vice, the perishable nature of goods shall no longer connote that the goods have an inherent vice; perishable nature is merely a physical hazard[92] which, coupled with a lengthy delay or lack of refrigeration, can lead to a loss.

2.18 Unsuitability of packing could also be an issue in respect of losses caused by inherent vice and delay. The Institute Cargo Clauses refer to the packing to withstand the 'ordinary incidents of the voyage'.[93] An ordinary delay in the voyage, if considered as an ordinary incident of the voyage may be treated as part of the unsuitability of packing exclusion and it may raise the question of whether the unsuitability of packing would be the cause of the loss rather than delay. Consequently, a delay that would exceed an ordinary time may be accepted as not making part of the definition of the unsuitability of packing and arguably may be excluded by the delay exclusion clause.

(g) Deprivation perils and delay

2.19 In some cases an insured peril may result in the partial loss of the cargo and there may also be a risk of an ensuing delay which may aggravate the loss

---

89 *Cory v Boylston Insurance Company* 107 Mass. 140 a cargo of champagne was spoiled by mold in the hold, there was also a delay in the voyage. In *Brandyce v United States Lloyds* 207 A.D. 665, the case involved perils of the sea, inherent vice and delay. Delay in this case was an event contributing to the loss of the rotten potatoes. In *Perry v Cobb* 88 Me. 435, 34 A. 278 a cargo of lime suffered a loss of content from the shrinking of the staves of the barrels, and slacking up of the cooperage. It was claimed that it had resulted from the rolling and pitching of the vessel caused by the storms of an unusually protracted voyage. The Supreme Judicial Court of Maine concluded that the damage came from the inherent qualities of the cargo, 'excited by the long-continued transit' at 282. Delay in this case was accepted as an event aggravating the loss which was mainly caused by the nature of the cargo.

90 (1796) 6 TR 656.

91 (1869) LR 4 CP 206.

92 Physical hazard is any fact increasing the risk of loss and in life insurance may include elements such as age, health or occupation; John Lowry, Philip Rawlings and Robert Merkin, *Insurance Law Doctrines and Principles* (3rd edn), 109.

93 ICC A 01/01/2009 cl 4.3.

and turn the partial loss into a total loss. In modern shipping one of the major problems is piracy which is an insured peril under some standard forms of marine policies.[94] The act of piracy results often in negotiations to save the ship and the cargo which are of relatively unforeseeable duration[95] and consequently involves a risk of delay. In *The Bunga Melati Dua*[96] a cargo of biodiesel carried on board a ship had to remain on the ship for 11 days before the ship was released. The cargo had not deteriorated during this delay as it was not a perishable cargo.[97] After the vessel and the cargo were released, the cargo was sold at the discharge port at less than half of the original value and the claim of the assured was for the balance. The court decided that the mere capture by pirates did not make the loss an actual total loss in this case as there was still a hope of release in the near future.

2.20 Another issue could have been whether the loss was a partial loss by virtue of s 56(1). In this case neither was there a loss of part of the goods[98] nor were they delivered in a damaged condition;[99] therefore claiming for partial loss would not have been an option for the assured. Had the cargo been perishable and deteriorated, one of the issues to be discussed would be whether the physical loss of goods by deterioration was proximately caused by delay or by piracy. Moreover, in this case the negotiations were conducted merely between the shipowners and pirates, accordingly the cargo owners were in any case not involved in the process. It could follow thence that the delay resulting from the piracy attacks could be qualified as 'delay beyond the control of the assured'.[100] Had it been a perishable cargo, it would be arguable whether the mere fact that the cargo was captured by pirates would give the assured a right to claim for an actual total loss of the goods on the basis of irretrievable deprivation.[101] The question whether the cargo would constitute an actual total loss would arise more likely where the cargo would be 'so damaged as to cease to be a thing of the kind insured'[102] because of the delay caused by the pirate attack and lengthy ransom negotiations. Currently no authority exists in England as to whether a loss caused by delay beyond the control of the

---

94 e.g. Institute Cargo Clauses A 1982 and 2009, cl 6.2.

95 In *Masefield AG v Amlin Corporate Member Ltd &Anor (The Bunga Melati Dua)* [2011] EWCA Civ 24 at para 7, reference was made to the 1st instance judge David Steel J in his finding that based on the communications with the Malaysian Security Council as to the negotiations with the pirates alone, the vessel with its crew and cargoes were likely to be released in short order. David Steel J had also referred to a circular received by the insured's insurance broker which stated that the process of release of a vessel normally lasts between six to eight weeks.

96 ibid.

97 ibid at para 12.

98 As per s 71(1).

99 As per s 71(3).

100 'Delay beyond the control of the assured' is an expression that appears in the Institute Cargo Clauses 1982 and 2009 cl 8.3 whereby the insurance remains in force during such delay.

101 In *Masefield v Amlin* it was held that the fact that the vessel and cargo were captured by pirates had not *per se* given a right to an actual total loss as during the negotiations there was still a hope that the cargo and vessel would be released, whereby the assured was not 'irretrievably deprived' thereof.

102 s 57(1).

assured shall not be recoverable[103] on the ground that the delay exclusion leaves out both delay within and beyond the control of the assured.[104] One may argue that in the absence of an ambiguous delay exclusion clause, any loss caused by delay beyond or within the control of the assured would not be recoverable. However, the current wording of the delay exclusion clause in the Institute Cargo Clauses is not so clear. The Clauses provide that the insurance remains in force during delay beyond the control of the assured,[105] yet no distinction is made with respect to delay within or beyond the control of the assured in the exclusion clause. This arguably gives rise to the argument that the exclusion clause is ambiguous and shall be interpreted *contra proferentem*, in which case a loss caused by a delay beyond the control of the assured can arguably be recoverable.

2.21 Many standard form policies include clauses excluding loss or damage caused by 'capture, seizure, arrest, restraint or detainment, and the consequences thereof'.[106] The Institute Cargo Clauses grant coverage for these perils if they occur in peace time.[107] Many standard form war risks cargo policies also provide cover for the same risks and their consequences.[108] Delay can be considered as 'the consequence' of these perils[109] and accordingly be either excluded as a consequence of the named perils. This issue would be of greater importance where the policy does not include any specific delay exclusion[110] although there is nothing barring courts from discussing whether this clause would alone be sufficient to exclude delay even where there is a specific delay exclusion. It was held in the

---

103 See *Lam Seng Hang Co Pte Ltd v The Insurance Corporation of Singapore Ltd* [2001] SGHC 31 for such an authority under the Singaporean law.

104 In *Schloss Brothers v Stevens* [1906] 2 KB 665 the policy was on 'all risks by land and water' and did not contain a delay exclusion. Delay in this case was a delay beyond the control of the assured and was due to abnormally disorganised transport arrangements arising from a revolution that was going on at the time. The loss, although caused by delay, was therefore held to be accidental and within the wording 'all risks by land and water'.

105 Institute Cargo Clauses 1982 and 2009 cl 8.3.

106 Institute Time Clauses – Hulls 01/10/1983 cl 23; Institute Voyage Clauses – Freight 01/11/1995 cl 14.2.

107 cl 6.2 of the Institute Cargo Clauses A-B-C 1982 is entitled 'war exclusion clause' and provides that the perils enumerated and their consequences shall not be covered. *A contrario* meaning of this clause suggests that these perils are covered if occurred in peace time. The same clause in 2009 forms do not include the same title nevertheless should the sub-clause be interpreted with the two other sub-clauses mentioning war perils, it shall be accordingly construed to exclude cover merely for these mentioned perils if they occur in war time. The fact that delay is caused by capture may nevertheless be considered separately as capture is only a war peril and cannot occur in peace time (a definition of capture was given by Channell J in *Andersen v Marten* [1907] 2 KB 248 involving taking by enemy and in time of open war; a similar definition was given by Lord Fitzgerald in *Cory & Son v Burr* (1883) 8 App Cas 393).

108 Institute War Clauses (Cargo) 01/01/2009 and 01/01/1982 cl 1.2; Institute War and Strikes Clauses – Freight – Time and Freight-Voyage 01/11/1995 cl 1.1.2.

109 For the view that the term 'consequences' represented a loss and not an independent peril, see Bennett, *The Law of Marine Insurance*, 13.53.

110 It was decided that where a loss comes within the general wording of the policy but is then specifically excluded by a particular exclusion, the specific exclusion takes priority: *Howard Farrow v Ocean Accident & Guarantee Corpn* (1940) 67 Ll L Rep 27.

US in *Blaine*[111] that a free from capture and seizure (FC & S) clause alone was considered as barring the recovery for delay due to detention.[112] However, it was held in a later decision[113] where Illinois law applied that the same clause did not bar coverage for losses caused by delay where delay had resulted from the closing of a river due to flooding by the Coast Guard. It was held that a delay clause in the same policy precluded coverage.

2.22 The American Institute Cargo Clauses All Risks 2004 contain a strikes, riots and civil commotions (SR & CC) clause[114] which excludes 'loss, damage, or expense caused by or resulting from' those risks. Cover is however provided in an endorsement[115] against, *inter alia*, 'physical loss of or damage to property insured directly caused by' strikers, locked-out workmen as well as vandalism, sabotage or malicious acts. The endorsement further provides:

> 'Nothing in this endorsement shall be construed to cover any loss, damage or expense directly or indirectly arising from, contributed to or caused by any of the following, whether due to a peril insured against or otherwise: . . . (c) loss of market or loss, damage or deterioration arising from delay'.

The wording used for causation is sufficiently broad to exclude instances such as where the assured incurs expenses in reconditioning the cargo which deteriorated during a delay resulting from a strike.

In *New Market Investment Corp v Fireman's Fund*[116] the assured was a fruit importer who had imported fruits from Chile to the United States which were detained for inspection due to terroristic threats that the fruits were injected with cyanide. Much of the goods were eventually spoiled, were destroyed, or were so damaged by inspection that they had to be destroyed. The action was brought by the assured under a Strikes, Riots, and Civil Commotions Endorsement to Open Marine Cargo Policy and the insurers sought to exclude liability in reliance of the Free from Capture and Seizure Warranty of the policy and in reliance of a clause which read:

> 'Nothing in this endorsement shall be construed to cover any loss, damage, deterioration or expense caused by or resulting from:
>
> . . .
>
> c. delay or loss of market'

---

111 *Blaine Richards & Co Inc v Marine Indemnity Insurance Company of America and William H. McGee & Co* 635 F.2d 1051, 1981 A.M.C. 1, US Court of Appeals, Second Circuit.

112 Circuit Judge Lumbard noted at 1056 that 'recovery for delay due to detention is barred by both the FC & S and Delay Clauses'. The FC & S Clause in this case excluded from cover all losses due to 'capture, seizure, arrest, restraint, detainment, . . . and the consequences thereof or any attempt thereat. . .'.

113 *Archer-Daniels-Midland Co v Phoenix Assur. Co of New York*, 975 F. Supp. 1137 (1997).

114 cl 4B. The wording used in the Clauses is 'warranty' although the clause does not operate as a warranty in the sense used in the Insurance Act 2015.

115 The American Institute of Marine Underwriters Endorsement for Open Policies (Cargo) Strikes, Riots & Civil Commotions (Form 12A) (1 January 2008).

116 774 F.Supp. 909 (1991).

Whether the proximate cause of the loss was the terroristic threats or delay was a matter of fact and not law, therefore the Court instructed to jury to find the dominant cause. The jury found that the proximate and real efficient cause of the assured's losses was the acts of terrorism, and not delay, loss of market, or the actions of the government in detaining the goods.

Delay being a contributing factor or a cause other than the proximate cause

2.23 The philosophical aspect of the word 'cause' brings about important results; firstly every event may have an infinite number of causes and secondly, each cause can be described in an infinite variety of ways.[117] In English law, 'cause' and 'causation' were considered by courts as concepts the interpretation of which 'does not involve any metaphysical or scientific view'.[118] This view was echoed in a delay case *Inman SS Co v Bischoff*[119] where it was stated that once there is a clear view of the fact, it would be best to keep away from philosophical mazes. Thus under an insurance policy 'cause' would mean 'what a business or seafaring man would take to be the cause without too microscopic an analysis but on broad view'[120] and finding the cause of the loss is mostly contemplated as a question of fact. Likewise in *Leyland*[121] it was stated by Lord Shaw that the causes need to be ascertained 'not in an artificial sense, but in that real sense which parties to a contract must have had in their minds when they spoke of cause at all'.[122] Albeit the approach to the ascertainment of 'cause' under the English law does not rest upon an artificial but upon real sense, rules applicable to ascertaining the cause or concurrent causes of a loss are fairly convoluted.

2.24 Whether delay may break the chain of causation between the initial peril resulting in delay and the loss is important to assess whether delay is a factor contributing to the loss or whether it is the proximate cause of the loss.[123] If an event is no more than a contributing factor to the loss, it may well not even be

---

117 Michael E. Bragg, 'Concurrent Causation and the Art of Policy Drafting: New Perils for Property Insurers', 20 *Forum* 1984–1985, 385–399, 385.

118 per Viscount Simon *Yorkshire Dale Steamship Co Ltd v Minister of War Transport (The Coxwold)* [1942] AC 691, 698. Likewise, in *Harrison Ltd v Shipping Controller (The Inkonka)* [1921] 1 KB 122, 130–1, McCardie J considered that causation 'is a topic of profound juristic complexity. The Courts cannot act as metaphysical analysts. They can only administer or state the law in practical language upon particular aggregates of circumstances'.

119 (1882) 7 App Cas 670.

120 *Yorkshire Dale Steamship Co Ltd v Minister of War Transport (The Coxwold)* [1942] AC 691, 706 per Lord Wright. Likewise in *Leyland Shipping Co Ltd v Norwich Union Fire Insurance Society Ltd* [1918] AC 350, 369 it was stated by Lord Shaw that the causes need to be ascertained 'not in an artificial sense, but in that real sense which parties to a contract must have had in their minds when they spoke of cause at all'.

121 *Leyland Shipping Co Ltd v Norwich Union Fire Insurance Society Ltd* [1918] AC 350.

122 ibid, 369.

123 Albeit it has been suggested in Bennett, *The Law of Marine Insurance*, 9.43 that the fact that a peril does not break the chain of causation between the peril meriting the proximate cause and the loss should not necessarily mean that it is excluded from being a proximate cause of the loss.

considered as 'a causal peril'.[124] It was also held that where the exclusion is the inevitable result of a peril, the exclusion has no independent effect and the peril is the proximate cause.[125] Some delay may be the inevitable result of perils such as perils of the seas or deprivation perils such as detention, capture and seizure and there are authorities in other jurisdictions that where delay results naturally from the deprivations perils, the ensuing loss should be attributed to the initial peril.[126] In decisions involving the loss of freight by loss of time, loss of time was not considered as a peril. It was stated in *The Playa de las Nieves*[127] that '. . .The intermediate event, loss of time, is not itself a peril though it may be the result of a peril.'[128] Some authors are of the same view in relation to deterioration cases and argue that delay is only a channel in the middle of a chain of causation through which insured or excepted perils may operate and that may have consequences, such as loss or damage.[129] A similar view was taken in a Canadian case[130] for windstorm followed by delay where it was considered that one may not say that these were distinct causes as neither can be separated from the other.

Delay was considered as not naturally resulting from collision in *Pink v Fleming*[131] where the policy covered losses 'consequent on collision' on the ground that they were too remote in time. If they had naturally resulted from the peril of collision, collision and not delay would have been the proximate cause of the loss. Given that the case adopted the last cause in time approach, whether delay was the natural result of the collision was assessed according to how far in time delay was placed from the collision, according to the events that occurred between the collision and the loss and according to whether they happen in every collision. Albeit the first criterion can no longer be supported on the ground that the last cause in time approach has been abandoned in *Leyland*, the latter two are somewhat viable. Where it is assumed that collisions usually involve some delay, the question would arise whether the delay shall be unreasonably long so as to break the chain of causation between the collision and the loss and whether relatively short delays are

---

124 Lord Mance, Lord Saville and Lord Collins recognised in *Global Process Systems Inc v Syarikat Takaful Malaysia Berhad (The Cendor Mopu)* [2011] UKSC 5, that there was only one causal peril which was perils of the seas. Lord Clarke recognised two perils; namely perils of the seas and inherent vice but concluded that only the perils of the seas were a causal peril.

125 *Mardorf v Accident Insurance Co* [1903] 1 KB 584 (an accident insurance case).

126 In the US case *Magoun v New England Marine Insurance Company, Fed. Cas.* No. 8,961, 1 Story 157 the underwriters contended that the long delay and exposure to hot climate were the immediate causes of the loss and detainment was the remote cause. Justice Story rejected this contention and stated that all the consequences naturally flowing from the peril insured against (in this case delay arising from detainment) shall be attributed to the peril itself.

127 *Naviera de Canarias SA v Nacional Hispanica Aseguradora SA (The Playa de las Nieves)* [1978] AC 853.

128 per Lord Diplock at 882. However in carriage cases, delay may be held to have no connection with another peril and may be held to be the responsible cause of the damage to the goods, see *The Renee Hyaffil* T.L.R. vol 32, 660 (CA).

129 Selmer, 13.

130 *Clark's Chick Hatchery Ltd v Commonwealth Insurance Company* 1982 CarswellNB 331, at para 11 per Stevenson J.

131 (1890) 25 QBD 396.

usually accepted as factors contributing to the loss rather than being a proximate cause of the loss.

2.25 Incidents which cannot be considered as the proximate cause of the loss may nevertheless aggravate the loss. In *Leyland*[132] Lord Shaw enunciated that there may be:

> 'attendant circumstances which may aggravate or possibly precipitate the result, but which are incidents flowing from the injury . . . The true and efficient cause never loses its hold'.[133]

Delay may sometimes be merely an event aggravating the loss already caused by a preceding peril, in which case delay would probably not be *the* or *a* proximate cause of the loss. The assured in such a case would have to prove that part of the loss was occurred before delay and was caused by an insured peril. This type of delay was illustrated in *Continental Insurance Co v Almassa*[134] where the loss was caused by the lack of ventilation in a ship's hold where the goods remained on board. Delay in this case was only a contributing factor that worsened the loss on the ground that had the cargo been properly ventilated there would have been no damage no matter how long the cargo remained on the ship. Considering that the pre-MIA judgments were delivered at a time where ventilated holds were not available on vessels, it is submitted that in the modern age, it is more likely that the lack of ventilation or unseaworthiness of the vessel and not delay will be taken to be the proximate cause of deterioration of perishable goods. Accordingly the general exclusion in s 55(2)(b) in the MIA or cl 4.5 in the Institute Cargo Clauses may not even come in to play. Clauses involving expressions such as '"caused by, resulting from, contributed to or aggravated by"[135] delay' or 'any increase of loss caused by delays'[136] would likely ensure that the exclusion comprises all delays, whether a proximate cause, a contributing factor or an event aggravating the loss.

2.26 It was suggested in Chapter 1[137] that ordinary delay may not be considered as a peril given that it is not accidental. This suggestion gives rise to the question of whether this type of delay can be a proximate cause of loss. A distinction was made in an early US case on delay[138] between the ordinary operation of the elements and their perilous action[139] and it was suggested that the latter must be the

---

132 *Leyland Shipping Co v Norwich Union Fire Insurance Society Ltd* [1918] AC 350.

133 ibid, 370–371.

134 *Continental Insurance Co v Almassa International Inc* (2003) 46 C.C.L.I. 3d 206 (Ontario Superior Court of Justice).

135 Such a wording was used in the policy in *Safeco Ins. Co v Guyton*, 692 F.2d 551 (9th Cir. 1982).

136 *Okanagan Prime Products Inc v Commercial Union Assurance Co of Canada* 1994 Carswell BC 874 (British Columbia Supreme Court) was with respect to a policy including the clause 'any increase of loss caused by delays or loss of time due to the presence of strikers . . .'.

137 See paras 1.13–1.17.

138 *Perry v Cobb* 49 L.R.A. 389, 88 Me. 435, 34 A. 278 (1896) given by Supreme Judicial Court of Maine.

139 per Haskell J at 281.

proximate cause of the loss. The decision was given prior to *Leyland*;[140] however the court stated that a protracted voyage is not a peril as it is not an unusual event but one of the natural events of the transit. It is therefore submitted that only extraordinary delay is capable of being the proximate cause of loss, however in some circumstances it may be taken to be an element aggravating the loss rather than being the proximate cause.

Delay and concurrent causation

2.27 The rules as to concurrent causation are fairly convoluted. Under this heading the relevant case law will be analysed together with speculations on how the authorities can be applied in circumstances involving delay. In *The Aliza Glacial*[141] Potter LJ stated that 'it is only when a Court is driven to the conclusion' of more than one proximate cause, that the concurrent cause rule will apply.[142] It was also submitted in *Wayne Tank & Pump Co Ltd v Employers' Liability Assurance Corp Ltd*[143] that unless one cause is clearly more decisive than the other, it should be accepted that there are two causes of the loss and no attempt should be made to give one of them the quality of dominance; and it was held that where one of the causes of the loss is excluded, the loss would not be recoverable.[144] Applying this is reasoning would result in the outcome that where delay is one of the causes of the loss, the loss would not be recoverable. The *Wayne Tank* approach to concurrent causation has not been challenged in English law to a great extent; nevertheless because the policy in that case was a liability and not first-party policy, this may give rise to the question of whether the decision should also apply to first-party policies. One should refer to the coverage provided and the nature of the risks involved in liability and first-party policies so as to answer this question. There ought to be a motive behind favouring the exclusion clause where it is one of the concurrent proximate causes in liability policies.[145] It was suggested that the approach of favouring the exclusion clause in liability policies arises because the liability insurer agrees to cover a wider range of risk than the property insurer,[146] and therefore intends to relieve the insurer from more liability.

2.28 This issue was raised in the US in *Garvey v State Farm Fire and Casualty Co*[147] delivered by the Supreme Court of California. In this case the insured peril was the negligence of the construction company and the excluded risk was the earth movement. The Court mentioned *State Farm Mutual Auto Ins Co v*

---

140 *Leyland Shipping Co v Norwich Union Fire Insurance Society Ltd* [1918] AC 350.
141 *Svenska Handelsbanken AB v Dandridge (The Aliza Glacial)* [2002] EWCA Civ 577.
142 ibid, para 48.
143 [1974] QB 57.
144 Ibid, 68–69 per Cairns LJ.
145 Questions of causation cannot be answered in the abstract. An informed response requires an understanding of the purpose and context of the causation test: *Scott v Copenhagen Reinsurance Co (UK) Ltd* [2003] EWCA Civ 688, [2003] Lloyd's Rep IR 696, para 68.
146 Lowry and Rawlings, 318.
147 770 P 2d 704 (1989), at 710 per Chief Justice Lucas.

Partridge[148] which involved a liability policy and which held that where the loss is caused by two concurrent proximate causes, one of which is an insured peril and the other is excluded, that the insured peril should prevail. The Court in *Garvey* stated that this approach to concurrent causation may not be applied in property insurance policies. The *obiter dictum* of *Wayne Tank* was rejected in *Partridge*.[149] Some American commentators enunciated on the basis of the decisions like *Partridge* that 'when there are several distinct or distinguishable factors which contribute to a loss, a persuasive case can be made for the proposition that courts will apply the causation theory that will relate the loss to a covered peril'.[150] This approach suggests that delay as a 'cause' in property insurance and liability insurance may be viewed differently[151] where the issue turns upon whether delay is a concurrent cause of the loss.

2.29 *The Cendor Mopu*[152] brought a different approach to concurrent causation as was discussed in *Wayne Tank*, particularly in respect of perils of the seas and inherent vice. Lord Mance, although he did not express a concluded view on the point, suggested that there can be a situation of concurrent causes capable of attracting the rule in *Wayne Tank* only where each of the two perils operating independently is of itself able to cause the loss.[153] This situation should be distinguished from the circumstance where each of the perils are capable of causing a loss independently and occur together.[154] A line of judgments was delivered in Australia to the effect that where a loss results from two or more concurrently operating interdependent

---

148 10 Cal. 3d 102 (Supreme Court of California, 1973).

149 *State Farm Mutual Auto Ins Co v Partridge* 10 Cal. 3d 102 (1973).

150 R.E. Keeton and A.I. Widiss, *Insurance Law: A Guide to Fundamental Principles, Legal Doctrines and Commercial Practice* (St Paul: West Publishing 1988). They also refer to the reasonable expectations of the assured doctrine which is not adopted in English law *(Smit Tak Offshore Services Ltd v Youell (The Mare)* [1992] 1 Lloyd's Rep 154, although it has been stated that a policy should not be construed in a way which would 'unwarrantably diminish the indemnity which it was the purpose of the policy to afford', *Morley v United Friendly Insurance plc* [1993] 1 Lloyd's Rep 490, 505 per Beldam LJ). This doctrine is not always applied in American law; the general view is that the court will construe the policy according to the reasonable expectations of the assured where there is ambiguity in the wording of a clause (*Montrose Chemical Corp v Admiral Ins Co* 42 Cal Rptr2d 324 (1995)).

151 For the suggestion that the 'cause' of loss in the context of property and liability insurance contracts are different and that the distinction is critical for the resolution of losses involving multiple causes, see M.E. Bragg, 'Concurrent Causation and the Art of Policy Drafting: New Perils for Property Insurers', 20 *Forum* 1984–1985, 385–399, 387.

152 *Global Process Systems Inc v Syarikat Takaful Malaysia Berhad (The Cendor Mopu)* [2011] UKSC 5.

153 Rob Merkin, 'Perils of the seas, inherent vice and causation', *Insurance Law Monthly* 23(3) March 2011, 1–5, 5.

Malcolm A. Clarke, *The Law of Insurance Contracts* (4th edn), i-law – Service Issue 35–1 April 2016, para 25–6B classifies this type of causes as 'independent causes' and cites *Ford Motor Co of Canada Ltd v Prudential Assurance Co Ltd* 14 DLR (2d) 7 (Ont, 1958), affirmed [1959] SCR 539. Clarke also cites *Guaranty National Ins Co v North Rivers Ins Co* 09 F 2d 132, 137 (5 Cir, 1990) where the court had decided that the assured could recover in full.

154 The causes of loss in *Wayne Tank* were the dangerous nature of the installation and negligence of one of the employees of the assured. This was classified in Malcolm A. Clarke, *The Law of Insurance Contracts* (4th edn), i-law Service Issue 35–1 April 2016, para 25–6A under the heading 'concurrent and interdependent causes'.

proximate causes, the loss is attributable to each of them.[155] If the rule in *Wayne Tank* applies only to concurrent interdependent causes, a different rule shall govern concurrent independent causes such as that the assured will recover the part of the loss caused by the insured peril. It would follow that even where the above argument that *Wayne Tank* shall apply merely to liability policies is not tenable,[156] the next question is whether delay can be an independent or interdependent cause.

(a) Limits to the rule in *Wayne Tank*: ordinary delay and delay
    beyond the control of the assured as uninsured perils

2.30 It was discussed in Chapter 1 that ordinary delay and delay beyond the control of the assured may arguably be excepted from the scope of the general delay exclusion. These types of delay may accordingly be considered as uninsured perils which would make the rule of *Wayne Tank* inapplicable. They would nevertheless attract the rule in *The Miss Jay Jay*[157] where it was held that where the loss is caused both by an insured and uninsured peril, the assured would recover under the policy. Notwithstanding the correctness of the foregoing, it was stated obiter in *HIH Casualty & General Insurance Ltd v Waterwall Shipping Inc*[158] that the statutory exception of wear and tear clarified the scope of cover rather than enunciating an exclusion. Moreover in *The Cendor Mopu*[159] Lord Clarke enunciated that s 55(2)(c) excluding losses caused by inherent vice did not mean an exclusion yet merely an amplification of the proximate cause rule, and an example of a loss not proximately caused by a peril insured against. Lord Mance, although he did not conclude the point, suggested that the exclusion of inherent vice in the contract (which was subject to the Institute Cargo Clauses All Risks 1982) did not make any difference to its reflection as an uninsured peril under s 55(2)(c). These two types of delay may accordingly be considered as events which result in a loss that is not proximately caused by an insured peril.[160]

---

155 *City Centre Cold Store Pty Ltd v Preservatrice Skandia Insurance Ltd* (1985) 3 NSWLR 739, 745 per Clarke J; *McCarthy v St Paul International Insurance Co Ltd* [2007] FCAFC 28; (2007) 157 FCR 402, [93] per Allsop J.

156 In the context of carriage of goods by sea, Lord Mance focussed on finding 'the' proximate cause (a single proximate cause rather than two causes which do not have to be proximate) instead of relying on the relatively flexible approach of *Wayne Tank* in *ENE Kos 1 Ltd v Petroleo Brasileiro SA (The Kos)* [2012] UKSC 17. Lord Sumption in this case concluded that the charterers' order to load was *an* effective cause of the owners' loss (and not the proximate or dominant cause). This approach was supported by Lord Clarke who stated that the order was an effective cause 'in the sense that it was not a mere 'but for' cause which did no more than provide the occasion for some other factor unrelated to the charterers' order to operate, it does not matter whether it was the only effective cause', at para 61.

157 *JJ Lloyd Instruments Ltd v Northern Star Insurance Co Ltd (The Miss Jay Jay)* [1987] 1 Lloyd's Rep 32. In this case the Court of Appeal allowed recovery where the ship was lost as a result of the combination of two events: adverse condition of the sea (an insured peril) and defects in the boat's design of which the assured was unaware (an uninsured peril).

158 (1998) 146 FLR 76, judgment given by the Court of Appeal of New South Wales.

159 *Global Process Systems Inc v Syarikat Takaful Malaysia Berhad (The Cendor Mopu)* [2011] UKSC 5.

160 As to the Institute Clauses, delay losses are usually mentioned under headings entitled 'Exclusions', cf. Institute Cargo Clauses A-B-C 1982 and 2009 cl 4.5. It is controversial whether this wording

(b) Whether delay can be an independent cause of loss

2.31 There may be two instances where delay may be regarded as an independent cause of loss; namely where it is able to cause a loss on its own, and when it occurs independently from any other peril. An analogy may be drawn with the risk of 'unseaworthiness' in determining whether delay can cause a loss independently. Unseaworthiness is usually accompanied by another peril[161] and was held not to be able to operate independently because it depended upon another peril for a casualty to occur in *Monarch Steamship Co Ltd v Karlshamns Oljefabriker*.[162] In this case, a cargo of soya beans was shipped on board a ship which sailed in May 1939. The voyage was expected to last for 60 days; however owing to the unseaworthiness of the vessel which slowed the vessel and caused a delay, the ship could not arrive at the port of discharge before the outbreak of the war in September. According to the Court the breach of warranty of seaworthiness operated directly as a cause and as a dominant cause.[163] Moreover it was held in *The Miss Jay Jay*[164] that unseaworthiness could be a concurrent proximate cause of the loss.

Concurrent causation where perils of the seas are involved was also analysed by Lord Clarke in *The Cendor Mopu*[165] where he enunciated that:

> 'The sole question in a case where loss or damage is caused by a combination of the physical condition of the insured goods and conditions of the sea encountered in the course of the insured adventure is whether the loss or damage is proximately caused, at least in part, by perils of the seas (or, more generally, any fortuitous external accident or casualty). If that question is answered in the affirmative, it follows that there was no inherent vice, thereby avoiding the causation issues that arise where there are multiple causes of loss, one of which is an insured risk and one of which is an uninsured or excluded risk.'[166]

Following this statement, it is likely that wherever perils of the seas proximately cause the loss, at least in part, there can be no concurrent causation issues between unseaworthiness and perils of the sea. The same can be suggested for delay and perils of the seas.

---

shall be interpreted as an exclusion rather than an exception clarifying the scope of cover. For the view that it constitutes an exclusion, see Bennett, *The Law of Marine Insurance*, 9.31.

161 In both *Dudgeon v Pembroke* (1877) 2 App Cas 284 and *JJ Lloyd Instruments Ltd v Northern Star Insurance Co Ltd (The Miss Jay Jay)* [1987] 1 Lloyd's Rep 32 unseaworthiness was followed by perils of the seas and caused a loss.

162 [1949] AC 196.

163 This case is on carriage of goods by sea and not insurance. It was mentioned that causation in carriage cases is to be different from causation in insurance cases in *Pink v Fleming* (1890) 25 QBD 396 and in *Thomas Wilson, Sons & Co v Owners of the Cargo per the Xantho (The Xantho)* (1887) 12 App Cas 503, at 510 (opposite view was expressed in *Leyland* by Lord Shaw of Dunfermline at 368).

164 *JJ Lloyd Instruments Ltd v Northern Star Insurance Co Ltd (The Miss Jay Jay)* [1987] 1 Lloyd's Rep 32.

165 *Global Process Systems Inc v Syarikat Takaful Malaysia Berhad (The Cendor Mopu)* [2011] UKSC 5.

166 ibid, para 137.

2.32 In *Clark's Chick Hatchery Ltd v Commonwealth Insurance Company*[167] the policy covered 'loss of birds resulting directly from windstorm' and excluded 'loss of market or loss or damage caused by delay'. Delay in this case was accepted as a concurrent cause together with other causes such as windstorm, although concurrent causation was not interpreted as requiring both of the causes to be capable of causing loss independently. The court decided that although 'the windstorm was the direct or proximate cause of the loss'[168] 'it was also a loss caused by delay and recovery must be denied'.[169] The court then proceeded by stating that courts should strain to find a dominant cause as there were two causes both of which can be properly described as effective causes of the loss and applied the reasoning of *Wayne Tank*. In *Continental Insurance v Almassa*[170] where lack of ventilation and delay were the possible causes of the loss, the court held that the exclusion could exclude losses caused solely by delay; nevertheless it would not extend to exclude also the situations where delay operates concurrently with a number of other factors.

2.33 Insurers may develop standard terms to avoid the unforeseeable application and results of causation rules. A clause to the following effect may accordingly be stipulated in the insurance contracts so as to exonerate insurers from liability whether or not delay is taken to be an independent cause of a loss: 'Where a loss occurs which would not have happened in the absence of an excluded event, there is no coverage regardless of: (a) the cause of the excluded event; or (b) other causes of the loss; or (c) whether other causes acted concurrently or in any sequence with the excluded event to produce the loss'.[171] Part (a) would particularly be important in respect of delay as delay is always caused by a preceding event.

Agreements altering the proximate cause rule and delay

2.34 In insurance law the proximate cause rule is a term implied into the insurance contract as representing the 'real meaning of the parties'[172] and parties are free to agree on wordings altering the proximate cause rule.[173] Nevertheless courts do not readily hold that the policy wording is sufficient to adopt a different test other than this rule as the test is a default and its applicability 'does not depend

---

167 1982 CarswellNB 331.

168 At para 7.

169 At para 13.

170 *Continental Insurance v Almassa* (2003) 46 C.C.L.I. 3d 206 (Ontario Superior Court of Justice).

171 In terms of delay exclusion in the MIA and Institute Clauses, this part of the wording is similar to 'even though delay be caused by a peril insured against'.

172 *Becker, Gray and Co v London Assurance Corpn* [1918] AC 101, at 112 per Lord Sumner. See also *Reischer v Borwick* (1874) 2 QB 548, 550 per Lindley LJ.

173 In *Coxe v Employers' Liability Assurance Corp. Ltd* [1916] 2 KB 629 parties agreed that the policy did not insure against death 'directly or indirectly caused by . . . war'. The Court decided that this wording could not be reconciled with the proximate cause rule.

on nice distinctions between the particular varieties of phrase used in particular policies'.[174] The Institute Cargo Clauses 1982 cl 4.5 is a similar reproduction of s 55(2)(b) in that it uses the same wording 'proximately caused by delay'. The wording in the Institute Cargo Clauses dated 2009 is slightly different and reads 'caused by delay'. The Joint Cargo Committee had firstly drafted the delay exclusion with the wording 'attributable to delay'[175] however later on the expression was changed to 'caused by delay'.[176] The wording 'attributable to' appears also in s 55(1)(a) and it was decided in *Trinder, Anderson & Co v Thames & Mersey Marine Co*[177] that it clearly varies the proximate causation rule.[178] The wording appeared in several cases on delay such as *Wilson Brothers Bobbin v Green*[179] and *Roura v Forgas*[180] as well as in some standard market terms.[181] In the former case the policy contained an exclusion clause reading 'all claims arising from delay'; however the court did not decide as to whether the 'arising from' is an equivalent of the proximate cause rule. It was held that the storage charges incurred for preventing a loss of adventure was considered as arising from delay. In the latter case the same expression was included in the policies; however no reference was made to proximate causation.

2.35 The wording 'arising from delay' has been considered in two decisions in the United States, namely *Archer*[182] and *Blaine Richards*[183] where both policies included the exclusion 'Warranted free of claim for loss of market or for loss, damage or deterioration *arising from* delay, whether caused by a peril insured against or otherwise'.[184] In the former case the assured argued that 'arising from delay' must be considered as an equivalent wording of 'proximately caused by delay' and that the detention and not delay was the proximate cause of the loss. The court has not expressed a conclusive view on whether 'arising from' should be interpreted as such.

---

174 *Lloyds TSB General Insurance Holdings v Lloyds Bank Group Insurance Co Ltd* [2001] EWCA Civ 1643, [2002] Lloyd's Rep IR 113, para 40 per Potter LJ.

175 JCC memo JC2008/008 dated 3 October 2008.

176 JCC memo JC 2008/019 dated 10 October 2008, cl 4.5.

177 [1898] 2 Q.B. 114.

178 Contrast with *Handelsbanken Norwegian Branch of Svenska Handelsbanken AB (PUBL) v Dandridge (The Aliza Glacial)* [2002] EWCA Civ 577, [2002] 2 Lloyd's Rep 421, para 60, the policy was on Institute Mortgagees Interest Clauses (Hulls) 1986 and included 'loss, damage, liability or expense arising from. . .'.

179 In *Wilson Brothers Bobbin v Green* [1917] 1 KB 860 likewise the same expression was included in the policies in *Roura v Forgas* (which was also a case of loss of adventure) and no reference was made to proximate causation.

180 [1919] 1 KB 189.

181 Institute War and Strikes Clauses Hulls-Time 1/11/95 cl 4.4 'any claim for expenses arising from delay'.

182 *Archer-Daniels-Midland Company v Phoenix Insurance Company of New York* 975 F.Supp.1137. Both policies included 'Warranted free of claim for loss of market or for loss, damage or deterioration *arising from* delay, whether caused by a peril insured against or otherwise' (emphasis added).

183 *Blaine Richards & Co Inc v Marine Indemnity Insurance Company of America and William H. McGee & Co* 635 F.2d 1051, 1981 A.M.C. 1.

184 Emphasis added.

The 'caused by delay' wording and whether it alters the proximate causation rule has not yet been litigated. In case it is interpreted as changing the proximate cause rule, the exclusion can nevertheless be triggered if delay is merely *a* cause of the loss,[185] and not *the* proximate cause. A more conservative view as to the fact that the wording does not alter the proximate cause rule can be found in *Coxe v Employers' Liability Assurance Corp. Ltd*[186] where Scrutton J stated that 'caused by' and 'arising from' has always been construed as relating to proximate cause.[187]

---

185 One of the views supporting this approach rests upon the fact that the wording serves to render the English drafting more easily accessible to foreign insureds, K.J. Goodacre, *Goodbye to the Memorandum: an in-depth study of standard cargo, war and strikes clauses* (London: Witherby 1988), 21.

186 In *Coxe v Employers' Liability Assurance Corp. Ltd* [1916] 2 KB 629.

187 At 634.

CHAPTER 3

Issues arising from delay in delivery of cargo

Introduction

3.1 A delay during sea transit together with a delay in delivery may result mainly in three types of losses. These are physical damage to or loss of goods;[1] economic loss as a result of the decrease in the market value of cargo between the time of the expected delivery and actual delivery; and pure economic loss where, by way of example, an industrial plant cannot operate given that parts of an essential machine are delivered after the date of delivery[2] or where a cargo owner loses his sale contract. Whereas the first category of loss results from delay in transit, the second and third categories rather arise in consequence of delay in delivery. The third category of loss may or may not be covered under marine delay in start-up insurance or business interruption policies depending on their respective wordings. This being said, there is a general view based on pre-MIA case law that the loss of market value caused by delay in delivery is not recoverable under cargo policies on the ground that mere delay in a voyage does not result in loss of the adventure insured and that this type of loss is consequential to cargo policies. This chapter will look at the pre-MIA authorities and assess whether they could survive the enactment of the Act. It will further elaborate on the meaning of delay in delivery in the context of insurance contracts; on whether the assured can claim for a total loss of goods where the delivery of goods is delayed and whether the generic exclusion of delay would strike out such claim; and on the scope of loss of market and loss of market value caused by delay.

Meaning of delay in delivery

3.2 Under a contract of carriage, delay in delivery may arise where the parties explicitly agree a delivery time in the contract and such agreement is not

---

1 This was dealt with in Chapter 2.
2 See United Nations Commission on International Trade Law, Fortieth session, Vienna, 25 June–12 July 2007, Report of Working Group III (Transport Law) on the work of its eighteenth session (Vienna, 6–17 November 2006), A/CN.9/616, at 42–43.

43

complied with;[3] where such delivery time is not expressly stated yet is implied or where a reasonable time required for delivery is exceeded.[4] In the absence of an agreed time, some international conventions such as the Hamburg Rules[5] provide a formula resting upon reasonable time required for a diligent carrier to deliver, having regard to the circumstances of the case.[6] As for the Rotterdam Rules,[7] an agreement as to the time of delivery can be both express and implied.[8]

3.3 Under cargo policies, as the time of delivery of the goods insured would be an element related to the contract of carriage, reference would have to be made to the contract of carriage and to whether it has an express or implied condition in interpreting delay in delivery. Certain cargo policies available in the market contain express references to 'delay in delivery' without actually defining it.[9] Standard form market terms such as the Institute Cargo Clauses 2009 contain references to the contract of carriage through which certain charges and liabilities or the termination of the policy are determined.[10] The Clauses do not however refer expressly to the contract of carriage in the clause which excludes 'losses caused by delay'[11] and this raises the question of whether 'delay' would extend to delay in delivery ascertainable by reference to the contract of carriage despite the absence of express reference thereto in the clause.[12]

---

3 For a common law example of delay in delivery under a contract of carriage, see *Horne v Midland Railway Company* (1872–73) LR 8 CP 131 where the parties had agreed a specific date for delivery of the goods.

4 For a common law example of not delivering within reasonable time under a contract of carriage see *Wilson v Lancashire and Yorkshire Railway Company* (1861) 9 Common Bench Reports (New Series) 632.

5 United Nations Convention on the Carriage of Goods by Sea 1978.

6 Art 5(2). Under the Carriage of Goods by Sea Regulations 1998 of Australia, if the contract does not specify a time for delivery, the goods are delayed if they are not delivered 'within a reasonable time for delivery, at that port, of similar goods carried by a diligent carrier (having regard to any particular circumstances of the case and the intentions of the shipper and the carrier)', Schedule 1A, art 4A(2) (b). No express provision exists in the Hague Rules (the International Convention for the Unification of Certain Rules of Law relating to Bills of Lading 1924) or the Hague-Visby Rules (the Protocol to Amend the International Convention for the Unification of Certain Rules of Law Relating to Bills of Lading 1968) as to the meaning of delay in delivery.

7 United Nations Convention on Contracts for the International Carriage of Goods Wholly or Partly by Sea 2008.

8 A. Diamond, 'The Rotterdam Rules', *Lloyd's Maritime and Commercial Law Quarterly*, 2009 (4), 445–536, at 479; Berlingieri, 'Revisiting the Rotterdam Rules', *Lloyd's Maritime and Commercial Law Quarterly*, (2010), 583–639, 603.

9 'Consequential Loss

This policy is extended to include reasonable costs necessarily incurred by you as a result of:

(...)

c) delay in delivery due to closure of any transport route following accident, fire, flood or act of God'.

10 Institute Cargo Clauses All Risks 2009, cl 2 general average and salvage charges are determined according to the contract of carriage; cl 8.3 the policy remains in force if a liberty granted under the contract of carriage is exercised; cl.9 the policy terminates if the contract of carriage comes to an end unless continuation of cover is requested and additional premium is paid.

11 cl 4.5.

12 An affirmative view can be expressed through an analogy with freight policies whereby loss of freight is determined by reference to delay frustrating the object of the contract of carriage. For

Where the contract of carriage does not refer to a specific period for delivery, such period can be determined by Courts by reference to ancillary elements such as the type of cargo (where goods are seasonal which require delivery in a particular season); and the intention of the assured to sell the goods in a particular market and the loss of that market. An example to the former can be found in *Federation Insurance v Coret*[13] where the goods which were seasonal handbag parts were temporarily lost and were delivered after the season where the assured had intended the goods to be sold. The Court opined that 'there was no obligation to deliver within a specified delay'[14] yet the loss of the assured resting upon the goods missing their market was held to be within the scope of application of the exclusion 'loss or damage arising from loss of market, or for loss, damage or deterioration arising from delay'.

In the absence of clear indication as to the time or interval for resale of the goods in the market, Courts may take notice of a particular period where the market prices are high so as to determine the most likely delivery period for the resale of the goods by the assured. In *Lewis Emanuel v Hepburn*[15] where the goods had deteriorated in value given the delay following a strike, the Court emphasised that the goods would have been sold at a time which was not precisely stated and accepted the evidence submitted by the assured as to an interval of a week where the market prices were high.[16]

3.4 In addition to the criteria determining whether there is delay in delivery in an insurance dispute, another complexity lies in the calculation of the loss of the assured, in particular the loss of market value. Despite that a reasonable time may be allowed or an interval may be anticipated for delivery,[17] the exact time or day when the goods should have been delivered is difficult to determine. This would consequently affect the calculation of the measure of damage, i.e. the difference in the value of the goods between the time the goods should have been delivered and the time of their actual delivery.

Marine Insurance Act 1906 and delay in delivery

3.5 The Marine Insurance Act expressly deals only with two modes of delay: delay at the commencement of the voyage,[18] and delay in voyage.[19] The sole

---

examples of loss of freight by delay frustrating the charterparty, see *Jackson v Union Marine Insurance Co Ltd* (1874) LR 10 CP 125; *Re Jamieson v Newcastle SS Freight Ins Assn* [1895] 2 QB 90. Frustrating delay and loss of freight is discussed in Chapter 5 of this work.

13 *Federation Ins. Co of Canada v Coret Accessories Inc* [1968] 2 Lloyd's Rep 109.

14 At 111. It is submitted that 'delay' in this context was used in the sense of 'time frame'.

15 *Lewis Emanuel & Son, Ltd v Hepburn* [1960] 1 Lloyd's Rep 304.

16 See *Lewis Emanuel & Son, Ltd v Hepburn* [1960] 1 Lloyd's Rep 304, 307.

17 See *Clark's Chick Hatchery Ltd v Commonwealth Insurance Co* 1982 CarswellNB 331, the expected interval for delivery was given with reference to the time of shipment for a cargo of perishable goods. There was no loss of market on the facts of the case.

18 s 42.

19 s 48.

express reference to delay in delivery is found in the context of insurable interest with respect to seller's delay in making delivery.[20] There is *dicta* to the effect that delay in delivery losses are excluded under s 55(2)(b) albeit they are not expressly excluded thereunder. In *Weissberg v Lamb*[21] where under an all risks policy the goods were damaged while being loaded on board the ship, the assured paid charges to the removal contractors who then sought to claim that amount back from the insurers under the sue and labour clause. The Court opined that had the assured not paid the charges there could have been delay in delivery of the goods which would be a peril outside the scope of the policy as per s 55(2)(b) and that therefore the sum could not have been recovered as sue and labour.[22]

Mere delay not resulting in loss of marine adventure and common law authorities

3.6 Prior to the enactment of the MIA, there had been several common law authorities whereby the courts had held that so long as non-perishable goods could be forwarded to their destination, there would be no actual loss of goods other than the expense in forwarding them if they were merely delayed on the voyage.

In some of the pre-MIA authorities, the disputes turned on whether it was a mere delay upon the voyage or the initial peril causing damage to the ship which required repairs (and consequently delay in the arrival of goods for the season) or depriving it from prosecuting the voyage (such as detention) that resulted in the impossibility of prosecuting the voyage to the port of destination. In *Barker v Blakes*[23] a non-perishable cargo was carried upon a vessel which could not prosecute the voyage due to a prolonged detention in consequence of which the cargo had to be sold. Lord Ellenborough enunciated that:

> 'The impossibility of prosecuting the voyage to the place of destination, which arose during and in consequence of the prolonged detention of the ship and cargo, may be properly considered as a loss of the voyage and such loss of voyage, upon received principles of insurance law, as a total loss of goods which were to have been transported in the course of such voyage'.[24]

Delay was involved in this case merely as part of the detention peril and the crucial point was that it was impossible to prosecute the voyage by reason of the detention. The goods were lost as a result of the loss of adventure due to detention and not due to delay arising from such detention.

3.7 Several decisions were given prior to the enactment of the MIA where, upon the facts of the cases, delay in the arrival of the goods to their destination was caused by damage to the ship which necessitated lengthy repairs. For instance

---

20 s 7(2).
21 [1950] 84 Ll L Rep 509.
22 At 512.
23 *Barker v Blakes* (1808) 9 East 283.
24 At 293, 294.

in *Anderson v Wallis*[25] the ship carrying non-perishable cargo was damaged during the voyage and repairs could not be completed until the new season. Another ship could also not be procured to forward the cargo which meant that it could not reach the destination on time. The claim of the assured based on loss of adventure was rejected on the ground that the goods were not perishable and the adventure had not become impossible by reason of the peril damaging the vessel. According to the Court, the adventure could have been prosecuted subsequent to the repairs; there was therefore still the possibility of conveying the goods to their destination, albeit with some delay. These circumstances qualified as a temporary suspension of the voyage and not as its destruction.[26] In addition, it was enunciated that 'if retardation of the voyage be a cause of abandonment; the happening of any marine peril to the ship by which a delay is caused in her arrival at the earliest market, would be also a cause of abandonment'.[27]

Similarly, it was stated *obiter* in *Roux v Salvador*[28] that it follows from the concept of irretrievable deprivation that mere retardation of itself cannot constitute an actual total loss of goods.[29] Lord Abinger CB stated the principle as follows:

> 'If the goods are of imperishable nature, *if the assured become possessed or can have control of them, if they have still an opportunity of sending them to their destination*, the mere retardation of their arrival at their original port be of no prejudice to them beyond the expense of re-shipment in another vessel. In such a case, the loss can be but a partial loss, and must be so deemed, even though the assured should, for some real or supposed advantage to themselves, elect to sell the goods where they have been landed, instead of taking measures to transmit them to their original destination.'[30]

This *obiter dictum*[31] recognises that mere delay in the arrival of the goods cannot result in the total loss of goods where the assured has control over them; however the expenses incurred so as to forward the goods to their destination could be recoverable under a cargo policy as partial loss. Lord Abinger CB further enunciated that:

> '. . . if, though imperishable, they are in the hands of strangers *not under the control of the assured*; if by any circumstance over which he has no control they can never, or *within no assignable period*, be brought to their destination; (. . .) The loss, is in its nature, total to him who has no means of recovering his goods, whether his inability arises from their annihilation or from any other insuperable obstacle'.[32]

This passage would give rise to the following suggestions. First, there may be a total loss of goods where the goods are delayed due to a deprivation peril (e.g.

---

25 *Anderson v Wallis* (1813) 2 Maule and Selwyn 240.

26 The Court thereby distinguished *Manning v Newnham* (1792) 3 Douglas 130.

27 At 247.

28 *Roux v Salvador* (1836) 3 Bing NC 266.

29 See MIA ss 57 and 60 on respectively actual and constructive total loss.

30 *Roux v Salvador* (1836) 3 Bing NC 266 at 278–279 (emphasis added).

31 The goods in that case were perishable.

32 At 279 (emphasis added).

detention or piracy) whereby the assured has no control or possession of the goods. Secondly, the deprivation of possession or control over the goods may merely be temporary, in situations where for instance imperishable goods go missing and are found much later than the date they should have arrived at their destination.[33] It can be fairly controversial to determine whether the adventure and accordingly the goods are totally lost or whether they are merely delayed, the discussion of which would turn upon the exact point of time where the loss must be identified.[34] Lastly, it can be suggested that the expression 'within no assignable period' in the *obiter dictum* refers to a situation where the deprivation peril is of unknown length whereby the assured, upon the condition of not having control over the goods during such deprivation, could claim for total loss of goods even where the goods eventually reach their destination, albeit with some delay.

Loss of adventure and the MIA 1906

3.8 Under a cargo policy, the main interest covered is the goods as tangible objects[35] and accordingly 'physical loss of or damage to goods' is insured particularly where the policy expressly so provides.[36] This being the case, another interest covered under a cargo policy is the loss of the adventure insured. Before the MIA 1906 was enacted, the draftsman of the Act Sir Mackenzie Chalmers had noted:

> 'Strictly speaking, it is the risk or adventure of the assured, and not the property exposed to peril, which is the subject of insurance. *Ex hypothesi*, the ship or goods may be lost. What is really insured is the pecuniary interest of the assured in or in respect of the property exposed to peril, in other words, the risk or adventure.'[37]

The passage cited was the note to s 3 of the MIA 1906 on marine adventure and the example given was the total loss of goods when the adventure is frustrated although the goods are not physically lost or damaged. The references in the Act to the expression 'adventure' are confined to the sections relating to the definition

---

33 As in *Federation Insurance Company of Canada v Coret Accessories* (1968) 2 Lloyd's Law Rep 109 and *Phoenix Assurance Plc v Golden Imports Ltd* 1989 CarswellBC 555. These decisions will be elaborated under the heading 'Temporary deprivation of cargo and delay'.

34 This issue will be covered below at paras 3.16–3.19.

35 The MIA 1906 states that where the policy designates the subject matter insured in general terms, it shall be construed to apply to the interest intended by the assured, see s 26(3). The subsection is founded on a speech delivered by Brett J, in *Allison v Bristol Marine Insurance Co* (1876) 1 App Cas 209. In this case the policy was on 'freight' and upon the facts of the case, Brett J opined that the assured had not intended to insure the whole charterparty freight yet only the part which had not been paid to him when the ship sailed.

36 See *Lewis Emanuel & Son, Ltd v Hepburn* [1960] 1 Lloyd's Rep 304.

37 McKenzie Chalmers, *A Digest of the Law relating to Marine Insurance* (1901), 5. For the distinction between 'subject insured' and 'subject matter of insurance' see Lord Escher *Rayner v Preston* (1881), 18 Ch D 1 at p 9, CA, as cited in Chalmers, at p 5.

of marine adventure,[38] to insurable interest,[39] to the warranty of legality[40] and to sections on delay[41] and do not appear in sections on causation or indemnity. This could give rise to the question of whether 'loss of adventure' can no longer be a claim for indemnity under the MIA.[42] This argument was however rejected by the House of Lords which held that the enactment of the MIA 1906 had not altered the pre-MIA rule that the assured can recover for constructive total loss of goods as per s 60 where the adventure contemplated is frustrated by the detention of goods for an indefinite time.[43] In particular, it was emphasised that:

> '. . . where goods are insured at or from one port to another port the insurance is not confined to an indemnity to be paid in case the goods are injured or destroyed, but extends to an indemnity to be paid in case the goods do not reach their destination. This may be variously described as *an insurance of the venture*, or an insurance of the voyage, or *an insurance of the market, as distinguished from an insurance of the goods simply and solely.* Goods delivered at the port of destination may be of value very different from their value at the port of loading. The underwriter's obligation is to pay money in the event of the goods failing to arrive at their destination uninjured by any of the perils insured against.'[44]

In other judgments delivered subsequent to the enactment of the MIA, several speeches were delivered to the effect that the subject-matter insured under a cargo policy is the goods as tangible objects as well as the adventure they embarked upon, in the sense that the assured has a benefit in the safe arrival of the goods.[45]

It would follow that unless there is clear and unambiguous wording covering only physical loss of or damage to goods or an exclusion clause for loss of adventure, goods do not have to incur only physical loss or damage for the assured to recover under a cargo policy. Cargo policies of that type cover losses suffered

---

38 s 3.

39 s 5.

40 s 41.

41 ss 42 and 48.

42 This was argued in *British and Foreign Marine Insurance Company, Limited v Samuel Sanday & Co* [1916] AC 650.

43 See in particular *British and Foreign Marine Insurance Company, Limited v Samuel Sanday & Co* [1916] AC 650, 657–658 per Earl Loreburn. In Lord Atkinson's speech, there were also references to *Barker v Blakes* (1808) 9 East 283 (loss of voyage in consequence of a prolonged detention of the ship and cargo); *Anderson v Wallis* (1813) 2 Maule and Selwyn 240 (mere suspension of the voyage does not result in loss of voyage where the goods are capable of being forwarded with delay); *Rodocanachi v Elliott* (1873) LR 9 CP 649 (loss of adventure given the goods were indefinitely detained and not merely delayed).

44 *British & Foreign Marine Insurance v Samuel Sanday* [1916] 1 AC 650, 652–653 per Lord Wrenbury (emphasis added). It is not clear whether 'Goods delivered at the port of destination may be of value very different from their value at the port of loading' refers to a delay in delivery of the goods.

45 See for instance *Rickards v Forestal Land, Timber and Railways Co* [1942] AC 50 where Lord Wright stated that the primary subject of the insurance on goods is the goods themselves, however an element of safe arrival of goods is also superimposed. See s 5(2) for interest in safe and due arrival of the goods, which will be discussed below.

by reason of the goods not arriving safely at their destination, though the goods themselves are undamaged.[46]

3.9 Identifying the scope of 'loss of adventure' is of importance for determining its relevance to delayed delivery of goods. In the passage from Lord Wrenbury's speech in *British & Foreign Marine Insurance v Samuel Sanday* cited above,[47] loss of adventure was used in several instances as being equivalent to loss of market. In *Rickards v Forestal*[48] loss of adventure was considered as a more general instance comprising the benefit from the arrival of the goods[49] which can include the sale of the goods at a profit at the port of destination as well as the use of the goods as raw material at the port of destination.[50] It may therefore be argued on the ground of both speeches that loss of market caused by delay can be considered as an instance by which the assured fails to obtain the benefit sought from the arrival of the goods. This could give rise to the question of whether, unless specifically excluded, loss of market caused by delay could be recoverable on the ground that it is a sub-category of loss of adventure, particularly leading to a commercial frustration of the adventure insured.[51]

3.10 Except for the foregoing suggestion, loss of adventure occurs where the transit is terminated or where the object of the adventure is frustrated. Regard must accordingly be taken to two types of delay so as to assess loss of adventure. The first type is mere delay or suspension of the voyage which, according to the pre-MIA authorities, does not result in loss of adventure in case of non-perishables; yet the transit may be considered as terminated where the goods cannot be forwarded to their destination. The second type is frustrating delay (where delay can be actual as well as anticipated) which may or may not give the assured the right to claim for the loss of adventure both for perishable and non-perishable goods. Both of these instances would also require the assured to take precautions against loss of goods or delay in the arrival of the goods by forwarding the goods to their destination in consequence of which forwarding expenses would be incurred.[52]

---

46 *Forestal Land, Timber & Railways Company, Ltd v Rickards; Middows Ltd v Robertson and Others* (1941) 70 Ll L Rep 173 at 184 per Viscount Maugham.

47 At para 3.8.

48 *Rickards v Forestal Land, Timber and Railways Co* [1942] AC 50.

49 *Rickards v Forestal Land, Timber and Railways Co* [1942] AC 50, 90–91 per Lord Wright.

50 *Rickards v Forestal Land, Timber and Railways Co* [1942] AC 50, 90 per Lord Wright.

51 Commercial frustration was defined in *Admiral Shipping Co v Weidner* (1916) 1 KB 429, at 436–437 by Bailhache J: 'The commercial frustration of an adventure by delay means, as I understand it, the happening of some unforeseen delay without the fault of either party to a contract, of such a character as that by it the fulfilment of the contract in the only way in which fulfilment is contemplated and practicable is so inordinately postponed that its fulfilment when the delay is over will not accomplish the only object or objects which both parties to the contract must have known that each of them had in view at the time they made the contract, and for the accomplishment of which object or objects the contract was made.' This decision was reversed in *Scottish Navigation Co Ltd v W.A Souter & Co* [1917] 1 KB 222 and *Admiral Shipping Co v Weidner* [1917] 1 KB 222 however the definition of Bailhache J was found entirely in line with previous authorities, at 243.

52 These expenses that can otherwise be named 'expenses caused by delay' and their recoverability under cargo insurance policies shall be discussed in Chapter 4.

3.11 Assuming that the concept of loss of adventure survived the MIA[53] would give rise to another query which is whether 'adventure' is a concept inconsistent with the modern market wordings and that loss of adventure is therefore not recoverable thereunder. Following the authority of *British and Foreign Marine Insurance v Samuel Sanday*, a clause was inserted into the Institute Cargo Clauses on war risks to exclude any claim based on loss of or frustration of the adventure[54] to abrogate the effect of *Sanday*. This clause does not appear in the Institute Cargo Clauses All Risks 2009 although the adventure insured can also be lost by perils insured under these Clauses or by delay. Whether the exclusion 'loss of or damage to the subject-matter insured proximately caused by delay' in the Clauses would exclude, *inter alia*, loss of market by delay which can be considered as a type of loss of adventure has not yet been tested by courts. It is submitted that it would exclude this type of loss where 'loss of or damage to the subject-matter insured' is interpreted as applying to all types of losses including loss of adventure as well as physical losses.[55]

*Marine adventure and 'due arrival of insured property'
under the MIA 1906*

3.12 Reference must be made to the definition of marine adventure under the MIA so as to comprehend loss of marine adventure and whether non-perishable goods could be taken to have been totally lost subsequent to a delay in delivery. According to MIA s 3(2) there is marine adventure where any ship, goods or other movables are exposed to maritime perils. Maritime perils are enumerated by way of example in the same subsection without specific reference to delay. Section 90(2) provides that the earlier case law would still apply where the provisions of the Act are not inconsistent therewith. In light of the definition of marine adventure in s 3 and the definition of insurable interest which refers to marine adventure in s 5, the question arises as to whether the previous case law holding that mere delay would not result in loss of adventure[56] is still tenable.

(a) 'Due arrival of insurable property'
3.13 According to the MIA s 5(1), every person has an insurable interest who is interested in a marine adventure. The Act goes on illustrating that a person is interested in a marine adventure in which he has a 'legal or equitable relation to the adventure or to any insurable property at risk in consequence of which he may benefit by the *safety or due arrival of insurable property*'.[57] The meaning of 'due

---

53 *British & Foreign Marine Insurance Company, Limited v Samuel Sanday & Co* [1916] AC 650.
54 For the most recent version, see Institute War Clauses (Cargo) 2009, cl 3.7.
55 The expression 'loss of or damage to the subject-matter insured' appears also in Institute War Clauses (Cargo) 2009, cl 3.7 which also contains a loss of adventure exclusion.
56 *Anderson v Wallis* (1813) 2 Maule and Selwyn 240; *Roux v Salvador* (1836) 3 Bing NC 266.
57 s 5(2) (emphasis added).

arrival of insurable property' has not been the subject of considerable litigation[58] nevertheless it can be interpreted by reference to the following part of the subsection, namely '. . . *or may be prejudiced by its loss, or by damage thereto, or by the detention thereof*'. Insurable property includes goods[59] and whereas safety may refer to the goods arriving with no loss or damage; due arrival may in turn refer to goods arriving without detention in the absence of which the goods, albeit not having been physically lost or damaged, could arrive to a falling market. Detention is a peril that includes an element of delay which may result in late delivery of the insured goods.[60] In the absence of clear guidance as to the meaning of 'due arrival of insurable property'[61] what can accordingly be deduced from this subsection is that insurable interest in property includes a benefit in due arrival of the property to its destination, i.e. an assured insuring goods would benefit both from the goods arriving to their destination without loss or damage, and from their timely delivery. This suggestion would also denote that whoever has an interest in the timely delivery of the goods is entitled to insure them (which can be considered as an economic interest), upon the condition that he has a legal or equitable relationship to the goods.[62]

3.14 Hence, marine adventure should be more than a mere exposure of the insurable property to the enumerated maritime perils under the cargo policy. One of the reasons why it should not be confined to the exposure of the subject-matter insured to maritime perils can be explained by the fact that in policies on freight, frustrating delay, although it is not mentioned among the marine perils, would cause a loss of adventure by frustrating the object thereof and consequently result in loss of freight.[63] The object of the adventure in this category of cases is usually determined by reference to a contract other than a marine insurance contract, for instance a charterparty under which the relevant adventure is prosecuted. By way

---

58 Chalmers, *A Digest of the Law relating to Marine Insurance* (1901) does not cite any specific judgment in this respect.

59 See s 3(2)(a); for the meaning of goods see MIA 1906, First Schedule, r 17.

60 See *Canadian Encyclopedic Digest: Insurance* (4th edn, Carswell 2010), III.7, § 197 providing in respect of s 5(2) which is equivalent to s 8(2) of the Canadian Marine Insurance Act 1993 (c.22), that: "Every person with an interest in a marine adventure has an insurable interest if he or she has a legal or equitable relation to the adventure or to any insurable property at risk therein, and may benefit from the safe or *due arrival of the insurable property*, or be prejudiced by its loss or *delay* or incur liability in respect *of such an adventure*" (Emphasis added).

61 Chalmers and Owen, *A Digest of the Law Relating to Marine Insurance* (1901) at 9 cites Arnould (6th edn), p 101 in support of s 5(2). The relevant part in Arnould mentioned that a party interested in cargo alone has no insurable interest in the ship, given that the goods may arrive safe though the ship be lost.

62 By virtue of s 5(2). *Feasey v Sun Life Assurance Corporation of Canada* [2003] Lloyd's Rep IR 637 per Waller LJ stated at para 92: 'It is not a requirement of property insurance that the assured must have a "legal or equitable" interest in the property as those terms might normally be understood . . . It is sufficient under Section 5 of the Marine Insurance Act for a person interested in a marine adventure to stand in a "legal or equitable relation to the adventure". That is intended to be a broad concept.'

63 See Chapter 5 and in particular *Jackson v Union Marine Insurance Co Ltd* (1874) LR 10 CP 125; *Re Jamieson v Newcastle SS Freight Ins Assn* [1895] 2 QB 90; *Bensaude v The Thames and Mersey Marine Insurance Company Ltd* [1897] AC 609.

of analogy, the object of the adventure for an assured may well be to receive the goods in a certain period for selling them in a specific market or under a number of sale contracts, in which case one of the objects of the marine adventure would be the timely delivery of the goods. There may accordingly be room for the suggestion that the marine adventure is an instance not limited to the safe delivery of the goods, yet a term that would also extend to timely delivery. The question which would accordingly ensue could be whether there can be a loss of adventure where the goods miss their market because of delay, given that the interest of the assured is to sell its goods in a given market in a given period as well as their safe arrival at their destination. If interest in a marine adventure comprises both safe and due arrival of insurable property, where cargo policies insure marine adventure and contain no express exclusion on late delivery losses, any loss resulting from late arrival of property can be recoverable. However one of the motives behind the general view that loss of market by delay in delivery is not recoverable under cargo policies rests upon the paradigm that it is a type of loss of profit, which shall be elaborated below.

(b) Loss of profit, loss of market and loss of adventure by delay

3.15 Goods are usually sent to profitable markets,[64] i.e. to markets where the assured will be able to sell its products at a higher figure than the invoice price.[65] The assured has therefore an economic interest in the safe and timely delivery of goods in the absence of which one of the outcomes could be the diminution in value of the goods. Therefore where a rising market is intended, any delay in delivery of the goods would have at least two consequences: first, the fall in the market value of the goods may result in the loss of a sale contract under which the assured could have sought to gain a fixed profit; and secondly, in consequence of delay in the arrival of goods the assured may have to sell his goods at a lower price than what was intended had the goods arrived on time. Whether the economic benefit behind both of these instances where the goods are undamaged should be treated as part of the 'marine adventure insured' or as 'profit' which is not recoverable under cargo policies could be a pertinent question.[66] Loss of profit is usually not recoverable under hull and cargo policies[67] unless specifically covered

---

64 This was considered in *Usher v Noble* (1810) 104 ER 249, at 253.

65 Insurable value for goods is the prime cost of the property insured, plus the expenses of and incidental to shipping and the charges of insurance upon the whole (MIA s 16(3)). Prima facie evidence of the prime cost of the property is the invoice price paid by the assured, Merkin et al, *Marine Insurance Legislation* (5th edn), 18.

66 With respect to safe arrival of goods and loss of adventure, see *British and Foreign Marine Insurance Company, Limited v Samuel Sanday & Co* [1916] AC 650 (frustration of the adventure of goods due to the port of destination becoming enemy territory); *Rodocanachi v Elliott* (1873) LR 9 CP 649 (constructive total loss of goods by restraints of princes which might extend to an indefinite time causing a loss of the particular adventure).

67 *Lucena v Craufurd* (1806) 2 Bos & PNR 269. See also *Maurice v Goldsbrough Mort & Co Ltd* [1939] 64 Ll L Rep 1, at 3 where Lord Wright stated 'an insurance described as an insurance on goods does not cover profits'. The loss of profit was described as the commission on sale of the goods lost

therein.[68] This is mainly due to the fact that it is considered as an instance of a loss arising by virtue of the physical loss of goods or loss to the ship and therefore consequential to cargo policies[69] and hull policies.

In *Anderson v Morice*,[70] it was stated that the assured would derive benefit from the policy if the market was a rising market and would sustain loss in a falling market and that the interest in profits arising collaterally from a policy relating to goods cannot be recoverable thereunder.[71] Whether the authority of *Anderson v Morice* is now obsolete by virtue of the expression 'due arrival of insurable property' in s 5(2) of the Marine Insurance Act 1906 is yet to be seen. The argument in favour of this suggestion could be supported with the express reference in *Anderson v Morice* to the earlier authorities on insurable interest[72] which is now a broader concept given the development of the doctrine in recent years.[73] Moreover, authorities discussing s 5(2) after the enactment of the MIA 1906 were merely with respect to safe arrival of goods and not to 'due arrival' such as *British & Foreign v Samuel Sanday*,[74] therefore the meaning of the expression is yet to be tested by the courts in England.

Temporarily missing goods and delay

3.16 Where there is a delay in the arrival of the goods or where goods that are intended for a specific market are temporarily missing, one of the issues that arises is whether the assured can claim for a constructive total loss as having been deprived of the possession of the goods. The assured would have to prove that the goods were unlikely to be recovered.[75] The test for unlikelihood of recovery assumes that there has to be a reasonable time at the expiration of which the subject-matter insured can be considered as having been a constructive total loss.[76] Moreover some standard form hull and freight clauses also specify the length of

---

by the assured in consequence of the peril insured against. It is noteworthy that the policy in this case specifically excluded loss of profits of any kind.

68 *Hibernia Foods plc v McAuslin (The Joint Frost)* [1998] 1 Lloyd's Rep 310.

69 There are consequential loss policies available in the market; see *Glengate-KG Properties Ltd v Norwich Union Fire Insurance Society Ltd* [1996] CLC 676 for an example of such a policy.

70 (1874–75) LR 10 CP 609.

71 At 621 per Blackburn J.

72 (1874–75) LR 10 CP 609, at 621: 'For the subject-matter of this insurance is on "rice" and though that is to be construed liberally as covering any interest in the rice, it cannot be construed as covering an interest in profits that might arise collaterally from a contract relating to the rice. For this it is enough to refer to *Lucena v Crauford*'.

73 See for instance *Feasey v Sun Life Assurance Corporation of Canada* [2003] Lloyd's Rep IR 637.

74 See *British & Foreign Marine Insurance v Samuel Sanday* [1916] 1 AC 650.

75 MIA s 60(2)(i)(a).

76 In respect of a vessel, this period was held to be 12 months in *The Bamburi* [1982] 1 Lloyd's Rep 314. Cf. also *Wong Wing Fai Co SA v Netherlands Insurance Co* (1945) [1980–81] 1 SLR 242 where nine months was deemed sufficient. For cargo, a lesser period would be considered as reasonable time.

time spent during the deprivation peril in consequence of which the loss shall be characterised as constructive total loss.[77] Under English law, it was decided that if a thing is missing or has disappeared and a reasonable time has elapsed without the goods having been found despite diligent research, then the goods are properly be said to be lost.[78] It is submitted that 'reasonable time' for goods shall depend upon the type of the goods insured and in any event shall be lesser than the period required for vessels. For the purposes of delay, irretrievable and temporary deprivation of goods could be relevant for two types of delay: delay during transit and delay in delivery.

In relation to the former, some jurisdictions such as Norway have introduced time limits by the expiration of which delay not resulting in physical loss under the cargo policy was deemed total.[79] As to the latter, an analogy can be drawn from the context of carriage of goods by sea Conventions whereby the goods are deemed lost if they are delivered after the expiry of a period of time following the time for delivery.[80] The risk of not having a time frame for unlikelihood of recovery is that even if a claim is made for constructive total loss of goods and is paid accordingly by the insurers, the goods may later on be delivered to their destination with some delay. The unlikelihood of recovery would subsequently turn into a temporary deprivation of goods and the insurers may argue that the claim was paid by mistake and that the claim was in any event not recoverable given the exclusion of delay. This matter has been the subject of two decisions which shall be analysed below.

---

77 The Detainment Clause in Institute War and Strikes Clauses Hulls-Time and Hulls Voyage of 1983 and 1995 cl 3 provides that if the vessel has been subject to capture, seizure or detainment and the assured has thereby lost the free use and disposal of the vessel for a continuous period of 12 months, for the purpose of ascertaining whether the vessel is a constructive total loss the assured shall be deemed to have been deprived of the possession of the vessel without any likelihood of recovery. A similar clause can be found in Institute War and Strike Clauses Freight-Time 1983 and 1995 cl 3.

78 *Holmes v Payne* [1930] 2 KB 301, 310.

79 Under Norwegian Cargo Clauses (All Risks) Version 2004, total loss by delay which does not result in physical loss of or damage to goods may be covered if it is agreed by the assured and the insurer, and the Cargo Clauses suggest a draft clause which provides as follows:

'Total loss as a result of delay (not resulting in the physical loss of or damage to the goods)'

The Assured is entitled to claim for a total loss pursuant to §§ 35 and 36 of the Cargo Clauses when:

a)   a domestic transit has been delayed for at least 30 days, or
b)   an international transit has been delayed for at least 30 days as a consequence of theft, piracy, damage to other goods carried by the means of transport, or the means of transport onto which the goods are loaded having suffered a casualty, disappeared or been abandoned, or harbours or transit routes having been destroyed or blocked, but not as a result of protest actions, riots, strikes, or similar occurrences, cf. § 18, no. 3 of the Cargo Clauses.'

80 art 5(3) of the Hamburg Rules provides that the cargo interest may treat the goods as lost if they have not been delivered within 60 consecutive days following *the expiry of the time for delivery* (emphasis added). No equivalent provision exists under the Rotterdam Rules.

3.17 In the Canadian case *Phoenix Assurance Plc v Golden Imports Ltd*[81] a consignment of fashion wear had disappeared and was subsequently found in a warehouse six months after the payment of the claim. As the goods had been intended as prototypes they had become worthless to the assured. The policy was on the Institute Air Cargo terms and included a delay exclusion[82] which was relied on by the insurers to recover back the proceeds paid at the time when the goods had been known as having been totally lost; the insurers further argued that there had been no 'loss' in the sense of an irretrievable loss.[83] The Court opined that the word 'loss' in the policy was used in two different senses; it was a term of general sense referring to goods not being able to be found, and a term of insurance law art referring to the right of recovery when an assured's interest had been injuriously affected. The word 'loss' in the exclusion of delay was used in the latter sense given that goods could not be missing by delay[84] and it was decided that the exclusion merely denied coverage consequent upon the disappearance of the insured goods whether the goods were never recovered or were recovered after a lapse of time. Delay did not necessarily exclude recovery where goods went missing but were recovered later.[85]

In an earlier Canadian decision *Federation Insurance Company of Canada v Coret Accessories*,[86] a similar exclusion clause was held not to respond to the claim of the assured where the goods were found after the payment of the claim. The Court held that the insurers only insured goods which were permanently lost, not the ones delayed in transit or which were lost temporarily but subsequently delivered. According to this reasoning, in all the circumstances where goods disappear and are subsequently found, assureds will have to reimburse insurers given the delay exclusion, despite that at the time of the claim the goods were characterised as 'lost'.

3.18 In situations similar to the above, it is crucial to identify at which point of time the loss must be identified: at one point of time the loss may be characterised as a total loss caused by a peril insured against and at a later point as a loss caused by delay where the goods are subsequently found and delivered.[87] In practice, against the risk of the goods temporarily missing and the possible rejection thereof by the cargo owner at the time of the delayed delivery, cargo insurers may require

---

81 *Phoenix Assurance Plc v Golden Imports Ltd* 1989 CarswellBC 555 (British Columbia County Court).

82 'This insurance is against all risks of loss or damage to the subject matter insured which shall in no case be deemed to extend to cover loss, damage or expense proximately caused by delay or inherent vice, or nature of the subject matter insured'.

83 This was a defence against a claim of actual total loss. According to MIA s 57(1), there is an actual total loss where the assured is irretrievably deprived of the possession of the subject-matter insured. The equivalent section in the Canadian Marine Insurance Act 1993 is s 56(1).

84 At para 15.

85 At para 16.

86 *Federation Insurance Company of Canada v Coret Accessories* (1968) 2 Ll L Rep 109 (Quebec Supreme Court).

87 This was the case in *Phoenix Assurance Plc v Golden Imports Ltd* 1989 CarswellBC 555.

their assured to sign a document entitled a 'loan receipt' whereby the assured undertakes to take delivery of the goods if they go missing and to refund the insurance payment where the claim is settled after the goods are delivered with delay.[88] The receipt characterises the payment received as a 'loan' and not as payment of the claim and allows the assured to keep the difference between the amount paid and the amount of loss or damage if during the temporary deprivation of the goods they were damaged or partially lost.[89] Another possibility for the insurers would be to insert clauses in the policy to that effect.[90]

Duties of the assured subsequent to the delayed delivery of goods

3.19 Where goods are damaged by a peril insured against and the cost of forwarding the goods to their destination would exceed their value on arrival, assureds can elect to abandon the goods and claim for constructive total loss.[91] Likewise, the goods can also be abandoned if they are missing and their recovery is unlikely. In both of these circumstances, insurers could accept the notice of abandonment, elect to take over the subject-matter,[92] pay the insured value of the cargo to the assured and be subrogated to all the rights and remedies of the assured in respect of the subject-matter as from the time of the casualty causing the loss.[93] This would accordingly entitle them to sell the goods at the port of distress and keep the proceeds of sale as 'salvage'. However, the assured, as the holder of a bill of lading would still be the person who could claim the goods from the carrier and who can accept delivery of the goods unless the bill of lading is assigned to the insurers upon their election to take over the goods or their payment of the claim. The scenario above where goods disappear and are subsequently delivered to the assured with delay would give rise to the question of whether the assured is bound to accept the delayed delivery of the goods under reservation,[94] sell them and tender the sale proceeds to the insurers and if affirmative, whether the nature of such duty would relate to sue and labour.[95]

---

88 George R. Strathy and George C. Moore, *The Law and Practice of Marine Insurance in Canada* (Butterworths 2003), 113.

89 Strathy and Moore, 461–462.

90 Such a clause was found in *Federation Insurance Company of Canada v Coret Accessories* (1968) 2 Ll L Rep 109.

91 Institute Cargo Clauses A-B-C 2009 cl 13.

92 As per s 63(1). This would give the insurers the right to an equitable lien at that point over the subject-matter which would, upon payment, entitle them to legal ownership as per s 79(1).

93 MIA s 79(1).

94 In order for the insurers who are subrogated to the rights of the assured to claim against the carrier.

95 This scenario assumes that the policy does not contain a clause requiring the assured to accept the goods upon their delivery and to reimburse the insurer accordingly for the insured value of the goods that was paid by the insurers upon their acceptance of the notice of abandonment, as in *Federation Insurance Company of Canada v Coret Accessories* (1968) 2 Ll L Rep 109. The scenario further excludes the situation where the assured signs a 'loan receipt'.

Most standard form policies contain clauses requiring the assured 'to take such measures as may be reasonable for the purpose of averting or minimizing a loss'[96] and it was disputed in *Phoenix Assurance v Golden Imports*[97] where the policy was on Institute Cargo Clauses (Air)[98] terms whether the assured was bound to sell the goods and tender the sale proceeds to the insurer. The Court concluded that under the mitigation of loss clause, the assured had to make arrangements for the goods in which he retained property and title even though they were delivered with delay. Nevertheless, under English law, it was held in *Kuwait Airways Corp v Kuwait Insurance Co SAK*[99] that the duty to sue and labour would cease when the insurers admit liability and commence payment which would denote that the assured would not be bound to accept and sell the goods if they arrive subsequent to the payment of the claim by the insurers.

Cargo policies and absence of physical loss of or damage to goods

3.20 All risks cargo policies essentially cover loss of or damage to goods as well as loss of adventure if that type of loss is not specifically excluded therein. Whether the wording 'loss of or damage to goods' in a cargo policy implies only physical losses in the absence of the expression 'physical' is a curiosity. In *Quorum v Schramm*[100] the value of the goods had depreciated because of a suspicion that the goods were physically damaged. It was held that that type of loss could not have been recoverable in the absence of physical damage; this decision therefore suggests that where there is only a loss in value without any direct physical change there is no damage to goods. Conversely, in a New Zealand authority *Technology Holdings Ltd v IAG New Zealand Ltd*[101] where the goods were insured against 'loss or damage' the Court held that if goods had to be stored in specific conditions which were not met by reason of an insured peril, that of itself could constitute 'damage' even though there was no physical alteration to goods yet merely because the goods were no longer fit for use. The decision relied on *Ranicar v Frigmobile Pty Ltd; Royal Insurance Pty Ltd*[102] where it was enunciated that under some circumstances goods could be said to have been damaged although no physical change had been caused to the goods. The example given was food handled in a way which violated the religious dietary laws of the country to which it was exported. On the facts of the case, the storage of the perishable goods above a certain temperature had affected their exportability whereby their value was

---

96 See e.g. Institute Cargo Clauses A 2009 cl 16.1.
97 *Phoenix Assurance PLC v Golden Imports Ltd* 1989 CarswellBC 555.
98 Institute Cargo Clauses (Air) 1982 cl 13.1 is almost identical to Institute Cargo Clauses A-B-C 1982 and 2009 cl 16.1.
99 *Kuwait Airways Corp v Kuwait Insurance Co SAK* [1997] 2 Lloyd's Rep 687, at 696.
100 [2002] 1 Lloyd's Rep 249.
101 (2009) 15 ANZ Insurance Cases 61–786.
102 BC8371124 (Unreported Judgment by Green CJ, Supreme Court of Tasmania).

reduced. The loss had arisen from the inability of the assured to export the goods and this was considered as 'damage' within the meaning of the policy.

3.21 In *Lewis Emanuel & Son, Ltd v Hepburn*[103] the policy covered 'physical loss or damage or deterioration caused by or arising out of riots, strikes and civil commotions and delay consequent thereon'. Loss of market by delay was not therefore expressly excluded and the issue was whether claims for loss of market caused by delay due to strikes were recoverable. But for the strike and delay consequent thereon, the goods which were of perishable nature would have been sold at a higher figure. Insurers argued that 'physical' was meant to apply to damage and deterioration and not to loss of market value, and the premium could not have been assessed in relation to market prices which could vary in the short term. The Court looked into the meaning of 'physical loss or damage or deterioration' and decided that it merely referred to physical loss, physical damage and physical deterioration; loss of market, although a 'loss' was not a 'physical loss' within the meaning of the policy and therefore not recoverable. The decision was given upon the construction of the policy wording and cannot constitute an authority establishing that loss of market is not recoverable under cargo policies. The ratio of the decision raises the query as to whether the word 'loss', in the absence of the adjective 'physical', could be sufficient to include loss of market value. It was argued on behalf of the insurers that they could not have intended to cover loss of market caused by delay given that no insurer could assess a premium in relation to variation of market prices.[104]

It is noteworthy that the essential motive behind the exclusion of loss of market value would arguably lie in the distinction between speculative and pure risks. Risk is generally known as the possibility of loss; however when there is also the possibility of gain for the assured, the risk is termed as 'speculative risk'.[105] Most policies, notably property policies insure against pure risks; which, in contrast to speculative risks, involves only the possibility of loss.[106] Speculative risks, given their nature and the possibility of gain as well as of loss can be considered as a business risk to be borne by the assured.[107] For instance loss of market value caused by delay in delivery can be classified as a speculative risk given that in consequence of delay in delivery, the goods may have to be sold at a lower price

---

103 [1960] 1 Lloyd's Rep 304.

104 At 305.

105 James L. Athearn, *Risk and Insurance* (West Publishing Co 1977), 6. The author gives the example of a person who purchases a share of common stock with the expectation that the stock will rise; the person also runs the risk that the prices may fall.

106 Athearn, 6.

107 It was stated in Greene, 11 that an insurer who agrees to cover an assured against price decline, would 'in effect, become a business partner with the insured and would be asked to assume serious risks at a set price but without the corresponding opportunity to share in profits if there should be any'. A price fall in the market may also occur where another kind of cargo similar to the one insured arrives to the market where the goods are delivered with delay, this was the case in *Koufos v C. Czarnikow Ltd (The Heron II)* [1969] 1 AC 350.

but can also be sold at a higher price where goods arrive to a rising market. This being said, physical damage to goods by delay can be characterised as a pure risk.

The importance of *Lewis Emanuel & Son, Ltd v Hepburn* other than the part of the case on loss of market lies in that the goods in that case had been damaged by delay caused by a strike. Delay had therefore caused two separate types of losses: physical loss whereby the value of the goods had diminished and the goods were sold for less than they otherwise would have been sold for; and loss of market value as the goods could not have been sold at the time where the market was more favourable to the assured than the one following delay. Damage in this case was considered as a physical happening given the wording 'physical' whereas loss of market was stated as a financial happening.[108] The former type of loss was a physical loss by delay caused by the strike which resulted in a financial disadvantage, the same delay had also caused another financial disadvantage which was the missing of a good market price. This case is therefore a good example that delay can cause physical loss having a financial consequence (in which case it can be recoverable if the policy does not contain a clear exclusion clause as to delay losses) and financial loss (i.e. loss of market value). The policy in *Lewis Emanuel & Son, Ltd v Hepburn* particularly insured against 'physical loss' and therefore can accordingly not be relied upon to support the view that loss of market is excluded in cargo policies on the ground that it is not a physical loss.

3.22 As far as the Institute Cargo Clauses are concerned, nowhere in the clauses appears a specific expression of 'physical loss'. In *Coven SPA v Hong Kong Chinese Insurance Co*[109] it was suggested that 'all risks cover applies only to physical loss or damage';[110] however this can arguably not be authority for the proposition that financial losses are not recoverable under cargo policies, as on the facts of the case the goods did not exist in the first place and there was merely a 'paper loss', not a 'financial loss'. 'All risks including shortage in weight' was construed as meaning that only shortage in weight resulting from physical loss or damage to cargo could be recoverable under the policy. The Court in that case relied upon *Fuerst Day Lawson v Orion Insurance*[111] in support of the proposition that all risks policies covered merely physical loss of or damage to the goods.[112] With due respect, this reliance is controversial given that the relevant part of the decision turned upon arguments of the parties as to the insurable interest of a CIF buyer in the goods until the time of shipment. It was submitted by the insurers in that case that the buyers would have had insurable interest had they insured against loss of profits or the seller's default in shipment, yet that they would have no insurable interest in the goods until the time of shipment under an all risks policy.[113] The Court did not express an opinion upon these arguments on the ground that they

---

108 At 309.
109 *Coven SPA v Hong Kong Chinese Insurance Co* [1999] Lloyd's Rep IR 565.
110 At 568 per Clarke LJ.
111 *Fuerst Day Lawson Ltd v Orion Insurance Co Ltd* [1980] 1 Lloyd's Rep 656.
112 [1999] Lloyd's Rep IR 565, at 568.
113 *Fuerst Day Lawson Ltd v Orion Insurance Co Ltd* [1980] 1 Lloyd's Rep 656, 664.

did not arise for decision, therefore it is doubted that *Fuerst Day Lawson v Orion Insurance* can stand as authority for suggesting that all risks policies cover merely physical loss of or damage to goods.[114] Given all these observations, it would not be a fallacy to argue that so far no authority under English law has strictly held that all risks policies cover merely physical loss of or damage to goods in the absence of express provision to that effect.

Scope of loss of market and loss of market value caused by delay in delivery

3.23 In other jurisdictions loss of market is usually excluded from cargo policies by clear wording[115] along with losses caused by delay.[116] The association of loss of market with delay was considered as a combination with indirect and economic loss and as a standard practice.[117] Exclusion clauses in cargo policies referring merely to losses caused by delay with no reference to loss of market would arguably exclude loss of market caused by delay especially in the case of non-perishable goods.[118] The main intention of excluding delay losses rests upon the approach that cargo owners should be indemnified if the cargo is lost or damaged by an insured peril such as fire or perils of the seas, whereas in case of a delay in the arrival of cargo either in the port or on a vessel trying to access a port the

---

114 These two judgments were mentioned in favour of the suggestion that cargo policies cover merely physical losses in Gilman and Merkin, *Arnould's Law of Marine Insurance and Average* (18th edn), para 23–72, fn 490.

115 American Institute of Marine Underwriters (AIMU) Cargo Clauses 2004 All Risks cl 4 is entitled 'Paramount Warranties' and includes 'Delay Warranty' at point C which provides 'Warranted free of claim for loss of market or for loss, damage, expense or deterioration arising from delay, whether caused by a peril insured against or otherwise'.

116 *Blaine Richards & Co Inc v Marine Indemnity Insurance Company of America and William H. McGee & Co* 635 F.2d 1051, 1981 A.M.C. 1 (delay clause in the all risks policy excluding 'loss of market and loss, damage or deterioration arising from delay' and the clause in the war risks policy excluding 'delay, deterioration and/or loss of market'); *Federation Insurance Company of Canada v Coret Accessories* (1968) 2 Lloyd's Law Rep 109 ('loss or damage arising from loss of market, or for loss, damage or deterioration arising from delay'); *Clark's Chick Hatchery Ltd v Commonwealth Insurance Company* 1982 CarswellNB 331 ('loss of market or loss or damage caused by delay'); *Boyd Motors Inc v Employers Ins of Wausau* 880 F.2d 270 (10th Cir. 1989) ('loss or damage resulting from delay, loss of market'); *Ontario Inc v Commonwealth Insurance Co* 2005 CarswellOnt 2605 75 O.R. (3d) 653, 26 C.C.L.I. (4th) 225 ('delay, loss of market or loss of use or occupancy and consequent loss of any kind'). See also *A. Tomlinson (Hauliers) Ltd v Hepburn* [1964] 1 Lloyd's Rep 416 ('excluding deterioration through delay and loss or [sic] market').

117 *Boyd Motors Inc v Employers Ins of Wausau* 880 F.2d 270 (10th Cir. 1989) citing *inter alia Blaine Richards & Co Inc v Marine Indemnity Insurance Company of America and William H. McGee & Co* 635 F.2d 1051, 1981 A.M.C. 1.

118 Frozen Food Extension Clauses 1/1/86 which can be used with Institute Frozen Food Clauses A 1/1/86 contains cl 4.5: claims arising from loss of market' as exclusion. The earlier version of this clause excluded claims caused by delay. So far as the Institute Cargo Clauses 1982 and 2009 are concerned, this gives rise to the question of whether 'loss caused by delay' excludes merely loss of market caused by delay and not the physical loss or damage caused by delay.

cost should be borne by cargo owners.[119] Another motive for insurers for insertion of the exclusion is to avoid any deliberate delays should the cargo owner no longer want the shipment.[120] This suggestion may however not be tenable given that standard form market policies used in London contain an 'avoidance of delay clause' which serves to prevent specifically this type of deliberate delays.[121]

Goods arriving late and undamaged

3.24 There are several types of cargo which are susceptible of losing their market in case of delay in delivery; fashion wear, oil and generally seasonal goods are only some of them. A delay in delivery could result in the twin consequences of the goods losing their market completely if they cannot be sold to their prospective purchasers, or their market value where they still have a commercial value subsequent to delay although they cannot be sold at the initially aimed price. These types of loss are most likely to be the ones that are sought to be excluded by a clause containing the wording 'loss caused by delay'[122] or other similar expression.[123] In other jurisdictions, clauses excluding 'loss or damage arising from loss of market, or for loss damage or deterioration arising from delay'[124] and 'loss, damage or expense proximately caused by delay'[125] were held to strike out any claim for the depreciation in value of the goods following a delay in delivery. Moreover, courts in the United States emphasised the difference between loss of market and loss of market value arising from delay in deciding whether a clause excluding 'loss of market' could be interpreted as referring also to loss of market value.

Under US law, market was defined as 'geographical or economic extent of commercial demand for any particular product and generally refers to a more or less identifiable group of prospective purchasers seeking a particular type of product offered by a more or less identifiable group of sellers'.[126] Market was generally taken to be referring 'collectively to matters external to any particular product item, namely those conditions that determine the degree to which supply of that

---

119 The statement of a London underwriter published in Jon Guy, 'Africa's Cargo Insurance Dilemma', *Fairplay* 2013, 378(6738), 20.

120 Guy, 'Africa's Cargo Insurance Dilemma', 20.

121 See Chapter 10 for more information on the Avoidance of Delay Clause.

122 As in the Institute Cargo Clauses A-B-C 2009 cl 4.5 'loss damage or expense caused by delay'.

123 Institute Cargo Clauses A-B-C 1982 cl 4.5 'loss damage or expense proximately caused by delay'.

124 *Federation Insurance Company of Canada v Coret Accessories Inc. & Hirch* [1968] 2 Lloyd's Rep 109.

125 *Phoenix Assurance Plc et al. v Golden Imports Ltd* 1989 CarswellBC 555. The policy in this case was on Institute Air Cargo terms and the facts of the case can be found elsewhere in this work under the section 'Temporary deprivation of cargo and delay'.

126 *Boyd Motors Inc v Employers Ins of Wausau* 880 F.2d 270 (10th Cir. 1989) citing *Webster's New International Dictionary* at 1504 (2d edn, 1950); *Black's Law Dictionary* at 874 (5th edn, 1979); *Encyclopedia Britannica*, Vol 11 at 511 (15th edn, 1982).

commodity exceeds or falls short of demand'.[127] Accordingly the strict meaning of 'loss of market caused by delay' could extend to situations where a market is lost when there is delay in distribution or changes in consumer habits, and where a 'certain type of product is no longer in demand with its intended purchasers'.[128] However 'market value' denotes a 'function of qualities (i.e. age, state of repair) inherent to the individual item itself, and refers to the price that that specific article with those qualities would command in a given market'.[129]

It was held by the US courts that 'loss of market' must occur in the originally intended market[130] in that if there is no evidence that the assured lost its customers at the intended market loss of market exclusion does not apply.[131] If the assured is able to sell its goods elsewhere though at drastically lower prices than they would have received in the originally intended market where the originally intended market still exists, this would amount to a 'loss of market value' and not to 'loss of market'.[132] Furthermore, it was also held that for triggering the exclusion of loss of market by delay actual delivery of goods has to have been made; that where they are never delivered to their intended destination and missing there is a physical loss of goods rather than loss of market.[133]

3.25 The exclusion of loss of market value may seriously prejudice the assured under a cargo policy particularly where seasonal goods suffer delay in transit due to piracy peril. In *Masefield v Amlin*,[134] a cargo of biodiesel oil had lost its market value following a piracy attack to the vessel carrying the cargo. Accordingly the assured had to sell it at a substantially lesser price than the insured value. The policy was an all risks policy which excluded 'capture, seizure, arrest, restraint or detainment (piracy excepted)' and the insurer observed, *inter alia*, that the claim was for loss of market and not for physical loss of goods and therefore excluded by s 55(2)(b).[135] In that particular case, the issue turned on the alternative ground of defence of the insurers, therefore it was untested whether an assured could claim financial loss following a piratical detention and ensuing delay. Assureds whose cargo runs the risk of being captured by pirates where the carrying vessel enters

---

127 *Boyd Motors Inc v Employers Ins of Wausau* 880 F.2d 270 (10th Cir. 1989), 273.

128 At 273.

129 At 273.

130 See *The Parana* (1877) 2 P.D. 118; *American National Fire Insurance Co v Mirasco Inc* 249 F.Supp.2d 303 (S.D.N.Y. 2003).

131 *American National Fire Insurance Co v Mirasco Inc* 249 F.Supp.2d 303 (S.D.N.Y. 2003), 322.

132 *American National Fire Insurance Co v Mirasco Inc* 249 F.Supp.2d 303 (S.D.N.Y. 2003). In this case, there was still market for the sale of goods but the goods could not be sold at the intended market given the denial of importation of the government. There was merely a diminution of value in the goods, the market was not lost and a claim for the diminution in value could not be excluded by a loss of market exclusion.

133 *Nationwide Brokers Inc v C & G Trucking Corp.* No. 87-C-5770, 1988 WL 116827 (N.D.Ill. 21 Oct 1988). The Court rejected the argument that loss of market exclusion precluded recovery where outdated magazines have no market on the ground that the exclusion appeared to assume actual delivery of goods.

134 *Masefield v Amlin* [2010] EWHC 280 (Comm).

135 At para 12.

piracy prone areas may protect themselves against this type of loss by requesting the extension of cover and paying extra premiums. This option would seem viable particularly on the ground that negotiations which can be lengthy for release of the vessel and cargo are usually carried out between pirates and the ship and the cargo interests may incur serious losses for events totally beyond their control. Contractual extensions for that particular type of case must be made available for assureds.[136]

3.26 In the case of a valued policy, an element of loss of profit from the sale of goods can be included in the valuation of the cargo[137] and if the insurer agrees to the valuation, the assured recovers that sum in the event of loss. Therefore in the absence of clear wording excluding loss of market value by delay, this type of loss can be recoverable by the assured if it is included in the valuation of the cargo.

Damaged goods and loss of market value by delay

3.27 Consequential losses under insurance policies are those losses which are not proximately caused by an insured peril but by the loss of the subject matter insured, i.e. by the physical loss of or damage to the subject matter. Hence, any loss of market value which comes into existence by delay in delivery can be taken to be out of the scope of a cargo policy on the ground that it is not a direct yet a consequential loss.

Where cargo is damaged by an insured peril such as perils of the seas, the measure of indemnity would be the diminution in value of the goods and any cost of replacing the goods where the goods are replaceable.[138] The diminution in value which is attributable to damage to property can be contemplated as being covered by the wording 'loss of or damage to'[139] and not excluded by the exclusion of 'loss or damage resulting from . . . loss of market'. In *Boyd Motors Inc v Employers Ins of Wausau*[140] the policy was an all risks inland marine policy which insured against 'direct physical loss or damage to the insured automobiles, except [. . .] loss or damage resulting from delay, loss of market. . .'. The first question in this case was whether the expression 'direct loss and damage' covered diminution in value of the subject-matter insured after repairs when the subject-matter was damaged and whether such diminution was recoverable given the 'loss of market' exclusion. Diminution in value was considered as a direct physical loss as it resulted from

---

136 Kate Lewins and Robert Merkin, '*Masefield AG v Amlin Corporate Member Ltd, The Bunga Melati Dua*: Piracy, Ransom and Marine Insurance' (2011) 35(2) *Melbourne University Law Review* 717–734, 733.

137 See *The Corporation of the Royal Exchange Assurance v M'Swiney* (1849) 14 Queen's Bench Reports 646.

138 Note that property could suffer damage without necessarily diminution in value, *Jan de Nul v Axa Royal Belge SA (Formally NV Royale Belge)* [2001] EWCA Civ 209, para 92.

139 See also *Quorum v Schramm* [2002] 1 Lloyd's Rep 249 where the value of a painting had diminished following damage by fire and the diminution in value was calculated with reference to the market value of the painting right after the fire.

140 880 F.2d 270 (10th Cir. 1989).

repairs for the damaged vehicle and not an excluded loss that is consequential to the physical loss. In this case the insurers had undertaken under the policy to repair or replace the damaged property and the Court was of the view that the coverage extended therefore not only to the cost of repairs but also to the diminution in value of the repaired property.[141]

3.28 In circumstances where goods are held up due to deprivation perils such as detention or seizure and are both damaged and delayed, elaborate issues may arise as to the types of losses incurred by the assured and their recoverability under a cargo policy containing a delay exclusion. This is given that where goods are both damaged and delayed, loss of market value incurred by the assured can either have been caused by delay or by damage to goods which results in depreciation in their value. There is *dicta* to the effect that 'loss of market' with no specific reference to delay would also extend to loss of market by delay. In *Russian Bank for Foreign Trade v Excess Insurance Company Ltd*[142] the policy contained clauses excluding 'deterioration or loss of market' as well as 'all claims due to delay' exclusions. Bailhache J stated in respect of the 'all claims due to delay' exclusion "They may cover the same ground, but they are certainly of wider import."[143] It is also possible to argue that loss of market which is mentioned along with deterioration merely refers to loss of market value arising from deterioration of goods. Nevertheless 'all claims due to delay' exclusion could exclude both loss of market caused by delay, loss of use of cargo due to delay and physical damage to cargo by delay.

3.29 All these types of losses and their recoverability were discussed in the US case *Blaine Richards v Marine Indemnity Insurance Company of America*[144] where a cargo of beans were improperly fumigated and were detained by the US authorities. The assured incurred expenses to recondition the cargo and also lost the original sale contracts, accordingly the beans had to be sold at lower prices. The goods were insured under an all risks policy against 'all risks of physical

---

141 Norwegian Cargo Clauses 2004 § 6 provides: 'Unless otherwise specially agreed, the Insurer shall not be liable for–

1. General capital loss, including loss of time, loss due to economic fluctuations, loss of market, operating loss or similar losses.'

In the Commentary to Norwegian Cargo Clauses: Conditions relating to Insurance for the Carriage of Goods of 1995, Version 2004, CEFOR Form No 261A, issued by The Central Union of Marine Underwriters (CEFOR), Oslo, Norway October 2004, available at www.cefor.no/Clauses/Cargo-Clauses/, general capital loss was defined as losses which can be incurred by the assured as a result of loss of or damage to goods and includes damages that have to be paid due to the loss of delivery contracts and costs for replacing the damaged goods with more expensive ones.

According to the Commentary, the other exclusions refer to charges and losses generated in connection with a delay. More specifically, 'loss due to economic fluctuations' refers to depreciation in the value of the goods and can be partly recovered under the rules governing the calculation of the insurable value which includes the anticipated profit.

142 [1918] 2 KB 123.

143 At 128.

144 *Blaine Richards & Co Inc v Marine Indemnity Insurance Company of America and William H. McGee & Co* 635 F.2d 1051, 1981 A.M.C. 1

loss or damage from any external cause' which contained an FC & S Clause[145] and also a Delay Clause excluding coverage 'for loss of market or for loss, damage or deterioration arising from delay, whether caused by a peril insured against or otherwise'. They were also insured under a war risks policy excluding losses caused by 'delay, deterioration and/or loss of market'. It was decided that unless it could be shown that the original purchasers rejected the cargo due to their physical condition no damages could have been recovered on the ground that the loss of original sale contracts would have been attributable solely to delay caused by detention which was excluded.[146] Likewise, the Court ordered that whether the sale of goods at lower price was caused by delay or contamination of goods (i.e. 'damage' under the all risks policy) had to be found.

3.30 Another issue that requires emphasis is whether the assured can recover under an all risks policy which contains a clause excluding loss arising out of delay and loss of market where due to damage to cargo the assured is deprived of selling his cargo for some time and then because the reputation of the cargo is bad. In the US case *Interpetrol Bermuda Ltd v Lloyd's Underwriters*[147] the issue was whether a temporary contamination of the cargo that deprives the cargo owner of free access to the market is ground for recovery under an insurance policy on all risks terms. The cargo which could have been sold en route was not marketable for a while (which was described as 'the delay period') due to contamination and afterwards for a few weeks because the cargo's reputation was bad. Between the contamination and the sale of cargo the market fell and the cargo had to be sold at a much lower figure than its invoice price. The assured claimed damages not only for the loss of market but also for the cost of financing the cargo from the beginning of the delay period until the time of sale. The policy was 'against all risks whatsoever' excluding 'loss arising out of delay, deterioration, or loss of market, unless otherwise provided elsewhere in this policy.' The assured argued that the expression 'unless otherwise provided under the policy' left the exclusion ineffective and that the loss of market caused was recoverable under 'all risks whatsoever' wording. It was held that to prevail upon a trial, the assured must nonetheless overcome the requirement that the loss be proximately caused by an insured peril. A pertinent aspect of the decision in *Interpetrol* was that under an all risks policy, economic damage such as loss of market proximately caused by an insured peril was stated to be within the cover.[148] It is submitted that the cost

---

145 The clause excluded all losses due to 'capture, seizure, arrest, restraint, detainment, confiscation, pre-emption, requisition or nationalization, and the consequences thereof or any attempt threat, whether in time of peace or war and whether lawful or otherwise'.

146 At 1056.

147 *Interpetrol Bermuda Ltd v Lloyd's Underwriters* 1984 588 F. Supp 1199 (United States District Court, S.D New York).

148 By reference to *Stanley v Onetta Boat Works*, Inc, 303 F.Supp. 99, at 106. It was decided in that case that under an all risks builder's policy, economic loss (lost profits and loss of use) proximately caused by an insured peril would be deemed 'not consequential'.

of financing the cargo during the period of delay can be exactly the type of loss or expenditure that is sought to be excluded under cargo policies.

3.31 Under many business interruption policy forms, coverage is subject to the interruption being caused by physical loss of or damage to the subject-matter insured. One can expect that so long as the physical loss of the subject matter is caused by a peril insured against under the relevant property policy, the resulting business interruption claim (i.e. loss of market) arising from delay could be recoverable under business interruption policies. Nevertheless most business interruption policies contain specific clauses excluding delay and loss of market on the ground that they do not directly flow from a covered loss. In the absence of unambiguous wording as to the exclusion of these types of losses, it can be argued that business interruption policies are the type of policies which can specifically grant cover for loss of market by delay, upon the condition that the assured proves the direct connection between the loss of the subject-matter and the loss of market by delay.[149] It is submitted that this can be possible where for instance delay in delivery and the consequent economic loss is caused by the fumigation of a contaminated cargo.

Whether loss of market value is a consequential loss in cargo policies

Loss of market value and directness under general contract law and carriage of goods by sea

3.32 In contract law, foreseeable losses are held to be those which are reasonably supposed to be in contemplation of both parties at the time they made the contract. They are those which are fairly or reasonably considered to arise naturally, and those which arise from any special circumstances communicated at the time of the contract.[150]

In *The Parana*[151] where there was a long delay in the arrival of the vessel to the port of destination, the price of the goods had fallen between the time when the goods should have arrived and when they actually did. The Court decided that the consignee was not entitled to recover damages arising from the loss of market; however it emphasised that the loss of market could be recoverable if goods are

---

149 In the US, it was held in *Duane Reade, Inc. v St. Paul Fire & Marine Ins. Co*, 279 F. Supp. 2d 235, 240, aff'd as modified, 411 F.3d 384 (2d Cir. 2005) that the exclusion of 'loss of market' did not 'bar recovery for loss of ordinary business caused by a physical destruction or other covered peril', as cited in Bernard P. Bell, 'Time Element (Business Interruption) Insurance' (Chapter 46) in *New Appleman on Insurance Law Library Edition* accessed at www.lexisnexis.com/legalnewsroom/insurance/b/applemaninsurance/archive/2011/08/23/time-element-business-interruption-insurance-new-appleman-on-insurance-law-library-edition-chapter-46-insurance-coverage.aspx

150 *Hadley v Baxendale* (1854) 9 Ex 341.

151 (1877) 2 PD 118, not followed in *Koufos v C. Czarnikow Ltd (The Heron II)* [1969] 1 AC 350.

INSURANCE LAW IMPLICATIONS OF DELAY

sent to be sold at a particular market and where they do not arrive at their destination by reason of the breach of contract (delay) on the part of the carrier.[152] Moreover such loss could be recoverable where it was known to both parties that the goods would sell at a better price if they arrive at one time than if they arrive at a later stage.[153] It was enunciated that:

> 'In order that damages may be recovered, we must come to two conclusions- first, that it was reasonably certain that the goods would not be sold until they did arrive; and, secondly, that it was reasonably certain that that was known to the carrier at the time when the bills of lading were signed.'[154]

3.33 The suggestion that the damages could be recoverable where it was known to both parties that the goods would sell at a better price if they arrive at one time than if they arrive at a later time can be considered as the second limb of *Hadley v Baxendale*[155] which would apply where goods are delivered to a carrier with notice that delivery of the goods within a certain period is an essential part of the contract. *The Parana* was later on applied in *The Notting Hill*[156] where the cargo owners having their cargo on board a ship which had collided with another ship sued the owners of the latter for the loss of market. The fact that this was a case of tort and not contract did not prevent the application of *The Parana*[157] where Mellish LJ enunciated that loss of market is on an ordinary voyage so uncertain that it cannot be the natural and reasonable consequence in every case and not the natural and reasonable result in a collision case. These two cases were not followed in *Koufos v C. Czarnikow Ltd (The Heron II)*[158] where the question was whether damages for breach of contract were of a loss of a kind which the other party, when he made the contract, ought to have realised was not unlikely to result from a breach of contract causing delay in delivery. It was stated that:

> 'The parties are not supposed to contemplate as grounds for the recovery of damage any type of loss or damage which on the knowledge available to the defendant would appear to him as only likely to occur in a small minority of cases'.[159]

---

152 (1877) 2 PD 118, 121.

153 (1877) 2 PD 118, 121.

154 At 123. A similar view was taken in the American case *Aktieselskabet Stavangeren v Hubard-Zemurray Shipping Co*, 250 F. 67, 162 C.C.A 239 (5th Cir.1918) where under a time charterparty the owners who carried the goods had no obligation to deliver the goods within any stated time, the shipper/charterer's loss was the difference between what the value of the goods would have been had they been sold at the intended market and what the shipper/charterer would have received had the advance orders which had been given not been cancelled because of the delay in delivery.

155 In this case one of the questions was whether the carriers knew that delay could cause loss of profit to the cargo owners.

156 (1884) 9 PD 105.

157 This reasoning was based on *Hadley v Baxendale* (1854) 9 Ex 341. In *Koufos v C. Czarnikow Ltd (The Heron II)* [1969] 1 AC 350, 386 Lord Reid distinguished between contract and tort law in terms of remoteness of damage yet stated that this shall not mean that *Hadley v Baxendale* would be decided differently.

158 [1969] 1 AC 350.

159 At 385.

and:

> 'Where there's a market it must be assumed to be in contemplation of the parties as a grave danger that the goods may be sold on arrival so that if there's a delay one of the consequences may be loss of market'.[160]

Where the delivery of goods is delayed, the difference between the market value of the goods at the destination on the date of their intended delivery and their market value at the actual delivery date is the measure of damage.[161]

Whether loss of market value is a consequential loss in cargo policies

3.34 Under an insurance contract, a consequential loss is not recoverable either given that it is not proximately caused by an insured peril but by the loss of the subject-matter insured against[162] and because it is in nature distinct from physical damage. Under the common law, it was not unusual to recover on a policy of goods the depreciation in their value where they were not physically damaged.[163] The earlier authorities shall however be treated with caution in a possible attempt to draw an analogy to depreciation in value caused by delay, on the ground that the losses there at issue were arguably the direct consequences of the insured peril (disallowance of discharge of cargo by government authorities) whereas the main argument behind the exclusion of loss of market value by delay rests upon the suggestion that that loss is not proximately caused by an insured peril, yet by an excluded peril that is delay.

It can be submitted that in shipping circles, goods are usually traded for sale with profits and are therefore sent to markets where goods can be sold accordingly during particular seasons. It may therefore be known to the parties of a contract of carriage that any delay in delivery of the goods may result in the loss of market value of the goods, hence losses resulting from delay can arguably be recoverable thereunder. However, recoverability of such losses under insurance policies, in the assumption that the policy contains no ambiguous exclusion clause or no express exclusion whatsoever,[164] would entail an inquiry into whether a possible loss in the

---

160 At 426.

161 *Wilson v Lancs & Yorks Ry* (1861) 9 CB (NS) 632; *Collard v S.E. Ry* (1861) 7 H & N 79; *Schulze v G.E. Ry* (1887) 19 QBD 30; *Heskell v Continental Express Ltd* [1950] 1 All ER 1033, 1046; *Koufos v C. Czarnikow Ltd (The Heron II)* [1969] 1 AC 350.

162 *Shelbourne & Co v Law Investment and Insurance Corporation Ltd* [1898] 2 QB 626, 627. In this case the insurers had accepted payment for damage to barges consequent upon collision yet had rejected payment for loss in consequence of detention during repairs on the ground that that loss was not proximately caused by the perils insured against (i.e. was not proximately caused by collision) and was therefore a remote loss.

163 *Puller v Glover* (1810) 12 East 124. In this case insurers had agreed to pay for total loss if the goods were not allowed to have been discharged by authorities. It was held that although there was no physical damage to goods, the loss which ensued from the disallowance of discharge (i.e. depreciation in value of the goods) was recoverable. See also *Puller v Staniforth* (1809) 11 East 232.

164 An exclusion entitled 'Consequential Loss/Delay Exclusion Clause' which provides: 'This Policy does not cover loss of market and/or loss or damage arising from delay or consequential loss

market value of goods by delay ought to have been contemplated by insurers when the policy is made, in particular where seasonal goods are insured. Another related question could be whether the rules of the Insurance Act 2015 as to disclosure by the assured and the information which ought to be known by insurers in the ordinary course of their business could be referred to in determining whether loss of market value by delay was in the contemplation of the insurers.[165]

Loss of use of cargo and resulting loss of sale contracts

3.35 As a result of delay in delivery of goods, the assured can be deprived of honouring sale contracts entered into prior to the occurrence of delay in delivery. This type of loss can be considered as a loss of use of cargo and may equally occur where the cargo is held up due to perils such as detention or congestion. Under cargo insurance policies the exclusion of loss of use of cargo can appear along with the exclusion of loss of market.[166] It shall be noted that the intention of the assured in the sale of goods at a profit and the resulting loss of a sale contract is a different instance from loss of market value. The latter may be categorised as a sub-category of loss of adventure which is insured under a cargo policy as well as the loss of or damage to goods[167] whereas the former is a loss of profit and therefore a consequential loss not recoverable under a cargo policy.

Under the common law, anticipated profits from the sale of cargo were insurable so long as they were certain[168] and not where they were merely speculative, i.e. where no binding agreement had yet been reached by the assured for reselling the goods.[169] Examples can be found of cargo policies where only loss of profit to be made upon resale of cargo was insured such as in *The Corporation of the Royal Exchange Assurance v M'Swiney*.[170] In this case while part of the cargo of rice was loaded on board, the ship got disabled by perils of the seas and the rice got spoiled. Accordingly the cargo had to be discharged and it was eventually not delivered to its destination which resulted in the upsetting of the sale contracts entered into by the assured. It was held that loss of profit was insurable and insured in respect of

---

of any description' could be an example of a clear clause excluding all types of delay loss. The wording was used in the policy which was at issue in *Clothing Management v Beazley Solutions* [2012] Lloyd's Rep IR 329.

165 See s 3 of the Insurance Act 2015 on the duty of fair presentation of the risk by the assured and s 3(5) for the circumstances which do not require disclosure.

166 *Ontario Inc v Commonwealth Insurance Co* 2005 CarswellOnt 2605 75 O.R. (3d) 653, 26 C.C.L.I. (4th) 225 ('delay, loss of market or loss of use or occupancy and consequent loss of any kind'); *Triple Five Corp v Simcoe & Erie Group* 1994 CarswellAlta 451 Alberta Court of Queen's Bench ('loss caused by delay, loss of market or loss of use, except as may be provided under Business Interruption covers of the Policy').

167 In the absence of an express clause having effect of excluding loss of adventure, see e.g. Institute War Clauses (Cargo) 2009 cl 3.7; Institute Strikes Clauses (Cargo) 2009 cl 3.8 'any claim based upon loss or frustration of *the* voyage or adventure' (emphasis added).

168 *Grant v Parkinson* (1781) 3 Doug 16, 18.

169 *Lucena v Craufurd* (1806) 2 Bos & Pul NR 269, 321.

170 (1849) 14 Queen's Bench Reports 646.

the cargo loaded; however the loss of profit as regards the unloaded cargo was not occasioned by perils of the seas but was consequential upon the loss of the cargo loaded as the profit to be made upon the whole cargo depended on the safe arrival of the whole cargo on board a particular vessel and in a certain time frame.

3.36 Loss of profit can equally be incurred following a delay in delivery of the goods at their destination.[171] If the ship with goods laden on board is damaged by perils of the seas and the goods are sent on another ship to their destination and arrive on time, no loss of profit would have occurred. Where the goods cannot however be forwarded to their destination which results in delay in delivery of the goods, it can be argued that profits are lost by delay in delivery and not by perils of the seas.[172] Insuring loss of profits could give rise to the question of whether a delay of one day in the arrival of goods to their destination could amount to a total loss, the answer seems to be affirmative where cover against delay in delivery is expressly granted under the policy,[173] in the absence of which insuring loss of profit under a cargo policy would not extend to 'events collateral to those on which ordinary profit on goods depends',[174] such as retardation of the voyage.

The recoverability of that loss under a policy covering profits can be challenged on the ground that that would otherwise be considered as a policy on the arrival of the ship in a given time and the ability of the assured to perform his sale contracts.[175] It is however possible for the assured to insure the loss of profit to be earned by the arrival of goods by a certain date upon the condition that the date by which the goods should arrive is disclosed to the insurer. This would be on the ground that information as to the arrival of goods by a certain date could be considered as an event which would influence the decision of the insurer in fixing the premium and in determining whether he would take the risk as per s 3(4) of the Insurance Act 2015. Cover would most likely be granted by insurers against the payment of additional premium.[176]

---

171 See *The Corporation of the Royal Exchange Assurance v M'Swiney* (1849) 14 Queen's Bench Reports 646, 663.

172 *The Corporation of the Royal Exchange Assurance v M'Swiney* (1849) 14 Queen's Bench Reports 646.

173 *The Corporation of the Royal Exchange Assurance v M'Swiney* (1849) 14 Queen's Bench Reports 646, 660. It is submitted that after the enactment of the MIA, the expression "due arrival of insurable property" in s 5(2) could be interpreted such that the assured could incur loss of adventure by delay in delivery of the goods even where the goods are late for one day, where the date on which the goods should have arrived is disclosed to the insurer.

174 Ibid, at 663.

175 Argued in *The Corporation of the Royal Exchange Assurance v M'Swiney* (1849) 14 Queen's Bench Reports 646, 658.

176 It was suggested that it would be 'strange' if the insurers insure the arrival of goods by a certain day at the ordinary premium in *The Corporation of the Royal Exchange Assurance v M'Swiney* (1849) 14 Queen's Bench Reports 646, 655 per Parke B.

CHAPTER 4

Cargo insurance and expenses arising during the period of delay

Introduction

4.1 This chapter analyses the recoverability of general average expenses that arise during the period of delay that shall be contributed to by the cargo interests; sue and labour charges arising in preventing or minimising a loss by delay and expenses incurred in forwarding the goods so as to prevent a delay in transit or in delivery.

General average expenses

4.2 The Institute Cargo Clauses 2009 and the Institute Strikes Clauses 2009 contain the identical delay exclusion[1] which reads that

> 'loss, damage or expense caused by delay, even though the delay be caused by a risk insured against (except expenses payable under Clause 2 above)'

is not recoverable. The Institute Strikes Clauses (Cargo) 2009 provide cover against loss of or damage to the subject-matter insured caused by, *inter alia*, strikers, riots, civil commotions and terrorism.[2] Perils such as strikes and riots, as well as other deprivation perils such as detention or capture almost invariably contain an element of loss of time during which several expenses may occur. The type of expenses payable under Clause 2 of both the Institute Cargo and Strikes Clauses are salvage charges and expenses arising in general average incurred to avoid or in connection with the avoidance of loss from any cause except those causes excluded in the Clauses. The type of expenses payable would therefore be, among others, the general average portion of the cargo for wages and maintenance expenses,[3]

---

1 Institute Strikes Clauses 2009 cl 3.5 and Institute Cargo Clauses A-B-C 2009 cl 4.5.
2 cl 1.
3 Wages and maintenance expenses during the prolongation of the voyage occasioned by a ship entering a port of refuge or returning to her port of loading shall be admitted as general average if those expenses are incurred for common safety or where the ship is necessarily removed to another port for carrying out repairs (YAR 1994, 2004, 2016, Rule XI(a)); recovery of those expenses is also available if they are incurred at the port of refuge (YAR 1994 Rule XI(b); 2016 Rule XI(b)(i), with the exception of YAR 2004 where such expenses are not recoverable) and while the vessel sails from the port of refuge to a second port where repairs are taking place (YAR 1994 Rule X(a); YAR 2004 Rule X(a(ii)); YAR 2016 Rule X(a(ii))).

72

port charges[4] and fuel and stores[5] incurred in entering and/or at a port of refuge.

4.3 Another issue relating to expenses arising during the period of delay is whether the expenses arising during ransom negotiations are allowable in general average. In view of the frequency of lengthy negotiations involved in piracy attacks, delay to the common maritime adventure can occur in the below situations:

- Until the first demand for ransom is made by the pirates after the vessel is hijacked,
- After the pirates make the first demand and before the shipowners accept it,
- Where further ransom demands are being considered by pirates following the shipowners' acceptance of the initial demand, and
- Between the agreement on the ransom and release of the vessel by the pirates.

4.4 The expenses that could possibly arise during these periods of delay encompass 'high risk area bonus' paid to the crew if the vessel is detained in piracy-prone zones, food and supplies for the crew, bunkers consumed, crew wages, and professional media response services, the recoverability of which were discussed in *Mitsui v Beteiligungsgesellschaft LPG (The Longchamp)*.[6] The issue in this case was whether those expenses were recoverable in general average under Rule A and F of the York Antwerp Rules 1974 which were incorporated into a bill of lading. The shipowners' vessel was hijacked by a group of pirates as it was transiting the Gulf of Aden who directed the vessel to Somalia where the vessel arrived two days after its hijacking. Three days following the arrival of the vessel, the pirates made their first ransom demand which initiated a negotiation process between them and the shipowners. The vessel was finally released 51 days after the vessel was captured following the payment of a ransom much lower than the initially requested sum. In deciding whether the above-mentioned expenses were recoverable in general average and what would their quantum be if they were, the average adjusters reasoned that they could be allowed as per Rule F as expenses substituted for the higher ransom sum that would have otherwise been paid had the owners not reached the final and lower figure. However the expenses would be paid only up to the amount of general average expense which had been avoided.[7]

4.5 In 2010, the Association of Average Adjusters had been asked to provide an opinion on another incident relating to Somali piracy as to whether wages and maintenance expenses for the crew and expenses arising from consumption of

---

4 YAR 1994 Rule XI(b); YAR 2004 Rule XI(c)(ii); YAR 2016 Rule XI(b)(iii).

5 YAR 1994 Rule XI(b); YAR 2004 Rule XI(c)(i); YAR 2016 Rule XI(b)(ii).

6 *Mitsui & Co Ltd and Others v Beteiligungsgesellschaft LPG Tankerflotte MBH & Co (The Longchamp)* [2016] EWCA Civ 708.

7 ibid, para 18.

bunkers during a delay arising from detention could be recoverable in general average. An Advisory Committee of the Association was of the view that they were not allowed in general average, *inter alia*, because they would represent a loss incurred by reason of delay which was excluded under the second paragraph of Rule C.[8] In 2012, parties had submitted to the Committee for the adjustment regarding the hijacking and the Committee had considered that the expenses claimed were not allowed in general average under Rule F on the ground that negotiation is a common incident in piracy cases; the expenses incurred were not extraordinary in nature and could not be categorised as 'substituted expenses for costs normally and reasonably allowed in general average'.[9] Costs normally and reasonably allowed in general average, according to the Committee, meant the actual figure of ransom for which the parties settled and that given the absence of saving (it would not have been reasonable for owners to accept the pirates' initial demand, hence there could have been no saving that could be allowed in general average as per Rule A and Rule Paramount) no substituted expenses could be claimed under Rule F. This opinion was not binding on the Court of Appeal.

4.6 The Court held that for Rule F to operate, there must have been extra expenses incurred in place of another expense and that would have required the shipowners to make a choice between two alternative causes of action. According to the Court, abandoning the vessel and cargo after they were hijacked was not an alternative cause of action to the payment of ransom; and the payment of a lower ransom could not have been classed as the alternative to the payment of a higher sum, they were essentially about doing the same thing. The expenses arising during the period of delay had accordingly not been incurred in place of another expense within the meaning of Rule F. They were also i) ordinary expenses ii) incurred by reason of delay; the former preventing their recoverability under Rule A and the latter under Rule C.[10] If it had been that the payment of the initial ransom was an alternative cause of action to the payment of the lower ransom, it was also reasonably made.[11] The most reasonable means of securing the release of the vessel by pirates was to agree to their initial demand and not involve the vessel and cargo in lengthy negotiations to obtain an offer for a lower ransom given the pirates were violent and armed criminals. The protraction of the negotiations would therefore constitute a risk for the lives of the crew and the safety of cargo and vessel generally. As a result, all the expenses except for media response costs were found not recoverable in general average. It is submitted that the wording of Rule C in YAR 1974 is fairly similar to the one contained in YAR 1994, 2004 and 2016. Therefore the part of the decision in relation to expenses incurred by reason of delay could also be relevant where the latter versions apply.

---

8 ibid, para 28.
9 ibid, para 29.
10 ibid, para 51.
11 ibid, para 82.

Loss of market caused by delay and general average

4.7 So as to be recoverable under the MIA the loss ought to be a loss that is the direct consequence of the general average act;[12] and under the York-Antwerp Rules losses such as loss of market that are considered as indirect losses are not allowed in general average.[13] Rule C of YAR 2016 provides:

> '1. Only such losses, damages or expenses which are the direct consequence of the general average act shall be allowed as general average.
>
> (. . .)
>
> 3. Demurrage, *loss of market*, and any loss or damage sustained or expense incurred by reason of delay, whether on the voyage or subsequently, and any indirect loss whatsoever, shall not be allowed as general average.'[14]

The disallowance of loss of market was introduced for the first time in the York-Antwerp Rules 1924.[15] The case law prior to 1924 is therefore crucial to interpret the exclusion and the ground upon which the necessity for its introduction was based. One of the reasons why loss of market through delay was excluded under the York-Antwerp Rules 1924 was suggested to be *The Parana*[16] in *Australian Coastal Shipping Commission v Green.*[17] It is noteworthy that albeit in *The Parana* loss of market by delay was held not to be recoverable, this rule was made subject to two exceptions: if goods are sent to be sold in a particular season to higher price compared to other seasons, and if it is known to both parties of the contract that the goods will sell at a better price if delivered on time.[18] Assuming therefore that the exclusion of loss of market by delay in the York-Antwerp Rules 1924 rested upon the authority of *The Parana*, it did not extend to the two exceptions mentioned hereabove. In addition to the foregoing, the authority of *The Parana* as to directness of loss of market was not followed in *Koufos*[19] and it was enunciated that loss of market by delay was directly caused by the breach of the contract. The crucial question according to Lord Reid was rather whether

> 'on the information available to the defendant when the contract was made, he should, or the reasonable man in his position would, have realised that such loss was sufficiently likely to result from the breach of contract to make it proper to hold that the loss flowed naturally from the breach or that loss of that kind should have been within his contemplation'.[20]

---

12 MIA s 66(1).

13 York-Antwerp Rules 1924, 1974, 1994, 2004, 2016 Rule C.

14 Emphasis added.

15 The York-Antwerp Rules 1890 did not contain any general rules similar to the current Rule C in terms of losses through delay.

16 (1877) 2 PD 118.

17 [1971] 1 QB 456, at 481.

18 (1877) 2 PD 118, 121.

19 *Koufos v C. Czarnikow Ltd (The Heron II)* [1969] 1 AC 350, 385 per Lord Reid.

20 At 385.

4.8 It was stated that the word 'direct' in Rule C of the York-Antwerp Rules 1950 which was essentially found in all the subsequent versions of the Rules has a narrower meaning compared to directness as was considered to be the test in relation to remoteness of damage,[21] although under English law loss of market was regarded as a direct loss.[22] Accordingly where goods intended for a specific market arrive at the port of destination safely however with some delay, and the loss of market arises from market fluctuations during the period of delay, claims for such a loss would according to the Rules not be recoverable in general average.

The earlier decisions assessed directness with reference to mainly two tests, one based on the foreseeability of the general average loss by the master at the time of the general average sacrifice,[23] and the other based on the existence of *subsequent accidents* to the general average act breaking the chain of causation between the act and the loss.[24] It is submitted that these tests are not readily reconcilable although earlier cases cited both with approval.[25] It is not very clear whether the two tests should be applied together, and it is submitted that their application to circumstances involving delay may have fairly different and irreconcilable results. The test for direct consequence based on 'subsequent accidents' was rejected by the Court of Appeal in *Australian Coastal Shipping Commission v Green*[26] where it was enunciated that an event does not break the chain of causation when the claimant, when he does the general average act, does actually foresee the

---

21 *Australian Coastal Shipping v Green* [1971] 1 QB 456, 487 per Carins LJ.

22 *Australian Coastal Shipping v Green* [1971] 1 QB 456, 481 *per* Lord Denning MR.

23 This test was established by Lowndes in *The Law of General Average: English and Foreign* (4th edn, Stevens and Sons 1888), 36 in the following passage: 'We have to determine quod pro omnibus datum est, and since giving must always imply an intention to give, what we have here to ascertain must be what loss at once has in fact occurred, and likewise must be regarded as the natural and reasonable result of the act of sacrifice? Or in other words, what the shipmaster would naturally or might reasonably have intended to give for all when he resolved upon the act? If then upon the act of sacrifice any loss ensues, which the master did not in fact bring before his mind at the time of making the sacrifice, it would have to be considered whether it were such a loss as he naturally might or reasonably ought to have taken account of.'

24 It was cited in *Anglo-Argentine Live Stock Agency v Temperley Shipping Co* [1899] 2 QB 403, 410 that 'Ulrich, in his Grosse-Haverei, p 5, says: "General average comprises not only the damage purposely done to ship and cargo, but also (1.) all damage or expense which was to be foreseen as the natural (immediate) consequence of the first sacrifice, since this unmistakably forms part of that which was given for the common safety; (2.) all damage or expense which, though not to be foreseen, stands to the sacrifice in the relation of effect to cause, or in other words was its necessary consequence. Not so, however, those losses or expenses which, though they would not have occurred but for the sacrifice, yet likewise would not have occurred but for some subsequent accident."'

25 It was stated in *Anglo-Argentine Live Stock Agency v Temperley Shipping Co* [1899] 2 QB 403, 410 that the master knew or ought reasonably to have known that the general average sacrifice could result in the losses incurred (Lowndes test); and that the damage was the necessary consequence of the general average act (Ulrich test). Likewise in *Austin Friars Steamship Co Ltd v Spillers & Bakers Ltd* [1914] 1 KB 833 where the master had decided to put into a port of refuge yet the vessel had struck the pier, Bailhache J applied first the foreseeability test and decided that what in fact occurred (damage to pier and liability to third parties arising by damaging the pier) was in contemplation of the master. In relation to the subsequent accident test, he enunciated that the collision with the pier was a foreseen result and not the result of a subsequent accident.

26 *Australian Coastal Shipping Commission v Green* [1971] 1 QB 456.

consequence, ought reasonably to have foreseen that a subsequent accident of the kind might occur or even that there was a distinct possibility of its happening.[27] It would follow that whereas delay could be considered as an event breaking the chain of causation between the general average act and loss of market according to the 'subsequent accident' test, the same argument may not be readily advanced on the basis of the foreseeability test.

4.9 If the assured incurs loss of market in consequence of a general average act leading to a delay such as where the vessel proceeds to a port of refuge to avoid damage to cargo by perils of the seas; this loss is expressly excluded as an indirect loss to the general average act and therefore not recoverable under the York-Antwerp Rules.[28] It was however recognised in *Anglo v Temperley*[29] that loss of market by delay could desirably have been recoverable yet that the common law was clear as to its non-recoverability.[30] Following the rejection of the subsequent accident test in favour of the reasonable foreseeability test, it is now debatable whether loss of market by delay could still be considered as an indirect loss. According to this test, it can be suggested that delay is usually foreseeable where a general average act occurs, for delay, as has already been discussed in this work, is almost always preceded by other events. In this respect delay may not break the chain of causation between the general average act and the loss and that losses resulting from delay may therefore be considered usually as direct consequences of the general average act. However, albeit delay may generate losses which can be considered as 'direct consequence of general average act' under the common law, Rule C § 3 of the York-Antwerp Rules expressly excludes any loss incurred by reason of delay.

This being said, loss of market which does not arise through delay (where goods cannot arrive at their initial destination and have to be sold elsewhere) is recoverable in general average under English law.[31] Under the common law, it was held that expenses for keeping the cargo in good condition during delay were held to be not recoverable.[32]

Sue and labour expenses

4.10 As per s 78(3) of the MIA, expenses incurred for the purpose of averting or diminishing any loss not covered by the policy are not recoverable as sue and labour expenses. This provision presents several issues so far as delay in delivery is concerned. Firstly, expenses arising during delay such as the ones occurring during necessary repairs of the vessel or during the period of storage

---

27 ibid, at 482 per Lord Denning MR. This reasoning follows the test established by Lowndes.
28 YAR 1974, 1994, 2004 and 2016 Rule C.
29 *Anglo-Argentine Live Stock Agency v Temperley Shipping Co* [1899] 2 QB 403.
30 At 412.
31 *Anglo-Argentine Live Stock Agency v Temperley Shipping Co* [1899] 2 QB 403.
32 *Anglo-Argentine Live Stock Agency v Temperley Shipping Co* [1899] 2 QB 403, 413.

of the goods are not necessarily excluded if they are incurred to prevent a loss otherwise recoverable under the policy. The authority illustrating this point was *The Pomeranian*[33] which was decided prior to the enactment of the MIA where a consignment of cattle was insured under an all risk policy on war risks including mortality and it contained a sue and labour clause. The vessel was exposed to bad weather and accordingly had to be repaired whereby extra fodder was needed for the cattle during repairs. The court ruled that the expenses for the purchase of extra fodder had to be reimbursed by the insurers accepting the possibility of a total loss of the cattle in case of not purchasing the extra fodder. For this reason, the essential question would be whether the loss is a 'loss by an insured peril' under the policy,[34] which in relation to delay, poses further issues of causation given that many deprivation perils such as strikes, detention or capture have an element of delay. Disputes on the recoverability of sue and labour expenses would therefore likely turn on whether the loss, the prevention of which results in expenses, is a loss by the deprivation peril or by delay.

4.11 Goods which are time-sensitive may be forwarded so as to prevent or minimise delay in the arrival of the goods. Another reason why such goods can be forwarded is to circumvent any deterioration during the marine adventure. The recoverability of sue and labour expenses incurred to prevent delay in delivery was discussed in *Weissberg v Lamb*[35] where under an all risks policy the goods were damaged while being loaded on board the ship. The assured paid charges to the removal contractors who then sought to claim that amount back from the insurers under the sue and labour clause. The Court opined that had the assured not paid the charges there could have been delay in delivery of the goods which would be a peril outside the scope of the policy by way of s 55(2)(b) and that therefore the sum could not have been recovered as sue and labour expenses.[36] The Duty of Assured Clause under the Institute Cargo Clauses A-B-C 2009 contain a similar wording to s 78(3) and provides:

> 'It is the duty of the Assured and their employees and agents *in respect of loss recoverable hereunder* 16.1. to take such measures as may be reasonable for the purpose of averting or minimising such loss,'[37]

According to this clause, where measures are taken to minimise or prevent a loss that is not recoverable such as a loss caused by delay, expenses incurred for that end shall not be recoverable.

---

33 (1895) P 34.

34 An insured peril must have occurred to recover under the suing and labouring clause as it relates to the prevention or mitigation of a loss arising from that insured peril; for illustrations please see *Xenos v Fox* (1868) LR 3 CP 630; *Integrated Container Service Inc v British Traders Insurance Co* [1984] 1 Lloyd's Rep 154.

35 [1950] 84 Ll L Rep 509.

36 At 512.

37 cl 16, emphasis added.

4.12 Under the US law, a similar approach was adopted in *Archer-Daniels-Midland Co v Phoenix Assur. Cp. of New York*[38] where a cargo insurance policy contained a Delay Clause which read

'Warranted free of any claim for loss of market or for loss, damage or deterioration arising from delay, whether caused by a peril insured against or otherwise.'

It was held in this case that the clause precluded coverage for losses caused by delay in shipment when a river was closed by the Coast Guard due to flooding as well as expenses due to delay including sue and labour expenses. In *Witcher v Saint Paul Fire*[39] the policy was a non-marine all risks property insurance policy and it excluded business losses due to delay. In this case a gas explosion occurred at a close distance to a construction site and the construction contractor incurred a delay of one month so as to have the structure inspected against possible physical loss due to explosion. His business loss was held to be solely due to temporary construction delay caused by the gas explosion and was held not to be a covered risk. Therefore the expenses incurred for the inspection of the structure were not recoverable, having occurred so as to prevent business losses due to delay which were excluded under the policy.

Forwarding and storage charges

4.13 The Forwarding Charges Clause of the Institute Cargo Clauses 2009[40] provides:

'Where, as a result of the operation of a risk covered by this insurance, the insured transit is terminated at a place other than that to which the subject-matter is covered under this insurance, the Insurers will reimburse the Assured for any extra charges properly and reasonably incurred in unloading storing and forwarding the subject-matter to the destination to which it is insured.

This Clause 12, which does not apply to general average or salvage charges, shall be subject to the exclusions contained in Clauses 4, 5, 6 and 7 above, and shall not include charges arising from the fault negligence insolvency or financial default of the Assured or their employees.'[41]

The forwarding expenses arising from delay in transit or delay in delivery can be recoverable where the policy expressly states so.[42] Where no such extension is

---

38 975 F.Supp. 1137(1997).

39 *Witcher Construction Company v Saint Paul Fire and Marine Insurance Company* 1996 550 N.W. 2d 1 (Court of Appeals of Minnesota).

40 As well as the Institute Commodity Trades Clauses 1983 cl 12.

41 cl 12.

42 For such an example, see:

'This policy is extended to include reasonable costs necessarily incurred by you as a result of:

a) loss or damage to the subject matter insured recoverable under this policy

b) *as a result of delay to the subject matter insured whilst in transit caused by the carrying vessel or*

provided under the policy two points would require a more detailed analysis in respect of the clause as regards delay.

4.14 The first point is the requirement of 'termination of the transit by a covered peril'. Under an all risks policy, the covered perils that could result in the termination of the adventure can be perils such as detentions and requisitions whereby the vessel and consequently the goods are unable to proceed to the destination. Delay is not a covered peril under the Institute Cargo Clauses.[43] Furthermore, the Transit Clause[44] in the Institute Cargo Clauses refers to delay beyond the control of the assured as an event which does not terminate the transit. *A contrario* meaning of this clause could suggest that a delay within the control of the assured could be an event terminating the transit, nonetheless it would not fulfil the requirement that the transit must be terminated as a result of a 'covered peril'. Therefore forwarding charges incurred cannot be claimed under this clause also where the transit is terminated by delay within the control of the assured. However where forwarding charges are incurred following a delay beyond the control of the assured, such delay would not be of a nature to terminate the transit and it is likely that the peril preceding delay – where it is a covered peril – will be deemed to have terminated the transit. Forwarding charges arising from the occurrence of that covered peril terminating the transit can be recoverable.

4.15 Transit can be terminated following a delay frustrating the object of the adventure caused by a peril such as restraint of princes or detention. The obvious question that would follow would be whether the forwarding charges incurred where the adventure is frustrated by delay following a deprivation peril could be recoverable despite the delay exclusion in the Institute Cargo Clauses. The answer to that question would essentially depend on whether the expense was incurred as a result of delay or the insured peril resulting in delay. Forwarding charges and other like expenses incurred in order to prevent a loss of adventure are usually occasioned by a peril depriving the vessel to continue to the port of destination such as restraint of princes or detention and resulting delay.

4.16 In *Wilson Bros Bobbin Company Ltd v Green*[45] a claim was made for sue and labour charges to prevent loss of the adventure when the cargo was prevented by warships from completing its voyage. Shortly after sailing, the ship was

---

conveyance suffering loss or damage from:

i)   *fire or explosion*
ii)   *stranding, grounding, capsizing or sinking*
iii)   *overturning or derailment of land conveyance*
iv)   *collision or contact of vessel, craft or conveyance with any external object other than water*
v)   *general average sacrifice*

c)   *delay in delivery due to closure of any transport route following accident, fire, flood or act of God.'* (emphasis added)

43   Institute Cargo Clauses All Risks A-B-C 2009 cl 4.5 is an exclusion.
44   cl 8 of Institute Cargo Clauses 2009.
45   *Wilson Bros Bobbin Company Ltd v Green* [1917] 1 KB 860.

stopped by enemy vessels and was put to a port where the cargo was discharged and stored and subsequently reshipped and forwarded to its destination. The policy excluded 'all claims arising from delay' and it was argued that the claim to recover the storage charges and forwarding expenses was expressly excluded as the claims arose from delay.[46] Bray J stated that the clause excluding all claims arising from delay had not affected in any way the sue and labour clause[47] and that the assured was entitled to recover the cost of storage for a reasonable time and the proper cost of forwarding the cargo to its port of destination at the expiry of that time. The storage and forwarding expenses were incurred by reason of the detention of the ship; delay in this case was an event which determined the measure of expenses and was not the reason why the expenses were incurred.

A similar decision was given in the United States *Firemen's Fund Ins. Co v Trojan Powder Co*[48] where the cargo policy was governed by English law and customs. In this case the vessel carrying the goods had stranded in consequence of which she had to be repaired; given the delay during repairs, the goods were forwarded to their destination on another vessel and additional freight had to be paid accordingly. The insurers had expressly undertaken to pay for forwarding charges under the policy, however the policy also contained a clause 'freight warranted free from any claim consequent upon loss of time, whether arising from a peril of the sea or otherwise'. It was held that the clause did not prevent the assured from recovering the extra freight paid for forwarding the goods (which were otherwise expressly recoverable under the policy) given that the expenses were the consequence of stranding and not of loss of time. According to the Court, stranding was the proximate and sole cause of the forwarding charges and the expenses were not excluded by the effect of s 55(2)(b) on the ground that the case was not with respect to damage to goods by delay;[49] yet to extra freight paid for forwarding the goods for which the insurers were expressly liable under the policy.

4.17 A different approach was adopted in *Russian Bank for Foreign Trade v Excess Ins Co Ltd*[50] where the assured shipped on board the steamship *Wolverton* a parcel of barley in September and October 1914. The cargo was insured against restraints of princes and against the risks excluded by the free of capture and seizure clause, but the policy excluded 'all claims due to delay.' Owing to the closing of the Dardanelles and the declaration of war against Turkey the ship was unable to make the voyage insured, and the cargo was landed. Subsequently while at the loading port, the ship was requisitioned by the Admiralty. The cargo could not be reloaded because of the requisition and the assured claimed for a

---

46 ibid at 861 by Leck KC and R.A. Wright KC. The goods were discharged on 15 December 1914 and were stored until they were forwarded in September 1915.

47 ibid at 862, 863.

48 *Firemen's Fund Ins. Co v Trojan Powder Co* (1918) 253 F.205 (Circuit Court of Appeals, Ninth Circuit, California).

49 The Court also rejected the contention that *Taylor v Dunbar* (1869) LR 4 CP 206 and *Russian Bank for Foreign Trade v Excess Insurance Company Ltd* [1918] 2 KB 123 shall be relied upon.

50 [1918] 2 KB 123.

constructive total loss of the cargo of barley by the restraint of princes which was covered under the policy on the ground that the adventure was frustrated owing to the restraint of princes. The insurers, in turn, argued that the loss was due to delay and was within the exclusion contained in the policy. The Court held that this was a case that could not be distinguished from *Bensaude v Thames and Mersey Marine Insurance Co*[51] because the House of Lords had pronounced in that case that where a propeller shaft had been broken by perils of the seas which resulted in a frustrating delay, a claim for loss of freight was excluded by the operation of the clause 'any claim consequent upon loss of time'. The Court in *Russian Bank* therefore equated 'all claims due to delay' and 'any claim consequent upon loss of time, whether arising from a peril of the sea or otherwise'. Moreover Bailhache J in *Russian Bank* stated obiter that 'whether arising from a peril of the sea or otherwise' was a mere surplusage on the ground that every claim in a policy must arise from a peril insured against. The House of Lords in *The Playa de las Nieves* found that the words were not a mere surplusage, and that:

> 'They are there to make it plain that the clause is concerned with an intermediate event between the occurrence of a peril insured against and the loss of freight of which the peril was, in insurance law, the proximate cause.'[52]

The Court's approach in *Russian Bank* was doubted in the following passage in *Naviera de Canarias SA v Nacional Hispanica Aseguradora SA (The Playa de las Nieves)*:[53]

> 'When a voyage charter is frustrated by the actual destruction of the major part of the carrying vessel or of the machinery essential to enable the vessel to carry the agreed cargo or is frustrated by outbreak of hostilities, it may not spring to one's lips to describe the resulting loss of freight under the voyage charter as 'consequent on loss of time'. These . . . may well be the kind of cases to which Lord Atkin refers as possibly having placed too wide a construction on that phrase'.[54]

---

51 [1897] AC 609.
52 per Lord Diplock, at 882.
53 [1978] AC 853.
54 per Lord Diplock, at 882.

CHAPTER 5

Marine delay in start-up insurance

Introduction

5.1 Many infrastructure and construction projects worldwide require the shipping of specialised material for use on the construction site, the delay of which can cause various types of financial losses to contractors. Delay in start-up (DSU) insurance (also known as 'advance loss of profits insurance') is a product offered in the market for the purpose of insuring against the risk of delay to the timely prosecution and completion of projects and is usually taken out separately from the business interruption cover. The subject-matter insured under a marine delay in start-up policy is the financial losses caused by delay to the commencement of a project and not equipment or material carried by sea as marine cargo for the purpose of use on the project site, which are otherwise known as 'project cargo'. Project cargo carried by sea to the construction site would have to be insured under a marine cargo policy against physical loss of or damage thereto and the insurer of the marine DSU may also be the primary insurer of the marine cargo policy.

5.2 This being the case, the interconnection between the project cargo and delay in start-up lies in that any loss of or damage to the goods or to the conveyance carrying them or any delay during the transit may in turn cause delay to the commencement of the project and result in financial losses to the project owners. For this reason, so as to have a better control over the whole process, insurers provide cover both against the risk of physical damage to the goods or to the carrying conveyance and the risk of delay under the same policy.

No standard form wording existed on project cargo and marine delay in start-up until the Joint Cargo Committee of Lloyd's Market Association released the 'Project Cargo Insurance and Project Cargo Delay in Start Up Wording'[1] (hereinafter referred to as 'the Wording') which contains two sections: the first section where the marine cargo policy is to be inserted; and the second section on marine delay

---

1 JC 2009/020, published on 2 November 2009 http://www.iuaclauses.co.uk/site/cms/content DocumentDownload.asp?filename=232.pdf&id=232&windowed=1&r=2756 (last accessed, 8 November 2016).

83

in start-up.[2] This chapter shall analyse the wording released by the Joint Cargo Committee and attempt to raise issues which can turn contentious in the future along with a particular focus on the relevant MIA provisions.

'Insured' under the marine DSU cover

5.3 In marine DSU policies, site owners (also known as 'project owners' or 'principals') can be insured[3] along with banks as lenders.[4] These parties may have an insurable interest both in the project cargo that is carried in transit to the construction site as well as in the timely arrival of the project cargo to the site. It would therefore not be surprising to see all of these parties to be named as insured both under the marine cargo and marine DSU sections of the policy. For the sake of determining their respective interests, it would be necessary to identify the scope of the 'project' which is defined as:

> 'the transportation of goods, materials and equipment for the purpose of construction, erection, testing, start-up, commissioning, operation and maintenance of the . . . project and all ancillary and associated works, in conjunction with the construction project.'[5]

Any changes in the definition of 'project' could potentially have an impact on insurable interest. The following paragraphs will attempt to analyse the possible interests of the parties to a project and whether and under what circumstances they can have insurable interest under the cargo or marine DSU sections of the policy.

Site owners

5.4 Principals or project owners have interest firstly in the safe arrival of the project cargo[6] in the sense that if the goods arrive in a damaged state, there would be a need to replace the goods or recondition them: these matters are within the scope of the marine cargo section of the cover. Where the cargo section covers merely physical loss of or damage to cargo and does not expressly cover consequential losses arising from a delay in the arrival of the goods, delayed arrival of the goods would cause nothing more than financial loss not otherwise recoverable under the cargo section. The principal's project would be directly affected by indemnifiable events under the marine cargo policy where a delay to the scheduled operation date accordingly occurs. Principals would therefore also have insurable

---

2 For a wording in similar format, see the policy in *Assicurazioni Generali S.P.A. v Black & Veatch Corp.* 362 F.3d 1108, 2004 A.M.C. 773. The marine cargo policy in this case offered cover under two different sections: cover against physical losses in the first section and against delay in start-up losses and expenditures incurred to avoid or diminish such losses in the second section.

3 See the Wording, Project Overview, Insured Section 2, box 7.

4 See the Wording, Project Overview, Insured Section 2, box 9

5 Project Overview, s 2.

6 MIA 1906 s 5(2) provides that a person has insurable interest in a property if he benefits from the safe arrival of goods or where he is prejudiced by its loss.

interest in the marine DSU section of the policy given that they would have an interest in the due arrival of the goods[7] the failure of which would result in a loss of revenue of the commercial operations carried out.

Contractors

5.5 Suppliers of cargo to a project site can be insured as contractors under marine cargo insurance policies.[8] However whether contractors have insurable interest in a marine DSU section is a matter which needs further attention.[9] The late arrival of goods to a project site would cause a delay in commencing the construction which may accordingly expose contractors to penalties (which are considered as liquidated damages) under their contracts with principals. However the interest in the timely commencement of the commercial operation on the project site would be that of the principal (site owner) and not of the contractor. For this reason, marine DSU policies are not designed to benefit contractors, but site owners.

As seen above, insurable interests of the parties to a project differ in each section of the policy and it is therefore crucial for insurers that parties having insurable interest are accordingly clearly provided for. In the absence of this, the question may arise as to whether a builder having an insurable interest under a marine cargo policy shall be indemnified for mitigation expenses that he has incurred so as to avoid delay in start-up losses that could have otherwise been incurred by a site owner who has an insurable interest in the delay in start-up policy. By way of example, in *Assicurazioni Generali S.P.A. v Black & Veatch Corp.*,[10] the contractor was not expressly insured under the marine DSU section of the policy; however the reading of the definition of 'assured' in the policy together with the duty of assured clause resulted in the finding that the contractor could recover the expenses made in order to prevent a delay in start-up of the project.[11]

Lenders (banks)

5.6 In practice, banks which are the financiers of large projects may take out marine DSU on behalf of project owners or operators. Lenders undoubtedly have insurable interest in due arrival of goods like principals, given that any delay in

---

7 MIA 1906 s 5(2).

8 See *Alstom Ltd v Liberty Mutual Insurance Co (No 2)* [2013] FCA 116 where Alstom (supplier of the goods to the project site) was a named insured under the policy along with 'all contractors and subcontractors in any tier engaged on the project, manufacturers and/or suppliers. . .engaged in the project. . .' which included *inter alia* the manufacturer of the goods. See also the Wording, Project Overview section 1 (marine cargo section) where contractors and sub-contractors are named as insured.

9 The Wording does not expressly enumerate contractors in section 2 contrary to section 1.

10 362 F.3d 1108, 2004 A.M.C. 773.

11 ibid, 1116. See also the policy in dispute in *Ace European Group Ltd v Chartis Insurance UK Ltd* [2012] 2 Lloyd's Rep 117; aff'd [2013] Lloyd's Rep IR 485.

start-up would generate a loss in the revenue to the principal which in turn could risk the reimbursement of the loan.

Scope of cover and duration of risk

5.7 According to the Wording, the policy covers the assured for actual loss sustained to the assured's business[12] where the following events cause a delay to the scheduled commercial operation date of the project:

a. 'Loss of and/or damage to and/or delay in arrival of the project cargo which results from an event giving rise to an indemnifiable claim' under the marine cargo section of the policy,[13]

b. 'Loss of or damage to or mechanical breakdown of the hull or machinery and/or equipment of the vessel, craft or aircraft, on which any of the project cargo is being carried or is intended to be carried which would be covered under the Institute Voyage Clauses- Hulls 1/10/83 (CL 285) and/or Institute War and Strikes Clauses Hulls- Voyage 1/10/83 (CL 285)',[14]

c. 'Loss of or mechanical breakdown of, any motor or rail vehicle or attachment thereto upon which any of the project cargo is being transported or is intended to be transported',[15]

d. 'The vessel, aircraft or other conveyance on which any of the project cargo is carried or is intended to be carried, being involved in a general average salvage or a life-saving operation'.[16]

For the last three circumstances, the duration of risk under the marine delay in start-up section runs from the time that such vessels, craft and conveyances come alongside the berth or mooring point at which the project cargo is to be loaded thereon.[17] With respect to the first circumstance the policy attaches when the marine cargo policy attaches (yet no earlier than the commencement of loading of the project cargo at the suppliers' premises) and terminates in line with the termination provisions applicable under the marine cargo section of the policy or on completion of unloading at project laydown area, whichever is the sooner.[18]

5.8 It is submitted that the phrase 'Loss of and/or damage to and/or delay in arrival of the project cargo which results from an event giving rise to an indemnifiable claim' in point (a) requires further consideration. It is to be noticed that the presence of the connector 'and/or' found between 'damage to' and 'delay in arrival' suggests that the clause includes both circumstances where delay

---

12 The Wording, section 2, para 1.
13 The Wording, section 2, para 1.1.
14 Section 2, para 1.2.
15 Section 2, para 1.3.
16 Section 2, para 1.4.
17 Section 2, para 4.2.
18 Section 2, para 4.1.

is incurred as a result of a physical loss of or damage to goods and where it is incurred independently from any tangible loss thereof. The latter type of situation may arise from perils which are either within or outside the scope of cover of a cargo policy and therefore determining the meaning of 'delay in arrival of the project cargo which results from an event giving rise to an indemnifiable claim' becomes of prime importance.

Delay in delivery of the project cargo may be caused by events under a cargo policy such as capture or seizure of the cargo. These events may result only in delay in delivery of the goods without actually causing a physical loss of or damage to them. These are excluded perils under the Institute Cargo Clauses (All Risks) 2009[19] and they would not give rise to an indemnifiable claim under the marine cargo section of the policy as required by section 2, ss 1.1 of the Wording. For this reason even if the marine cargo policy is on the Institute Cargo Clauses (All Risks) 2009 terms and these perils may result in delay in delivery of the goods to the project site, any loss to the principals arising from such delay cannot be recovered under the marine DSU section of the policy. The situation would differ however where the marine cargo section of the policy is on the Institute War Clauses (Cargo) 2009 terms and the risk of capture or seizure is due to a war or revolution.

5.9 Another point that requires further attention is the consequence of an exclusion under the marine DSU section of the policy when read together with the scope of cover provided for physical loss to the project cargo transported to the project site. The occurrence of insured perils under a marine cargo insurance policy such as perils of the seas or fire which may result in physical loss of or damage to the project cargo may require some degree of improvement of the goods or their replacement which could accordingly cause delay in their delivery and in turn delay to the scheduled commencement date of the project. Under the DSU Wording, delay as a consequence of alteration, additions, improvements or elimination of any deficiencies in the project cargo carried out after the occurrence of damage is excluded.[20] This would connote that where there is physical loss of or damage to cargo, delay in delivery of the project cargo which would occur as a result of the improvement, replacement or repairs of the cargo would not give rise to an indemnifiable claim under the marine DSU section of the policy even if there is a delay to the commencement date of the project.

5.10 The phrase 'indemnifiable claim' under the cargo policy which is contained in ss 1.1 of section 2 of the Wording would allude not only to cargo losses but also to expenses incurred such as storage or forwarding expenses as a result of the operation of insured perils. In these cases, any delay in the arrival of the goods arising from the insured perils could trigger the DSU cover even though the goods are physically unaffected by the operation of the perils.

---

19 cl 6.2.

20 Section 2, para 6.3.

Measure of indemnity

5.11 Under the Joint Cargo Committee's Wording, the measure of indemnity is subject to the choice of the assured and is either the loss of gross profit calculated 'by applying the rate of gross profit to the difference between the turnover which would have been achieved during the indemnity period and the actual turnover during that period as a result of the occurrences'[21] which trigger the cover under the DSU section of the policy; or making good the inability to proportionally pay fixed costs and debt servicing incurred by the insured's project which are not affected by any change in the output of the insured project.[22] Whichever is opted for by the assured, increased costs of working expenses which are the additional expenditure necessarily and reasonably incurred by the assured for the sole purpose of avoiding or diminishing the reduction in turnover[23] are recoverable in addition thereto.

Exclusions

5.12 The exclusions under a delay in start-up policy vary in practice according to the insuring company policy wording. There are nonetheless certain provisions which have been observed by the Joint Cargo Committee as appearing commonly in most marine DSU policies and have been included in the Wording. One of the exclusions is the loss of or damage to project cargo or any expenses recoverable under the marine insurance section of the policy[24] as these relate to the scope of cover provided under the first section of the policy and not under the marine DSU section. A second exclusion is delay as a consequence of fines, penalties and damages for breach of contract, or late or non-compliance of orders, or any penalties of whatever nature[25] which would include penalties imposed by public authorities to the principals,[26] as well as penalties found in the contract between the principals and contractors.

Other exclusions consist of, *inter alia*, delay as a consequence of alteration, additions or improvements of the project cargo carried out after the occurrence of damage,[27] delay as a consequence of lapse or cancellation of a lease, import licence or regulation unless resulting from the insured events under the delay in start-up section of the policy,[28] delay as a consequence of physical loss of or damage to contractors' or subcontractors' materials other than project cargo

---

21 Section 2, para 3.1(a).
22 Section 2, para 3.1(b).
23 Section 2, para 3.1(c).
24 Section 2, para 6.1.
25 Section 2, para 6.2.
26 Although this might also come under the exclusion in Section 2, para 6.8. which provides that no cover shall be provided under the marine DSU section of the policy for delay as a consequence of any restrictions imposed by a public authority other than where covered under the marine cargo section.
27 Section 2, para 6.3.
28 Section 2, para 6.4.

procured thereby.[29] It is submitted that loss of market caused by delay in delivery of the goods to their destination cannot be indemnified under marine delay in start-up policies given that although loss of market can arguably be considered as a consequential loss not recoverable under a cargo policy, the goods carried to the construction site are carried for the purpose of use on the site, and not for the purpose of sale in the market.

5.13 One of the exclusions that requires specific emphasis is 'delay as a consequence of commandeering, requisition or destruction or damage by order of any government de jure or de facto or by any public authority other than where covered under the Institute War & Strikes Clauses Hulls – Voyage 01/10/83 (CL 295), and other than where specifically covered under section 1'.[30] The wording is cryptic; however the expression 'other than where the carrying vessel is covered by the Institute War & Strikes Clauses Hulls-Voyage' is likely to connote that the acts of the government or public authorities should be directed to the vessel carrying the goods, in which case the exclusion would operate where requisition of the vessel is covered under the named Clauses and results in delay of delivery of the project cargo.[31] The second part of the exclusion which states 'and other than where specifically covered under section 1' arguably means that where goods are specifically covered under the marine cargo policy against commandeering, requisition or destruction or damage by order of any government, delay resulting therefrom and consequent losses are recoverable under the marine DSU policy and the exclusion does not apply. It is noteworthy that cargo may be requisitioned or destroyed by a public authority independently from the vessel, where for instance the cargo does not have an import licence.

The 'duty of insured' clause

5.14 Subsection 10 of the Wording enumerates the circumstances which are considered by the insurers as the duties of the insured, their servants and agents. Those duties are, *inter alia*, the duty to act with reasonable dispatch;[32] the duty to sue and labour;[33] the duty to notify the insurers of any revisions to the scheduled shipping dates of all project cargo critical items;[34] of any delays to programme, of extensions of time being granted or changes to the scheduled commercial operation date.[35] Two of these duties, the duty to act with reasonable dispatch and to sue and labour are of particular importance and will be dealt with below.

---

29 Section 2, para 6.7.
30 Section 2, para 6.5.
31 Under Section 2, para 1.2, any actual loss of the insured arising from delay in delivery of the project cargo due to loss of or damage or mechanical breakdown of the carrying vessel covered under the Institute Voyage Clauses-Hulls 1/10/83 and/or Institute War and Strikes Clauses Hulls- Voyage 1/10/83 is covered.
32 Section 2, para 10.1.
33 Section 2, para 10.2.
34 Section 2, para 10.5.
35 Section 2, para 10.6.

Mitigation of losses and recoverability of mitigation expenses

5.15 The complex co-existence of marine cargo and marine DSU cover in the same contract raises intricate issues with respect to sue and labour. The main grounds which have so far appeared in judicial decisions were whether the provider of a project cargo (and contractor on the project site) can be indemnified under a duty of the assured clause of a delay in start-up section of a policy for mitigating consequential losses which would otherwise have been incurred not by themselves but by the site owner due to delay to the operation date of the project. Another issue that was raised was whether the costs of repairing or replacing the goods can be claimed by a contractor as sue and labour expenses incurred in order to avoid a much greater delay in start-up loss under a marine project cargo/delay in start-up policy.

5.16 With respect to the second query, in *Assicurazioni v Black & Veatch*,[36] the builder had taken out a marine cargo insurance policy from a syndicate of underwriters at Lloyd's through its broker. The first section of the policy covered physical loss to the project cargo and the second section provided coverage for delay in start-up losses and expenditures incurred to avoid or diminish such losses through a duty of insured clause. The consequential losses arising from delay in start-up were recoverable solely by the site owner and not by the builder. The duty of insured clause read: 'It is the duty of the Assured and their servants and agents *in respect of loss recoverable hereunder. . .*'.[37] The parties to the dispute had agreed that there was a general framework to the insurance contract and the risk for a particular project was added to the framework policy by way of endorsement. The general framework provided that both the builder and site owner were assureds thereunder, in other words the word 'assured' which is critical for the 'duty of assured' clause did not particularly appear neither in the marine cargo nor in the delay in start-up section of the policy.

The project cargo, whilst on its voyage from Japan to the United States was damaged by a severe typhoon and was replaced, which accordingly caused a delay of six months to the originally scheduled delivery date. The builder in anticipation of this delay incurred several expenses to avoid delay in the start-up of the plant and managed to meet the deadline for completing it; otherwise the site owner would have incurred consequential delay in start-up losses (lost revenue). The builder argued that they were entitled under the duty of insured clause to be indemnified for mitigation expenses incurred so as to prevent a loss recoverable under the delay in start-up section of the policy even though the site owner and not themselves would have incurred the losses. The Court accepted this argument and observing that the phrase 'loss recoverable hereunder' was not specifically limited either to the builder's or the site owner's loss, ruled in favour of the builder.

---

36 *Assicurazioni Generali S.P.A. v Black & Veatch Corp.* 362 F.3d 1108, 2004 A.M.C. 773.
37 Emphasis added.

5.17 A similar issue was raised in *Ace European Group Ltd v Chartis Insurance UK Ltd*[38] where a marine cargo/DSU insurer had agreed that contractors who were named as co-assureds under the policy could recover costs of repair and replacement of damaged goods as sue and labour expenses if those expenses were incurred in avoiding the greater loss of delay in start-up which would have arisen under the DSU section of the policy.[39] Under the common law, whether there is a duty to sue and labour or whether sue and labour is merely a matter of causation is an issue yet to be resolved by the courts.[40] The courts nonetheless recently applied the causation test[41] which seeks to establish whether the loss is proximately caused by the assured's act of not mitigating the loss or by an insured peril. The rationale behind the test is that the assured ought not to have caused his own loss by failing to mitigate it. It is therefore debatable whether a contractor who has an interest in the marine cargo policy yet not in the marine DSU policy can be held to have failed his duty to sue and labour if he fails to mitigate the site owner's loss (and not his own loss) recoverable under the DSU policy, unless he himself was named as an assured thereunder. His own loss recoverable under the marine cargo section of a Marine Cargo/DSU policy could be loss of or damage to goods arising from an insured peril. Otherwise the loss of the contractor resulting from delay in delivery of the goods to the project site would for instance be penalties that shall be paid to the site owner for delaying the commencement date of the construction which would not otherwise be recoverable in neither cargo nor DSU sections.

5.18 Another question would arise as to whether the failure of the contractor to mitigate losses otherwise recoverable by the principals under the marine DSU section of the policy where the contractor is not named as a co-assured could be regarded as a cause that would give rise to an indemnifiable claim under the DSU section. The Joint Cargo Committee Wording provides a list of the events that would result in delay to the scheduled commercial operation date of the principal's project which would accordingly be indemnified by the insurers.[42] One of those events is delay in the arrival of the project cargo, which can arise from the failure of the contractor in forwarding the goods to the project site by a different

---

38 *Ace European Group Ltd v Chartis Insurance UK Ltd* [2012] 2 Lloyd's Rep 117; aff'd [2013] Lloyd's Rep IR 485.

39 At para 38.

40 According to *Yorkshire Water v Sun Alliance & London Insurance* [1997] 2 Lloyd's Rep 21 the common law does not impose a duty to sue and labour. According to Chalmers, s 78(4) of the MIA 1906 which established that it is the duty of the assured to mitigate losses recoverable under the policy was based upon four cases: *Kidston v Empire Marine Insurance Co* (1866) LR 1 CP 535, *Currie v Bombay Native Insurance Co* (1869) LR 3 CP 72, *Benson v Chapman* (1849) 2 HLC 496 and *Notara v Henderson* (1872) LR 7 QB 225 although arguably only the *Currie* case was directly relevant and decided that the loss was proximately caused by the master's conduct and not by an insured peril (as cited in Merkin et al, *Marine Insurance Legislation* (5th edn), 129).

41 For examples, please see *Integrated Container Service Inc v British Traders Insurance Co Ltd* [1984] 1 Lloyd's Rep 154; *State of Netherlands v Youell* [1998] 1 Lloyd's Rep 236; *Strive Shipping Corporation v Hellenic Mutual War Risks Association (Bermuda) Ltd, The Grecia Express* [2002] Lloyd's Rep IR 669.

42 Section 2, para 1.

conveyance where for instance a fire occurs on the vessel requiring the vessel to be repaired. Losses to the principal arising from delay in the arrival of the project cargo can be recoverable upon condition that such delay results from an event giving rise to an indemnifiable claim under the marine cargo section of the policy. In the example given, two potential causes of delay exist in this respect; fire on board the vessel carrying the project cargo and the failure of the contractor to forward the goods. Where the marine cargo policy is on 'all risks' terms, fire could constitute a fortuity; and the failure of the contractor to forward the goods could constitute a fortuity only in respect of the principal who is insured as assured thereunder.

Duty to act with reasonable dispatch

5.19 The Wording provides:

'10. DUTY OF INSURED
It is the duty of the insured, their servants and agents that they shall:
10.1. Act with reasonable dispatch in all circumstances within their control.'

This clause is found in the modern standard form clauses on cargo insurance and is entitled 'avoidance of delay clause' thereunder.[43] The clause has been discussed in detail in Chapter 10[44] and it will be analysed in this chapter with pointing out the differences of the clause from its equivalents and its interrelation with other clauses in the Wording.

5.20 The most obvious difference of the clause from its counterpart in the Institute Cargo Clauses is that under the Wording, the duty is one of the assured as well as of its servants and agents whereas under the Cargo Clauses merely the assured is required to act with reasonable dispatch. One of the issues that has to be noted is that lenders, their servants and agents will have this duty as lenders are mentioned as 'insured' under the Wording along with principals/site owners.[45] Another issue that requires further attention is what acts would be considered as within the duty. It is submitted that the duty would comprise appointing a surveyor for the inspection of loading, stowage and unloading of the project cargo,[46] informing relevant authorities promptly where the project cargo is stolen, or providing

---

43 See the Institute Cargo Clauses A-B-C 2009 cl 18.

44 See paras 10.59–10.77. There is currently no binding authority under English law as to whether the avoidance of delay clause operates as a warranty; however it was enunciated in *Ostra Insurance Public Company Ltd v Kintex Shareholding Company (M/V Szechuen)* [2004] EWHC 357 (Comm) that: 'There are plainly strong arguments in favour of treating this as a breach of warranty' (per Cooke J at para 52). In the leading cases decided in Australia, the avoidance of delay clause was held to operate as a promissory warranty whereby the insurer is discharged from liability when the assured does not act with reasonable despatch: *Wiggins Teape Australia Pty Ltd v Baltica Insurance Co Ltd* [1970] 2 NSWR 77, 80–81 per Macfarlan J. Also see *Verna Trading Pty Ltd v New India Assurance Co Ltd* [1991] 1 VR 129 per Kaye and McGarvie JJ.

45 Project Overview, Section 1.

46 Section 2, General Policy Conditions Applicable to Section 1 and 2, para 2 is entitled 'survey warranty' and sets out the duties of surveyors to be appointed for inspecting the Project cargo and approving loading, stowage and unloading thereof.

adequate space on site for storing the project cargo upon on arrival,[47] failure of which may result in damage to cargo upon loading and accordingly delay to the scheduled commercial operation date.

5.21 The Wording provides that:

> 'The indemnity afforded by paragraph 1.1 above shall operate, whilst the Project Cargo is in the normal course of transit, as per the attachment provisions contained in Section 1 of this policy, but no earlier than commencement of loading at suppliers.'

It is noteworthy that this subsection covers only the indemnity afforded by para 1.1 which is for any delay to the scheduled commercial operation date arising from loss of and/or damage to and/or delay in the arrival of the project cargo. The phrase 'in the normal course of transit' alludes to 'ordinary course of transit' found in the Institute Cargo Clauses A-B-C 2009 cl 8.1 and should particularly be interpreted as such where the marine cargo insurance is made on these terms. One of the questions that could arise is whether the duty to act with reasonable dispatch could have an impact on the transit so as to terminate it where the duty is not observed by the assured, its servants or agents.[48] This can be illustrated by where the cargo is no longer in the ordinary course of transit because the goods are unreasonably delayed as a result of the provision of incorrect or missing information on the place of unloading by the site owners and failure to correct such information in good time. This failure can both terminate the transit and result in that the indemnity afforded under para 1.1 would no longer operate.

5.22 The reasonable dispatch clause in para 10.1 can now arguably be regarded as a term that would come under s 11 of the Insurance Act 2015 where compliance with it would tend to reduce the risk of loss of a particular kind, loss at a particular location or at a particular time. Indeed, the non-compliance with the reasonable dispatch clause may aggravate the risk of delay in the arrival of the goods and accordingly in the scheduled operation date of the project.

---

47 Where onsite storage is agreed to by the insurers, see Section 2, para 4.1.

48 This query is based on the suggestion that the reasonable dispatch clause is a clause governing all other clauses in the policy, which was mentioned in *Wiggins Teape Australia Pty Ltd v Baltica Insurance Co Ltd* [1970] 2 NSWR 77, at 80 per Macfarlan J.

CHAPTER 6

Freight insurance and the loss of time clause

Introduction

6.1 Delay in voyage can take several forms which may subsequently result in loss of freight, both in the sense of freight *stricto sensu* and freight in the sense of charter hire: Delay in earning freight contracted for may induce the assured to contract for substituted freight; delay can frustrate the object of the adventure together with a peril from which it ensues; and it can induce loss of hire where it results from an off-hire event under a time charterparty.

6.2 The exclusion of delay losses in s 55(2)(b) applies to policies on ships and goods leaving out policies on freight. The law on delay in relation to freight insurance, both in the sense of freight *stricto sensu* and freight in the sense of charter hire has been developed in light of common law authorities. Currently, the former is insured under the Institute Voyage Clauses-Freight and the latter under the Institute Time Clauses-Freight. The loss of hire is also separately insured under loss of hire policies[1] and therefore the distinction between this type of policy and time policies on freight must be made for the purposes of losses consequent upon loss of time and their recoverability. The distinction between freight policies on time basis and loss of hire policies was clarified in *The Wondrous*[2] where it was observed that loss of hire policies cover a fixed sum to be paid by reference to a period of time whereas valued time policies on freight insure the part of the adventure represented by the hire to be earned under a particular contract.[3] Moreover the latter requires a loss in respect of the subject matter insured to be proved and is concerned 'with the earnings or potential earnings of the vessel and not with the expenses of earning these sums'.[4] A calculation of loss suffered under a time charterparty may therefore be relevant in assessing whether the assured has successfully mitigated losses under a freight policy; however, it cannot be taken to answer the question whether there was a loss of freight. Unvalued policies on freight are now overtaken by loss of earnings or loss of hire policies.[5] Loss of

---

1 Loss of hire insurance is covered in Chapter 8.
2 *Ikerigi Compania Naviera SA v Palmer (The Wondrous)* [1991] 1 Lloyd's Rep 400.
3 At 417.
4 At 417.
5 Gilman and Merkin, *Arnould's Law of Marine Insurance* (18th edn), 12–54.

94

hire policies will be analysed in Chapter 8 and this chapter will merely be concerned with freight policies on time and voyage basis.

6.3 The Loss of Time Clause which now reads 'This insurance does not cover any claim consequent on loss of time whether arising from a peril of the sea or otherwise'[6] was introduced against the background of some of the common law authorities with the aim of relieving the insurers from liability for any claim consequent upon loss of time. This chapter will scrutinise the common law background of the law on delay in regards to freight policies and shed light upon the scope of application of the Loss of Time Clause.

Early authorities on delay in earning freight

6.4 Pre-MIA decisions on mere delay on the voyage[7] which were decided on the basis of policies on freight followed or cited authorities decided upon policies on cargo.[8] It is submitted that those decisions should be considered separately with respect to the effect of delay on marine adventure and losses arising therefrom. It would arguably not be a fallacy to suggest that delay in earning freight would not amount to a loss of freight by loss of adventure on the ground that freight is a fixed sum, the measure of which would not depend on the timing of the arrival of the goods to their destination. Accordingly, there would be no loss of adventure in a freight policy in so far as the freight is eventually earned, albeit with some delay. The interest of the assured in that case would be the safe arrival of the goods upon which the earning of freight would depend. Nonetheless, the interest sought in a marine adventure in so far as goods are concerned is not merely the safe arrival of goods, yet also their timely arrival.[9] Delay in the marine adventure resulting in the impossibility of selling seasonal goods would not merely delay the earning of the interest contemplated by the assured (as in delay in earning freight) yet could arguably destroy the adventure contemplated.

6.5 The common law judgments delivered prior to the enactment of the MIA 1906 consistently held that a mere retardation on a voyage where freight was eventually earned did not give the assured a right to claim for a total loss of freight.[10] In *M'Carthy v Abel*,[11] the assured had abandoned the freight upon a hostile embargo to the freight insurers which was accepted by them; the embargo

---

6 Institute Time Clauses-Freight 1983 cl 14; Institute Voyage Clauses-Freight 1983 cl 12; Institute Time Clauses-Freight 1995 cl 15; Institute Voyage Clauses-Freight 1995 cl 12.

7 'Mere delay' is used in the sense of a delay which does not reach the point of a delay frustrating the adventure insured.

8 e.g. *Everth v Smith* (1814) 2 M & S 278 (policy on freight) followed *Anderson v Wallis* (1813) 2 M & S 240 (policy on cargo) where it was said that 'if the retardation of the voyage be a cause of abandonment, the happening of any peril by which a delay is caused in the arrival of the ship would also be a cause of abandonment'.

9 See s 5(2) of the MIA 1906 for the interest in safe and due arrival of the subject-matter insured.

10 *M'Carthy, Corner and Henderson v Abel* (1804) 5 East 388; *Everth v Smith* (1814) 2 M & S 278.

11 (1804) 5 East 388.

having subsequently ceased, the ship continued the adventure and in fact earned freight. The assured claimed for a total loss of freight subsequent to the abandonment and the cessation of embargo, however the Court held, *inter alia*, that there was no total loss of freight as the freight had actually been earned, albeit with some delay.

6.6 This decision was followed a few years later in *Everth v Smith*[12] where the assured had insured freight that was planned to be earned from the carriage of a cargo of hemp between two ports and the carriage of another homeward cargo. The vessel could have discharged her outward cargo, yet was detained at an intermediate port and was prevented from loading her homeward cargo. The master finally procured some substitute cargo for the homeward voyage and the vessel could eventually prosecute the adventure, however with some delay due to the detention. The assured incurred detention expenses which exceeded the freight eventually earned from the substitute homeward cargo and claimed for total loss of freight arguing that the freight actually earned was not the specific freight contracted for. Lord Ellenborough enunciated that it was certainly a loss of the particular trade which the assured had personally in contemplation, but that it was not within the intention of the policy. He found that the insurance was on freight generally,[13] and that it was therefore not material if the freight eventually earned was the one contracted for or a posterior one. The mere retardation of the adventure, and 'the consequent inconvenience and expense arising from it', were not a substantive cause of loss where the particular thing insured had not received damage and where freight was eventually fully earned, though with some delay.

6.7 The decision in *Everth v Smith* is authority for the proposition that the substituted freight could not give rise to a total loss of freight, if freight – albeit not the freight contracted for – is actually earned with some delay. It is not entirely clear whether this line of reasoning could apply to freight which is commensurate with a particular charterparty which may arguably not be considered as freight on general terms, but specific freight contracted for.[14] It can therefore be suggested that unless the assured can prove the freight was not on general terms,[15] the substituted freight would not be covered under the policy and the assured can claim the difference between the substituted freight and the freight contracted for, a claim for partial loss of freight.

Nevertheless, even in the event that the assured is allowed to claim for a partial loss, such a claim can effectively be considered as a claim 'consequent upon loss of time' on the ground that the freight had to be substituted because of a delay on the voyage and be excluded under the current Loss of Time Clause. In

---

12 (1814) 2 M & S 278.

13 The policy was expressed to be on 'freight valued at £1,200'.

14 Birch H. Sharpe, 'Substituted Freight' (1904) 20 LQR 160, 164.

15 See the speech of Gorell Barnes J in *The Main* [1894] P 320, at 324: 'It is clear that the Court held that, in a policy in similar terms, the freight which was actually earned on a voyage would be covered, although the assured in taking out his policy contemplated having a specific freight, but when he went to the underwriters he insured the freight in general terms' with reference to *Everth v Smith*.

Turnbull, Martin & Co v Hull Underwriters'Association, Ltd[16] the subject-matter insured was 'freight of frozen meat, chartered or as if chartered'. The policy also contained the special clause 'chartered freights and freights are warranted free from any claim consequent on loss of time whether arising from a peril of the sea or otherwise.' The earning of freight had been rendered impossible due to a fire occurring on board and the impossibility to have the ship repaired on site. According to the court, 'chartered or as if chartered' meant 'contracted for, or as if contracted for' and it was held that the loss of time clause applied not only to chartered freights, but to all freights.[17]

6.8 Another category of claim in a freight policy like in *Everth v Smith* could have been expenses arising from detention. The assured in that case had not particularly claimed these expenses, yet had claimed total loss of freight on the ground that the detention expenses had exceeded the freight eventually earned. It is submitted that these expenses can properly be characterised as expenses arising from delay and would give rise to the question of whether they would be excluded by virtue of the Loss of Time Clause. To the best knowledge of the author, this issue has not yet been canvassed by courts; however it was stated in *The Wondrous*[18] that

> 'Freight insurance is concerned with the earnings or potential earnings of the vessel, not with the expenses of earning those sums. It is not concerned as such with the fact that the voyage took longer nor with the fact that the costs of performing it were higher than were expected".[19]

There is therefore room to suggest that detention expenses can be excluded under the Loss of Time Clause.

6.9 It can be assumed, therefore, that where the adventure insured is merely delayed and not ruined by frustrating delay, a mere delay not reaching the point of frustrating delay would solely delay the earning of freight and not terminate the adventure. Consequently, no claim for a total loss of freight can be made by the assured with success.

Introduction to the loss of time clause

6.10 It was established under common law that the insurer on ship or goods was not liable for losses caused by delay yet the insurer on freight was liable where freight ceased to be payable by virtue of a contractual term or frustration.[20] Whereas the rule on ship and goods was codified in the MIA,[21] the Act is silent as to loss of freight caused by delay. However in practice loss of freight caused by

---

16 [1900] QB 402.
17 See the speech of Mathew J at 405.
18 *Ikerigi Compania Naviera SA v Palmer* (*The Wondrous*) [1991] 1 Lloyd's Rep 400.
19 ibid, at 417. An exception to the non-recoverability of these expenses could arguably be where they are incurred in general average.
20 *Re Jamieson v Newcastle SS Freight Ins Assn* [1895] 2 QB 90.
21 MIA s 55(2)(b).

INSURANCE LAW IMPLICATIONS OF DELAY

delay is excluded from freight policies on time and voyage basis by the standard loss of time wording 'This policy does not cover any claim consequent on loss of time whether arising from a peril of the sea or otherwise'.[22]

6.11 The Loss of Time Clause has been the subject of several judgments in respect of both claims for loss of freight under voyage charters and loss of charter hire.[23] In the most recent authority on the scope of the loss of time clause *The Playa de las Nieves*,[24] it was enunciated that the clause postulates a chain of events: the occurrence of a peril insured against, which results in loss of time; and consequently in loss of freight which he would have earned from the use or hire of his vessel.[25] It was held that the clause would exclude any loss where delay was merely an intermediate event between the loss and the peril insured against. Moreover authorities pointed out that the clause applies both to chartered and not chartered freight,[26] and both to claims for constructive total loss of cargo by frustration[27] and to the withholding of hire under an off-hire clause under a time charterparty.[28] The scope of the clause and its effect on loss of freight and hire will be discussed under the following headings.

Loss of freight, loss of adventure and the loss of time clause

Loss of marine adventure and delay

6.12 There must be a delay of nature destructive or frustrating for the marine adventure to come to an end; otherwise the mere loss of time on a voyage shall not terminate or frustrate the adventure and cause loss of freight. It is noteworthy that delay in this context is an event frustrating the object of a contract other than a marine insurance contract, which consequently causes the loss of the subject matter of the latter. In assessing the circumstances where loss of freight would be excluded by virtue of a loss of time clause, it is essential to determine at what point of time delay would become frustrating.

The leading test applied in deciding whether a particular contract has been frustrated by delay used to be the 'implied term test' established by *Taylor v*

---

22 Institute Time Clauses-Freight 1983 cl 14; Institute Voyage Clauses-Freight 1983 cl 12; Institute Time Clauses-Freight 1995 cl 15; Institute Voyage Clauses-Freight 1995 cl 12.

23 The most recent example of the latter is *Naviera de Canarias SA v Nacional Hispanica Aseguradora SA (The Playa de las Nieves)* [1978] AC 853.

24 *Naviera de Canarias SA v Nacional Hispanica Aseguradora SA (The Playa de las Nieves)* [1978] AC 853.

25 *Naviera de Canarias SA v Nacional Hispanica Aseguradora SA (The Playa de las Nieves)* [1978] AC 853, 879–880.

26 See, for instance, *Turnbull, Martin & Co v Hull Underwriters' Association, Ltd* [1900] QB 402, 405.

27 *Russian Bank for Foreign Trade v Excess Ins Co Ltd* [1918] 2 KB 123; appealed on other grounds [1919] 1 KB 39.

28 *Naviera de Canarias SA v Nacional Hispanica Aseguradora SA (The Playa de las Nieves)* [1978] AC 853, 882.

Caldwell[29] which provides that there is an implied condition in the contract which operates to release the parties from performing it. This test has been replaced by the 'radical change test' according to which a contract is considered to be frustrated where without default of either party a contractual obligation becomes incapable of being performed because a fundamental or radical change from the obligation originally undertaken occurs.[30] The test is an objective one[31] and does not deal with the actual or presumed intentions of the parties as the implied term test. In this respect a mere change in the expenses or onerousness would not be sufficient to decide whether the contract has been frustrated, yet a significant change in the nature of the obligations would be required.[32]

6.13 Delay may seriously affect the commercial object of the adventure as the ship's expenses may continue during delay,[33] yet it is difficult to lay down strict rules as to when delay causes frustration of a contract. The nature of the underlying contract, the ship, the type of the cargo, and the contemplated duration of the voyage must be taken into consideration while deciding whether a delay is frustrating.[34] To fall outside what the parties could reasonably have contemplated at the time of the contract, it must be 'abnormal in its cause, effects or its expected duration'.[35] Therefore a frustrating delay is required to be sufficiently long to frustrate the commercial adventure of the parties,[36] and a delay which is within the commercial risk undertaken by the parties would be unlikely to frustrate the contract.[37] It was suggested that even a delay of considerable length and of uncertain duration can be an incident of the marine adventure if it is clearly within the contemplation of the parties; delay which is ordinary in character accordingly makes it something other than the cause of frustration.[38]

---

29 *Taylor v Caldwell* (1863) 3 B & S 826. In *Jackson v Union Marine Insurance Co Ltd* (1874) LR 10 CP 125 Cleasby B referred at 140–141 to the judgment of Blackburn J in *Taylor v Caldwell* (1863) 3 BS 826. See also *Re Jamieson v Newcastle SS Freight Ins Assn* [1895] 2 QB 90.

30 In *Tatem v Gamboa* (1938) 61 Ll L Rep 149, 156 the new test was stated by Goddard J as 'if the foundation of the contract goes . . . by reason of such long interruption or delay that the performance is really in effect that of a different contract . . .' then the performance of the contract is regarded as frustrated. A similar view was expressed in *Davis Contractors Ltd v Fareham U.D.C* [1956] AC 696 which was approved by the House of Lords in *National Carriers Ltd v Panalpina (Northern) Ltd* [1981] AC 675 and in *Pioneer Shipping Ltd v B.T.P Tioxide Ltd (The Nema)* [1982] AC 724.

31 *Davis Contractors Ltd v Fareham U.D.C* [1956] AC 696, 728 per Lord Radcliffe: '. . . the true action of the court . . . consists in applying an objective rule of the law of contract'.

32 *National Carriers Ltd v Panalpina (Northern) Ltd* [1981] AC 675.

33 If for instance delay is caused by ice or neaping, the margin of profit is quickly run off despite the benefit of P & I Club policies, *Bank Line v Capel* [1919] AC 435, 458–459 per Lord Sumner.

34 Maurice E.V. Denny, *Freight Insurance: A Commentary (The Insurance of Shipowners' Interest in Freight for the Carriage of Goods)* (Witherby 1986), 69.

35 Hugh Beale et al, *Chitty on Contracts* (32nd edn), Vol 1, para 23–035 citing *Blankley v Central Manchester and Manchester Children's University Hospitals NHS Trust* [2014] EWHC 168 (QB), para [40] upheld on appeal [2015] EWCA Civ 18.

36 *Pioneer Shipping Ltd v B.T.P Tioxide Ltd (The Nema)* [1982] AC 724.

37 *Davis Contractors Ltd v Fareham U.D.C* [1956] AC 696.

38 Stated by Lord Sumner in *Bank Line v Capel* [1919] AC 435 at 458–459. The contemplation of the parties must be sufficiently clear and if expressly clear, sufficiently wide to cope with the new

*Can the loss of time clause be triggered where delay is not the cause
of the loss of adventure*

6.14 The role of delay in frustration can be categorised under two types of cases: the first category is where some loss of time is caused by a deprivation peril; and the second encompasses cases where the ship becomes a constructive total loss due to a damage by perils of the seas. An example for the former is *Atlantic Maritime v Gibbon*[39] where during a civil war, an adventure had had to be abandoned due to a restraint of princes and it was held that the restraint and not delay had caused the loss of adventure.[40] The charterparty in this case was terminated due to its own provisions and not owing to frustration in the strict legal sense. The time element had only been essential in order to estimate correctly the extent of the peril. It was held that:

> 'if because of the length of time which is likely to subsist during which the peril lasts, it is justifiable to say 'This finally disposes of the bargain' then the freight is lost then and there immediately upon the happening of the insured peril and is attributable solely to that peril'.[41]

However, even though delay was not the frustrating event, the loss of time clause was nevertheless held to have defeated the assured's claim. This decision is to be contrasted with *Roura & Forgas v Townend*[42] where it was held that the lapse of time during which a ship is captured cannot be regarded as the cause of loss of profit on charter and would not be excluded by the wording 'claims arising from delay'.[43]

6.15 The second category is where the loss of time is a consequence of a mishap[44] such as perils of the seas resulting in constructive total loss of vessel or a breakage of shaft. The loss of time exclusion was tested for the first time in *Bensaude v The Thames and Mersey Marine Insurance Company Ltd*[45] in such a context where the policy was against total loss of freight. It was argued on behalf of the assured that the claim was consequent upon the peril insured against and had happened then and there as the adventure became impossible upon its occurrence, therefore it was submitted that the loss of time was merely an element for

---

situation; otherwise it will not prevent frustration, *Fibrosa v Fairbairn* [1943] AC 32, 40 per Viscount Simon.

39 *Atlantic Maritime v Gibbon* [1954] 1 QB 88.

40 *Obiter* support for this suggestion can also be found in *Robertson v Petros Nomikos Ltd* [1939] AC 371, 377. A similar example can be found in *Russian Bank for Foreign Trade v Excess Ins Co Ltd* [1918] 2 KB 123. The case involved frustration of the voyage by the closure of Dardanelles upon declaration of war.

41 *Atlantic Maritime v Gibbon* [1954] 1 QB 88, at 126–127.

42 [1919] 1 KB 189.

43 ibid, at 197 per Roche J.

44 *Atlantic Maritime v Gibbon* [1954] 1 QB 88, 127 per Lord Evershed MR.

45 [1897] AC 609.

measuring the extent of the loss.[46] Lord Watson used the 'but for' test[47] to assess the cause of the loss of freight and according to him the loss would not have arisen but for the delay occasioned by the breaking of the shaft and that this would be excluded by the loss of time clause. The House of Lords decided that the freight was lost by perils of the seas but the claim depended on loss of time and therefore was struck by the exclusion. According to Lord Herschell, 'any claim consequent upon loss of time' meant that although the freight was lost by a peril insured against (in this case perils of the seas) if the claim depends on loss of time in the prosecution of the voyage and that the voyage cannot be completed within the time contemplated, then the insurer is not liable for the loss.[48] The decision gives rise to the question of whether Lord Herschell construed 'whether arising from a peril of the sea or otherwise' as referring to the loss and not to the 'loss of time'.

6.16 In *Carras*,[49] the same peril (stranding) produced the twin consequences of the loss of the ship and the loss of freight where the ship could not make the cancelling date. It was not controversial that the adventure was frustrated by the casualty which by the following inevitable delay made it impossible to carry out the contract. It was admitted that the loss of time clause would defeat a claim based on loss of the adventure, but the claim for freight on this occasion rested upon the loss of the ship due to perils of the seas, on the ground that it was impossible in a commercial sense to repair her. The loss of time clause was held not applicable.

6.17 Similarly in *Robertson v Petros Nomikos*[50] the assured's vessel had become a constructive total loss, and the charterparty which would have been performed when she was repaired was accordingly never performed. The lost freight was recovered under the total loss clause as the loss had occurred immediately when the vessel was totally lost and the House of Lords held that the claim was not defeated by the loss of time clause. Lord Atkin pronounced his famous sentence that the loss of time clause 'received too wide a construction in some of the cases'.[51] This expression was interpreted as referring to the fact that it shall not be construed to protect underwriters in all frustration cases, even where delay was no part of the frustration.[52]

6.18 Lord Atkin's *dictum* was cited by Lord Diplock in *The Playa de las Nieves*[53] who was of the view that it encompassed situations such as where the voyage charter is frustrated because of the destruction of the carrying vessel,[54]

---

46 At 610.

47 At 613.

48 At 613–614.

49 *Owners of the Yero Carras v London & Scottish Assurance Corp Ltd (The Yero Carras)* [1936] 1 KB 291.

50 *Robertson v Petros Nomikos Ltd* [1939] AC 371.

51 At 377–378.

52 Argued by the insurers in *Naviera de Canarias SA v Nacional Hispanica Aseguradora SA (The Playa de las Nieves)* [1978] AC 853, 860.

53 *Naviera de Canarias SA v Nacional Hispanica Aseguradora SA (The Playa de las Nieves)* [1978] AC 853, 883.

54 As in *Robertson v Petros Nomikos Ltd* [1939] AC 371.

because of the destruction of the machinery essential to carry the agreed cargo[55] and where it is frustrated by the outbreak of hostilities.[56] He pronounced that although in these cases where under a voyage charter the loss of freight may not be defeated by the loss of time clause, under a time charter such as in *Bensaude*, the clause would defeat any claim based upon loss of time.

Actual and apprehended loss of time and the loss of time clause

6.19 One of the questions that can be raised in relation to the loss of time clause is whether it merely applies to claims where loss of time has already occurred or whether it also strikes out claims which rest upon not an actual yet an apprehended loss of time. In determining whether the adventure insured is frustrated, 'the probabilities as to the length of the deprivation, and not the certainty arrived at after the event are . . . material'.[57] Therefore in assessing whether delay frustrates the object of the adventure insured, the potential duration of the delay at the time of the event is to be looked at rather than the actual duration of the delay.[58] The loss of time clause defeats claims based on loss of adventure by frustrating delay, which shall connote that although there is no actual yet an apprehended delay, this can be sufficient to strike out claims based on loss of adventure. This suggestion is however controversial given that the wording 'consequent upon loss of time' can be interpreted as alluding to a loss occurring after the loss of time begins operating. The common law authorities shall accordingly be scrutinised so as to determine the scope of application of the clause in relation to the foregoing controversy.

6.20 Several authorities can be cited where the application of the clause has been analysed by courts in cases involving both actual and apprehended loss of time. In *Turnbull*[59] the insurance was effected on the outward voyage of a steamer from London to Australian ports for freight expected to be earned on the homeward voyage. The policy was warranted 'free from any claim consequent upon loss of time'. While the vessel was discharging the cargo a serious fire broke out which destroyed the refrigerating apparatus which rendered the carriage of frozen meat upon the return voyage impossible. The owners elected not to have the ship repaired as it was obvious that repairs would be of great length and in order to avoid such delay they arranged another cargo. It was decided that had the ship been repaired promptly there would have been no loss of freight. There was accordingly no actual loss of time due to repairs, yet an apprehension of delay on the possibility that the repairs would be carried out and the loss was held to have been within the words 'consequent upon loss of time'.[60] Later on, it was doubted

---

55 As in *Turnbull, Martin & Co v Hull Underwriters' Association Ltd* [1900] QB 402.

56 As in *Russian Bank for Foreign Trade v Excess Ins Co Ltd* [1918] 2 KB 123. The case involved frustration of the voyage by the closure of Dardanelles upon declaration of war.

57 *Bank Line Limited v Arthur Capel & Co* [1919] AC 435, 454.

58 J.E. Stannard, 'Frustrating Delay' 46 *Modern Law Review* 738–753, at 745.

59 *Turnbull, Martin & Co v Hull Underwriters' Association Ltd* [1900] QB 402.

60 ibid, at 406 per Mathew J.

in *Atlantic Maritime v Gibbon* that the clause applied to estimated loss of time situations where loss of freight was expected to occur upon the happening of a deprivation peril resulting in loss of time.[61]

6.21 Despite the foregoing, there have been instances where loss of freight was not considered as 'consequent upon loss of time' even though there was actual, and not apprehended loss of time. In *Petros M Nomikos v Robertson*[62] the ship had to undergo repairs following a fire; however the repairs caused some loss of time as they could not have been completed on time and the charterparty could not have been performed as expected which resulted in loss of freight. The loss had occurred at the time of fire and the loss of time had not even entered into play after the casualty. It was stated that every case of constructive total loss of ship based on cost of repairs or deprivation of possession implies some loss of time and that arguing that any claim for freight resting upon constructive total loss of the ship should be excluded by the operation of the loss of time clause is not acceptable.[63]

There is an obvious controversy between the authority in this case and the decision in *The Playa de las Nieves* where the House of Lords held that both in voyage and time policies on freight, loss of time clause would defeat claims wherever loss of time is an intermediate event between the loss and the peril preceding delay. Nevertheless it is noteworthy that on the facts of the case in *The Playa de las Nieves* the freight policy was on a time basis and involved a time charterparty which included an off-hire clause. For this reason, the part of the decision relating to freight policies on voyage basis can be considered as *obiter*.

'Consequent on loss of time' and causation

6.22 Whether a loss is consequent on loss of time is a question of fact and the authorities should be treated accordingly.[64] So as to have a better understanding of the wording and its causative meaning as to whether it imports the proximate cause rule into the policy as in the MIA s 55(2)(b) or suggests a different rule, it would be necessary to analyse the relevant authorities. The Institute War and Strikes Clauses on freight were drafted with an exclusion that reads 'loss proximately caused by delay or any expenses arising from delay' instead of the loss of time clause.[65] There have been examples in case law where these two clauses

---

61 *Atlantic Maritime v Gibbon* [1954] 1 QB 88, 127 per Evershed MR.

62 *Robertson v Petros Nomikos* [1939] AC 371 per Lord Wright at 387.

63 The distinction of *Nomikos* from *Bensaude v The Thames and Mersey Marine Insurance Company Ltd* [1897] AC 609 was that in the latter the loss was caused simply by delay in repairing the partial loss arising from perils of the seas, whereas in the former the loss of freight was caused by constructive total loss of the ship which was complete at the date of the fire.

64 *Robertson v Petros M Nomikos Ltd* [1939] AC 371, 377.

65 e.g. Institute War and Strikes Clauses, Freight-Time and Freight-Voyage 1/10/83 cl 4.4; Institute War and Strikes Clauses, Freight-Time and Freight-Voyage 1/11/95 cl 4.5 provide 'loss proximately caused by delay or any claim for expenses arising from delay except such expenses as would be recoverable in principle in English law and practice under the York-Antwerp Rules 1994'.

co-existed in the same policy. By way of example in *Atlantic Maritime v Gibbon*[66] the policy was warranted free of claims based on loss of or frustration of, any voyage or adventure caused by restraint of princes, as well as on loss proximately caused by delay. The policy also incorporated the Institute Time Clauses-Freight which contained the loss of time exclusion. Albeit the court did not decide on the point, Evershed MR admitted that there may be distinctions between the two clauses without further elaborating on the matter.[67]

6.23 Two differences between the clauses are readily noticeable: the causation wordings 'consequent upon' and 'proximately caused by', and the use of the terms 'loss of time' and 'delay'. With respect to the former, it was rejected in the House of Lords that 'consequent on' was identical to 'proximately caused by'.[68] Lord Diplock emphasised that 'consequent on' and 'arising from' were similar by enunciating that the exclusion '. . . contemplates a chain of events expressed to be either consequent on or arising from one another'.[69] It was sufficient in that respect if the loss of time was within the chain of events between the 'event which is in marine insurance law the proximate cause of that loss' and the loss for which the claim is made; accordingly the loss of time ought not to be the proximate cause of the loss of freight. Hence, unless a freight policy contains proximate causation wordings, 'consequent upon loss of time' *per se* would not import the proximate causation rule.

The issue of whether 'loss of time' and 'delay' are identical concepts in respect of the loss of time clause was raised previously in two instances where the assured had argued that the loss of time exclusion was inserted to bring freight insurance in line with s 55(2)(b) of the MIA.[70] The House of Lords in *The Playa de las Nieves* did not expressly pronounce any view on this matter and rather emphasised the causation point.

Time charters and the loss of time clause

Origins of the clause

6.24 It is not entirely clear whether the loss of time clause was inserted into time and voyage clauses on freight following pre-MIA judgments on frustration[71]

---

66 [1954] 1 QB 88.

67 ibid, at 122.

68 *Naviera de Canarias SA v Nacional Hispanica Aseguradora SA (The Playa de las Nieves)* [1978] AC 853, 882 per Lord Diplock.

69 ibid.

70 The owners in *Naviera de Canarias SA v Nacional Hispanica Aseguradora SA (The Playa de las Nieves)* [1978] AC 853, 876 contended that loss of time in the context meant in effect delay. This argument was also made in *Russian Bank for Foreign Trade v Excess Insurance Co Ltd* [1918] 2 KB 123 at 126–128.

71 This was enunciated by Donaldson J in *Naviera de Canarias SA v Nacional Hispanica Aseguradora SA (The Playa de las Nieves)* [1975] 1 Lloyd's Rep 259 at 260 and had also been argued by the assured.

FREIGHT INSURANCE

such as *Jackson v The Union Marine Insurance*[72] or cases such as *The Alps*[73] and *The Bedouin*[74] where the issue was whether loss of hire was occasioned by the off-hire clause in time charterparties or the peril insured against under the policy. The rationale behind arguing the latter rests upon the similarity between the wording of the loss of time clause later on introduced ('Warranted free from any claims consequent upon loss of time, whether arising from a peril of the sea or otherwise')[75] and the off-hire clauses contained in the charterparties which were the subject of *The Alps* and *The Bedouin* ('in the event of loss of time by. . . payment of hire to cease. . .').

The distinction between the foregoing cases is crucial given that where the clause is taken to have originated from cases on frustrating delay, it can be submitted that the clause essentially purports to exclude total loss of freight occasioned by the frustration of the objects of the adventure by delay. On the other hand, should the clause be taken to have originated from *The Alps* and *The Bedouin*, the clause may be construed to exclude mainly partial loss of hire arising from the happening of an off-hire event and resulting loss of time.

6.25 In *Jackson v Union Marine Insurance Co Ltd*[76] which was a leading judgment on frustrating delay, the vessel got aground and was delayed due to the getting of the vessel off the rocks and repairs, during which the charterer had abandoned the vessel and arranged another vessel to carry the cargo. The assured claimed that there had been a total loss of freight[77] on the ground that he was prevented by sea perils from earning it. The issues were whether the time necessary for repairing the ship was so long as to make it unreasonable for the charterers to supply the agreed cargo at the end of that time, whether there was a total loss of freight to be earned under a charterparty by perils of the sea, and whether such time was so long as to put an end to the commercial speculation entered upon by the shipowner and charterers.[78] The policy also did not contain any loss of time exclusion. Bramwell J held that the proximate cause maxim did not apply;[79] the loss of freight was caused by perils of the seas and that delay was only an event frustrating the charterparty.

6.26 According to Bramwell J the issue was not whether the perils of the seas or the delay were the proximate cause of the loss of freight, but was

---

72 (1874) LR 10 CP 125.

73 *Mersey Steamship Company Ltd v Thames and Mersey Marine Insurance Company Ltd (The Alps)* [1893] P 109.

74 *The Bedouin* [1894] P 1.

75 This wording is very similar to the equivalent clause in the Institute Clauses Time and Voyage Freight 1995 (cl 15 and cl 11 respectively) and has the same effect although 'Warranted free from' is replaced by 'This insurance does not cover any claim'. This difference was not considered as creating a difference in meaning in *Naviera de Canarias SA v Nacional Hispanica Aseguradora SA (The Playa de las Nieves)* [1978] AC 853.

76 (1874) LR 10 CP 125.

77 There is no specific reference in the case as to whether the shipowners' claim was for constructive or actual total loss.

78 At 125–126 per Cleasby B.

79 (1874) LR 10 CP 125, 148.

105

whether the perils of the seas or the refusal of the charterers to load were the cause. Delay frustrating the charterparty was not even considered as a peril for the purpose of the insurance contract that may or may not have been the cause. Bramwell J held that there would have been a new adventure after the frustration of the charterparty by perils of the seas and that the perils of the seas did not cause something which caused something else.[80] Cleasby B dissenting in that judgment approached delay as being caused by perils[81] and not by the fault of the charterers[82] or the breach of a stipulation by the owners. It was found that delay frustrated the charterparty; it was the event which gave the charterers the right not to load the ship but not the event which caused the loss of freight. The loss of freight was accordingly held to be caused by the perils of the seas.

Should it be submitted that *Jackson* was the ground upon which the loss of time clause was introduced into both time and voyage policies on freight, the main purpose behind this introduction was arguably to exclude total loss of freight by frustrating delay and any delay which was not as lengthy as to be frustrating the commercial speculation of the adventure undertaken by the charterparty would not suffice to trigger the clause.

6.27 It could alternatively be argued that the main purpose of the clause was to exclude partial loss of hire arising from an off-hire clause being triggered. Several judgments on loss of hire after *Jackson* had referred to *Re Jamieson v Newcastle SS Freight Ins Assn*[83] for the suggestion that loss of hire by an off-hire event and consequent delay are the types of losses sought to be excluded under time policies on freight. In *Re Jamieson v Newcastle SS Freight Ins Assn*[84] the risks insured against included perils of the seas and it was provided that 'no claim arising from the cancelling of any charter, *nor loss of time under a time charter*' shall be allowed.[85] The claim in this case and the main discussion turned upon the meaning of 'cancelling the charter', and the second part of the clause as to the loss of time was *obiter*.[86] In this case the shipowner had chartered his ship to carry a cargo at an agreed freight. While the ship was sailing for the port of loading she was damaged through perils of the sea and was unable to fulfil her engagement. It took her so long to get repaired that the adventure contemplated by the charterparty was frustrated; therefore the shipowner was not bound to proceed with the voyage and charterers were not bound to load. The freight to be earned should the voyage be proceeded with was hence lost to the shipowner. It

---

80 At 148.
81 Lord Esher MR also stated in *Re Jamieson v Newcastle SS Freight Ins Assn* [1895] 2 QB 90 at 93–94 '. . . if the ship is so delayed, whether by a peril of the sea or by any other cause. . .'.
82 At 132.
83 [1895] 2 QB 90.
84 [1895] 2 QB 90.
85 Emphasis added.
86 per A.L. Smith LJ at 96.

was held that the loss was occasioned directly by the perils of the sea and not by delay. It was stated:

> '. . . what this clause means is that, if under a time charter the ship is laid up and by agreement time is then not to count, the underwriters will not be responsible for loss of freight arising therefrom'.[87]

6.28 In policies which expressly limit the scope of application of the loss of time clause to cases where the vessel is fulfilling a special charter containing a cancelling date,[88] the clause would only apply to defeat claims for loss of freight which arise from the cancellation of the charterparty by the parties.

6.29 Some loss of time is inevitably linked to loss of hire arising from an off-hire event; conversely loss of freight consequent on loss of time requires the delay to be very lengthy for the voyage to put an end thereto. Delay that is of nature to frustrate the contract is in this respect distinct from mere passage of time. Albeit the clause operates both to exclude loss of freight arising from frustrating delays and loss of charter hire caused by an off-hire event; the latter has received criticism which will be examined below.[89]

Off-hire clauses and the loss of time clause

(a) Early cases on loss of hire and off-hire clauses

6.30 In early cases on loss of hire where policies did not include the loss of time clause, courts had consistently held that this type of loss could be recoverable from the insurers where it had resulted from loss of time. In *Inman v Bischoff*[90] the Court of Appeal held that the insurers were not liable on the ground that the perils insured against were not the proximate cause of the loss; however in the House of Lords Lord Selbourne LC stated that although the proximate cause rule was intelligible and applicable in many cases, in a case such as *Inman* a too literal application of it could have caused injustice.[91] Lord Watson also enunciated:

> 'If it had been expressly stipulated in the charterparty that freight should cease to be payable so long as the ship was incapable from that cause of efficiently performing her contract, I do not doubt that the insurers would have been liable'[92]

given that that would have been a case of loss of freight through perils of the seas.

---

87 ibid.

88 Such as in *Scottish Shire Line, Limited and Others v London and Provincial Marine and General Insurance Company Limited* [1912] 3 KB 51, although in this case the contract was held not to be a special charter containing a cancelling date and therefore the loss of time clause had not applied.

89 See para 6.35.

90 *Inman SS Co v Bischoff* (1880–1881) LR 6 QBD 670.

91 *Inman SS Co v Bischoff* (1881–1882) LR 7 App Cas 670, 675–676 per Lord Selbourne LC. According to Lord Blackburn, the real question in the case was not whether the proximate cause would apply, yet whether there was any loss of freight.

92 *Inman SS Co v Bischoff* (1880–1881) LR 6 QBD 670, 690.

6.31 Following this *obiter dictum*, two important decisions were delivered in respect of loss of hire where time charterparties contained off-hire clauses, which they now almost invariably do.[93] In two similar cases decided after *Inman* namely *The Alps and The Bedouin*,[94] the time charterparties contained off-hire clauses and loss of time was caused during repairs of the damaged vessel. In both instances the courts decided that what triggered the off-hire clause in the charterparty was the immediate action of the perils of the seas and thereby applied the proximate cause rule. The result was that the inefficiency of the vessel was due to a peril insured against which was the proximate cause of the loss and given also the absence of the loss of time clause in the policies the insurers were held liable for the loss.

(b) Time charterparties, off-hire clauses and the meaning of
   'loss of time'

6.32 According to the terms of a time charterparty, loss of time can be considered as the result of an off-hire event or the off-hire event itself.[95] In the latter case, what would differentiate delay or loss of time from other off-hire events which could contain an element of loss of time (e.g. detention) would be considered to be a delay of the service immediately required.[96] Therefore a vessel could be said to have been both detained and delayed where the detention causes the vessel to delay the service immediately required. In standard form time charterparties such as NYPE 46 the off-hire clause is taken not to be concerned with the entire marine adventure or the chartered service as a whole.[97] In that type of charterparties, loss of time resulting in loss of hire is considered as actual time lost during the inefficiency of the vessel and not an identifiable length of time by which the chartered service could be said to have been delayed.[98] This approach could give rise to the question of whether judgments relating to frustration of voyage charterparties by excessive delay could be taken as authorities for cases of partial loss of hire by loss of time. This suggestion accordingly doubts whether the authority

---

93 The time charterparties in standard forms such as NYPE Time Charter 1946 cl 15 contains the wording '. . . in the event of loss of time from . . .' and enumerates off-hire events. The revised version of 1993 preserved the same wording.

94 *Mersey Steamship Company Ltd v Thames and Mersey Marine Insurance Company Ltd (The Alps)* [1893] P 109 was followed by *The Bedouin* [1894] P 1.

95 In *Nippon Yusen Kaisha Ltd v Scindia Steam Navigation Co (The Jalagouri)* [1998] CLC 1054, the charterparty included an additional clause (cl 53) which would put the vessel off-hire where she is 'seized or detained or arrested or delayed'. In this case the vessel was removed from her berth and was prevented by the port authorities from discharging her cargo.

96 *Nippon Yusen Kaisha Ltd v Scindia Steam Navigation Co (The Jalagouri)* [1998] CLC 1054, 1057, Rix J, as he then was, considered that according to time charter interpretation delay was 'a word of broad meaning and had to be measured by reference to the service immediately required'.

97 *Minerva Navigation Inc v Oceana Shipping AG; Oceana Shipping AG v Transatlantica Commodities SA (The M/V Athena)* [2013] EWCA Civ 1723.

98 Given the expression 'time thereby lost' in cl 15 of NYPE 46.

of the House of Lords in *The Playa de las Nieves*[99] which was decided following *Bensaude*[100] is tenable.

(c) Whether loss of time a cause of loss or merely a measure of loss

6.33 The connection between loss of hire and loss of time would inevitably depend upon the terms of the charterparty. By way of example, where a time charterparty contains an off-hire clause providing that the hire shall cease to be payable where the vessel is prevented from performing for more than twenty-four working hours[101] it would follow that hire would not have been lost in the first twenty-four hours of inefficiency, albeit time would definitely have been lost by the shipowner. This can accordingly be an example of a circumstance where loss of hire shall not strictly mean that its loss directly depends upon loss of time, yet also upon the terms of the charterparty. Nonetheless, whether the terms of the charterparty shall also determine the cause of the loss of hire is a question that requires further analysis.

It can be submitted that but for the existence of off-hire clauses in charterparties, hire thereunder would not be lost; nevertheless this shall not necessarily denote that the proximate cause of the loss of hire is the terms of the charterparty and not the insured perils. The more fundamental question would perhaps be whether it is still necessary to identify the proximate cause of the loss[102] in order to decide whether the loss would be excluded by the loss of time exclusion. The House of Lords in *The Playa de las Nieves*[103] focused on the distinction between proximate and 'consequent upon' causation. According to this authority, for the loss of time exclusion to apply, it would suffice that the loss of hire is merely 'consequent upon' loss of time; i.e. that loss of time is merely an event in the chain of causation.

6.34 The loss of hire by the happening of an off-hire event that triggers an off-hire clause shall be distinguished from loss of hire by frustrating delay. In the former case it may be argued that the hire is lost by virtue of the contract[104] (but

---

99 *Naviera de Canarias SA v Nacional Hispanica Aseguradora SA (The Playa de las Nieves)* [1978] AC 853.

100 *Bensaude v The Thames and Mersey Marine Insurance Company Ltd* [1897] AC 609.

101 As in *Mersey Steamship Company Ltd v Thames and Mersey Marine Insurance Company Ltd (The Alps)* [1893] P 109.

102 As was the case in *Mersey Steamship Company Ltd v Thames and Mersey Marine Insurance Company Ltd (The Alps)* [1893] P 109 and *The Bedouin* [1894] P 1.

103 *Naviera de Canarias SA v Nacional Hispanica Aseguradora SA (The Playa de las Nieves)* [1978] AC 853.

104 In the context of voyage charters where the vessel had to incur lengthy repairs, the use of the cancelling option in the charterparty was regarded as the cause of the loss of freight in *Mercantile v Tyser* (1880–81) LR 7 QBD 73. It can be argued that the happening of an off-hire event triggering the off-hire clause in the charterparty can be regarded in the same way, which was the case in *Mersey Steamship Company Ltd v Thames and Mersey Marine Insurance Company Ltd (The Alps)* [1893] P 109.

for the off-hire clause, the loss of time would not cause the loss of hire)[105] whereas in the latter it happens with the occurrence of a frustrating delay. The loss of time in the former context can arguably be regarded as an event quantifying the amount of loss;[106] the lengthier the loss of time is, the greater the extent of loss shall be. In this sense, identifying whether the loss of hire is consequent on loss of time and therefore excluded by the loss of time clause in freight policies or whether it is consequent on the off-hire event is important. There is considerable authority now that such loss is excluded by the loss of time exclusion[107] as none of the cases decided on time charters and loss of time other than *The Playa de las Nieves* included a loss of time exclusion.[108] The decision of the House of Lords shall be analysed along with the views expressed in the Court of Appeal as to the fact that the cause of the loss of hire was the off-hire event and not the loss of time.[109]

6.35 Under a voyage charterparty, the freight can be lost in several ways such as where the vessel or the cargo becomes a constructive total loss or if delay or the peril preceding delay frustrates the object of the adventure. Therefore one may argue that the loss of time clause in a freight policy has a specific role to strike out all the claims which are consequent on loss of time. Nonetheless the same argument may not be tenable in respect of loss of hire under time charters as that loss mainly depends on the existence of an off-hire clause in the charterparty the trigger of which depends on the happening of an off-hire event. It is crucial to identify the situations where hire will be lost under a freight policy other than the off-hire event situations, as it may not be appropriate to construe the loss of time clause barring all the claims for loss of hire if the most frequently occurring type of loss thereunder is one by the occurrence of an off-hire event. One of the most obvious benefits sought by taking out a freight policy would probably be covered in case of loss of hire where an off-hire event occurs.[110] Holding that loss of time exclusion strikes out any loss of hire by an off-hire event shall signify that the only loss of hire recoverable under such a policy would be loss of hire consequent on total loss of the ship whereby it becomes impossible to perform the service for which she is chartered.

6.36 On the other hand, holding the insurers liable for the loss of hire under a freight policy during an excessively long delay could raise the suspicion whether

---

105 Although in certain charterparties such as in BIMCO Supplytime 2005, loss of hire can occur independently from the off-hire clause. Clause 14(f) provides that where hazardous cargo is carried, the Charterers shall be liable for any loss 'directly or indirectly' caused to the shipowners. A delay resulting from the carriage of hazardous cargo and the consequent loss of hire can arguably be an event that would come under this clause.

106 This point was argued by the assured in *Naviera de Canarias SA v Nacional Hispanica Aseguradora SA (The Playa de las Nieves)* [1978] AC 853.

107 *Naviera de Canarias SA v Nacional Hispanica Aseguradora SA (The Playa de las Nieves)* [1978] AC 853.

108 *Inman Steamship Co v Bischoff* 7 App Cas 670; *Mersey Steamship Company Ltd v Thames and Mersey Marine Insurance Company Ltd (The Alps)* [1893] P 109; *The Bedouin* [1894] P 1.

109 The decision was given with a majority of Lord Denning MR and Shaw LJ; Goff LJ dissenting.

110 *Naviera de Canarias SA v Nacional Hispanica Aseguradora SA (The Playa de las Nieves)* [1976] 3 WLR 45 per Lord Denning MR.

the insurers might have intended to cover such a risk without having requested higher premiums. Subsequent to *The Playa de las Nieves*, standard terms covering loss of charter hire was made available in the market known as London ABS Form 1983.[111] The cover provided under these clauses extends to loss of hire caused by loss of or damage to the vessel preventing it from operating and earning hire, however does not extend to loss of hire where the vessel is not on charter or to loss of hire incurred for the purposes of ensuring the health of a crew member. These types of losses can be considered as consequent upon loss of time and be excluded under both time-freight policies and loss of charter hire policies.

---

111 This will be analysed in Chapter 8.

CHAPTER 7

Hull and machinery insurance and delay considerations

Introduction

7.1 The MIA 1906 provides that an insurer of a ship is not liable for any loss proximately caused by delay, although the delay is caused by a peril insured against.[1] The common law origin of the provision goes back to *Shelbourne v Law*[2] where it was held that loss of earnings due to detention and delay of a vessel during repairs necessitated by a collision are not recoverable under a hull and machinery policy. The origin was therefore with respect to the exclusion of this type of consequential losses arising from delay from the scope of hull and machinery policies. In *Phoenix Shipping Co v Apex Shipping Corp*[3] it was enunciated:

> 'It is clear beyond doubt that an insurance on a subject matter, whether described as 'hull and machinery' or 'ship' or 'vessel' does not indemnify the assured against loss of earnings, or wasted expenditure during periods of delay.'[4]

Those claims all have an element of loss of time given that in order to calculate the exact measure of losses, the number of weeks, days and hours during which the vessel is deprived of earning must be taken into consideration. In other words, loss of earnings can be considered as a consequence of loss of time occasioned by damage to hull and therefore excluded from the scope of hull and machinery policies. Part of the type of expenses arising from delay otherwise excluded under this type of insurance can be insured in the market under loss of hire (loss of earnings) policies which shall be dealt with in Chapter 8.

7.2 This being the case, hull and machinery policies provide however liability cover for owners against the detention and demurrage claims of third parties

---

1 MIA s 55(2)(b).

2 *Shelbourne & Co v Law Investment and Insurance Corporation Ltd* [1898] 2 QB 626 cited in Chalmers and Owen, *A Digest of the Law Relating to Marine Insurance* (William Clowes and Sons Ltd 1901), 64. The decision was also found in later editions, see E.R. Hardy Ivamy, *Chalmers' Marine Insurance Act 1906* (9th edn, Butterworths 1983), 80 and in E.R. Hardy Ivamy, *Marine Insurance* (3rd edn, Butterworths 1979), 257.

3 [1982] 2 Lloyd's Rep 407.

4 ibid, at 414 per Mustill J.

112

where the owners' vessels collide with other vessels.[5] Delay also may not only be involved in the chain of causation where consequential losses such as loss of earnings due to detention are incurred, but also where there is damage to the hull, increased cost of repairs where a delay in carrying them out occurs, and expenses incurred during repairs. This chapter will analyse the law on the recoverability of each of these separate heads of claim.

Damage to the hull and delay: introduction

7.3 Damage to the hull of the vessel which involves an element of loss of time may occur essentially in two cases; namely first where the vessel deteriorates pending repairs to average damage and second, where the event causing delay does not damage the hull of the vessel yet results in an excessively lengthy delay that accordingly produces deterioration of the hull of the vessel.[6] In the former case the damage is usually caused by a preceding event such as collision or perils of the seas which require repairs, and delay intervenes where repairs are pending. The deterioration of the hull of the vessel by delay in these situations is rare mainly because the deterioration is essentially caused by the peril preceding delay and delay can only be the event aggravating the deterioration already caused if it is sufficiently lengthy. It is therefore controversial whether delay in these cases can be regarded as *a* or *the* proximate cause of the loss. With respect to the latter type of loss, the current standard market terms used in the UK contain no express exclusion. The International Hull Clauses 2003 provides that it 'covers loss of or damage to the subject matter insured' caused by perils insured against such as perils of the seas,[7] fire[8] or jettison.[9] Delay can be an event which ensues from the preceding perils, and could result in consequential losses as well as deterioration of the hull if sufficiently lengthy. Section 55(2)(b) and (c) could both be invoked by insurers in this case to exclude any liability for the deterioration of the hull by lengthy delays.

Deterioration of the hull by lengthy delays and ordinary wear and tear

7.4 Ships do not usually navigate for any length of time without a certain degree of deterioration and diminution in value, which is usually referred to as wear and tear. Ordinary wear and tear may result from excessive delays following a detention, capture or seizure which was illustrated by *Magoun v New England*

---

5 e.g. 3/4th collision liability clause as found in the International Hull Clauses 2003 cl 6.1.2; Institute Voyage Clauses Hulls 1983 cl 8.1.2; Institute Time Clauses Hulls 1983 cl 6.1.2.

6 The latter seldom happened during the World War II detentions.

7 cl 2.1.1.

8 cl 2.1.2.

9 cl 2.1.4.

Marine Insurance Company in the United States.[10] In that case, excessive delay due to an earlier detention combined by hot weather and exposure of the vessel to an open roadstead had caused damage to the hull of the vessel requiring great repairs that cost more than the vessel was worth. The Court rejected the argument that the long delay and exposure to the climate was the proximate cause of the loss; the detention was the cause and that the insurers were not liable for wear and tear and delays on the voyage. It was held that:

> 'The argument is, that the injury to the vessel, by the long delay and exposure to the climate, was the immediate cause of the loss, and the seizure and detainment the remote cause only; and that, therefore, the rule applies, "Causa proxima, non remota, spectatur," and the underwriters are not liable for injury by mere wear and tear, or by delays in the voyage, or by worms, or by exposure to the climate. But it appears to me, that this is not a correct exposition of the rule. All the consequences naturally flowing from the peril insured against, or incident thereto, are properly attributable to the peril itself.'[11]

The earlier detention resulting in delay was a peril insured under the policy and the hull damage was therefore recoverable. This example must now be considered in the light of *The Cendor Mopu*[12] where Lord Mance stated that 'ordinary wear and tear and ordinary leakage and breakage would thus cover loss or damage resulting from the normal vicissitudes of use in the case of a vessel . . . without any fortuitous external accident or casualty'.[13] The exclusion in s 55(2)(c) can therefore be successfully invoked by insurers in the absence of an insured peril such as the perils of the seas.[14]

7.5 Delay can operate following damage to the hull of the vessel and result in the deterioration of the vessel which can cause the assured to incur expenses for its removal and destruction. In *St. Margaret's Trust Ltd v Navigators and General Ins Co Ltd*[15] the vessel which was covered against losses by 'accidental external means including stress of weather, stranding, sinking, collision' was put on mud berth and had subsequently shifted across river to another mud berth, where she slipped over a low tide and filled with water on the flood tide owing to the neglected state of her topside caulking which caused her to sink. The vessel was left at that position for nearly a month, and then was refloated and towed to a place where she was left until another mud berth became available. As it was not possible to get any berth at the time, the vessel eventually gradually deteriorated and had no more than a break-up value. Later orders were given by the harbour authority for the removal of wreck. The issue in this case was whether the vessel

---

10 *Magoun v New England Marine Insurance Company*, 1 Story 157, 16 F.Cas. 483, C.C.Mass. (1840).

11 ibid, 485–486.

12 *Global Process Systems Inc v Syarikat Takaful Malaysia Berhad (The Cendor Mopu)* [2011] UKSC 5.

13 ibid, para 81.

14 *Wadsworth Lighterage and Cooling Co Ltd v Sea Insurance Co Ltd* (1929) 34 Ll L Rep 285.

15 *St. Margaret's Trust Ltd v Navigators and General Ins Co Ltd* (1949) 82 Ll L Rep 752.

was a total loss, whether the expenses for refloating and payment due for destroying and removal of the wreck could be recoverable under the policy.

It was held that there was only evidence to the effect that the vessel when raised could have been made approximately into the condition in which she was when first submerged. The claimants were accordingly not entitled to recover for a total loss but for a partial loss which was the amount paid by them in connection with the refloating of the vessel and the estimated damage to the fittings caused by the submersion. The Court agreed with the insurers' submission that the costs of destroying and removal of the wreck were expenses caused by delay within the meaning of s 55(2)(b) of the Marine Insurance Act 1906 and that they were not recoverable under the policy.

Delay in carrying out repairs and increased cost of repairs

7.6 Prior to the entry into force of the Marine Insurance Act, Lord Blackburn had enunciated in *Marine Insurance Co v China Trans-Pacific SS Co*[16] that charging insurers for the increased cost of repairs delayed by the assured would not be fair.[17] In this case the repairs were carried out a year after the damage had occurred. This statement was however merely an *obiter dictum* as on the facts of *Marine Insurance Co v China Trans-Pacific* no extra cost had arisen for delaying repairs.

Delay in effecting repairs may arise due to circumstances within or beyond the control of the assured. If the repairs are delayed by the assured and increased cost of repairs accrue therefrom, one of the questions that would arise would be whether these costs would be considered as the result of the delay or the peril preceding delay. In the former case insurers may invoke the delay exclusion in s 55(2)(b) of the MIA; in the latter case the costs may arguably not be recoverable on the ground of the failure to sue and labour an insured loss if the peril preceding delay is an insured peril under the policy.[18]

7.7 Contrary to the standard cargo forms currently in use, the standard hull forms do not impose a general duty on the assured to act with reasonable despatch in all circumstances within their control.[19] Both the Institute Time Clauses – Hulls 1983 and the International Hull Clauses 2003 contain provisions on the measure of indemnity of unrepaired damage and provide that the measure of indemnity 'shall be the reasonable depreciation in the market value of the Vessel at the time [the] insurance terminates arising from such unrepaired damage, but not exceeding the reasonable cost of repairs'.[20] What can be regarded as 'reasonable

---

16 *Marine Insurance Co v China Trans-Pacific SS Co* (1886) 11 App Cas 573. In this case the repairs were carried out a year after the damage had occurred.

17 ibid, 591–592.

18 MIA s 78(4); International Hull Clauses 2003 cl 9.1. The event resulting in need for repairs that are delayed must be an insured peril.

19 See cl 18 (avoidance of delay clause) in the Institute Cargo Clauses 2009.

20 Institute Time Clauses – Hulls 1983 cl 18.1; International Hull Clauses 2003 cl 20.1. See also the American Hull Clauses 2009, lines 170–172: 'No claim for unrepaired damages shall be allowed,

cost of repairs' was discussed in *Irvin v Hine*[21] where it was decided that where an insured peril causes damage to the ship which requires repairs, the costs of repair can be recoverable as partial loss and the measure of indemnity should be assessed by reference to the time where the repairs could have been effected albeit with some delay beyond the control of the assured, not by reference to the time where they should have been. In this case the ship got damaged in 1942 due to stranding and was never repaired by the assured; yet it was proved that owing to the wartime licensing system then in force, she could not in any event have been repaired before 1946 or 1947. The depreciation arising from the unrepaired damage exceeded the estimated cost of repair in 1946. The assured argued that there was constructive total loss as it was at all material times unlikely that the assured would have been able to obtain a licence to repair the ship within a reasonable time; and alternatively claimed for a partial loss. It was contended by the insurers that the depreciation arising from the unrepaired damage had to be reduced to what the repairs would have cost in 1942. This was rejected on the ground that the measure of indemnity should be the cost of repairs at the time when they could have been effected.[22] Per Devlin J's words:[23]

> 'In estimating the cost of repair for the purpose of a partial loss, I think that the court has to arrive as near as possible at the actual figure which would have been expended had she been repaired; and if it be proved to my satisfaction, as it is, that she could not have been repaired earlier than the early part of 1947, I think that I ought to take the figures appropriate to that time.'

7.8 Provisions in some other jurisdictions expressly cover the situation where repairs are not carried out with reasonable despatch by the assured. The Nordic Marine Insurance Plan of 2013 Version 2016 cl.12.6 which is entitled 'deferred repairs' provides that 'If the repairs have not been carried out within five years after the damage was discovered, the insurer is not liable for any increase in the cost of the work that is incurred later.' According to this sub-clause, the insurer will be liable for the costs of repair incurred within the five-year period, however any increased cost of repairs after that period will be borne by the assured.

Expenses incurred during repairs

Are they losses proximately caused by delay?

7.9 Whether expenses arising during repairs can be claimed as part of the costs of repair or whether they are excluded as losses proximately caused by delay

---

except to the extent that the aggregate damage caused by perils insured against during the period of the Policy and left unrepaired at the expiration of the Policy shall be demonstrated by the Assured to have diminished the actual market value of the Vessel on that date if undamaged by such perils.'

21 *Irvin v Hine* [1950] 1 KB 555.

22 ibid, per Devlin J at 572.

23 ibid.

within the meaning of s 55(2)(b) is a question of fact and would depend upon the evidence submitted by the parties. In *The Jascon 5*[24] damage to the vessel caused delay in the completion of the contract between the owner of the vessel and the shipyard given that repairs needed to be carried out. Expenses arising during repairs, i.e. costs of labour, materials in effecting the work itself and additional expenses such as planning and supervision of the repairs and provision of the yard services which delayed the completion of the work were claimed as repair costs. The policy was a standard form of builder's risk policy which contained no express exclusion clause for loss, damage or expense caused by delay, however the insurers invoked s 55(2)(b) to argue that the expenses claimed were not within the scope of cover. The Court held that the policy was a marine hull policy covering all risks whilst the work was being done to the vessel and the fact that expenses arising during repairs over a 60-day period are calculated on a time basis would not necessarily mean that these should be considered as costs of delay or amount to a loss proximately caused by delay.[25] It was further enunciated that whether or not costs incurred are costs of repair or costs proximately caused by delay – and hence excluded – was a question of fact and would depend on the evidence submitted by the parties.[26] The application was made for a summary judgment and the Court held that upon the evidence submitted, it was more likely that these costs would be considered as costs of repair and not losses proximately caused by delay.

Wages and maintenance expenses arising during repairs
at port of refuge

(a) Under the common law

7.10 Under the Common law, wages and maintenance expenses of crew during the stay of the vessel at the port of refuge were not recoverable in general average by the shipowner on two grounds. The first ground was that the general average act was taken to have terminated where the vessel reached the port of refuge and that accordingly all the expenses incurred following the termination of the general average operation were considered to be resulting not from the general average act yet from delay in port for repairs, which fell under the shipowner's duty under his contract.[27] The second ground was that those expenses constituted an increase in ordinary expenditure whereas a loss recoverable in general average had to be extraordinary in nature. The services of the crew during the entire voyage were

---

24 *Talbot Underwriting Ltd v Nausch Hohan & Murray Inc (The Jascon 5)* [2005] EWHC 2359 (Comm) affirmed by the Court of Appeal, *Talbot Underwriting Ltd v Nausch Hohan & Murray Inc (The Jascon 5)* [2006] EWCA Civ 889.

25 At para 136 per Cooke J.

26 At para 137.

27 R.R. Cornah and J. Reeder QC, *Lowndes and Rudolf: The Law of General Average and The York-Antwerp Rules* (14th edn, Sweet & Maxwell 2013), para 11.02. The early versions of this book (for instance Rudolf Lowndes, *The Law of General Average: English and Foreign* (4th edn, London: Stevens and Sons 1888), § 57) cites no authority in support of this rule.

deemed as due to the cargo on board and the shipowner had to bear the risk of a longer voyage.[28]

7.11 Doubt was cast in *Atwood v Sellar*[29] as to whether expenses for wages or provisions of crew in a port of refuge have ever been disallowed by the courts as constituting a claim for general average in a case where the ship puts into the port to repair a damage which itself belongs to general average. In this case, the repairs had been required in consequence of a damage to the ship by perils of the seas. The cargo had to be accordingly unloaded and warehoused for the repairs to be carried out and the question was whether the expenses of warehousing and reloading the unloaded goods for the purpose of repairing the injury and expenses incurred for pilotage were the subject of general average. Going into port, unloading, warehousing, reloading of the cargo and coming out of port were treated in this case as parts of one act or operation carried through for the common safety and were regarded as continuous. It was also stated that wages and maintenance provisions at the port of refuge were recoverable under the laws of all the other countries except for England and the reason for this could have been that either the Courts had made a mistake to limit the application of the rule or that the disallowance rested upon public policy grounds.[30]

7.12 As to the first ground mentioned above for the disallowance of the expenses during repairs, i.e. that the general average act terminates when the ship arrives at the port of refuge, the main counter-argument could be the requirement of a danger to the common safety of the adventure.[31] This concept can either refer to the danger of actual injury to the ship and cargo, or alternatively danger of the ship with her cargo being prevented from prosecuting the voyage safely. Albeit in the former case, putting into a port of refuge can arguably terminate the general average situation, in the latter case the general average sacrifice would span to the expenses incurred until the ship leaves the port of refuge. Wages and maintenance expenses would therefore occur during the general average act.

A second question could be whether the wages and maintenance expenses are extraordinary sacrifice for the safety of the common maritime adventure[32] or a sacrifice merely made by the shipowner during the repairs necessary for the prosecution of the common adventure. Some of the earlier authorities referred to in *Atwood v Sellar* distinguished the situations of an injury to the vessel which is of itself the subject of general average (e.g. injury arising from a collision) and an injury caused by ordinary perils of the seas in consequence of which proceeding to port of refuge is necessary.[33] The cases mentioned therein are in no way direct

---

28 Ibid.

29 *Atwood v Sellar* (1880) 5 QBD 286, at 291.

30 *Atwood v Sellar* (1880) 5 QBD 286, 291.

31 See the definition in MIA 1906 s 66(2); YAR 1994, 2004 and 2016, Rule A/1.

32 ibid.

33 See, for instance, *Hallett v Wigram* (1850) 9 CB 580 where at p 603 Wilde CJ quoted with approval the following passage from Abbott (8th edn), p 497: 'It seems to result from these decisions that if a vessel goes into port in consequence of an injury which is itself the subject of general average,

authority for the suggestion that wages and maintenance expenses could be recoverable, yet can constitute a fair ground to argue the allowance of such costs as general average expenses where they are incurred as the result of a voluntary sacrifice. Accordingly the mere fact that these expenses were incurred at the port of refuge during delay pending repairs shall not necessarily mean that they are excluded from the scope of general average merely because they arise during delay.

7.13 After *Atwood v Sellar* was decided, it was recognised in an *obiter dictum* that loss of hire could be allowed in general average even if caused by delay at the port of refuge. It was stated in *Anglo-Argentine Live Stock Agency v Temperley Shipping Co*[34] that:

> 'Everyone concerned in the adventure suffers damage by delay at the port of refuge. Each cargo-owner is delayed in the use or the sale of his goods. The freight-owner is delayed in getting payment of his freight, and the shipowner is deprived of the use of his ship. Yet none of these cases afford the foundation of any claim in general average according to our common law. Perhaps it is desirable that they should; and when the York-Antwerp Rules are by contract made applicable, some of them do form the subject of contribution. But the common law is clear, and it will be found laid down in the cases collected by Mr. Lowndes . . . '.[35]

This decision was made against the background of the York-Antwerp Rules 1890 where a clause similar to the current Rule C did not exist. Rule C of the YAR 1994, 2004 and 2016 provides as follows:

> '1. Only such losses, damages or expenses which are the direct consequence of the general average act shall be allowed as general average.
> 2. In no case shall there be any allowance in general average for losses, damages or expenses incurred in respect of damage to the environment or in consequence of the escape or release of pollutant substances from the property involved in the common maritime adventure.
> 3. Demurrage, loss of market, and any loss or damage sustained or expense incurred by reason of delay, whether on the voyage or subsequently, and any indirect loss whatsoever, shall not be admitted as general average.'

(b) Under the York-Antwerp Rules

7.14 According to the York-Antwerp Rules, wages and maintenance expenses during the prolongation of the voyage occasioned by a ship entering a port of refuge or returning to her port of loading shall be admitted as general average if

---

such repairs as are absolutely necessary to enable her to prosecute her voyage, and the necessary expenses of port charges, wages, and provisions during the stay, are to be considered as general average; but if the damage was incurred by the mere violence of the wind or weather, without sacrifice on the part of the owners for the benefit of all concerned, it falls, with the expenses consequent upon it, within the contract of the shipowner "to keep his vessel tight, staunch, and strong" during the voyage for which she is hired.'

34 [1899] 2 QB 403.
35 [1899] 2 QB 403 at 412.

those expenses are incurred for common safety or where the ship is necessarily removed to another port for carrying out repairs.[36] Recovery of those expenses is also available if they are incurred at the port of refuge[37] and while the vessel sails from the port of refuge to a second port where repairs are taking place.[38] The Rules use the term 'prolongation of the voyage' for the part of the voyage which involves a deviation from the original route to proceed to the port of refuge and which also inevitably involves some loss of time during the original voyage. Therefore the prolongation of the voyage begins where the vessel deviates and ends where the vessel resumes the originally intended course.[39] Whereas 'prolongation' as a term could have either a geographical or a temporal meaning in other contexts,[40] in respect of Rule X, it is submitted that even if it is used in its geographical meaning, its temporal meaning shall also be implied where because of the deviation, the voyage cannot be terminated within the expected period of time.

There is no international uniformity as to calculating the extent of prolongation of voyage however many of the calculation methods combine distance with the time involved. When Rule X is considered together with Rule C, some ambiguity may arise as to the difference between 'prolongation of the voyage' and 'delay on the voyage' and expenses resulting therefrom. The inter-relation between the lettered and numbered rules is set forth in the Rule of Interpretation in YAR 1994, 2004 and 2016 providing that 'Except as provided by the Rule Paramount and the numbered Rules, general average shall be adjusted according to the lettered Rules'. Accordingly, given the express and specific rule described in Rule X as to the recoverability of wages and maintenance expenses, they are allowed as general average expenses even though they are expenses arising during the period of delay.

---

36 YAR 1994, 2004, 2016, Rule XI(a).

37 YAR 1994 Rule XI(b); 2016 Rule XI(b)(i), with the exception of YAR 2004 where such expenses are not recoverable.

38 YAR 1994 Rule X(a); YAR 2004 Rule X(a(ii)); YAR 2016 Rule X(a(ii)).

39 R.R. Cornah and J. Reeder QC, *Lowndes and Rudolf: The Law of General Average and The York-Antwerp Rules* (14th edn, Sweet & Maxwell 2013), 11.10.

40 In *Union Castle Mail Steamship Co Ltd v United Kingdom Mutual War Risks Association* [1958] 1 All ER 431 the assured was covered under a 1956–1957 standard form of war risks time policy on hull and machinery for expenses incurred by the assured by reason of prolongation of the voyage arising from compliance with directions of certain authorities. Diplock J in an *obiter* passage stated that 'prolongation' in that context was merely temporal given the word 'period of' preceding prolongation. Moreover he observed that there can be deviation without prolongation of the voyage if the voyage is terminated within the expected period of time and he assessed the prolongation of the voyage by reference to the dates the vessels were due to their port of loading from their round voyage. It is submitted that the *obiter dictum* of Diplock J would not apply in the case where the deviation from the agreed route for proceeding to port of refuge and the following loss of time are incurred because of a general average act. The type of expenses recoverable under the York-Antwerp Rules, i.e. wages and maintenance of the crew, do not arise after the expiry of the expected duration of the voyage (as was interpreted as 'prolongation' in this decision) yet during the deviation, i.e. during the stay at the port of refuge and on the voyage back to the point where the vessel deviated.

Wages and maintenance expenses arising during repairs other than in general average

7.15 Institute Time Clauses-Hulls 1983 and 1995 cl 16, Institute Voyage Clauses-Hulls 1983 and 1995 cl 14 and the International Hull Clauses 2003 cl 18 provide that except in the case of general average, the insurers will not be liable for wages and maintenance of the master, officers and crew or any member thereof, other than where these expenses are incurred solely in removing the vessel between ports for the repair of a damage covered by the insurers under the policy, or 'for trial trips for such repairs, and then only for such wages and maintenance as are incurred whilst the vessel is under way.' This clause would not exclude for instance additional payments made to the persons enumerated in shifting the vessel for tank cleaning[41] but would leave out wages and maintenance occurred during the repairs of a vessel allowable in general average.

The earlier common law authorities *Robertson v Ewer*[42] and *De Vaux v Salvador*[43] had held that wages and maintenance expenses were considered as a distinct subject matter than the one insured under a hull and machinery policy and therefore were not recoverable. In *Robertson v Ewer*,[44] the claim was to recover the expenses of wages and maintenance occurred during the detention of a ship under an embargo and it was enunciated by Buller J that the wages and provisions were no part of the thing insured under a hull and machinery policy.[45] In *De Vaux v Salvador*[46] where the claim was for expenses of wages and provisions of crew that arose during the detention of the ship for necessary repairs due to a damage resulting from a collision, Lord Denman stated that the sea peril could not be held as the proximate cause of the expenses and that the expenses resulted from delay incident to the damage.[47] The claim was therefore for consequential losses caused by delay not recoverable under the hull policy. *The Medina Princess*[48] where the issue was whether crew wages during repairs could be recoverable as part of the cost of repairs followed these authorities and disallowed recovery also on the additional ground that on the evidence submitted, the crew would not have done

---

41 See the American Hull Clauses 2009, lines 152–157: 'No claim shall be allowed in Particular Average for wages and maintenance of the Master, Officers or Crew, except when incurred solely for the necessary removal of the Vessel from one port to another for average repairs or for trial trips to test average repairs, in which cases wages and maintenance will be allowed only while the Vessel is under way. *This exclusion shall not apply to overtime or similar extraordinary payments to the Master, Officers or Crew incurred in shifting the Vessel for tank cleaning* or repairs or while specifically engaged in these activities, either in port or at sea.' (emphasis added)

42 (1786) 1 Term Rep 127.

43 (1836) 4 Adolphus and Ellis 420.

44 (1786) 1 Term Rep 127.

45 At 132.

46 (1836) 4 A & E 420.

47 At 431–432.

48 *Helmville Ltd v Yorkshire Insurance Company Ltd (The Medina Princess)* [1965] 1 Lloyd's Rep 361, not followed by *Connect Shipping Inc v Sveriges Anfgartygs Assurans Forening (The Swedish Club) ('The Renos')* [2016] 2 Lloyd's Rep 364 on different grounds.

INSURANCE LAW IMPLICATIONS OF DELAY

any work the cost of which could have been recoverable from hull and machinery insurers.[49]

Fuel and stores and port charges occurring in general average

7.16 Fuel and stores consumed during the extra period of detention are allowable in general average if they are incurred in effecting repairs which are themselves admitted in general average.[50] These expenses would include, *inter alia*, fuel consumed for maintaining the cargo carried on board the vessel and fuel for lighting. Like fuel and stores, port charges which are incurred within the extra period of detention are also allowable in general average except where these expenses occur solely as a result of repairs which are not general average repairs.[51] Port charges allowable in general average must be incurred for the common safety and this requirement was expressed in YAR 2016 to the effect that they would 'include all customary or additional expenses incurred for the common safety or to enable a vessel to enter or remain at a port of refuge or call in the circumstances outlined in Rule XI(b)(i)'.[52] Those circumstances are where 'a ship shall have entered or been detained in any port or place in consequence of accident, sacrifice or other extra-ordinary circumstances which render that entry or detention necessary for the common safety, or to enable damage to the ship caused by sacrifice or accident to be repaired, if the repairs were necessary for the safe prosecution of the voyage'.[53] Port charges allowable within this rule would encompass for instance port dues or charges paid for a stand-by tug[54] occurring during the period of repairs.

Fuel and stores and port charges occurring other than in general average

7.17 With respect to certain hull forms, recoverability of fuel and stores and port charges depend on whether they are reasonably incurred for the purpose of landing sick or injured persons or persons saved at sea, or for the purpose of awaiting a substitute for crew. In the former case the Institute Time Clauses Hulls – Port Risks 1987 provide that these expenses are allowed,[55] whereas the latter is excluded.[56]

Institute War and Strikes Clauses Hulls-Voyage and Hulls-Time 1983 provide that 'any claim for expenses arising from delay except such expenses as would

---

49 per Roskill J at 523.
50 YAR 1994 Rule XI(b); YAR 2004 Rule XI(c)(i); YAR 2016 Rule XI(b)(ii).
51 YAR 1994 Rule Rule XI(b); YAR 2004 Rule XI(c)(ii); YAR 2016 Rule XI(b)(iii).
52 YAR 2016 Rule XI(c)(ii).
53 YAR 2016 Rule XI(b)(i).
54 Cornah and Reeder, 11.29.
55 cl 9.2.1.
56 cl 9.3.8.

be recoverable in principle in English law and practice under the York-Antwerp Rules 1974' are not recoverable under the Clauses.[57] A very similar provision is found in the Institute War and Strikes Clauses Hulls-Voyage and Hulls-Time 1995 to the effect that 'any claim for expenses arising from delay except such expenses as would be recoverable in principle in English law and practice under the York-Antwerp Rules 1994' are disallowed.[58] Under both the 1974 and 1994 Rules, loss of or damage to the ship 'through delay'[59] resulting in demurrage is not recoverable in general average; and this type of expense is, *a fortiori*, excluded from the scope of hull and machinery policies. The exclusion in the War and Strikes Clauses must therefore be referring to expenses which can otherwise be indemnified if incurred in general average under the 1974 and 1994 York-Antwerp Rules. Expenses which can properly be characterised as 'expenses arising from delay' could therefore comprise fuel and stores and port charges arising during a period of detention.

Loss of possession and use of the vessel, delay and constructive total loss

7.18 The Marine Insurance Act 1906 provides that there is constructive total loss where the assured is deprived of the possession of his ship by a peril insured against;[60] and deprivation of use is usually caused by perils such as capture and seizure which inevitably contain an element of loss of time. For the purposes of this section attention will be drawn to circumstances whereby delay is part of the chain of causation resulting in the deprivation of use of the vessel.

In *Field Steamship Co v Burr*[61] the ship was insured under a time policy on hull against perils of the seas and all other perils. The vessel was injured by a collision and a hole was knocked in her bottom. Her cargo, through the action of the water and mud which came through the hole became rotten. Following the collision, the vessel was towed to discharge the rest of the cargo however discharge was not allowed because of the condition of the cargo which accordingly had to be discharged elsewhere. Owners claimed for the cost of dealing with the cargo during the delay occurred between the date of the collision and the discharge of the cargo. According to the assured the damage to the ship could not have been repaired unless the cargo was discharged and the cost of discharging the cargo was really part of the cost of repairing sea damage to the ship.[62] A.L. Smith LJ held that 'delay occasioned by discharging cargo is not a deprivation of the use of

---

57 cl 4.4.
58 cl 5.5.
59 Rule C.
60 s 60(2)(i).
61 *Field Steamship Co v Burr* [1899] 1 QB 579.
62 At 581–582.

the hull and machinery to the owner by reason of an injury to the subject-matter insured'.[63] The injury in that case was to the cargo and not to the hull.

7.19 Even if the above is correct, the position might be different where the cargo damages the hull of the vessel. An example was given in the above case[64] for a cargo of cement which encounters perils of the seas, solidifies and is affixed to hull and machinery. Removing the cargo in such a case would inevitably result in delay and consequently deprivation of use of the vessel. This would accordingly give rise to the question of whether the cost of removing the cargo from the hull and the cost arising from such deprivation would be recoverable under a hull policy. This can be answered if it is assessed whether the expense sustained has been incurred as 'owner of the structure of the ship' or as 'carrier'.[65] Expenses arising out of deprivation of use of the vessel are incurred as 'carrier' and for this reason they are excluded from the ambit of the hull policy. The most obvious example of loss occasioned by such deprivation is loss of hire which is not recoverable under hull policies on the ground that it is not a loss or damage to the ship itself. This type of loss can arguably be covered under loss of hire policies which will be discussed in Chapter 8.

7.20 Because there is constructive total loss where the assured is deprived of the use of the vessel by an insured peril, another issue that shall be tackled is how to determine whether the cause of the deprivation of the use of the vessel is perils of the seas or delay. It can be relatively easy to argue that the cause of deprivation of use is delay where perils of the seas causes injury to cargo which have to be discharged, therefore deprivation is an indirect consequence of perils of the seas. Likewise in *Field Steamship Co v Burr* it was held that the real sea damage was to the cargo and the incidental consequence was that the ship could not be used again until the damaged cargo was removed, and therefore it was suggested that the deprivation of use of the vessel was due to the delay and not perils of the seas.[66]

3/4th collision liability clause

7.21 Claims for loss of use arising from delay are subject to different rules in first party and liability claims. The 3/4th collision liability clause provides that the insurers will indemnify the assured for delay to or loss of use of any other vessel in consequence of the collision.[67] In the earlier version of the Insitute Time Clauses

---

63 At 585. Holding this, the mere extra expense of taking the cargo out of the vessel was *a fortiori* not part of this liability for L. Smith LJ.

64 At 587.

65 This difference was raised by reference to the defendants' arguments by Chitty LJ at 588.

66 The reference was made to *De Vaux v Salvador* (1836) 4 A & E 420 where Lord Denman stated that the sea peril in this case cannot be held as the proximate cause of the loss but that the damage results from delay incident to the damage. In this case the claim was for expenses of wages and provisions of crew that arose during the detention of the ship in repairing (necessary repairs) damage resulting from a collision. The claim therefore was for consequential losses caused by delay.

67 Institute Voyage Clauses – Hulls 1983 cl 6.1.2; Institute Time Clauses-Hulls 1983 cl 8.1.2; Institute Time Clauses-Hulls 1995 cl 8.1.2; Institute Voyage Clauses – Hulls 1995 cl 6.1.2; International Hull Clauses 2003 cl 6.1.2.

Hulls dated 22/07/1959 the policy was worded to cover the assured 'in respect of damage done in collision to another ship or vessel *including its demurrage*'.[68] It is however important to distinguish 'demurrage' that is used in the strict legal sense and the term that is used in the general sense. The former would connote 'the agreed amount of damage which is to be paid for the delay of the ship caused by a default of the charterers at either the commencement or end of the voyage'.[69] Accordingly the events where demurrage would arise would be confined to cases where collision occurs while the vessel is loading or discharging[70] or when it occurs when the vessel leaves the loading or discharging port temporarily.[71]

Although the new version of the clause has not yet been interpreted to a comprehensive extent, it would cover claims for loss of use of the vessel that the assured under the hull policy collides with. This loss can be considered as a loss incurred by way of delay resulting from collision and for which the assured of the insured vessel shall be liable by way of damages.

---

68 Emphasis added.

69 *Harris v Jacobs* (1885) 15 QBD 247 per Brett MR at 251.

70 The fact that demurrage goes on running when the loading or discharging is interrupted by collision was mentioned in *Petrinovic & Co Ltd v Mission Française des Transports Maritimes* (1941) 71 Lloyds Law Rep 208 per Atkinson J at 216.

71 *Cantiere Navale Triestina v Handelsvertretung der Russe Soviet Republik Naphtha Export* (1925) 21 Lloyds Law Rep 204 per Atkin LJ at 211.

CHAPTER 8

Loss of charter hire insurance and loss of time

Introduction

8.1 One of the most obvious types of loss that is sought to be excluded by the delay exclusion in s 55(2)(b) is loss of hire (loss of earnings) arising from the loss of use of the vessel which can otherwise be recoverable under loss of hire policies. According to the drafters of the Act, the exclusion rests upon the authority of *Shelbourne v Law*[1] where loss of earnings due to the detention of an insured vessel during repairs necessitated by a collision was not allowed on the ground that it was remote to the hull policy.[2] In this case a 'river insurance policy' that was a time policy covered the assured against 'loss or damage by reason of the collision' of the barges insured and excluded 'loss or damage . . . in respect of the cargo or engagements' of the barges. There was also a clause whereby the insurer had the option to make good the loss or damage instead of paying for it. Two barges collided with a vessel and the assured suffered loss of earnings during delay arising from detention, as well as physical damage to the barges.

The Court accepted the insurer's argument that the loss was not proximate to the injury by collision but was a fact which existed in consequence of the injury and that it was rather proximate to the repairs. The Court further opined that the clause granting the insurers the option to make good the loss could merely refer to the damage to barges and not to loss occasioned by the loss of time. Accordingly the 'claim for damage for loss of time while the barges were detained for repairs', wages and maintenance of the crew were held not to be recoverable under the policy. Kennedy J opined that 'there can be no question that on an ordinary marine policy there would be no right to claim for loss of time, or for the wages and maintenance of the crew'.[3] This judgment emphasises the fact that such losses are caused by delay and are remote to the damage to barges by collision, therefore

---

1 *Shelbourne & Co v Law Investment and Insurance Corporation Ltd* [1898] 2 QB 626.

2 Chalmers and Owen, *A Digest of the Law Relating to Marine Insurance* (1901), 64. The same judgment was given as example also in later editions, see E.R. Hardy Ivamy, *Chalmers' Marine Insurance Act 1906* (9th edn, London: Butterworths 1983), 80; and in E.R. Hardy Ivamy, *Marine Insurance* (3rd edn, London: Butterworths 1979), 257.

3 At 629.

not recoverable under policies covering merely the vessel and not the consequent losses arising from the deprivation of its use.[4]

8.2 Currently loss of time and the resulting loss of charter hire is covered under standard form policies such as the Loss of Charter Hire Insurance Including War (ABS 1/10/83 Wording)[5] and the Loss of Charter Hire Insurance Excluding War (ABS 1/10/83 Wording)[6] which are widely used in the market.[7] Below is an attempt to analyse the relevant clauses of these two Forms and controversial issues which may give rise to disputes in relation to the recoverability of loss of hire and other losses and expenses incurred during delay.

Events triggering the cover under the ABS forms

8.3 Loss of hire may be occasioned by loss of or damage to hull by the perils insured under the hull policies, by delay in delivery of a new-build vessel[8] or by events which do not result in damage to the hull yet merely loss of use of the vessel, such as port congestions. Under the ABS forms, loss of hire is covered where the vessel is prevented from earning hire due to 'a loss, damage or occurrence covered by', *inter alia*,[9] Institute Time Clauses-Hulls (1/10/83) and Institute War and Strikes Clauses Hulls-Time 1/10/1983.[10] Albeit there is room to argue that the word 'occurrence' may allude to wider circumstances than loss or damage to the hull such as a general average act or collision resulting in loss of hire,[11] its exact meaning has not yet been tested in court. 'Occurrence' in the

---

4 Contrast with *Owners of the Steamship Gracie v Owners of the Steamship Argentino (The Argentino)* (1889) 14 App Cas 519 where loss of earnings incurred while a vessel was undergoing necessary repairs were held to be the direct consequence of the collision.

5 Hereinafter referred to as the 'ABS Form Including War'.

6 Hereinafter referred to as the 'ABS Form Excluding War'.

7 See the address of the former Chairman of the Association of Average Adjusters Paul Silver 'Stuck in the Doldrums? A Consideration of whether the ABS Loss of Charter Hire Insurance Wording is still Fit for Purpose', 10 May 2012, available at www.ctplc.com/media/268702/2012-P-Silver-Stuck-in-the-doldrums-A-consideration-of-whether-the-ABS-Loss-of-Charter-Hire-Insurance-wording-is-still-fit-for-purpose.pdf, at p 2 (last accessed, 26 November 2016). For a recent example of a policy written on the ABS Form, see *Sealion Shipping v Valiant Insurance Co (The Toisa Pisces)* [2013] 1 Lloyd's Rep 108 where the dispute arose out of misrepresentation and excess applicable to a period of delay which will be further elaborated in para 7.18 below.

8 See for e.g. the policy in *Hong Kong Borneo Services Co Ltd v Anthony David Pilcher* [1992] 2 Lloyd's Law Rep 293.

9 The ABS Form in cl 1(a) provides 'loss, damage or occurrence covered by Institute Time Clauses – Hulls (1/10/1983) or Norwegian Hull Form or American Institute Hull Clauses (2nd June 1977)'.

10 The ABS Form – Including War cl 1(a) and (b); and the ABS Form – Excluding War cl 1(a) and (b).

11 This was argued in two unpublished papers cited in Silver's address, at p 6, namely by G.D. Kemp in a paper entitled 'Loss of Hire' written in 1963 for the Chartered Insurance Institute and by Geoffrey Hudson in a paper entitled 'Claims on Loss of Earnings Insurances' written in 1978. The former paper discussed the wording then in use 'if in consequence of loss, damage or occurrence covered by I.T.C etc. or Breakdown of Machinery occurring during period of this insurance, the vessel is prevented from earning hire in excess of X days any one accident, this policy will pay . . .'. Kemp argued that 'occurrence' was inserted to cover situations such as a general average deviation to a port

context of the ABS Form other than in cl 1(b) is mainly used along with 'accident'[12] to allude to a cause of the loss or damage rather than the loss or damage itself. It is used in the same context in the Institute Time Clauses-Hulls[13] and in the American Institute Hull Clauses 1977.[14] Therefore it is submitted that the expression should arguably refer either to general average act[15] or to collision resulting in loss of hire which is not otherwise recoverable under the hull clauses.[16]

8.4 Whether the loss of hire should strictly be resulting from a loss of or damage to the hull was discussed in *The Wondrous*[17] in respect of a policy which stated that the policy was only to pay if the vessel was prevented from earning hire in consequences of the risks enumerated in the Institute War and Strikes Clauses Hulls-Time 1983.[18] Accordingly two possible interpretations were available: either the policy would pay where the risks enumerated under the hull policy would result in loss of hire, or where those risks would cause a loss of or damage to vessel in consequence of which loss of hire would be incurred. On the facts of the case the vessel was detained for a year by reason of the failure of the assured to pay the port dues, therefore the vessel was not lost or damaged. In the first instance, Hobhouse J rejected the argument that the reference in a loss of hire policy to 'risks enumerated' in the hull policy did not mean that these risks had to cause 'loss of or damage to the vessel'.[19] This decision was upheld by the Court of Appeal;[20] however it is noteworthy that both of the decisions were delivered upon the construction of the policies there at issue and the Court of Appeal decision cannot be authority for a generic suggestion that loss of or damage to vessel is required for triggering claims under loss of hire policies.

In this respect, the wording under the ABS Form is clearer in terms of the requirement of a loss of or damage to the vessel for triggering the loss of hire cover compared to the wording discussed in *The Wondrous*. The approach adopted by the Court of Appeal that loss of or damage to vessel was germane to a loss of hire

---

of refuge. As cited in Silver, p 6, based on the 1971 wording which was very similar to the ABS Forms 1983, Hudson had given the example of a vessel running aground and being put off-hire for which loss of hire insurers would be liable given the wording 'occurrence', although no damage to the hull was in place.

12 cl 1(b)–cl.8 (deductible clause) – 'any one accident or occurrence'.

13 cl 12 provides 'all such claims arising out of each separate accident or *occurrence* (including claims under Clauses 8, 11 and 13)' (emphasis added).

14 Line 92.

15 cl 11 of the Institute Time Clauses-Hulls 1983.

16 As per cl 8 of the Clauses, the insurers cover 3/4th of the owner's collision liability, however the loss of hire of owners arising from the collision is covered by the Clauses.

17 *Ikerigi Compania Naviera SA v Palmer (The Wondrous)* [1991] 1 Lloyd's Rep 400.

18 The loss of hire policy was subject to the Jardine Glanville Ltd War Loss of Hire Wording No 1 which provided that the policy shall only pay if in consequence of the risks enumerated in the Institute War and Strikes Clauses Hulls-Time 1.10.1983 including London Blocking and Trapping Addendum LPO444 the vessel is prevented from earning hire.

19 See *Ikerigi Compania Naviera SA v Palmer (The Wondrous)* [1991] 1 Lloyd's Rep 400, 416 per Hobhouse J.

20 *Ikerigi Compania Naviera SA v Palmer (The Wondrous)* [1992] 2 Lloyd's Rep 566, at 573, 577.

policy was based on the argument that the policy incorporated the Hull Clauses rather than the Freight Clauses[21] which was, according to the Court, the expression of their intention to limit the loss of hire cover to the circumstances of loss of or damage to the vessel. Albeit the risks enumerated under both Clauses are fairly similar – if not identical – incorporation of the Freight Clauses would run the risk of the loss of hire claims being excluded by the loss of time clause[22] if it could be contended that the incorporation encompassed not only risks enumerated but also the exclusions.[23] In *The Wondrous*, it was submitted that the risks enumerated referred merely to the perils 'in consequence of which' the vessel was prevented from earning hire, and loss of time being merely the consequence of those perils could not be included in the 'risks enumerated'.

8.5 A large number of circumstances may give rise to loss of time without any damage to vessel, such as time lost during surveys following a stranding where the vessel is not damaged, loss of time due to a congestion or strike in port, loss of time as a consequence of removing a damaged cargo, as a consequence of an event that is allowed in general average[24] and time lost in consequence of death or illness on board. Therefore restricting the cover for loss of hire merely to incidents resulting in loss of or damage to hull would leave out a considerable number of loss of hire claims unrecoverable.[25] Removal of damaged cargo shall be elaborated under the next heading given its relevance to hull insurance and common law origin.

Loss of time in removing cargo and consequent loss of hire

8.6 The ABS Form provides that loss of hire is covered if it is incurred following loss, damage or occurrence covered by Institute Time Clauses-Hulls 1983. This would first of all exclude any loss of hire incurred due to the time lost in discharging cargo damaged where the peril causes no damage to the hull of the vessel.[26] However if damage to the vessel is caused both by the operation of one of

---

21 *Ikerigi Compania Naviera SA v Palmer (The Wondrous)* [1992] 2 Lloyd's Rep 566, 573.

22 Institute Time Clauses Freight 1/10/1983 cl 14. This clause is discussed in Chapter 5.

23 It was decided that the 'risks enumerated' included both the covered perils and exclusions in the incorporated text, *Ikerigi Compania Naviera SA v Palmer (The Wondrous)* [1991] 1 Lloyd's Rep 400, 416 per Hobhouse J.

24 Loss of hire arising from loss of time consequent on these enumerated risks are recoverable under The Nordic Marine Insurance Plan of 2013 Version 2016, Chapter 16, Loss of hire insurance, cl 16–1.

25 cl 10 of the ABS Form provides that the policy is automatically cancelled if the vessel insured under the Form is sold or is unchartered. The Form is therefore charter contingent. However, even a policy is made on 'chartered or unchartered' terms, the assured's loss of earning must be caused by the loss of or damage to the vessel and not by the fact that the vessel would have been out of the market anyway, *Cepheus Shipping Corporation v Guardian Royal Exchange (The Capricorn)* [1995] 1 Lloyd's Rep 622. In this case a vessel sustained a generator damage and was laid up in the close season, it was decided that the loss was caused because of the close season and not because of the damage to the vessel and consequent repairs.

26 See *Field Steamship Co v Burr* [1899] 1 QB 579 where the policy was on hull and machinery for an example where the casualty damaged the cargo and not the hull of the vessel. The vessel was

INSURANCE LAW IMPLICATIONS OF DELAY

the perils insured under the Institute Time Clauses-Hulls 1983 and of the damage to cargo, loss of hire whilst removing damaged cargo can arguably be recoverable. The most obvious example would be where a cargo of cement which encounters perils of the seas, solidifies and is affixed to hull and machinery.[27]

'Expenses arising from delay'

8.7 The ABS Form – Including War 1983 provides that expenses arising from delay except such expenses as would be recoverable in principle in English law and practice under the York-Antwerp Rules 1974 are excluded from the scope of cover.[28] It shall accordingly be discussed below firstly the type of expenses which are susceptible of being excluded by this wording and secondly the circumstances giving rise to general average expenses which are recoverable under the ABS Form.

Loss of hire arising during general average repairs – expense arising from delay?

8.8 In the average adjusting practice, where the vessel is on time charter at the time of the average loss, the time charter hire does not contribute to general average.[29] The legal equivalent of this rule emanates from a set of common law authorities and has also been expressly regulated under the York-Antwerp Rules. Albeit the common law authorities seem to have established the law quite clearly, the application of some of these authorities to loss of hire policies is controversial given that they were decided with respect to claims arising under hull and machinery policies whereby loss of hire as a consequential loss to the loss of or damage to the vessel is by nature excluded thereunder. It was accordingly not surprising that loss of hire arising during general average repairs was held not recoverable in general average. A further analysis of the authorities and the York-Antwerp Rules 1974 shall shed light to the application of these authorities to loss of hire policies written in the ABS form.

8.9 In *The Leitrim*[30] the vessel was under a time charter which included a clause stating that the hire should cease in case of damage preventing the working of the vessel for more than 24 hours. The general average act in this case was the pouring of water into the hold where the cargo was stored so as to save the

---

injured by a collision and a hole was knocked in her bottom. Her cargo, cotton seed, had become rotten through the action of the water and mud which came through the hole.

This type of loss is expressly recoverable under The Nordic Marine Insurance Plan of 2013 Version 2016, Chapter 16, cl. 16(2)(c).

27 *Field Steamship Co v Burr* [1899] 1 QB 579, at 587.

28 cl 13.3.

29 Rule B26 of the Rules of Practice of the Association of Average Adjusters 1980 (as amended in 2015).

30 *The Leitrim* [1902] P 256. This case was decided under the 1890 York-Antwerp Rules which did not contain any provision similar to Rule C of the 1974, 1994, 2004 and 2016 versions of the Rules.

ship and cargo from destruction. The vessel had delayed at a port of refuge while undergoing repairs for the water damage and one of the main issues was whether the loss of hire was due to the general average act or due to the off-hire clause in the charterparty. It was decided that recovery of the loss of hire incurred during general average repairs should not be allowed as general average expense on mainly two grounds: that the loss of time is common to all the parties interested so that the damages by delay may be considered proportionate to the interests of the parties and may be disregarded; that were these losses to be calculated, there would have been difficulties in ascertaining the exact amount of loss on each of the interests as losses arising from delay would have been estimated and speculative.[31]

It is noteworthy that the loss of time incurred by the shipowner was not merely due to repairs, yet also due to the act of extinguishing the fire on board and the removal of the cargo for repairs to the hull, i.e. loss of time or delay was part of the general average act and had occurred during the currency of the common adventure. It may be necessary to draw a distinction between loss of time and loss of hire in this respect on the ground that not every loss of time could amount to loss of hire as the latter would also depend on the wording of the off-hire clause in the time charter. In the example of *The Leitrim*, the loss of time in extinguishing the fire on board could not have amounted to loss of hire if the off-hire clause in the charterparty had not extended to cover situations of the like. Accordingly the main issue in that case was whether the shipowner was entitled to some compensation in general average for the delay caused by the sacrifice, as opposed to whether he was entitled to recover the particular consequences of delay. This was on the ground that if losses due to delay had to be calculated it would cause inconvenience to the other interested parties because loss of hire is an accidental circumstance peculiar to the shipowner and charterer arising from the terms of their contract.[32]

8.10 This decision was followed later on in *Wetherall v The London Assurance*[33] where a claim was made under a hull and machinery policy for loss of use of the vessel damaged by a general average act and repaired after the termination of the adventure. The claim was disallowed by the Court, however in this case the dispute had turned on the recoverability of the loss incurred not during delay 'on the voyage' yet during delay subsequent to the termination of the voyage. The 'voyage' referred to was the voyage in which all interests were concerned, i.e. the common adventure. The Court opined that if under the common law loss of hire during delay on the voyage was not recoverable in general average, loss of hire during delay subsequent to the termination of the voyage would *a fortiori* be disallowed.[34] This reasoning is tenable given that where the common adventure

---

31 At 269.

32 *The Leitrim* [1902] P 256, at 265.

33 [1931] 2 KB 448.

34 As far as YAR 1994, 2004 and 2016 are concerned, Rule C § 3 and YAR 1974 Rule C refers to delay 'on the voyage or subsequently'; accordingly this paragraph could exclude a claim for a loss incurred after the termination of the voyage.

terminates, any loss arising subsequent to the termination cannot be determined as general average loss, yet could be considered as particular average loss. Nevertheless given that the policy at issue in this case was a hull and machinery policy to which loss of hire is a consequential loss, it is submitted that it cannot be authority for loss of hire policies.

8.11 Albeit the common law authorities are clear as to the disallowance of such losses in general average, doubt was cast in one particular occasion in an *obiter dictum*. It was stated in *Anglo-Argentine Live Stock Agency v Temperley Shipping Co*:[35]

> 'Everyone concerned in the adventure suffers damage by the delay at the port of refuge. Each cargo-owner is delayed in the use or the sale of his goods. The freight-owner is delayed in getting payment of his freight, and *the shipowner is deprived of the use of his ship*. Yet none of these cases afford the foundation of any claim in general average according to our common law. Perhaps it is desirable that they should; and when the York-Antwerp Rules are by contract made applicable, some of them do form the subject of contribution. But the common law is clear . . .'[36]

This decision was made against the background of the York-Antwerp Rules 1890 where a clause similar to the current Rule C § 3 did not exist.

The below subsections shall discuss the grounds upon which the above mentioned decisions were made.

(a) 'Loss of time is proportionate to the interests of the parties'

8.12 In *The Leitrim*,[37] one of the reasons for the disallowance of loss of hire in general average was because it was submitted that in cases like the one in *The Leitrim*, the damages by loss of time could be considered proportionate to the respective interests and be disregarded.[38] The Court had recognised that there might be situations where loss of time is not common to all concerned and this could give rise to the question of whether in such a case damages by loss of time could not be set off and disregarded. By way of example, there may be some loss of time at the port of refuge arising from repairs and although the shipowner may incur loss of hire, the assureds under a cargo policy insuring the goods on board such vessel may not incur any loss where the goods are still marketable. Moreover, even if all the interested parties suffer losses, it is controversial whether these losses can be proportionate to the interests and be set off in all circumstances.

It was submitted by *Lowndes* that the proportion of the loss of interest during delay to the cost of the goods would most of the time bear the same proportion as the one of the loss of hire to the value of the ship[39] which appears to have been

---

35 [1899] 2 QB 403.

36 at 412.

37 [1902] P 256.

38 at 268–269.

39 Rudolf Lowndes, *The Law of General Average: English and Foreign* (4th edn, Stevens and Sons 1888), 242.

recognised in *The Leitrim*. Some thoughts can be expressed with respect to this submission. Firstly, it is not controversial that in both cases there is a deprivation of use during delay: in the former case deprivation of use of the cargo and in the latter case deprivation of use of the ship. Nevertheless, it can be argued that in assessing the proportion in the latter case, the efficiently working state of the ship rather than the value of the ship shall be taken as the basis for the interest of the shipowner. This is given that although the value of the cargo is indispensable in assessing the loss of the cargo interest in case of deprivation of use of the cargo, the value of the ship could have been relevant in assessing the loss of the ship-owner as to the cost of repairs, and not as to the loss of hire. Secondly, the loss of time may not necessarily be proportionate to the interests in situations where, for instance, on the second day of a delay the cargo loses its entire market (this may occur particularly for goods that require prompt delivery) whereas the shipowner incurs a loss of hire merely for two days or less, depending on the wording of the off-hire clause. For these reasons, it is submitted that the argument resting upon proportionate losses during delay shall be approached cautiously.

(b) 'Delay is not a direct consequence of general average act'

8.13 Another ground upon which loss of hire during delay was not allowed in general average is that it is not accepted as a direct consequence of the general average act.[40] Under the Marine Insurance Act 1906 and the York-Antwerp Rules the loss ought to be a loss that is the direct consequence of the general average act so as to be recoverable in general average.[41] Directness was assessed with reference to mainly two tests; one based on the foreseeability of the loss by the master at the time of the general average sacrifice,[42] and the other based on the existence of subsequent accidents to the general average act breaking the chain of causation between the act and the loss.[43] Both of these tests were applied with approval in

---

40 Argued in *Wetherall v The London Assurance* [1931] 2 KB 448.

41 MIA s 66 provides: 'A general average loss is a loss caused by or directly consequential on a general average act.' See also YAR 1974 and 1994 Rule C; YAR 2004 and 2016 Rule C § 1: 'Only such losses, damages or expenses which are the direct consequence of the general average act shall be allowed as general average'.

42 This test was established by Lowndes in *The Law of General Average: English and Foreign* (4th edn) at para 36 in the following passage: 'We have to determine quod pro omnibus datum est, and since giving must always imply an intention to give, what we have here to ascertain must be what loss at once has in fact occurred, and likewise must be regarded as the natural and reasonable result of the act of sacrifice? Or in other words, what the shipmaster would naturally or might reasonably have intended to give for all when he resolved upon the act? If then upon the act of sacrifice any loss ensues, which the master did not in fact bring before his mind at the time of making the sacrifice, it would have to be considered whether it were such a loss as he naturally might or reasonably ought to have taken account of.'

43 It was cited in *Anglo-Argentine Live Stock Agency v Temperley Shipping Co* [1899] 2 QB 403 at 410, 'Ulrich, in his Grosse-Haverei, p. 5, says: "General average comprises not only the damage purposely done to ship and cargo, but also (1.) all damage or expense which was to be foreseen as the natural (imme-diate) consequence of the first sacrifice, since this unmistakably forms part of that which was given for the common safety; (2.) all damage or expense which, though not to be foreseen, stands to the sacrifice in the relation of effect to cause, or in other words was its necessary consequence. Not so, however, those losses

earlier cases.[44] It is not very clear whether they should be applied together, and it is submitted that their application to circumstances involving loss of hire the calculation of which depends on a time element may have fairly different and irreconcilable results. The latter test was most recently rejected and the former test was applied in assessing whether an accident following the general average broke the chain of causation,[45] this section shall therefore focus mainly on the application of the former test to situations involving delay.

8.14 According to the foreseeability test, an event does not break the chain of causation where the claimant, when he does the general average act, ought reasonably to have foreseen that a subsequent loss of the kind might occur or even that there was a distinct possibility of it.[46] The test is therefore mostly known as the 'reasonable foreseeability test'. Should this test be applied to situations involving general average repairs during which the owner incurs some loss of time, one of the questions that could arise would accordingly be whether a master could reasonably foresee that loss of hire would occur when he does the general average act, for instance where he deviates from the usual route for proceeding to a port of refuge.

Delay is usually foreseeable where a general average act occurs, for delay is almost always preceded by other events. In this respect delay may be considered as an event not breaking the chain of causation and losses resulting from delay may therefore be taken as direct consequences of the general average act according to the foreseeability test. However losses by delay were not allowed in general average by an express provision under YAR 1924 which provided 'damage or loss sustained by the ship or cargo through delay on the voyage, and indirect loss from the same cause, such as demurrage and loss of market, shall not be admitted as general average', which has subsequently been amended to reflect the current Rule C § 3. Direct and indirect losses incurred by delay are therefore disallowed according to this wording.

Loss of market and demurrage used to be considered as indirect losses to the general average act resulting from delay in earlier versions of the York-Antwerp Rules such as YAR 1924[47] and this was given the approach to loss of market at the

---

or expenses which, though they would not have occurred but for the sacrifice, yet likewise would not have occurred but for some subsequent accident."'

44 *Anglo-Argentine Live Stock Agency v Temperley Shipping Co* [1899] 2 QB 403, at 410, that the master knew or ought reasonably to have known that the general average sacrifice could result in the losses incurred (Lowndes test); and that the loss or damage was the necessary consequence of the general average act (Ulrich test). Likewise in *Austin Friars Steamship Co Ltd v Spillers & Bakers Ltd* [1914] 1 KB 833 where the master had decided to put into a port of refuge yet the vessel had struck the pier, Bailhache J applied first the foreseeability test and decided that what in fact occurred (damage to pier and liability to third parties arising by damaging the pier) was in contemplation of the master. In relation to the subsequent accident test, he enunciated that the collision with the pier was a foreseen result and not the result of a subsequent accident.

45 *Australian Coastal Shipping v Green* [1971] 1 QB 456, 482 per Lord Denning MR.

46 ibid.

47 e.g. Rule C of York-Antwerp Rules 1924 provided: 'Damage or loss sustained by the ship or cargo through delay on the voyage, and indirect loss from the same cause, such as demurrage and loss of market, shall not be admitted as general average'.

time.[48] Later on, loss of market was regarded as a direct loss under English law;[49] however Rule C of the latter versions of the York-Antwerp Rules, including YAR 1974, excluded loss of market and demurrage in their own right.

8.15 Whereas loss of hire during general average repairs would not be allowed in general average given the express provision in Rule C of the York-Antwerp Rules 1974 as to demurrage,[50] it is submitted that the exclusion in the ABS Form 1983 for expenses arising from delay, except those allowed in general average under YAR 1974 does not expand to loss of hire arising during general average repairs. The first ground for this submission rests upon the fact that the ABS Form uses the words 'loss', 'damage' and 'expense' separately in other clauses[51] and therefore 'expenses arising from delay' shall not include loss of hire. The second ground is that excluding loss of hire arising during general average repairs would not be compatible with the scope of cover of a policy which provides cover for loss of hire. The fact that loss of hire is calculated on a time basis shall not necessarily denote that it is caused through delay or loss of time. Arguing that loss of hire is not recoverable according to the ABS Form's delay exclusion could arguably be diametrically opposite to the very nature of the Form and would render the delay exclusion obsolete: a policy providing cover for a loss that is calculated on time basis would be struck out by the delay exclusion on the ground that common law authorities did not allow loss of hire incurred during average repairs to be recoverable in general average.

Given the express wording in the York-Antwerp Rules 1974 as to wages and maintenance expenses at the port of refuge, these expenses could be recoverable in general average and would not be struck out by the delay exclusion in the ABS Form. Expenses such as port dues payable during general average repairs in port, or wages and maintenance payable during such repairs would also be covered under the Form unless they are incurred other than in general average.

8.16 Another consideration can be that delay following deviation to the port of refuge can be the general average act itself.[52] Delaying the voyage in order not to enter a port in danger and losses resulting therefrom[53] may well be regarded as the direct consequence of the general average act, which is the decision to delay the voyage for the common safety. This loss could be considered as within the meaning of the Rule C § 1[54] and it is not clear whether Rule C § 3 excludes merely losses by delay as a consequence of the general average act or whether it

---

48 It was enunciated in *Australian Coastal Shipping v Green* [1971] 1 QB 456 at 481 per Lord Denning MR that the Rule C on delay had followed the authority in *The Parana* (1877) 2 PD 118.

49 *Australian Coastal Shipping v Green* [1971] 1 QB 456 at 481 per Lord Denning MR referring to *Czarnikow (C.) Ltd v Koufos* [1969] 1 AC 350, 385, per Lord Reid.

50 See also YAR 1994, 2004 and 2016 to the same effect.

51 See cl 13.1.

52 See York-Antwerp Rules Rule A for the definition of general average act.

53 'Wages and maintenance of crew' during the 'prolongation of the voyage' when entering a port of refuge is admissible in general average by virtue of Rule XI (a).

54 It provides: 'Only such losses, damages or expenses which are the direct consequence of the general average act shall be allowed as general average'.

also excludes delay being the general average act itself. In the context of the ABS Form losses arising from delaying the voyage for not entering a port with danger cannot arguably be recoverable in general average on the ground that the Form requires a loss or damage to the hull of the vessel which results in loss of hire in the absence of which cover may not be available.

Aggregation of losses and delay

8.17 The ABS Forms Including War and Excluding War provide that if the vessel is prevented from earning hire for a period in excess of a certain number of days (deductible) in respect of any one accident the insurers shall pay a daily sum for each 24 hours after the expiration of the number of days stipulated by the parties.[55] Where the vessel is prevented from earning hire on separate occasions, in respect of any one accident or occurrence, the total time that the vessel is off hire shall be taken into account for the purpose of ascertaining the amount that can be claimed under the policy.[56] Certain issues in respect of delay accordingly arise as to the sum recoverable per occurrence.

The number of occurrences would therefore affect the deductible to be paid by the assured per accident. Where for instance because of a collision the vessel's machinery is damaged and failing to properly manoeuvre it is then struck by perils of the seas in consequence of which on site delays occur; if the vessel subsequently collides with another vessel due to the damage caused by perils of the seas and is repaired for damages caused by both accidents, it may be argued on behalf of the assured that there was only one accident for the purposes of the deductible clause. The insurers may in that case have to pay the difference between the sum of the number of days of off hire resulting from both events and the deductible stipulated in the policy.

8.18 Determining the number of occurrences in loss of hire policies and its effect on policy deductibles was acknowledged as being distinct from the determination of the number of occurrences in hull and machinery policies.[57] This view can suggest that albeit the loss of hire is caused by damage to hull or machinery, the fact that three occurrences are treated as separate insured events under the hull and machinery policy cannot necessarily be a ground for considering them as separate occurrences for the purposes of deductibles payable under a loss of hire policy. By way of example, in *Sealion Shipping v Valiant Insurance*[58] the Court

---

55 cl 1(b).

56 cl 8. It is submitted that this clause could operate where the policy itself does not contain any limits; see *Sealion Shipping v Valiant Insurance Co (The Toisa Pisces)* [2013] 1 Lloyd's Rep 108 where the policy had the following limits clause: 'Limited to 30 days each accident or occurrence or series of accidents or occurrences arising out of one event and in all.' It also contained an excess clause providing '14 days any one occurrence, 21 days in respect of machinery claim'.

57 *Sealion Shipping v Valiant Insurance Co (The Toisa Pisces)* [2013] 1 Lloyd's Rep 108, at para 28.

58 *Sealion Shipping v Valiant Insurance Co (The Toisa Pisces)* [2013] 1 Lloyd's Rep 108.

of Appeal approached the issue of determination of the number of occurrences for the purpose of the policy excesses from the point of causation and affirming the first instance decision, ruled that one excess should be payable where one occurrence led to another and the chain of causation was therefore not broken by a *novus actus interveniens*. It is submitted that for only one deductible to be payable under the ABS form, the events must involve both loss of or damage to the vessel or to its components and cause loss of hire; and that they must lead one to another.

Mitigation of losses by the assured and loss of time

8.19 The ABS Form requires the assured to effect, or cause to be effected, all repairs (temporary or permanent) with due diligence and despatch and provides that the insurers have the right to require the assured to incur any expense which would reduce insurers' liability provided that such expense is for insurers' account.[59] The duty to effect all repairs with reasonable or due despatch may at first sight recall the duty of the assured to prosecute the voyage with reasonable despatch in the absence of which insurers are discharged from liability where the delay becomes unreasonable.[60] It is noteworthy however that s 48 duty merely applies to voyage policies as its wording suggests, and not to time policies.

8.20 The ABS Form does not impose upon the assured a general duty to sue and labour of the sort provided for in s 78 of the MIA 1906 or in standard forms such as the Institute Time Clauses Hulls 1983[61] and the Institute Cargo Clauses 2009.[62] The only provision under the Form which comes close to a sue and labour clause whereby the assured is required to mitigate losses is cl 12 which concerns carrying out of repairs with despatch. Even in the event that the clause is admitted as a sue and labour clause, it is far from being clear as to its scope. Section 78(1) of the MIA 1906 recognises the situation where the policy contains a sue and labour clause and provides that the assured is entitled to claim from the insurer the expenses properly incurred to mitigate the loss. The remedy available to the insurer in the event where the assured fails to sue and labour is not entirely clear.[63] Where sue and labour is deemed to be a matter of causation,[64] the assured would not be entitled to claim sue and labour expenses incurred while mitigating the loss

---

59 cl 12.

60 MIA 1906 s 48. This section is dealt with in Chapter 11.

61 cl 13.

62 cl 16.

63 s 78(4) provides that there is a duty to sue and labour however does not mention the consequence of not complying with the duty.

64 In *State of Netherlands v Youell* [1998] 1 Lloyd's Rep 236, Phillips LJ commented that sue and labour was a separate obligation and that therefore insurers could not raise a defence on this ground under the policy. The matter was approached as one of causation whereby the assured would not be able to be covered for a loss which was caused by its own failure to sue and labour, see *Currie & Co v Bombay Native Insurance Co* (1869) LR 3 PC 72; *Ngo Chew Hong Edible Oil Pte v Knight* [1988] 1 SLR 414; *Fudge v Charter Marine Insurance Co Ltd*, 1991, unreported, Newfoundland Supreme Court.

if the loss was caused by its own conduct. Accordingly an assured who induces loss of time following the occurrence of a casualty by not acting with reasonable despatch in notifying the hull insurers of the casualty (and consequently delaying tenders) could be taken to have caused his own loss of hire. The loss of hire arising from his conduct would therefore not be recoverable on the ground of the failure to sue and labour.

8.21 Delay in effecting repairs can be caused by the assured's conduct where he selects a repair yard where repairs can be carried out at a lower cost but which is at a longer distance than a repair yard where repairs can be carried out at a higher cost yet which is at a shorter distance to the casualty. It is noteworthy however that repair yards are usually selected not by the assured, but by hull insurers.[65] Moreover, it is common practice for insurers to receive tenders prior to deciding at which yard the repairs shall be carried out,[66] meaning that further delays may be incurred by assureds which may result in loss of hire under their loss of hire policies. However a term in the hull policy requiring the assured – who is also an assured under a loss of hire policy – to comply with the insurer's decision as to the choice of repair yard would not be binding on the loss of hire insurer unless the loss of hire policy makes express provision in this respect. The assured may therefore run the risk of incurring delays beyond his control while awaiting his hull insurer to decide on the tender, in consequence of which he may breach his duty to sue and labour under his loss of hire policy. The dilemma between a hull insurer who would prefer to keep the repair costs at a minimum and a loss of hire insurer who would require the assured to effect the repairs as quickly as possible has not yet been solved by an express provision under the ABS Form or the Institute Time Clauses- Hulls 1983.[67] It can be submitted however that where the choice of repair yard is not within the control of the assured, the loss of hire

---

65 Institute Time Clauses – Hulls 1983 cl 10.2; International Hull Clauses 2003 cl 44.1.

66 Institute Time Clauses – Hulls 1983 cl.10.3; International Hull Clauses 2003 cl 44.2. Insurers may provide an allowance is made at the rate of 30% per annum on the insured value of the vessel for the time lost between the despatch of the invitations to tender and the acceptance of tender. However this amount covers merely fuel, stores and wages and maintenance of the Master Officers and Crew, including amounts allowed in general average, and any amounts recovered from third parties in respect of damages for detention and/or loss of profit and/or running expenses, see cl 10.3 and cl 44.3 respectively. This allowance does not therefore cover loss of hire of the assured incurred during the negotiations for the tender.

67 See the relevant clauses of the Nordic Marine Insurance Plan of 2013, Version 2016:

Part 2 Hull Insurance, cl.12–12. Choice of repair yard

'The tenders received shall, for the purpose of comparison, be adjusted by the costs of removal being added to the tender amount.

The assured decides which yard shall be used, but the insurer's liability for the costs of repairs and removal is limited to an amount corresponding to the amount that would have been recoverable if the lowest adjusted tender had been accepted, with an addition of 20% p.a. of the agreed insurable hull value for the time the assured saves by not choosing that tender.

If the assured, because of special circumstances, has justifiable reason to object to the repairs being carried out at one of the yards that have submitted tenders, he may demand that the tender from that yard be disregarded.'

insurers may not reject the claim on the ground that the assured failed to sue and labour or that loss of hire incurred during the choice of repair yard was caused by the failure of the assured to sue and labour.

8.22 The last point requiring elaboration is the connection between the exclusion of 'expenses arising from delay' under the ABS Form and s 78(3) of the MIA which provides that expenses incurred in minimising a loss not covered by a policy cannot be claimed as sue and labour expenses.[68] As submitted previously, loss of hire is by nature a loss or expense directly connected to and measured by loss of time and cannot be struck out by a clause excluding expenses caused by delay under a loss of hire policy.[69] The exclusion would therefore not apply to expenses incurred in minimising loss of hire.

Part 3 Other insurances for ocean-going ships, Chapter 16: Loss of hire insurance, cl 16–9 Choice of repair yard
'The insurer may require that tenders for repairs be obtained from repair yards of his choice. If the assured does not obtain such tenders the insurer may do so.

If, due to special circumstances, the assured has reasonable grounds to object to the repairs being carried out by one of the repair yards that has submitted a tender, he may require that the tender from that yard be disregarded.

The assured shall decide which yard is to be used. However, the liability of the insurer shall be limited to the loss of time under the tender that would have resulted in the least loss of time among the tenders for which the assured would have been able to claim compensation under the hull insurance. If the assured chooses this repair yard, the claim shall be settled on the basis of the actual time lost, even if this is greater than that specified in the tender. If the hull insurance has been effected on conditions other than those of the Plan, and these conditions have been accepted in writing by the insurer, the liability of the insurer shall be limited to the loss of time under the tender that would have resulted in the least loss of time plus half of any additional loss of time that may occur.'

68 cl 13.3.
69 See para 15 above.

CHAPTER 9

Implied condition as to the commencement of risk

Introduction

9.1 Section 42 of the MIA 1906 states that in voyage policies insured 'at and from' or 'from' a particular place, there is an implied condition that the adventure shall be commenced within reasonable time, failure of which gives the insurer the right to avoid the contract. The words 'at and from' or 'from a particular place' do not import a warranty or a representation that the vessel is already at the place when the policy is made.[1] The fact that s 42 applies merely to voyage policies rests upon the rationale that delay in the nature of abandoning the voyage or changing the risk undertaken with respect to the voyage initially insured should no longer be binding upon the insurer. Albeit there is a fair number of cases decided prior to the enactment of the MIA, the section has not been much litigated nor has it been the subject of considerable debate following its enactment.

There are mainly three aspects of s 42 which shall be analysed in this chapter namely the implied condition as to the commencement of risk in the period of pre-attachment of risk, pre-contractual non-disclosure of a circumstance which may result in delay at the commencement of the voyage; and insurers' discharge from liability for delay in the post-attachment of risk period, before the commencement of voyage. These aspects and the circumstances which negate the implied condition will be considered in the following parts of this chapter. The chapter generally aims at assessing whether and to what extent the MIA has changed the common law rules so far as s 42 is concerned, at identifying the possible motives behind such a change and at determining whether the wording of the section still allows the implication of certain common law concepts into the provision. The latter assessment will rest upon s 91(2) which provides that the rules of the common law including the law merchant shall continue to apply to marine insurance contracts save in so far as they are inconsistent with the express provisions of the MIA.

---

1 s 42(1). The relevant part of this subsection which states was a codification of *De Wolf v Archangel Maritime* (1874) LR 9 QB 451, 453.

IMPLIED CONDITION

Delay before the risk attaches

9.2 In a voyage policy on ship 'at and from' a particular place, if the vessel is not at the place when the insurance contract is made, the risk attaches as soon as she arrives there in good safety.[2] What is required for the attachment of risk is not merely confined to the vessel arriving at the port of departure,[3] the vessel should arrive at the port and without unreasonable delay. In the leading pre-MIA authority *De Wolf v Archangel Maritime*[4] where the policy was on freight, the ship finally arrived at the departure port however with some delay.[5] There was no representation as to the time of arrival of the ship and it was held that the risk had not attached. There were also several US decisions which held that even if a vessel arrived at the port of departure but stayed there without reference to any particular voyage, the policy attaches only from the time that preparations begin with reference to the voyage insured.[6] Similarly it was held that the risk did not attach where an entirely different voyage was intended although the ship was where the risk was to begin.[7] This would mean the mere arrival at the port without undue delay would not be sufficient for the risk to attach, there would also be the requirement of the vessel being or getting ready for the voyage insured.[8] The delay in commencing the voyage insured would consequently result in the non-attachment of the risk.

It may be submitted that this approach would also be in line with the concept of risk undertaken by the insurer under a voyage policy subject to the MIA, which is a marine adventure involved in a particular voyage of a particular vessel.[9] According to each policy, the particular voyage may have to commence within a given period or on a specific day, in the absence of which and prior to the enactment of the MIA, the common law implied in the policies that the adventure should be commenced in reasonable time *for that particular voyage*. Whether in policies 'at and from' the risk attaches when the ship arrives without unreasonable

---

2 Schedule I to the MIA 1906, r 3(b).

3 As per Schedule I to the MIA 1906, rr 2 and 3.

4 (1874) LR 9 QB 451.

5 See also *Seamans v Loring* (1816) 1 Mason, 128 (Circuit Court, D. Massachusetts) where it was stated that given the delay was not justified, there was a complete non-inception of the voyage insured. Contrast with *Martin v Fishing Ins. Co* (1838) 20 Pick. 389 (Supreme Judicial Court of Massachusetts) where the policy was 'at and from . . ., on the 16th day of July' the court held that the policy attached although there was no evidence that the vessel was at the named port on the specified day.

6 *Synder v Atlantic Mutual Ins. Co* (1884) 95 N.Y. 196, the policy was 'at and from'. For other cases which held that the risk attaches where the ship arrives at the departure port *and* starts preparing for the voyage insured, please see *Lambert v Liddard*, 1 Marsh. R. 149, (1814) 5 Taunt. 480; *Kemble v Bowne*, (1803) 1 Caines, 75 (Supreme Court of New York).

7 *Sellar v M'Vicar* (1804) 1 B & P 23.

8 The concept of 'voyage insured' has to do with the nature and circumstances of the risk undertaken by the insurer and is therefore crucial for the purposes of 'alteration of risk' which shall be dealt with below.

9 Howard Bennett, *Good luck with Warranties*, 594. By virtue of s 3(2)(a), there is a marine adventure where the ship, goods or other moveables are exposed to maritime perils, i.e. to 'perils consequent on, or incidental to, the navigation of the sea' (s 3).

delay *and* terminates where the preparations for the insured voyage are laid aside is important for the purposes of s 42. The section's title is 'implied condition as to commencement of risk', and not 'as to commencement of voyage' and the section arguably relates only to the period until the attachment of risk.[10] The risk attaches where the vessel arrives at the port of departure as per MIA Schedule I, r 3 and the period as to preparations for the insured voyage will be considered as pertaining to the period of post-attachment of risk.

9.3 The fact that the risk has attached in an 'at and from' policy does not necessarily mean that the voyage has started as from that date and that s 48 on delay in voyage may apply. In particular in terms of goods, as transit contemplates their movement from one place to another,[11] s 48 may begin to operate as from the moment where the vessel leaves the port of departure with the goods, or at the very least when the goods are laden on board for the insured adventure and are ready for the transit which is going to start immediately. It is important to note that delay in arriving at the loading port and delay at the loading port should be considered separately in terms of 'at and from' policies.[12] The situation can be briefly described as follows:

i. The voyage to the departure port shall be performed in reasonable time after the contract is made and without unnecessary delay before the risk attaches,

ii. The insured voyage which is usually due to commence after the attachment of risk shall be commenced within reasonable time.

This distinction emanates from Tindal CJ's speech in *Mount v Larkins*[13] where the difference as to delay before and after the risk is attached was made clear. Tindal CJ asked the question of what would be the difference between a delay in the outward voyage and a delay in the departure port and enunciated that the insurer had a right to calculate upon the outward voyage in order that the risk may attach:

'as he has that the voyage insured shall be commenced within a reasonable time after the risk has attached'[14]

and also:

'That an unreasonable delay in commencing the voyage insured against, after the policy has actually attached, discharges the underwriters from the policy appears not only from the thing itself, but from the opinion of Lord Kenyon in *Smith v Surridge* (4 Esp. 25)'.[15]

---

10 This is also supported by the fact that Chalmers, in his book *A Digest of the Law relating to Marine Insurance* (1901) referred merely to the case *De Wolf v Archangel Maritime* (1874) LR 9 QB 451, 453 which was a case on delay at the period of pre-attachment of risk and was with respect to a delay in the voyage to the departure port after the contract was made.

11 In the words of Roskill J in *Sadler Brothers Company v Meredith* [1963] 2 Ll L Rep 293, at 307, transit 'is being in motion'.

12 They were so considered in *Mount v Larkins* (1831) 8 Bing 108, by Tindal CJ.

13 *Mount v Larkins* (1831) 8 Bing 108.

14 At 122.

15 At 120.

IMPLIED CONDITION

This statement may be interpreted as identifying two periods of delay at the commencement of the voyage, i.e. before and after the attachment of risk.

In situation (i), the question is whether the risk has or has not attached, i.e. whether the vessel arrives at the port of departure and in reasonable time to commence the voyage. In situation (ii), where a delay occurs after the ship's arrival to the departure port, given that the risk will have attached, the sole question would be when the delay in commencing the insured voyage becomes unreasonable so that the insurers are discharged from liability. Therefore it may be argued that post-attachment delays which occur prior to the commencement of transit where the ship prepares for the voyage insured should be assessed according to the pre-MIA case law, and not according to the current s 42, the reason being that the section arguably covers only the pre-attachment period.

9.4 In a voyage policy 'from' a particular place, the risk does not attach unless the ship starts on the voyage insured[16] in a fit state and totally ready for that voyage.[17] This would denote that after the vessel sails from the departure port, s 48 would apply for the rest of the voyage, and any delay in sailing from the departure port would be subject to s 42.

Implied condition precedent to the attachment of risk

9.5 The remedy for pre-attachment delay was discussed in the leading case *De Wolf v Archangel*[18] where the court held that in the absence of a representation as to the time of arrival at the departure port, it was an implied understanding that the vessel shall be there within such time that the risk shall not be materially varied and that otherwise the risk does not attach. According to this authority, the subject-matter should arrive at the stated place and without unreasonable delay for the risk to attach.[19] The case was the sole authority referred to by the draftsman of the MIA 1906 Sir MacKenzie Chalmers with respect to the interpretation of s 42(1).[20] It is however a curiosity why the subsection states the remedy of 'avoidance' and not the non-attachment of risk as established by *De Wolf*. This may either rest upon the fact that the avoidance remedy invokes upon the situations where the assured fails to disclose a material circumstance which could amount to delay;[21] or alternatively that it is a term which is used in the sense of discharge from liability, a remedy that was available to insurers prior to the entry into force of the Insurance Act 2015 where a warranty was breached.

---

16 Schedule I to the MIA 1906, r 2.

17 *Pittegrew v Pringle* (1832) 3 B & Ad 514.

18 *De Wolf v Archangel Maritime* (1874) LR 9 QB 451 where delay in arriving to the loading port had altered the risk materially.

19 Representations made as to the time of arrival at the departure port or of sailing will be dealt with in paras 9.7–9.12.

20 MacKenzie Chalmers and Douglas Owen, *Digest of the Law Relating to Marine Insurance* (London: William Clowes and Sons 1901), 52

21 See paras 9.7–9.12.

It is submitted that the decisions of the Court of Appeal[22] and the House of Lords in *The Good Luck*[23] shed light on the controversy as to the latter possibility. The Court of Appeal in their judgment held that a breach of warranty could give the insurer a 'right to avoid' based on, *inter alia*, s 42 and that to read s 33(3) as conferring a right to avoid was not inconsistent with the recognition of waiver in s 34(2), since in s 42 both conditions were found. This analysis was rejected by the House of Lords leaving no room for doubt. According to the Court, the waiver in s 42 was a waiver of the implied condition, and not waiver of the right to avoid as was considered by the Court of Appeal. The waiver prevented any breach or any right to avoid arising at all whereas waiver in s 34(3) was a waiver of a breach of warranty after the breach occurs. This approach, although *obiter*, may be taken to mean that the implied condition in s 42 may not be equated to a warranty.

9.6 In other cases the remedy was not made as explicit as it was in *De Wolf*.[24] In *Bah Lias Tobacco & Rubber Estates, Ltd v Volga Insurance Company Ltd*[25] which involved a policy on cargo, a delay in the shipment of cargo due to war was waived by the insurers when the assured paid extra premium for that period. Delay in the commencement of the risk was qualified as a 'breach of condition', however no remedy was pointed out by the court. In *Hull v Cooper*[26] the initial position of the vessel when the policy was made had not been disclosed and there had been a delay resulting therefrom in the arrival of the vessel to the departure port. The main issue was whether there was a change of risk. The court did not refer specifically to discharge or non-attachment of risk; however it was suggested that the affirmative decision in this case was that a delay not varying the risk did not discharge the insurer.[27] The reasoning in *Hull v Cooper* was applied in *Mount v Larkins*[28] where the difference as to delay before and after the risk is attached was made clear. In this case the vessel had met with bad weather and was driven back to two ports in one of which the master had been building a house. It was held in this case that the insurers were discharged on the ground that the delay at the port of departure where the risk is to attach alters the risk undertaken by the insurer.[29]

---

22 *Bank of Nova Scotia v Hellenic Mutual War Risks Association (Bermuda) Ltd (The Good Luck)* [1990] 1 QB 818.

23 In *Bank of Nova Scotia v Hellenic Mutual War Risks Association (Bermuda) Ltd (The Good Luck)* [1991] 1 AC 233.

24 *De Wolf v Archangel Maritime* (1874) LR 9 QB 451, 453.

25 (1920) 3 Lloyd's List Law Reports 155.

26 (1811) 14 East 479.

27 *De Wolf v Archangel Maritime* (1874) LR 9 QB 451, 453.

28 *Mount v Larkins* (1831) 8 Bing 108.

29 'Upon this special verdict it has been argued before us on the part of Defendant, that the unreasonable and unjustifiable delay on the part of the captain in completing the outward voyage on which he was then engaged, and commencing the homeward voyage on which the risk was intended to attach, discharged the underwriters from this policy; and we are of opinion that such unreasonable and unjustifiable delay on the part of the insured, in commencing the voyage insured against, is in the nature of a deviation, and does amount to such an alteration of the risk insured against, as to discharge the liability of the underwriters upon this policy. That an unreasonable delay in commencing the voyage insured against, after the policy has actually attached, discharges the underwriters from the policy appears not only from the thing itself, but from the opinion of Lord Kenyon in *Smith v Surridge* (4 Esp. 25)' at 120.

Nevertheless this should not be considered as authority for the suggestion that pre-attachment delay discharges insurers, the case is distinguishable from *De Wolf*[30] on the ground that delay in the former was a delay after the risk had attached.

(a) Pre-contractual non-disclosure of circumstances which may result in delay

9.7 The remedy available to insurers where the assured does not commence the voyage in reasonable time as per s 42 is avoidance of the policy. Moreover under the 1906 Act this is an option, meaning that the insurers may or may not elect to do so. Where a loss occurs during the preliminary voyage between the date the policy is made and the attachment of the risk, the insurer would not be liable given that the risk is not yet attached. Determining avoidance of the policy *ab initio* as remedy for that limb of the voyage would not add considerably to the insurers' position. An insurer would be less likely to elect to avoid a policy where he is obviously not liable for a loss occurring before the risk has attached. Identifying a remedy for delay at the commencement of the voyage could mostly be relevant for the part of the voyage after the risk has attached until the vessel sails from the loading port.[31] Besides, the insurers would have to return the premiums earned until the moment the delay became unreasonable on the ground that there would be total failure of consideration[32] and this would not be the most favourable option for insurers who are not yet even liable for the loss.

In Sir MacKenzie Chalmers' work on the draft Bill of the MIA 1906,[33] the avoidance remedy was based on *De Wolf v Archangel Maritime*.[34] It is curious on which basis the remedy of avoidance of contract was inserted in the MIA and a tentative answer may be based, but may not be confined to, on the following points in light of an analysis of earlier case law.

(I) Cases on delay and concealment

9.8 Before the Insurance Act 2015 has entered into force, avoidance of the insurance contract was the only remedy for insurers where the assured had not disclosed a material fact or had made a misrepresentation about the risk.[35] Albeit the relevance of the breach of utmost good faith to delay at the commencement of the risk is not always very obvious, this may however be inferred from several

---

30 A similarity with *Mount v Larkins* can be drawn in *Driscol v Passmore* (1798) 1 B & P 202 although in that case, unlike *Mount v Larkins*, the course of the ship had to be changed by necessity and the insurers were therefore not discharged.

31 Support for this view can be found in *De Wolf v Archangel Maritime* (1874) LR 9 QB 451.

32 As per MIA 1906 s 84.

33 Chalmers and Owen, *Digest of the Law Relating to Marine Insurance* (1901), 52

34 (1874) LR 9 QB 451.

35 s 17 stated that if the utmost good faith be not observed by either the assured or the insurer, the other party may avoid the contract. Likewise, s 18 provided that the insurer may avoid the contract where the assured fails to disclose a material circumstance known to him before the contract is concluded. The remedy of avoidance is still available to insurers under the Insurance Act, albeit it is not the only remedy: see Schedule I.

pre-MIA cases. It is clear from the wording of s 42 that the vessel does not need to be at the loading port at the time when the policy is made, yet the assured needs to ensure that it arrives there within reasonable time. If at the time of the policy, the vessel is at a place other than the loading port, and if the assured, knowing that the vessel would not be at the loading port within a reasonable time conceals this fact from the insurer and does not inform the insurer as to the location of the vessel at the time, this fact could amount to a breach of utmost good faith as it would have constituted a non-disclosure of a material fact.[36]

9.9 This issue was discussed in *Hull v Cooper*[37] which was referred to by *De Wolf* as authority that the assured is not bound to communicate to the insurers the actual location of the ship when the contract is made.[38] *Hull v Cooper* was with respect to a cargo policy whereby the ship was insured at and from a certain place yet was not there at the time of the policy. The possibility that the ship could be delayed for the departure port was not communicated to the insurers who did not call for information on the subject. The question was whether the intervening delay materially varied the risk initially undertaken by the insurers. Arguably, *De Wolf*'s reference to the case is doubtful, given firstly that the ratio of the case was with respect to whether the risk was varied, and secondly that it was a mere example of the confirmation of s 42(1), in that the ship does not have to be in the place where the risk is going to attach at the time of the policy.[39] This would not necessarily mean that the assured does not have to disclose the actual location of the ship if the actual location is likely to cause a delay in the arrival of the ship at the loading port and accordingly in the commencement of risk.

9.10 Even where information is not communicated to the insurers that could potentially result in delay, it is not free from doubt that the pre-contractual avoidance remedy could apply in all circumstances. This may be supported by the fact that as per s 42(2) the implied condition may be negatived if delay was caused by circumstances known to the insurer 'before the contract was concluded'. This echoes s 18(1) and (3)(b) of the MIA[40] which, read in conjunction, may denote that the assured does not have to disclose circumstances known to the insurer which caused delay. The circumstances which do not require disclosure under the Insurance Act 2015 are provided for in s 3(5).

In the authorities prior to the MIA, Tindal CJ admitted in both *Vallance v Dewar*[41] and *Ougier v Jennings*[42] that a delay at the commencement of the risk would discharge the policy if an intermediate voyage was not communicated to the insurers, unless such voyage is made usually and according to the normal

---

36 Materiality was defined in s 18(2) as any circumstance which would influence the judgment of an insurer in fixing the premium or in whether he would accept the risk in the same terms as he did.
37 *Hull v Cooper* (1811) 14 East 479.
38 *De Wolf v Archangel Maritime* (1874) LR 9 QB 451, 456.
39 See the speech of Lord Ellenborough CJ, at 479.
40 s 18 has been omitted by virtue of the Insurance Act 2015.
41 (1808) 1 Camp 503.
42 (1808) 1 Camp 505 (both of these cases were cited in *Mount v Larkins*).

course of trade in which the ship was then engaged. Similarly in *Driscol v Passmore*[43] the representation made by the assured was that the insured voyage would be performed following other voyages which was in fact true, but due to subsequent events the vessel was prevented from so doing. It was held in this case that the representation being true, the subsequent events not happening through misconduct did not discharge the underwriters.

(II) Representations as to the time of sailing

9.11 Representations made by the assured as to the time of sailing may in particular be important in respect of 'from' policies as in this type of policy the risk attaches when the vessel sails from the departure port. Representations may be made by the assured before entering the contract as to some estimation regarding the date the ship would sail, yet this would not necessarily connote that the assured is bound to disclose the exact time and date of sailing.

In *Beckwith v Sydebotham*[44] where the policy was on ship, freight and cargo it was held that the assured did not have to disclose the communication between a master and owner as to the fact that the vessel had to be repaired before her homeward-bound voyage to the departure port and that it would take her longer to take in her cargo and to arrive at the departure port. Imposing a duty on the assured to disclose the time of sailing would entail that each time repairs are needed at the commencement of the voyage to make the ship seaworthy, this fact would also have to be disclosed. Accordingly the view that the insurers should ask the assured as to the date of sailing or should insert a sailing warranty into the policy rather than the assured having to disclose it was favoured.

9.12 If the insurance policy contains a warranty as to the date or the period of sailing of the vessel from the departure port and the vessel is delayed in the voyage thereto whereby the assured breaches the warranty, the insurers would no longer be automatically discharged from liability as from the date of the breach yet would be subject to s 10 of the Insurance Act 2015. The question would accordingly be confined to whether the insurers can also avoid the policy as per s 42 where delay in reaching the port of departure becomes unreasonable.

(b) Delay within and beyond the control of the assured

9.13 Delay within and beyond the control of the assured may have impacts both on the duty of good faith which shall be preserved by the assured in the pre-contractual phase; and on the remedies available to insurers during the period of pre-attachment of risk. As to the former, the materiality of information which relates to a delay at the commencement of the insured voyage could depend upon whether the assured has control over the circumstances resulting in delay. According to s 3(4)(a) of the Insurance Act, the assured is required to disclose every material information known to him or ought to be known by him. The assured shall

---

43 (1798) 1 B & P 202.
44 (1807) 1 Camp 118.

not be required to investigate matters outside his knowledge and the policy not be avoided for his failing to do so. Where the assured expects the vessel to arrive to the port of departure at a given time yet has no control over its arrival and the vessel delays, it would suffice that the assured has made a representation as to the likely arrival date of the vessel in good faith.[45] In *Bowden v Vaughan*[46] a representation was made by the brokers of a cargo owner who informed the brokers that the vessel carrying his goods would sail 'in a few days', although an attack was very much expected that could cause delay. The vessel did not sail until a month after the policy was made and was then stopped during sea transit by the enemy. It was held that the representation of the owner of the goods did not conclude the insurer and that he did not have any control over the time of the ship's sailing.

9.14 Where however there is no representation as to where the ship was when the policy was made, it is not material whether the delay which varies the risk is within or beyond the control of the assured, 'in either case the risk is equally varied'.[47] This may be the reasoning behind the omission of the concept of 'justifiable delay' in s 42,[48] given also that the draftsman's sole reference to an authority for s 42 was to *De Wolf v Archangel.*[49] Two points however need to be made with respect to this suggestion. Firstly, the *De Wolf* case was decided on the facts which were relevant to pre-attachment delay only, therefore the judgment may not be taken as authority for necessary delays occurring in the period of post-attachment of risk. It was submitted by Blackburn J that:

> 'Where the alteration in the course of the voyage after the risk has attached is justified by necessity it does not vary the risk.'[50]

Secondly, the decision could be sensible only with respect to losses arising until the attachment of risk. Whether or not the requirement of commencing the voyage in reasonable time is breached by a circumstance beyond the control of the assured, the losses would not be recoverable by the assured.

(c) Institute Cargo Clauses and s 42

9.15 The Institute Cargo Clauses 2009 do not contain an express clause as to delay at the commencement of the voyage. Although the application of s 42 may seem obsolete in light of the modern market terms on cargo, there is room to argue that it may be implied in so far as it is applicable. If affirmative and unless the avoidance of delay clause[51] unambiguously replaces s 42 the question that follows would be whether it would apply merely before the sea voyage

---

45 Insurance Act s 3(3)(c).
46 (1809) 10 East 416.
47 *De Wolf v Archangel Maritime* (1874) LR 9 QB 451, 456.
48 Hodges, 147. Hodges argues that the statements of Tindal CJ in *Mount v Larkins* as to the fact that necessary delays excused the assured for their breach were rejected in *De Wolf v Archangel.*
49 Chalmers and Owen, *Digest of the Law Relating to Marine Insurance* (1901), 52
50 At 456.
51 cl 18.

148

IMPLIED CONDITION

starts, or before the commencement of the land element.[52] Although the ICC 2009 comprises land elements and the adventure to be prosecuted may not be confined to 'marine adventure', any adventure analogous to a marine adventure is covered by a policy in the form of a marine policy. The provisions of the MIA, *in so far as applicable*, will therefore continue to apply.[53] This may accordingly support the view that the assured should act with reasonable dispatch to commence the land transit without unreasonable delay.

There is currently no authority which suggests that s 42 can apply before the land element of the voyage starts yet an analogy can be drawn from authorities regarding the application of s 48 to policies containing warehouse-to-warehouse or transit clause.[54] In order to draw an analogy between the two sections, the meaning of 'adventure' in s 42 and 'insured adventure' in s 48 need to be analysed. It is submitted that 'adventure' in s 42 is an equivalent of the 'adventure insured' in s 48 given that in some of the post-attachment delay cases the insurers were discharged where the vessel had not commenced the insured adventure in reasonable time because of lengthy repairs[55] and this was held to be a breach of the implied condition.

9.16 For ss 42 and 48 to apply, the policy has to be a voyage policy insuring a 'marine adventure' the definition of which was provided for in the MIA. The definition is not exclusive and includes ships, goods or other movables when they are exposed to maritime perils,[56] i.e. 'the perils consequent on, or incidental to, the navigation of the sea'.[57] The definition may suggest that land risks do not form part of perils incidental to the navigation of the sea and that therefore a voyage policy and accordingly ss 42 and 48 would not apply to the land leg of the voyage. This suggestion was rejected in *Verna Trading Pty Ltd v New India Assurance Co Ltd*[58] so far as the equivalent of s 48 in the Australian MIA 1909 was concerned.

---

52 Under ICC 2009, the risk attaches where the goods are first moved in the warehouse (cl 8) and therefore ICC covers certain risks occurring during land transit as well as sea transit.

53 MIA s 2(2) (emphasis added).

54 In *Verna Trading Pty Ltd v New India Assurance Co Ltd* [1991] VR 129 which was on the interpretation on s 54 of the Australian Marine Insurance Act 1909 which is identical to s 48 of the MIA 1906, was delivered by the Australian Supreme Court of Victoria Appeal Division. It was stated that the land transit element of a policy was covered by the Marine Insurance Act including the provisions which relate to 'voyages' (of which both ss 42 and 48 are parts) on the basis of the textbook of MacKenzie Chalmers, *Marine Insurance Act 1906* 7th edn), 4–5 and of *Leon v Casey* [1932] 2 KB 576, 585–7 per Scrutton LJ and 590 per Greer LJ. It is noteworthy that in *Verna*, the duration of the risk was from 'warehouse to warehouse', and not from shelf to shelf as in the current ICC 2009. Nevertheless it is submitted that this judgment can be authority for the suggestion that the land transit can be covered by the sections of the Marine Insurance Act as to voyage. In *Wiggins Teape Australia Pty Ltd v Baltica Insurance Co Ltd* [1970] 2 NSWR 77, at 78 and 80, Macfarlan J described the policy which incorporated the then conventional transit clause as a 'voyage policy' although the description of voyage policy was not there in issue. This finding is important for the purposes of s 42 as the condition in s 42 is implied only in voyage policies. For the view that s 48 of the MIA is confined to sea voyage, please see Victor Dover, *Analysis of Marine Insurance Clauses*, 19.

55 *Smith v Surridge* (1801) 4 Esp 25; *Motteux v London Ass. Co* 1 Atk 545.

56 s 3(2)(a).

57 s 3(2).

58 [1991] VR 12.

149

However, land risks which are incidental to marine adventure do not prevent a policy from being a policy of marine insurance.[59] Therefore if it can be argued that s 42 applies to land element of the policy, the land transit should also be commenced in reasonable time by virtue of s 42.

9.17 Whereas the above is plausible in respect of the land risks, the analogy between ss 42 and 48 as to their application to land risks is doubtful regarding the following points: distinctively from s 48, s 42 mentions that the adventure should start within reasonable time *although the ship is not at the place* where the adventure is to start. This may seem to import an element only as to the sea leg of the voyage. Moreover in s 42, voyage policy is defined as a policy 'at and from' or 'from' a particular place, namely from a port where the subject-matter insured is exposed essentially to maritime perils. The wording of s 42 therefore suggests that it shall not apply to the entire duration of risk under the Clauses whereby goods are covered 'from shelf to shelf'.[60] This being said, the contrary view was adopted in the *Verna* case in respect of pure voyage policies 'at and from'.

Where the approach in *Verna* is not accepted and the view that the expression of 'marine adventure' applies only to marine risks is adopted, delay at the commencement of the voyage may solely be relevant to the period prior to the commencement of the sea voyage. It would therefore not apply to the land leg of the insured transit whereby by virtue of cl 8.1. the risk attaches where the goods are first moved in the shelves for the commencement of the insured transit.[61] The sea leg of the adventure for goods commences at a later stage when they are laden on the ship. Therefore the policy would attach at an earlier stage according to the express provisions of ICC and the delay in the commencement of the land transit cannot result in the non-attachment of risk.

(I) Avoidance of delay clause and s 42

9.18 Avoidance of delay in cl 18 of the Institute Cargo Clauses 2009 reads that it is a condition of the insurance contract that the assured should act with reasonable dispatch in the circumstances within their control. There is no authority as to whether the clause can apply where the assured causes a delay in the commencement of the voyage before the risk attaches, and if affirmative, whether the clause replaces s 42 in the Institute Cargo Clauses. Avoidance of delay clause was analysed in Chapter 10[62] and it was submitted that it was usually considered by judicial authorities as a warranty.[63] It is yet to be seen how English courts will approach the remedy available to insurers where the clause is breached.

---

59 MIA 1906 s 2 reads that a contract of marine insurance may be extended so as to protect the assured against losses on any land risk which may be incidental to any sea voyage.

60 The contrary view was adopted in *Verna* case in respect of pure voyage policies 'at and from'.

61 This is a change to the classical attachment of risk in goods, whereby the risk does not attach until the goods are on board the ship, MIA 1906 Schedule 1, r 4.

62 In paras 10.59–10.77.

63 *Wiggins Teape Australia Pty Ltd v Baltica Insurance Co Ltd* [1970] 2 NSWR 77; *Ostra Insurance Public Company Ltd v Kintex Shareholding Company (M/V Szechuen)* [2004] EWHC 357 (Comm) (*obiter*).

IMPLIED CONDITION

Other standard market terms and s 42

9.19 Standard market terms on hulls do not contain a specific clause about delay at the commencement of the voyage[64] which is probably due to the fact that most hull policies are nowadays made on time and not voyage basis. However the position of War and Strikes Clauses on Hulls presents a certain degree of ambiguity.[65] The wording of the relevant clauses contains similarities to some standard market terms on freight which mention an automatic termination prior to the attachment of risk[66] in which case the insurers do not come on risk. This would mean that in case a war breaks out or requisition occurs prior to or following the attachment of risk, there may be automatic termination resulting therefrom. It would follow that a delay induced by the outbreak of war or any other peril enumerated under the relevant clause would not have any impact on the policy on the ground that the insurance will have already terminated. The rather doubtful issue is whether the insurer can cancel the policy[67] where there is delay prior to the attachment of risk and where delay does not result from the enumerated perils in the clause. If affirmative, the remedy of avoidance expressed in s 42 shall not apply. This suggestion presumes that avoidance of the policy and cancellation of the policy are different remedies, the former having effect *ab initio* and the latter having effect as from the date of cancellation.

Negating the implied condition

9.20 The circumstances which are capable of excusing a breach of s 42 are expressly stated in s 42(2). There is controversy and no case law as regards whether the subsection is confined merely to waiver and circumstances known to the insurer before the contract was concluded, or whether it could also include the aspect of usage of trade as an excuse for the breach. The subsection was altogether the subject of doubt expressed by Chalmers and Owen as according to their opinion the proposition in the subsection appeared to be unsettled law.[68] This part of the chapter will first provide analysis on s 42(2) and then seek to clarify the position of usage of trade as a possible excuse for the breach of the implied condition.

(a) Waiver by the insurer

9.21 The second part of s 42(2) states that the implied condition may be negatived by showing that the insurer waived the condition. The first part of the

---

64 Institute Voyage Clauses-Hulls 1983 and International Hull Clauses 2003.

65 Institute War and Strikes Clauses-Hulls-Voyage 1983 and 1995, cl 5 and cl 6.

66 Institute War and Strikes Clauses-Freight-Voyage 1995 cl 5, which is equivalent to Institute War and Strikes Clauses-Hulls-Voyage 1983 and 1995 cl 5 and cl 6.

67 As per cl 5.1.

68 Their work *A Digest of the Law Relating to Marine Insurance*, p v provided that the sections and sub-sections of the Bill as appeared in the work which contain square brackets are areas where the law is unsettled. Section 42(2) was one of the sub-sections put in square brackets.

sentence enunciates that the option to negative is available *before the contract was concluded*, the assured can accordingly prove that the insurer waived the delay before the contract was made by a representation or by stipulating a clause in the policy prevailing over the implied condition. The meaning of '*or by showing that he waived the condition*' is however not clear. It arguably enables the assured to prove that the insurer waived the condition after the contract was made and after finding out about the breach of the implied condition.[69] The Marine Insurance Bill was drafted slightly differently than the current subsection and read:

> 'The implied condition may be negatived by showing that the delay was caused by circumstances known to the insurer before the contract was made, or by showing that he *acquiesced in the delay*' (emphasis added)

The italicised part is distinct from the current version of the section in that the waiver of an implied condition (and not the waiver of the delay) is not necessarily equivalent to acquiescing in the delay, where the latter would presumably refer only to post-delay waiver.

9.22 The second part of the current s 42(2) may allude the waiver of an implied warranty[70] particularly because the predecessor of what was MIA s 33(3)[71] contained the term 'avoidance' for breach of warranty instead of 'discharge'.[72] However it is submitted that it cannot be treated so for several reasons. The option of avoidance granted to the insurer under s 42(2) would mean that the contract would remain in full force and effect until the insurer elects to avoid. The waiver of the implied condition in s 42, when considered in the context of the right to avoid could be read such that if the insurer waives the condition, the right to avoid the contract following the breach of the implied condition would not arise altogether. Another reason why the term 'waiver' in s 42(2) may not be considered as referring to a breach of warranty is that while s 34(3)[73] mentioned the *waiver of breach* of warranty, s 42(2) is about *waiver of the implied condition*, i.e. not about the waiver of the 'breach' of it. This may accordingly rather suggest that the waiver could operate after the delay occurs. In the sole case which was decided on waiver after the enactment of the MIA, the insurer by accepting extra premium for the lengthy delay after it occurred was taken to have waived the 'condition'. In *Bah Lias v Volga Insurance*[74] the insurance was taken out against fire including fire antecedent to the shipment under a voyage policy on cargo 'at and from'. There

---

69 This was the situation in *Bah Lias Tobacco & Rubber Estates, Ltd v Volga Insurance Company Ltd* (1920) 3 Lloyd's List Law Rep 155.

70 Under the US law, the waiver was considered as a waiver of implied warranty; Phillips, s 602, Buglass, *Marine Insurance and General Average in the United States*, 47.

71 The second part of the subsection has been repealed by the Insurance Act 2015.

72 The second sentence of s 33(3) read: 'If it be not so complied with, the insurer may avoid the contract as from the date of the breach of warranty, but without prejudice to any liability incurred by him before such date.'

73 The section has been repealed by the Insurance Act 2015.

74 *Bah Lias Tobacco & Rubber Estates, Ltd v Volga Insurance Company Ltd* (1920) 3 Lloyd's List Law Rep 155.

was a shortage of shipping of the cargo as a result of the war. A fire occurred on board the vessel one year after the policy of insurance was made and part of the cargo was accordingly lost. Notice of loss was given to the insurers and increased premium had been paid in respect of the delay during the two months in which the loss had occurred. It was held that the insurers had waived the breach of the condition in accepting the premium.

9.23 It was stated obiter in the House of Lords decision *The Good Luck*[75] that the waiver in s 42 was a waiver of the implied condition, and not waiver of the right to avoid. The waiver prevented any breach or any right to avoid from arising whereas the waiver in s 34(3) was a waiver of a breach of warranty after it occurs. The view expressed in *The Good Luck* by the House of Lords confines the waiver of the implied condition to the period before the delay becomes unreasonable.

(b) Circumstances known to the insurer

9.24 Section 42(2) reads that the implied condition may be negatived by showing that the delay was caused by circumstances known to the insurer before the contract was made. Prior to the enactment of the MIA 1906, this issue was discussed in *De Wolf v Archangel*[76] in two different instances. The first instance related to the statement that the delay may be excused on the ground that it is necessary where the insurer is aware of the event which caused the delay.[77] This does not form part of the ratio in *De Wolf* as the necessity of delay was not discussed, nor was there an issue about whether the insurers knew about the preliminary voyage. Nevertheless s 42(2) may have arguably settled this point. The second relates to two views previously expressed by Phillips[78] and they were mentioned in *De Wolf* as follows:

- That there is an implied understanding that the risk is to commence in reasonable time so that it shall not be varied unless the policy contains an express provision in this respect,[79] and
- That a representation, although not embodied in the policy may qualify or rebut the implied understanding.[80]

Firstly what needs to be distinguished is what type of representation may qualify or rebut the implied condition. According to Phillips:

'if the assured, prior to effecting the policy, discloses a fact, or an intention to do any act, not inconsistent with the express provisions of the policy, but which, if not

---

75 In *Bank of Nova Scotia v Hellenic Mutual War Risks Association (Bermuda) Ltd (The Good Luck)* [1991] 1 AC 233.

76 *De Wolf v Archangel Maritime* (1874) LR 9 QB 451.

77 The Court in *De Wolf* referred to *Mount v Larkins* (1831) 8 Bing 123 at p 455 where it was stated that the preliminary voyage in that case was in the knowledge of the insurers although the report did not give a specific information in that respect. The Court in *De Wolf* thought it was scarcely possible that it should be otherwise.

78 Phillips, *Treatise on the Law of Insurance,* ss 602, 690.

79 *De Wolf v Archangel Maritime* (1874) LR 9 QB 451, 457.

80 *De Wolf v Archangel Maritime* (1874) LR 9 QB 451, 457.

disclosed, would be a violation of a warranty implied by the fact of making the insurance, but not by the obvious and necessary construction of the language of the policy, the underwriters are bound by such representation, and the policy is valid notwithstanding such fact or the execution of such intention. . .'.[81]

The example given by Phillips for such representation was a representation of an intention to vary from usage. The reasoning upon which the statement was based was that usage of trade and implied warranties constituted part of the contract and preliminary and simultaneous statements could be introduced as intention of the parties. The consequence is that if the assured states a material fact which might have an effect on the breach of the implied condition as to the commencement of the voyage, the implied condition will be qualified by the representation.

9.25 As to representations about the location of the vessel when the contract is made, the *De Wolf* case referred to *Hull v Cooper*[82] as authority that the assured is not bound to communicate the location of the vessel to the insurer.[83] The reason for this was that the risk is not to attach unless the vessel arrives at the port of departure within reasonable time, therefore to be aware of the location of the vessel at the time of the contract is not material to the insurer. Conversely, it was stated that if the time when the risk is to attach might be indefinitely delayed by circumstances affecting the passage to the departure port from the place where the vessel was, to know the location of the vessel at the time of the contract would be material to the insurer. This aspect of *De Wolf* must be approached cautiously. Firstly because if *Hull v Cooper* can be authority with respect to materiality of representations of the assured, it can only be authority for representations as to the location of the vessel at the time the contract is made. There may be several other circumstances which may exist before the contract is made, and which may result in delay after the policy is made. Secondly, the policy in that case was a policy on goods, whereby the assured may not be expected to make representations as to the location of the vessel when the insurance policy is made given that either it may not be known to him, or that it may not have control over the timely prosecution of the voyage to the departure port.

Whether a representation needs to be made by the assured should be determined according to the materiality of the representation.[84] Except for the usage of trade which is a situation known or presumed to be known by the insurer,[85] other circumstances which may amount to delay may have to be disclosed to the insurer as they would be material; and if disclosed they would qualify the implied term.

---

81 Phillips, s 602.

82 *Hull v Cooper* (1811) 14 East 475.

83 At 456.

84 MIA s 18(2) has been repealed by the Insurance Act 2015. As per s 3(4) of the Insurance Act, the assured has to disclose all material information which is known or ought to be known by the assured.

85 The assured does not need to disclose any information which is known, presumed to be known or ought to be known by the insurer (s 3(5) of the Insurance Act 2015). However an intention to vary from the usage of trade may be considered as material and needs to be disclosed.

Where the insurer does not stipulate any particular term in the policy after the representation is made, he may be taken to have waived the implied term.

9.26 For the assured to negative the implied condition, the delay must be caused by circumstances known to the insurer 'before the contract was concluded'. The condition may be negatived for instance by wars and the like events occurring before the contract is made in the area where the vessel is to depart from. It is not clear whether it would also be negatived where there is an anticipation of war arising prior to the conclusion of contract, however breaking out after the contract is made and causing delay at the commencement of the voyage. There may be many such instances where delay occurring after the date of the policy is caused by circumstances arising before the date of the policy.

(I) USAGE OF TRADE

9.27 In the pre-MIA cases *Vallance v Dewar*[86] and *Ougier v Jennings*[87] the usage of trade as to an intermediate voyage meant that the assured did not have to disclose the fact that the ship would sail on such a voyage on the ground that the usage of trade was equivalent to a notice or representation to insurers. It was suggested that this point has been settled by s 42(2) which provides that the implied condition will be negatived where delay is caused by circumstances known to the insurer.[88] A strict interpretation of s 42(2) may however not necessarily allow this finding. The subsection refers only to 'circumstances known to the insurer' and not 'circumstances which are presumed to be known by the insurer'.[89] Accordingly insurers may argue that although usage of trade is expected to be known by the insurer, it was *actually* not known and that therefore the existence of usage of trade which caused delay at the commencement of the voyage may not negative the implied condition.

Usage of trade was expressly provided as an element that would negative any right, duty or liability that would arise under a contract of sale by implication of law under the Sale of Goods Act 1893[90] which was also drafted by Sir MacKenzie Chalmers. Chalmers stated that when one party relies on and gives evidence on trade usage, the other party can either prove the non-existence of the usage, or its illegality or unreasonableness or that it formed no part of the agreement between the parties.[91] The Sale of Goods Act 1893 and the concept of usage of trade as negativing an implied condition or warranty may not be authority for interpreting the MIA, yet may be of help in understanding the background against which the draftsman prepared the legislation.

---

86 *Vallance v Dewar* (1808) 1 Camp 503.
87 *Ougier v Jennings* (1808) 1 Camp 505.
88 *Arnould* (9th edn), vol 1, 643.
89 See s 3(5) of the Insurance Act 2015.
90 s 55.
91 Chalmers, *The Sale of Goods Act 1893*, 103.

Delay after the risk attaches, before the insured voyage commences

9.28 The previous part of this chapter focused on delay in the attachment of risk and it was submitted that the risk would attach where the vessel arrives at the port with no unreasonable delay. This part of the chapter will look at the delay after the risk has attached, before the insured voyage commences. Such delay has been discussed in detail in *Mount v Larkins*.[92] A delay occurring in this leg of the voyage would have an effect only on policies 'at and from' and not 'from', given that in the latter, the risk does not attach until the ship sails on the voyage insured[93] after which time s 48 would begin to operate.

9.29 It is necessary to determine the scope of s 42 in order to differentiate it from s 48. The scope of s 48 extends to the period after the *insured voyage* commences.[94] Most of the pre-MIA cases which were the authorities based on which the section 48 was drafted, 'delay in voyage' referred to situations where delay occurred after the vessel sailed from the departure port.[95] Likewise, in most of the pre-MIA cases, delay in the commencement of voyage for ships was the period of time until the sailing of the vessel from the departure port,[96] therefore the calculation of delay started as from the date of the policy until the date of the ship's sailing.[97] This being said, s 42 was purported to be the codification of *De Wolf* which arguably only applies to pre-attachment delay. One of the questions that can be raised accordingly is whether the delay after the risk attaches and before the ship sails from the port of departure will be governed according to the common law authorities on the assumption that the situation is not governed by neither s 42 nor s 48. The period after the risk attaches before the vessel sails from the port of departure may particularly be apparent where the vessel, having arrived in reasonable time and the risk having been attached, prepares for another voyage than the voyage insured, or that the vessel prepares for the insured voyage but the preparations delay the vessel.

9.30 It was enunciated in *Mount v Larkins*[98] that the effect of delay before and after the risk attaches would be the same for the insurer, i.e. discharge on the ground that he has another risk substituted instead of the one which he has insured

---

92 (1831) 8 Bing 123.

93 Schedule 1 to the MIA, r 4.

94 See s 48 '. . . the *adventure insured* must be prosecuted' (emphasis added).

95 This suggestion is illustrated in *Williams v Shee* (1813) 3 Camp 469; *Schroeder v Thompson* (1817) 7 Taunt 462; *Company of African Merchants v British and Foreign Marine Insurance Co* (1873) LR 8 Exch 154; *Hamilton v Sheddon* (1837) 3 M & W 49; *Phillips v Irving* (1844) 7 Man & G 325.

96 In *Palmer v Marshall* (1832) 8 Bing 317, where the policy was 'at and from', the Court meant sailing of the vessel from the departure port by 'commencement of the voyage'. See also *Hull v Cooper* (1811) 14 East 475; *Grant v King* (1802) 4 Esp 175; *Chitty v Selwyn and Martyn* (1742) 2 ATK 358. For the view that 'voyage' usually means the sailing from one port to another with all practicable, safe and convenient expedition, please see Phillips, *Treatise on the Law of Insurance*, vol 1, 563. This work of Phillips was also cited in *De Wolf v Archangel Maritime* (1874) LR 9 QB 451.

97 As in *Palmer v Marshall* (1832) 8 Bing 317.

98 (1831) 8 Bing 123.

IMPLIED CONDITION

against. It would follow that whereas a delay until the risk attaches is a condition precedent to the attachment of cover, a delay following the attachment of risk until the insured voyage commences and a delay in voyage both relate to the continuation of cover and their remedy could arguably be the same remedy of discharge.

Alteration of risk by delay at the commencement of the voyage

9.31 It was suggested that the implied understanding that the risk is to commence within a reasonable time rested upon the same principle upon which the doctrine of deviation is founded, *that the adventure is to be pursued in the usual manner*.[99] The main reason why delay can be considered as a form of deviation[100] is that at both instances there is an alteration of risk undertaken by the policy caused by the assured. According to pre-MIA case law, alteration of risk is not a concept akin merely to delay during sea voyage but also to delay before and after the risk attaches.[101] The reason why alteration of risk is not allowed in a voyage which commences after some unreasonable and unnecessary delay is that it is considered as a 'voyage at a different period of the year, at a more advanced age of the ship, and in short, a different voyage than if it had been prosecuted with proper and ordinary diligence'.[102]

9.32 The need for a delay capable of varying the risk undertaken by the insurer is not expressly codified in s 42(1). It is submitted that alteration of risk for pre and post-attachment delay must be analysed separately in this respect. Section 42(1) which codifies the *De Wolf* case does not expressly provide for the risk to have been altered by delay for the insurers to acquire the right to elect to avoid the contract. The omittance of alteration of risk requirement may well have been unintended by the draftsman of the MIA.[103]

It is submitted however that alteration of risk by delay was a requirement for post-attachment delay for the insurers to be discharged from liability.[104] While post-attachment delay is not expressly provided for under the MIA, it is submitted that the common law requirement of alteration of risk shall still apply for post-attachment delay. It is of no surprise that the remedy for alteration of risk by post-attachment delay is discharge from liability, i.e. the same remedy for deviation.

---

99 Phillips, 387.

100 It was comprehended within the concept of deviation in *Company of African Merchants v British and Foreign Marine Insurance Co* (1873) LR 8 Exch 154.

101 *De Wolf v Archangel Maritime* (1874) LR 9 QB 451 was on pre-attachment delay and whether there was alteration of risk was discussed by the court. See *Mount v Larkins* (1831) 8 Bing 108 for post-attachment delay where alteration was discussed.

102 *Mount v Larkins* (1831) 8 Bing 108.

103 *Arnould* (18th edn), para 13.50 submits that the principle on which *De Wolf v Archangel* was decided is no longer law even though the omittance of variation of risk requirement may well have been unintended. For the view that delay in commencing the insured voyage alters the risk in the same way as delay in prosecuting the voyage (s 48) does, please see Bennett, *Good Luck with Warranties*, 595.

104 *Mount v Larkins* (1831) 8 Bing 108.

As the MIA s 49 provides excuses for deviation which prevent the insurers from being discharged from liability, the common law decisions consistently held that a post-attachment delay can be excused and the insurers would not be discharged if delay can be justified.[105]

9.33 Therefore the cases on delay at the commencement of the voyage referring to deviation need to be carefully scrutinised as this may be either because the alteration is so material that, just as deviation, it causes an end to the policy;[106] or because there may indeed be a change of course which results in delay where such change cannot be deemed as 'deviation' in the sense given to it by the MIA. In the latter circumstance, so long as the change of course is justified, delay may not, on its own suffice to discharge the insurers.[107]

Types of alteration of risk

9.34 An adventure which is due to start in reasonable time after the date of the policy may be delayed and may have to be prosecuted in a different season.[108] The mere change of season does nevertheless not necessarily change the risk undertaken by the insurer especially where delay is not excessive.[109] Moreover even if there is a change of season, where the circumstances resulting in delay did not happen through misconduct of the assured or there is sufficient evidence to prove that the voyage was not abandoned, the change of risk does not discharge the insurers.[110] Change of season can be excused where delay is not voluntary;[111] however it cannot be excused where according to the usage of trade, the vessel in any event has to sail in the season which is reached by delay. It was argued in *Palmer v Marshall*[112] that given that the vessel was described as a yacht in the policy and that according to the usage as to yachts it was to sail only in summer, a delay from January to May did not change the risk undertaken by the policy.[113] The argument was rejected on the ground that the assured should have insured it accordingly if he wanted to be covered for a period exceeding the reasonable time. Conversely in *Vallance v Dewar*[114] and *Ougier v Jennings*[115] it was admitted that a delay at the commencement of the risk would discharge the policy if an intermediate voyage causing delay in the attachment of risk was not communicated to

---

105 See paras 9.46–9.48 below for justifiable delays.
106 As in *Palmer v Marshall* (1832) 8 Bing 317.
107 *Driscol v Passmore* (1798) 1 B & P 202.
108 As in *De Wolf v Archangel Maritime* (1874) LR 9 QB 451.
109 In *Hull v Cooper* (1811) 14 East 475 the delay was slightly more than two weeks. As to the fact that the change of season arising from delay does not necessarily vary the risk, please see *Driscol v Passmore* (1798) 1 B & P 202.
110 *Driscol v Passmore* (1798) 1 B & P 202.
111 *Smith v Surridge* (1801) 4 Esp 25.
112 *Palmer v Marshall* (1832) 8 Bing 317.
113 A decision to this effect was given in *Palmer v Fenning* (1833) 9 Bing 460.
114 *Vallance v Dewar* (1808) 1 Camp 503.
115 *Ougier v Jennings* (1808) 1 Camp 505.

IMPLIED CONDITION

the insurers, unless such voyage was made usually and according to the normal course of trade in which the ship was then engaged. The basis on which the insurers were not discharged was because the usage of trade had the effect of a notice to the insurers about a possible delay in the attachment of risk, i.e. a circumstance which was known to insurers before the contract was concluded.[116]

Delay has to be unreasonable

9.35 As the implied condition requires that the voyage has to be commenced in reasonable time, the delay has to be so unreasonable as to alter the risk undertaken by the insurers in the pre-attachment delay.[117] The exact meaning of 'reasonable time' as it appears in s 42 is not free from doubt and its meaning would not be a primordial issue where the policy contains a named day as to when the vessel should be at the loading port.[118] The controversy as to when the risk becomes varied would therefore be avoided. In policies which do not state an express time of arrival at the departure port or a sailing time therefrom, identifying the criteria which need to be taken into consideration in order to determine whether the voyage commenced in reasonable time are essential.

9.36 Reasonableness should be decided on a case-by-case basis as it is a question of fact[119] and in the pre-MIA cases this issue was mostly left to the verdict of the jury. It refers to the length of delay and not to its purpose or justification.[120] The House of Lords established with respect to contracts of affreightment that an obligation to discharge a ship in reasonable time must be construed with reference to the circumstances existing at the time of the performance; and that provided that the owner did not act negligently or unreasonably, he is not responsible for a delay arising from an event beyond his control.[121] It was stated that the rule was of general application and did not only apply to contracts for the carriage of goods.[122] This judgment raises the question of whether not commencing the voyage in reasonable time may discharge insurers and this may have to be decided

---

116 This echoes s 42(2) although the subsection was not drafted having taken these two judgments into consideration.

117 *De Wolf v Archangel Maritime* (1874) LR 9 QB 451.

118 Or if the policy allows a time frame allowing delay, an extension of that time could be considered as unreasonable delay, *Doyle v Powell* (1832) 4 B & Ad 267. This case was in respect of an allowed waiting period of two months in the discharge port, extension of that period by the assured had discharged the insurers.

119 MIA s 88.

120 That 'unreasonable time' was a question of fact was addressed in *Bain v Case* (1829) 3 Car & P 496 where a vessel had remained one hundred and nine days at a port because of a blockade. It was stated by the assured that the stay was for the hope of getting permission to land cargo as negotiations were pending with the government. The verdict of the jury was that the length of time was not unreasonable. The judgment did not state a particular reason, therefore it may be suggested that the purpose of delay could have been regarded as justifiable by the jury. However in many post-MIA cases on delay, unreasonable and unjustifiable delays were considered separately.

121 In *Hick v Raymond* [1893] AC 22.

122 ibid, 32 per Lord Watson.

159

according to the circumstances existing at the time of the performance, in that the assured is responsible for a delay where delay was caused by the assured's act or was within its control.[123] The counter-argument could be that the condition that the adventure should be commenced in reasonable time is not an obligation of the assured against the insurer.[124] In that sense it is different from the obligation of the shipowner against the consignee to discharge the ship in reasonable time the breach of which gives the consignee the right for an action for breach of contract and it is not clear whether the rule laid down by the House of Lords as to the determination of 'reasonable time' could apply for s 42 situations.

9.37 Where the remedy of avoidance in s 42 may be taken to be an initiative to make the condition an obligation of the assured the breach of which can be regarded as a breach of contract, this could justify the right of the insurer to avoid the contract in which case the reasoning of the House of Lords in *Hick v Raymond*[125] may well apply. It was suggested that the language of s 42 allows a construction that the reasonable time must be determined with reference to the risk contemplated at the time of the insurance and that this construction gives effect to the rule laid down in *De Wolf v Archangel*.[126] The complexity with this argument may lie in that firstly in some circumstances the risk may not be fully contemplated at the outset or to confine the calculation of reasonable time to the risk contemplated at the time of the insurance may run the risk of overseeing the mutual agreements between the assured and the insurer reached after the contract was made. Another option could be to construe reasonable time according to circumstances at the time when the voyage might reasonably be presumed to commence.[127]

9.38 Reasonableness under the MIA is a question of fact as was the reasonableness of delay in the pre-MIA judgments which referred merely to the length of delay. Whether a delay was justified was however a question of law,[128] therefore it could be submitted that even though a delay is beyond the control of the assured, this shall not necessarily denote that the delay is reasonable for the purposes of s 42.

9.39 Another important aspect that requires consideration is the time when the calculation of 'reasonable time' should commence and terminate in a situation

---

123 This was discussed in Edward Louis de Hart and Ralph Iliff Simey, *Arnould on the Law of Marine Insurance and Average* (9th edn), vol I, (Steven & Sons and Sweet & Maxwell 1914), 640 (Hereinafter referred to as 'Arnould (9th edn), vol I')

124 Arnould (9th edn), vol I, 640.

125 [1893] AC 22.

126 Arnould (9th edn), vol I, 641. This view was amended in the 17th edition at para 13–50, on the ground that the principle on which *De Wolf v Archangel* was decided is no longer law and remained in the 18th edition, see para 13–50. According to the editors, neither the rule in *Hick v Raymond* nor *De Wolf v Archangel* can apply so as to determine what is a reasonable time within the meaning of s 42.

127 This view was expressed in *Grant v King* (1802) 4 Esp. 175 in the context of unreasonable delay amounting to abandonment of the voyage insured.

128 See for instance the excuses for delay and deviation which are instances of justified delays and deviations at s 49.

IMPLIED CONDITION

which would require the application of s 42. According to earlier case law, it starts with the time when the policy is made[129] until the vessel arrives at the departure port or until the vessel sails therefrom, according to the place where the risk will attach. In *Grant v King*[130] there was a delay of six months after the signing of the policy and it was decided that a mere length of time elapsed between the signing of the policy and the commencement of the voyage would not be sufficient to avoid a policy.[131] In *Mount v Larkins*[132] the jury's verdict in the first instance[133] was that the delay between the making of the policy and the commencement of risk was unreasonable. In this case[134] reference was made to *Hull v Cooper*[135] where Lord Ellenborough had stated the principle that a delay in the arrival of the vessel at the place where the risk is to attach alters the risk undertaken by the insurer.[136] It is noteworthy that considering the increasing speed of maritime trade, some of the delays that were considered as reasonable in terms of their length in the pre-MIA cases would presumably not be so considered now.

Unreasonable delay amounting to the abandonment of the voyage

9.40 A voyage is abandoned where all thoughts of voyage are laid aside by the assured with whose privity the vessel lays in the port of departure for an unreasonable amount of time prior to the commencement of the voyage.[137] Any delay which is not for the purpose of preparing for the insured voyage alters the risk undertaken and discharges the insurers.[138] In *Grant v King*[139] there was a delay of six months after the signing of the policy and it was decided that a mere length of time elapsed between the signing of the policy and the commencement of the voyage would not be sufficient to avoid a policy.[140] Rather, so that the delay be

---

129 In *Grant v King* (1802) 4 Esp 175, there was a delay of six months after signing of the policy and it was decided that a mere length of time elapsed between the *signing of the policy* and the commencement of the voyage would not be sufficient to avoid a policy. In *Mount v Larkins* (1831) 8 Bing 108, the jury's verdict in the first instance (the case was appealed in different grounds) was that the delay between the *making of the policy* and the commencement of risk was unreasonable. For other cases mentioning signing of the policy as starting point for calculation of reasonable time, please see *Palmer v Marshall* (1832) 8 Bing 317; *Chitty v Selwyn and Martyn* (1742) 2 ATK 358; *Vallance v Dewar* (1808) 1 Camp 503.

130 (1802) 4 Esp 175.

131 For other cases mentioning signing of the policy as starting point for calculation of reasonable time, please see *Palmer v Marshall* (1832) 8 Bing 317; *Chitty v Selwyn and Martyn* (1742) 2 ATK 358; *Vallance v Dewar* (1808) 1 Camp 503.

132 (1831) 8 Bing 108.

133 The first instance decision was appealed on different grounds.

134 (1831) 8 Bing 120.

135 (1811) 14 East 479.

136 See also *De Wolf v Archangel Maritime* (1874) LR 9 QB 451.

137 *Chitty v Selwyn and Martyn* (1742) 2 ATK 358. In this case the vessel laid in port for four years before it sank.

138 *Palmer v Fenning* (1833) 9 Bing 460. The case was about a yacht, waiting at the port as there was an intention to sell it and no preparation was made for sailing for five months.

139 *Grant v King* (1802) 4 Esp 176.

140 Avoidance here was used in the sense of 'discharge'.

material, it should be such as to amount to an abandonment of the voyage.[141] According to Lord Ellenborough whether the voyage has been abandoned had to be decided according to the 'existing circumstances at the time when the voyage might reasonably be presumed to commence' and the circumstance that was taken into consideration was the extreme difficulty in procuring crew members which was the cause of the delay.[142] The speech also refers to the fact that so long as there is an explanation for delay and that the assured can prove that the delay was more than 'a mere waste of time', delay would not be sufficient to 'avoid'[143] the policy. This raises the question that although the excuses for delay enumerated in s 49 of MIA do not apply in the case of delay at the commencement of the voyage, whether necessary delays in commencing the voyage may excuse the assured and prevent insurers from being discharged regardless of the length of delay.

Justification for an unreasonable delay could mean that the voyage insured has not yet been abandoned; yet if the vessel lies at the departure port with no intention of the assured to sail in reasonable time for the voyage, the excessive length of time spent at the port may amount to the abandonment of the voyage and would take the insurers off risk. Support for this view can be found in the Marine Insurance Bill as commented on in the work of Chalmers and Owen[144] which was published before the MIA was enacted where a section 44 entitled 'abandonment of adventure by delay' was placed after the section on the implied condition as to commencement of risk.[145] Section 44 reads:

> 'Where the assured abandons the adventure insured, the contract of marine insurance is determined'.

The annotation of the section referred to the distinction between the 'implied condition that the risk shall not be altered by delay' and the 'abandonment of the voyage by not commencing the voyage within reasonable time'. It also contained references to decisions such as *Palmer v Marshall*[146] and *Palmer v Fenning*[147] however it was surprisingly not incorporated in the current version of the MIA 1906.

Consequence of alteration and post-attachment delay

9.41 Several cases which were decided prior to the enactment of the MIA where delay had occurred after the attachment of risk and before the sea voyage

---

141 *Chitty v Selwyn and Martyn* (1742) 2 ATK 358.
142 *Grant v King* (1802) 4 Esp 175.
143 In the sense of 'discharge'.
144 *A Digest of the Law Relating to Marine Insurance*, 1901, 53.
145 In that work, the implied condition as to the commencement of risk was provided under s 43.
146 (1832) 8 Bing 317.
147 (1833) 9 Bing 460.

IMPLIED CONDITION

commenced mention discharge as the remedy available to insurers.[148] The reasoning which underlies the fact that the insurer should be discharged if an unreasonable delay occurs is because otherwise it would be exposed to the risk of every accident which may happen in port because of the unreasonable delay, something which is not intended to be covered by the insurer in addition to the risk of the voyage.[149] It is submitted that s 42 does not apply to post-attachment delay on the ground that it codifies *De Wolf* where it was held that a delay in the arrival of the vessel to the departure port resulted in the non-attachment of the risk. Therefore any delay that occurs subsequent to the attachment shall be ruled by the common law authorities.

9.42 The fact that the remedy for delay after the risk attaches before the insured voyage commences is discharge may rest upon the fact that it was identified as a branch of the law relating to alteration of risk or alternatively that it was considered as an implied warranty by earlier authorities.[150] Warranties are enumerated in ss 36 through to s 41 under the title 'Warranties, etc' whereas an implied condition as to commencement of risk appears under the title 'The Voyage'. This suggests that the drafters of the MIA treated s 42 differently than warranties, considering also that the remedy for s 42 is avoidance and not discharge. It is submitted in this work that avoidance in s 42 means 'avoidance *ab initio*' for the circumstances where the assured makes a representation as to the time of arrival of the vessel at the departure port and this has not been complied with as a result of which a delay occurs. This being the case, it is noteworthy that the term 'avoidance of contract' was used in some of the earlier cases to mean 'discharge from the contract'.[151] Moreover avoidance was not an alien term to warranties before the MIA was enacted. In the Marine Insurance Bill the remedy for s 33(3) which was at that time s 34(3) read that if a warranty is not complied with, the insurer may avoid the contract.[152] The subsection also stated that this remedy applied to the promissory warranties in sections 35 to 42,[153] thereby excluding the section of delay at the commencement of the voyage from the class of promissory warranties. Therefore under the Bill,

---

148 *Grant v King* (1802) 4 Esp 175; *Smith v Surridge* (1801) 4 Esp 25; *Palmer v Marshall* (1832) 8 Bing 317; *Chitty v Selwyn and Martyn* (1742) 2 ATK 358; *Vallance v Dewar* (1808) 1 Camp 503; *Palmer v Fenning* (1833) 9 Bing 460. In *Hull v Cooper* (1811) 14 East 479 it was only mentioned whether there was change of risk, the decision did not expressly refer to discharge from liability; however in *De Wolf v Archangel Maritime* (1874) LR 9 QB 451, 453, it was stated that the affirmative decision in *Hull v Cooper* was that a delay not varying the risk does not discharge the insurer.

149 This was what happened in *Smith v Surridge* (1801) 4 Esp 25 where the vessel could not sail from the port in reasonable time firstly because of necessary repairs and subsequently because the water was uncommonly low.

150 Prior to the enactment of the Insurance Act 2015, the MIA provided that the remedy for the breach of a warranty is discharge from liability as from the date of the breach (s 33(3)). This rule has now been abolished following the entry into force of the Insurance Act 2015.

151 *Grant v King* (1802) 2 Esp 175; *Smith v Surridge* (1801) 4 Esp. 25; in *Bah Lias Tobacco & Rubber Estates, Ltd v Volga Insurance Company Ltd* (1920) 3 Lloyd's List Law Rep 155 the defence of the insurer was that the unreasonable delay 'voided' the policy.

152 See Chalmers and Owen, *Digest of the Law Relating to Marine Insurance*, 1901, 43.

153 Which are now MIA ss 34 (repealed by the Insurance Act 2015) to 41.

the section as to delay at the commencement of the risk was not considered as a warranty, yet had the same remedy as warranties. It was rather considered as a voyage condition.

The English and Scottish Law Commissions enumerated s 42 along with s 48 and others[154] respectively in their Consultation Paper No 204 and Discussion Paper 155[155] under the title 'implied warranties' and described them as 'conditions which operate in the same way as warranties, in that the risk may never attach or the insurer may be discharged from liability'.[156] This view curiously does not reflect the current remedy for delay at the commencement of the voyage that is avoidance of contract. In other paragraphs of the Consultation Paper, sections 43, 44, 45, 46 were considered as 'implied voyage conditions' under the heading of 'implied warranties' and it was submitted that the proposals on warranties did not affect them.[157] Finally the Law Commissions asked the consultees whether the implied voyage conditions from s 42 to s 49 should be repealed; although few had responded to their query, the majority of the consultees expressed the view that they should be retained.[158] In an earlier consultation paper[159] delay at the commencement of the voyage was mentioned as an implied voyage condition[160] however was not made part of the proposal as to whether the implied voyage conditions should be repealed or made subject to the same causal connection test as express warranties.[161]

9.43 Section 42 is identical to s 48 of the Australian Marine Insurance Act 1909. The Australian Law Reform Commission considered in their Review of the Marine Insurance Act 1909 Report No 91[162] that the effect of the section is 'to discharge the insurer from liability by some act of the insured or some other person which occurred after the contract was concluded'[163] and that the provisions about delay[164] should be treated in the same way as the reforms proposed in respect of warranties. The Australian Law Reform Commission proposed accordingly to

---

154 ss 40(2), 41, 42, 43, 44, 46, 48 and 49 respectively.

155 English Law Commission Consultation Paper No 204 and Scottish Law Commission Discussion Paper No 155, published on 26 June 2012 entitled *Insurance Contract Law: The Business Insured's Duty of Disclosure and the Law of Warranties*.

156 At 12.16.

157 From 16.19 to 16.24.

158 See The Law Commission of England and Wales and the Scottish Law Commission's joint paper *Insurance Contract Law: Summary of Responses to Third Consultation Paper, The Business Insured's Duty of Disclosure and the Law of Warranties*, Chapter 2: The Law of Warranties, paras 8.20–8.24 for the views expressed by the consultees. The Law Commissions' decision to retain the conditions is found at para 8.19.

159 The Law Commission Consultation Paper no 182 and the Scottish Law Commission Discussion Paper no 134 entitled *Insurance Contract Law: Misrepresentation, Non-Disclosure and Breach of Warranty by the Insured* published in 2007.

160 At 2.63.

161 At 8.131–8.132.

162 The Australian Law Commission, *Review of the Marine Insurance Act 1909 Report No 91* (hereinafter referred to as 'ALRC 91').

163 At 9.212.

164 Both s 48 of MIA 1909 and s 54 of MIA 1909 (which is equivalent to s 48 of MIA 1906).

repeal the provisions equivalent of ss 42 and 48 of the MIA 1906[165] for them to be dealt with as an express term of the contract. They regarded the provisions relating to the non-attachment of risk[166] differently and decided to retain them on the ground that they were not relating to a breach of a contractual term. Section 48 of MIA 1909 (equivalent to s 42 of the MIA 1906) was not considered within this classification, however if it can be demonstrated that the pre-MIA 1906 cases relating to pre-attachment delay referred to the non-attachment of risk rather than discharge from liability,[167] it may be the case that the Australian Commission's proposal to retain the sections on the attachment of risk could also apply for s 48 of MIA 1909.

(I) Whether post-attachment delay is a breach of warranty and the Insurance Act 2015

9.44 The assured does not have to ensure that the vessel is at the place where the adventure should commence at the time of the contract. Therefore it does not have to affirm the existence of the vessel at the place where the voyage insured is to commence from, a circumstance avoiding a warranty as to a present fact. However it may be argued that the assured promises to fulfil the condition that the voyage shall commence in reasonable time which can constitute a promise as to a future conduct. Post-attachment delay, so as to discharge the insurers, has to be unreasonable and the moment when delay becomes unreasonable in a specific circumstance cannot be easily identified. The Insurance Act provides that the breach of a warranty shall suspend the insurer's liability instead of automatically discharging it, so that if the breach is remedied before the loss the insurer has to pay the claim.[168] Given that to identify the moment when the delay becomes unreasonable is not straightforward, the time of breach and accordingly the starting point of the suspension would not be readily ascertained. Another complexity is how the assured is going to remedy the breach of not commencing the voyage in reasonable time. Breach of the requirement to commence the voyage in reasonable time may be an example of the circumstances where remedy may be impossible. Once the delay in commencing the voyage becomes unreasonable, it may arguably not be made good even though the assured acts with reasonable or even utmost despatch.

(II) Whether post-attachment delay is breach of a condition subsequent or innominate term

9.45 The concept of condition subsequent is an unsettled area in general contract law and insurance law. As regards the consequence of its breach, it was found similar to warranties in *The Beursgracht (No 1)*[169] which involved a charterers'

---

165 i.e. s 48 and s 54 of MIA 1909.
166 i.e. the sections as to alteration of port of departure and sailing for different destination.
167 *De Wolf v Archangel Maritime* (1874) LR 9 QB 451.
168 Insurance Act 2015 s 10(1) and (4).
169 *Glencore International A.G. v Ryan (The Beursgracht (No 1))* [2002] CLC 547.

liability insurance policy. This was an appeal made by the insurers who had alleged at first instance that the assured had to make declarations in reasonable time on the ground that that was a condition subsequent. At the appeal the issue discussed was whether it was a warranty or a condition and it was decided that the term was an innominate term. It was stated by the Privy Council in *Union Insurance Society of Canton v George Wills*[170] that warranties could sometimes be described as condition subsequent to insurer's liability, the breach of which would automatically discharge insurers. The assured in that case sued insurers for a total loss of shipment of goods as to which they had made a declaration after the attachment of risk but not 'as soon as possible after the sailing of the vessel' which was required by the policy. Although the following was not an obvious distinction made by the Court, it is submitted that the case can be authority for the suggestion that whereas the promise need not be material to the risk where it is a warranty, so that a promise can be qualified as a condition subsequent, the object of the promise has to be so material to the risk that it forms a substantive condition of the contract. A condition subsequent becomes effective following the inception of the risk, the breach of which gives the insurers the right to terminate the contract[171] and not to avoid it *ab initio*.[172] Usually the occurrence of an event determines the previously binding contract.

A term about doing something in reasonable time does not necessarily make time of the essence of the contract nor would the absence of reference to urgency be sufficient to justify elevating an implied term into promissory warranty or condition,[173] everything would depend on the context. It was discussed in *The Beursgracht (No 2)*[174] that so as to assess the *quality* of the breach, the length of delay had to be considered so as to determine whether the delay was so inordinate that the insurers should not be bound. As to the *effect* of the breach, the court asked whether the delay could cause real or serious prejudice to insurers.[175]

Limits to the remedy of alteration: justifiable delays

9.46 The MIA expressly provides in s 49 that delay in sea transit may be excused if it occurs owing to the circumstances enumerated in the section. The Act does not provide excuses for delay at the commencement of the voyage and

---

170 [1916] 1 AC 281.

171 In the context of sale of land, it was held that the breach of condition subsequent gave the right to elect to terminate the contract, and not to rescind ab initio, *Howard-Jones v Tate* [2011] EWCA Civ 1330.

172 In the South African case *Lehmbackers Earth Moving and Excavators (Pty) Ltd. v Incorporated General Insurances Ltd* (1984) (3) S.A. 513, the court considered the remedy for fraudulent claims (which was a post-contractual event) as breach of a subsequent condition, which could therefore not amount to avoidance *ab initio*.

173 *Glencore International A.G. v Ryan (The Beursgracht (No 1))* [2002] CLC 547.

174 *Glencore International A.G. v Ryan (The Beursgracht (No 2))* [2001] 2 Lloyd's Rep 608.

175 At 618.

IMPLIED CONDITION

it cannot be inferred from s 49 that the excuses would also apply to s 42. One of the main reasons for this is that delay in voyage was seen as a form of deviation and that therefore benefitted from the same excuses for deviation provided for in the pre-MIA cases.[176]

It was held in some earlier cases that the assureds were excused for post-attachment delays.[177] It was not allowed in *De Wolf v Archangel*[178] that the breach of the duty to commence the voyage in reasonable time could be excused and it is submitted this suggestion could merely apply to pre-attachment delays. Post-attachment delays occurring prior to the commencement of the voyage insured should be evaluated according to the pre-MIA cases in whether they allow excuses for delays. Several different wordings were used for justifiable or unjustifiable delays such as 'delay unaccounted for',[179] 'necessary delay',[180] 'delay not occasioned by the wrongful act of the insured himself'.[181] Pre-MIA cases allowed delay at the commencement of the voyage where delay was for the purpose of the voyage[182] and what was for the purpose of the voyage depended on each particular voyage. The justification for delay was widely interpreted, in the sense that so long as there is an explanation for delay and that the assured can prove that the delay was more than 'a mere waste of time', it would not be sufficient to discharge the insurers.[183] Some examples of justifiable delays were where delay was for the purpose of waiting for a wind or for provisions;[184] for necessary repairs or where delay was due to low level of water;[185] where delay occurred due to an intermediate voyage which was made usually and according to the normal course of trade in which the ship was then engaged[186] and the insurers were accordingly not discharged.[187]

---

176 *Company of African Merchants v British and Foreign Marine Insurance Co* (1873) LR 8 Exch 154.

177 *Grant v King* (1802) 4 Esp 175; *Driscol v Passmore* (1798) 1 B & P 202; *Ougier v Jennings* (1808) 1 Camp 505. However whether these cases may be authority after the enactment of the MIA was doubted in Hodges, *Cases and Materials on Marine Insurance Law*, 147 where it was submitted that they no longer stand as authority. This was on the ground that the fact that the circumstances where the implied condition as to the commencement of the voyage may be negative, in other words, where the assured would be excused in case of such delay, are expressly stated in s 42(2) and it may be suggested that they are enumerated in an exhaustive way.

178 *De Wolf v Archangel Maritime* (1874) LR 9 QB 451.

179 *Palmer v Marshall* (1832) 8 Bing 317.

180 *Chitty v Selwyn* (1742) 2 ATK 358.

181 *Mount v Larkins* (1831) 8 Bing 108.

182 In *Palmer v Marshall* (1832) 8 Bing 317, Park J stated that the language of the policy implied that if the vessel is ready for sea, she shall sail without delay unless the delay be accounted for. According to Alderson J, the delay in sailing must be a delay incurred 'for the purpose of the voyage' in order to be justified and he referred to *Langhorn v Alnutt* (1812) 4 Taunt 511 which was a case on delay in sea transit and not delay at the commencement of the voyage.

183 *Grant v King* (1802) 4 Esp 175.

184 *Palmer v Fenning* (1833) 9 Bing 460, 463 per Alderson J. The case was about a yacht, waiting at the port as there was an intention to sell it and no preparation was made for sailing for five months.

185 *Smith v Surridge* (1801) 4 Esp 25.

186 *Vallance v Dewar* (1808) 1 Camp 503; *Palmer v Fenning* (1833) 9 Bing 460.

187 *Smith v Surridge* (1801) 4 Esp 25.

9.47 In *Driscol v Passmore*[188] where delay at the commencement of the voyage was due to an earlier deviation which was justified, the resulting delay was also excused. However this case should be an exception and should apply only with respect to a voyage comprised of intervals. This is given that deviation which is a change of route to the destination can occur after the voyage starts. However in *Driscol* the voyage insured was one of the intervals and the delay in the commencement of the voyage was therefore the delay in starting that particular interval. In a voyage with no interval or with intervals which are not separately insured, deviation would normally result in a delay in sea voyage which is within the scope of s 48.

Where there is a sailing warranty in the policy as to a specific day, and if it is breached by the assured, whether delay in the post-attachment period is excused by the fact that it is due to a peril which is covered by the policy is controversial.[189] It is submitted that a peril such as detention resulting in delay could in some circumstances amount to an abandonment of the voyage.[190] In this case this would put an end to the insurance contract and it would probably be immaterial whether the warranty of sailing was complied with.

The relation of justifiable and unreasonable delays

9.48 If it is correct that post-attachment delays which are justifiable excuse assureds, it would be necessary to inquire into whether the delay has to be both unreasonable and unjustifiable so as to discharge insurers. The wording of s 42 implies[191] that in order to be 'unreasonable', the only element with respect to delay that should be taken into consideration would be the length of delay and not the purpose thereof.[192] This finds support in the speech of Tindal C J in *Palmer v Marshall*[193] which was a judgment on post-attachment delay where he submitted '. . .Where the delay is unexplained, and so great as to fix it with the character of unreasonableness in the mind of every reasonable person'.[194] It would follow that a delay 'unaccounted for' or 'unjustified' should be differentiated from 'unreasonable' delay, whereby the former rests upon the circumstances which would cause delay but would excuse the assured, and the latter being simply an excessive delay

---

188 *Driscol v Passmore* (1798) 1 B & P 202.

189 In *Hore v Whitmore* (1778) 2 Cowper 784, where the policy was 'at and from', stated that the ship was to sail on a specific day free from detention. The ship was ready to sail before the time however was detained by an embargo and had to sail later than the set date. It was held that the delay was not excused and the sailing warranty which was 'positive and express' was not complied with.

190 It is not clear whether, in light of the law decided in *Grant v King* (1802) 4 Esp 176 and *Chitty v Selwyn* (1742) 2 ATK 358 that delay would amount to abandonment of the voyage if it is caused by necessity or caused by other perils which are beyond the control of the assured and covered by the policy. The concept of 'abandonment of the voyage' is discussed above.

191 '. . . that the adventure shall be commenced within a reasonable time. . .'.

192 Unreasonable delay has been considered in other parts of this work in terms of s 48, unreasonable delay within the scope of s 42 was also considered in this chapter, under 2.1.

193 (1832) 8 Bing 317.

194 At 319.

IMPLIED CONDITION

for the purposes of the voyage insured. A lengthy delay which may however be justified does arguably not discharge insurers.

9.49 Justification of a lengthy delay may also rest upon an event which is beyond the control of the assured. In *Smith v Surridge*[195] there were two delays the first of which was due to repairs which were necessary and the second one was due to low level of water which prevented the vessel from sailing, it was an involuntary delay which did not discharge the insurers. If repairs are made for the purpose of the voyage, the risk will commence notwithstanding the length of repairs,[196] however they must be made without unnecessary and unreasonable delay, in which case the insurers will be discharged. Albeit transit risks which may cause delay can be more numerous compared to circumstances at the commencement of voyage, there should be nothing preventing assureds from relying on excuses for post-attachment delay, i.e. on unforeseeable events which are beyond their control.

---

195 (1801) 4 Esp 25.
196 *Motteux v London Ass. Co* 1 Atk 545.

CHAPTER 10

Delay in voyage

Introduction

10.1 The Marine Insurance Act 1906 provides that the adventure insured must be prosecuted with reasonable despatch and in the absence of a lawful excuse, the insurer is discharged from liability when the voyage is not so prosecuted.[1] It is also provided that if the cause excusing the delay ceases to operate, the ship must resume her course and prosecute the voyage with reasonable despatch.[2] The purpose of those provisions is 'to minimise the period of risk while the ship and goods are at sea'.[3]

10.2 This chapter will analyse firstly the common law origins of the sections with a particular focus on the concept of alteration of the risk initially undertaken by the insurer and secondly the criteria in determining whether a delay is unreasonable. Furthermore it will assess whether the entry into force of the Insurance Act 2015 would affect in any way the operation of s 48. In addition to the foregoing, the chapter shall focus on the inter-relations of ss 48 and 49 with standard market terms currently used in the insurance market, particularly with the Institute Cargo Clauses.

Delay and deviation

10.3 Before the MIA 1906 was enacted, delay was held to be an instance of deviation in several cases[4] on the ground that just as deviation, unreasonable or unexcused delay causes change in the risk undertaken by the insurer.[5] At the time, 'deviation' was a concept akin to voyages where the purpose of the voyage was not followed although there was no strict deviation from the course of the voyage

---

1 s 48.

2 s 49(2).

3 This was enunciated in *Verna Trading Pty Ltd v New India Assurance Co Ltd* [1991] 1 VR 129, 146 per Kaye J in the context of ss 55 and 56(2) of the Australian Marine Insurance Act 1909 which respectively are identical to s 48 and s 49(2) of the MIA 1906.

4 This was particularly expressed by Lord Mansfield in *Hartley v Buggin* (1781) 3 Dougl 39.

5 For the speech of Tindal CJ as to the alteration of risk by unreasonable delay, see *Mount v Larkins* (1831) 8 Bing at 122.

170

in the locality sense.[6] The distinction between deviation and delay has been made clear in ss 46 and 48 of the MIA and deviation can now accordingly be regarded as a change of the voyage insured in terms of locality, whereas an unreasonable or unexcused delay is an instance of a change of the voyage insured in terms of time. A deviation does not necessarily delay an adventure insured, however should it do so, the policy will be discharged as from the time where the deviation occurs, i.e. before even delay is in place. This would be subject to the terms of the policy which may provide that the insurance shall remain in force during any deviation,[7] in which case what could discharge the insurers can be an unreasonable delay caused by the deviation unless the policy contains a waiver on delay or qualifies the type of delay that would discharge the policy.[8]

10.4 The difference between delay and deviation has not been canvassed to a great extent by courts after the enactment of the Marine Insurance Act. The distinction between 'prolongation' of the voyage and deviation was nevertheless discussed in the context of their respective representation of time and locality. In *Union Castle Mail Steamship Co Ltd v United Kingdom Mutual War Risks Association*[9] a war risks policy taken out on time basis covering hull and machinery provided cover for the expenses incurred by the assured by reason of the prolongation of the voyage arising from the compliance with the directions of certain authorities; however the expenses incurred during the period of prolongation were not recoverable. In an *obiter* passage, Diplock J enunciated that prolongation of the voyage had merely a temporal and not a geographical meaning, referring also to the word 'period' preceding the word 'prolongation'. Moreover he observed that prolongation had not started until the voyage would have normally ended.

10.5 On the facts of the case, the prolongation could have readily been determined given that the insured vessels were due to their ports of loading on specific dates. The vessels had also deviated multiple times and one of the points discussed in the *obiter* passage was the connection between deviation and prolongation of the voyage. If the prolongation of the voyage was going to be treated as having a geographical sense, then the assured would have to be given credits for savings made during the deviations such as savings of canal dues, port charges at ports omitted and additional freight earned. Diplock J observed that there can be deviation without prolongation of the voyage if the voyage is terminated within the expected period of time and assessed the prolongation of the voyage by reference to the dates the vessels were due at their port of loading from their round voyage.

---

6 See *Hamilton v Sheddon* (1837) 3 M & W 49. Deviation can no longer be held to occur where the purpose of the voyage is not followed given the clear wording in s 46 as to locality.

7 See for instance the Institute Cargo Clauses (All Risks) 2009 cl.8.3.

8 Such as where the insurance remains in force during delay beyond the control of the assured under the Institute Cargo Clauses (All Risks) 2009 cl 8.3.

9 *Union Castle Mail Steamship Co Ltd v United Kingdom Mutual War Risks Association* [1958] 1 All ER 431.

Liberty clauses on deviation and their impact on delay

10.6 In most of the pre-MIA cases on delay and deviation involving policies which contained clauses granting liberty to deviate, delay amounting to deviation was often considered within the scope of the liberty clause. In *Hyderabad v Willoughby*[10] the policy contained a clause covering the assured 'in the event of deviation and change of voyage at a premium to be . . . arranged'. The goods having to be carried to a warehouse after having been rejected upon discharge had to be kept there for a month until the arrangements were made for delivery. Insurers sought to avoid liability on the ground that there was deviation and unreasonable delay. It was held that the deviation was for the purpose of the voyage and therefore justifiable; but the delay in the warehouse was unreasonably long and amounted to unjustifiable deviation. The insurers were nevertheless not discharged from liability because the liberty clause had allowed deviation upon payment of a reasonable additional premium. Delay was accordingly excused under a liberty clause allowing deviation. Other examples existed where 'delay' and 'deviation' were used interchangeably in the context of liberty clauses allowing delay, however 'deviation' was not used strictly in the locality sense. In *Syers v Bridge*[11] delay was allowed under a liberty clause excusing 'cruising for six weeks' and it was held that this deviation (in the sense of time and not locality) was allowed.

10.7 In the US case *The Citta di Messina*[12] a bill of lading contained a liberty clause which provided 'to proceed and stay at any port or place for loading and discharging or for any other purpose whatsoever'. The ship had waited for nearly two weeks for cargo at a port, of which she had obtained a small amount. District Judge Hough recognised that the MIA in the UK distinguished delay from deviation, however at the time the decision was made, delay in the course of transit was still equivalent to deviation under the US law. The judge therefore cited the pre-MIA authority of *The Company of African Merchants v Foreign Marine Insurance Company*[13] and stated that delay amounted to deviation even upon the course of the voyage prescribed in the policy and that therefore the scope of the liberty clause comprised delay.

10.8 Before the enactment of the MIA, in *Pearson v Commercial Union*[14] where the policy contained a clause which read 'liberty to go into dry dock' and both the deviation and delay were usual in the circumstances of the case, Lord Cairns in the House of Lords noted that 'any delay usual in the circumstances, any deviation usually or conveniently made from the straight line, provided the delay and deviation are connected with' would be justifiable in the words of the

---

10 *Hyderabad v Willoughby* [1899] 2 QB 530.

11 (1790) 2 Dougl 526.

12 *The Citta di Messina* (1909) 169 F. 472, District Court, S.D New York.

13 (1872–73) LR 8 Exch 154.

14 *Pearson v Commercial Union* (1876) 1 App Cas 498.

DELAY IN VOYAGE

policy.[15] Albeit in this case the liberty clause had a reference to locality, it was nevertheless held to encompass delay upon the condition that delay be usual in the circumstances.

10.9 Following the enactment of the MIA which distinguished delay and deviation, the application of s 48 would have the result that liberty clauses that expressly excuse merely deviation may no longer be taken to encompass delay whereby the earlier authorities to that effect[16] would no longer be good law. Nowadays, under the Institute Cargo Clauses, both deviation and delay beyond the control of the assured are enumerated separately as incidents which would not terminate the transit[17] the operation of which is similar to a liberty clause. Two possibilities may arise in this context, i.e. where there is a mere delay and a delay arising from a deviation from the intended course of the voyage. In both cases whether the insurance remains in force would be answered according to whether or not the delay is of a nature that is beyond the control of the assured.

Time policies, mixed policies and s 48

10.10 The wording of the current s 48 is to the effect that an unreasonable delay discharges the insurers in the case of a voyage policy, therefore the rule does not apply to time policies. According to s 91(2) the common law authorities continue to apply following the enactment of the MIA except where they are inconsistent with the express provisions of the Act. On the ground that s 48 refers expressly only to voyage policies, the common law authorities on time policies where delay is involved would continue to apply.

10.11 In the House of Lords decision *Pearson v Commercial Union Assurance*[18] the policy was a time policy against fire which described the ship as 'lying in the Victoria Docks' and gave the ship 'liberty to go into dry dock'. The ship before entering the dry dock had to remove paddle-wheels, which had to be re-fitted on the way back to the Docks. As it was more economic for the assured to re-fit the paddles before entering the Docks, they were re-fitted on a river which was not in the usual transit from the dry dock to the Docks, as a result of which a delay had occurred. The ship was covered by the policy for three months where she lay in the Docks, or where she proceeded to or was in a dry dock. In deciding whether the delay was occasioned by usage and therefore excusable, the Court approached delay in a time policy as a non-fulfilment of a contractual condition. It was held to be collateral to the object of the end in view and therefore

---

15 At 502.

16 For example *Phillips v Irving* (1844) 7 Man & G 325 and *Columbian Insurance Company v Catlett* (1827) 25 U.S. 383.

17 Institute Cargo Clauses (All Risks) 2009 cl 8.3.

18 *Pearson v Commercial Union* (1876) 1 App Cas 498.

unjustifiable, accordingly the ship was not covered by the policy as from the time when the delay occurred.[19]

10.12 Where the policy is both on voyage and time basis, i.e. where it is a mixed policy,[20] the question would arise as to whether an unreasonable delay could discharge the insurers. In this case, in principle, s 48 would apply for the part of the policy that is on voyage basis unless the policy is not altogether considered as a time policy;[21] and any delay would also discharge the insurers from liability where delay constitutes the breach of a condition that is found in the part of the policy that is on time basis.

10.13 In *The Company of African Merchants v Foreign Marine Insurance Company*[22] the policy was upon a ship at and from Liverpool to the west or south-west coast of Africa 'during her stay and trade there', at a premium varying with the duration of the risk. It was therefore a combination of a voyage policy and a time policy because the assured had the right to keep the ship in that area for an unlimited period upon the condition of staying and trading there.[23] After arriving at the coast of Africa, the ship stayed there for some weeks for a purpose not connected with the voyage, however the delay was within the currency of the policy. It was held by the court that the delay discharged the insurers on the ground that the ship had stayed there for a purpose not connected with trading. Delay in this case had occurred during the period which, according to the Court, makes the policy partly a time policy. The decision is fairly similar to *Pearson v Commercial Assurance* in the sense that in both cases delay discharged the insurers from liability because a contractual obligation had not been fulfilled.

10.14 More recently the Singapore Court of Appeal tackled the issue of whether s 48 could apply to mixed policies in *The Al-Jubail IV*.[24] The ship was insured 'at and from Singapore to the Persian Gulf' and 'for the period of 12 months' commencing from the date the ship left Singapore and was therefore held to be insured under a mixed policy.[25] On its voyage, the ship encountered heavy seas and had to be repaired whereby the voyage was delayed. Insurers argued that they were discharged from liability according to s 48 as the delay was allegedly unreasonable. So far as the voyage was concerned, the part of the cover had the attributes

---

19 Collateral purpose of delay which can be interpreted as commercial convenience for the assured has been the subject of many judgments after *Pearson v Commercial Union*. For a relatively recent example see *Fedsure General Insurance Limited v Carefree Investments (Proprietrary) Limited* (477/99) [2001] ZASCA 88.

20 See s 25(1).

21 A time policy with the intention of covering a voyage was held to be a time policy only, *Marina Offshore Pte Ltd v China Insurance Co (Singapore) Pte Ltd* [2007] 1 Lloyd's Rep 66.

22 *Company of African Merchants v Foreign Marine Insurance Company* (1872–73) LR 8 Exch 154.

23 At 156.

24 *M Almojil Establishment v Malayan Motor and General Underwriters (Private) Ltd (The Al-Jubail IV)* [1982] 2 Ll L Rep 637.

25 Lai J at 641.

DELAY IN VOYAGE

of a voyage policy. Lai J decided that the time spent for repairs was reasonable and that the insurers were therefore not discharged from liability.

10.15 According to *Pearson v Commercial Assurance* and *The Company of African Merchants v Foreign Marine Insurance Company*, it would not be a fallacy to argue that as far as time policies are concerned where cover is for a certain period of time if a condition is fulfilled, delay can be considered as a breach of a contractual condition and discharge the insurers if the purpose of delay is unjustifiable. In mixed policies, s 48 would apply to the part of the policy that has the attributes of a voyage policy and a delay could discharge the insurers altogether where the assured cannot prove that delay had occurred for a purpose connected to the voyage.

The meaning of 'unreasonable delay'

10.16 Section 48 of the MIA 1906 enunciates that the assured should prosecute the voyage with reasonable despatch and the insurers are discharged from liability when the delay becomes 'unreasonable'. Several decisions prior to the enactment of the MIA touched upon this term[26] and a recapitulation thereof is required so as to ascertain the criteria which determine when delay becomes unreasonable.

Common law authorities and unreasonable delay: purpose and length

10.17 Unreasonable delay was canvassed in many pre-MIA cases[27] although its criteria had not been pointed out as clearly as they were in *Langhorn v Alnutt*.[28] Prior to analysing this case and its significance, the decision in *Hartley v Buggin*[29] needs to be considered so as to determine the difference between the length and purpose of delay and their impact on the development of the concept of 'unreasonableness' of delay.

In *Hartley v Buggin*, the policy gave the assured the 'liberty to exchange goods and slaves' during the voyage insured. Instead of exchanging goods and slaves, the ship was used as a floating slave depot which had occasioned a delay of seven months. As the use of the ship as a depot was not within the purpose of the voyage and the liberty granted, delay was held to be unjustifiable and discharged the insurers from their liability. The length of delay and whether it was unreasonable

---

26 *Hamilton v Sheddon* (1837) 3 M & W 49; *Company of African Merchants v British Insurance Co* (1873) LR 8 Exch 154; *Pearson v Commercial Union Assurance Co* (1876) 1 App Cas 498; *Phillips v Irving* (1884) 7 Man & G 325; *Hyderabad (Deccan) Co v Willoughby* [1899] 2 QB 530; *Smith v Surridge* (1801) 4 Esp 25; *Grant v King* (1802) 4 Esp 175; *Schroder v Thompson* (1817) 7 Taunt 462; *Samuel v Royal Exchange Assurance* (1828) 8 B & C 119; *Bain v Case* (1829) 3 C & P 496; *British American Tobacco v Poland* (1921) 7 Ll L Rep 108; *Niger Co Ltd v Guardian Assurance Co* (1922) 13 Ll L Rep 175.

27 ibid.

28 (1812) 4 Taunt. 511.

29 *Hartley v Buggin* (1781) 3 Doug KB 39.

was not canvassed by the court. The fact that there was no account for delay was sufficient for the change of risk by delay and discharge of insurers from liability.

10.18 *Langhorn v Alnutt*[30] was delivered a few years later and clarified the position as to the criteria for deciding whether a delay is unreasonable. The policy contained a clause giving the assured liberty to touch and stay at all ports for all purposes whatsoever. The ship waited in port for about four months and according to the evidence provided, obtain forged documents. Chambre J stated that the 'Length of delay creates a degree of suspicion and calls for explanation'[31] and Gibbs J gave a detailed judgment as to the criteria of an unreasonable delay.

He enunciated that whether the ship's stay was for a purpose within the scope of the adventure was a question of law and would have to be answered by the courts, whereas whether the ship stayed for an unreasonable time for that purpose was a question of fact to be answered by the jury.[32] According to this judgment, a delay that is of a nature to discharge the insurers from their liability has two components, namely the purpose and length of delay. If delay is incurred for an unaccountable purpose and is therefore unjustifiable, the insurers are discharged. It follows that in this case whether the delay's length was unreasonable in the circumstances shall not have to be considered.[33] Nevertheless if the delay is justifiable or otherwise is for a purpose connected with the purpose of the voyage insured, the next issue is whether the delay occasioned for the purpose of the adventure was unreasonably long.[34]

10.19 This reasoning was also followed in *Phillips v Irving*[35] where the purpose of delay was within the scope of the adventure insured as it was due to necessary repairs, and when she was ready to take in cargo, the freight market was unusually low and the port was crowded with shipping. The freights offered, if accepted, would have occasioned great loss to owners. The delay therefore being justified, the next question was whether the length of delay for that purpose was unreasonable. A similar example was found in *Bain v Case*[36] where a delay in waiting permission to land cargo was for the purpose of the voyage and therefore justified, and the length of delay of one hundred and nine days was held to be not so unreasonable.

10.20 After the enactment of the MIA, in *British-American Tobacco Company Ltd v H.G. Poland*[37] a delay of three months was occasioned due to waiting to obtain a permit to forward the goods under a cargo policy. Having decided that the delay was for the purpose of the voyage, the court agreed with the first instance judge's finding that the goods were forwarded at the earliest convenience and

---

30 *Langhorn v Alnutt* (1812) 4 Taunt 511.
31 At 518.
32 At 519.
33 As was the case in *Hartley v Buggin* (1781) 3 Doug KB 39.
34 *Reed v Weldon* (1869) Carswell NB 23 following *Langhorn v Alnutt*.
35 (1844) 7 Man & G 325.
36 (1829) 3 Car & P 496.
37 *British-American Tobacco Company Ltd v H.G. Poland* (1921) 7 Ll L Rep 108.

therefore the length of delay was not excessive. On similar facts in *Hyderabad v Willoughby*,[38] a delay for a month having occurred in corresponding to arrange how the cargo could be sent on in order to continue the transit was held to be unreasonably long although it was for the purpose of the voyage and therefore justified.[39]

10.21 In examining whether the length of delay was so excessive for the voyage insured, which is a question of fact, one of the issues that can be contended by the assured is that such delay is within the usage of trade in which the voyage is embarked upon. As was stated in *Columbian Insurance v Catlett*,[40] whether delay is 'unreasonable' should depend upon the nature of the voyage and usage of trade.[41] The delay in this case was justifiable as it was for the purpose of selling the cargo and a price limit was set by the assured for such sale. Although the delay was long, considerable delays at that port were not uncommon and therefore the length of delay was held not to be unreasonable. It was also noted that if the owner of the goods (who was also the owner of the vessel) had set a very high limit for selling the cargo and had further delay been caused accordingly, that delay could have been 'unreasonable'.

10.22 However long a delay can be, it has to occur for the purposes of the voyage contemplated in the policy. It was noted by Blackburn J in *Company African Merchants* that the parties had known and contemplated that the ship could protract its course, yet the protraction could have been excused if it was for the purpose of trading as the policy covered the ship during her 'stay and trade'.[42] This case was cited as an illustration of a s 48 type of situation by the draftsman of the Marine Insurance Act 1906[43] and it is noteworthy that as the previously mentioned authorities, this decision supports the position that a delay incurred for a purpose unconnected with the voyage insured discharges the insurers. Because this requirement was not fulfilled by the assured, the court did not even assess whether the length of delay (on the facts of the case, four weeks) was excessive.

10.23 According to the common law authorities, it can be submitted that if a delay is incurred for a justifiable purpose and that the length of delay is not so excessive for that purpose, such delay does not discharge the insurers. The fact that the purpose rather than the length of delay is to be primarily looked at so as to determine whether a delay discharges the insurers can be further supported by the fact that unreasonable delay and deviation have the identical remedy[44] and the excuses[45] under the Marine Insurance Act rest solely on the basis of 'purpose'.

---

38 *Hyderabad v Willoughby* [1899] 2 QB 530.

39 This part of the decision was followed by *Tension Overhead Electric (Pty) Ltd v National Employers General Insurance Co Ltd* [1990] 4 SA 190, see the judgment of Van Schalkwyk J at 196.

40 *Columbian Insurance v Catlett* (1827) 25 U.S. 383 (US Supreme Court).

41 See below paras 10.34–10.35 for the position that usage of trade can also be considered as a circumstance that would justify a delay.

42 At 157.

43 See Chalmers and Owen, *A Digest of the Law Relating to Marine Insurance*, 1901, 57

44 s 46 provides that the insurer is discharged from liability as from the time of the deviation.

45 s 49.

It may accordingly follow that there must be a change of risk in terms of purpose of the voyage and length of delay for that purpose that would make the delay discharge the insurers from liability.

Excessive delay and the knowledge of the assured

10.24 The knowledge of the assured at the time of the contract as to the probability of the occurrence of an excessive delay and its concealment may be considered as a fact material to the risk that could give the insurers the remedies available in the Insurance Act 2015.[46] In *Schloss Brothers v Stevens*[47] it was argued on behalf of the insurers that it was known to the assured and concealed that the deficiencies of the means of transport were such as might involve an excessive delay. The court, without elaborating on the matter, pronounced that there had been no concealment of facts which were material to the risk and went on discussing whether an abnormal delay was within the wording 'all risks by land and by water'. This issue would not arise where knowledge of an event which could cause an ordinary delay is concealed given that an ordinary delay resulting from the perils insured against ought, or be presumed to be known by insurers.[48]

Unreasonable delay under s 48 and the delay exclusion

10.25 According to s 48, insurers are discharged from liability as from the time the delay becomes unreasonable. When this provision is read in conjunction with the exclusion of delay losses in s 55(2)(b), the most obvious finding would be that the insurer would be discharged as from the time the delay becomes unreasonable and therefore no question would arise as to whether there would be cover for losses that arise following the unreasonable delay. The delay exclusion in the Marine Insurance Act would therefore only apply to the losses which occur prior to the unreasonable delay.[49]

Justifiable delays

(a) Unreasonableness under s 48 and excuses for delay

10.26 It is not clear whether the notion of unreasonableness referred to in s 48 reflects the common law position, i.e. whether it involves both the length and purpose of delay. This observation is based on several grounds. The scope of s 49 where excuses for delay and deviation are enumerated in a non-exhaustive way is

---

46 Schedule 1, Pt 1.

47 *Schloss Brothers v Stevens* [1906] 2 KB 665.

48 Insurance Act 2015, Pt 2, s 3(5)(c) and (d).

49 For the view that even where the delay is not unreasonable, s 55(2)(b) will allow insurers to exclude losses proximately caused by delay, see Merkin, *The Marine Insurance Legislation*, 63. A similar view was expressed in Bennett, *The Law of Marine Insurance*, 15.29.

not entirely clear when considered together with s 48 if the concept of unreasonableness under s 48 is taken to reflect the same position as under the common law. Reading s 48 in conjunction with s 49 results in the suggestion that delay has to be unreasonable in the first place so that the question whether such delay can be excused under s 49 could arise.[50] This is given that not any delay, but unreasonable delays discharge insurers and therefore those are the only types of delays that can be excused under s 49. In other words, there has to be an unreasonable delay under s 48 which may or may not be excused under s 49.

10.27 Importing an element of excuse or justification into the concept of 'unreasonableness' under s 48 would therefore connote that delay, if justifiable and not extraordinary in its length for complying with the purpose of the voyage, would not be unreasonable as per s 48 in consequence of which s 49 would not need to be triggered. This accordingly raises the question of whether the concept of unreasonableness under s 48 refers mainly to the length of delay and not to its purpose. This reasoning can also be supported if the expression 'lawful excuse' in s 48 is taken to refer to s 49 excuses,[51] whereby unless a lengthy delay is not excused by one of the circumstances enumerated under s 49 or like circumstances, it would discharge the insurers. It can therefore be concluded that the concept of unreasonableness under s 48 can arguably be different than its counterpart under the common law and relate merely to the length of delay, and not also to its justification despite the fact that the drafters of the Marine Insurance Act had cited cases such as *Company of African Merchants* as the background of s 48 where the length of delay had not even been looked at.

10.28 For the unreasonable delay to be excused, the excuse must be lawful;[52] yet it is controversial whether lawful excuses are confined to the ones enumerated in s 49 or whether excuses such as delaying for the purpose of furthering the voyage insured or delays occurring in usage of trade could also be included in this wording. The way s 49 is drafted does not expressly result in an inference that the list of possible justifications for delay enumerated therein is exhaustive. This would give way to the argument that common law justifications for delay, i.e. delays incurred for the furtherance of the voyage insured and delays incurred in usage of trade could still excuse the assureds. As to the former, s 49 requires further elaboration.

10.29 The excuses in s 49 may or may not necessarily be triggered for the purpose of the adventure insured. By way of example, an instance similar to *Hyderabad v Willoughby*[53] may be an example for both delay for the furtherance

---

50 This was illustrated in *Hyderabad (Deccan) Co v Willoughby* [1899] 2 QB 530 where delay was held to be unreasonable, yet necessary for the prosecution of the voyage and therefore justified.

51 According to Bennett, para 18–42, 'since in the circumstances laid down by section 49, there would almost certainly be no discharging deviation or delay in the first place, section 49 would appear merely to provide clarification of what constitutes a lawful excuse and reasonableness'.

52 This wording is also provided in s 46(1).

53 *Hyderabad (Deccan) Co v Willoughby* [1899] 2 QB 530.

of the voyage insured and s 49(1)(a),[54] however delaying in order to help a ship in distress (as per s 49(1)(c)) would arguably not necessarily be for the purpose of a voyage insured. Therefore confining the phrase 'lawful excuse' in s 48 to circumstances mentioned under s 49 would considerably restrict the scope of justifiable delays and would oversee the approach taken in most of the pre-MIA common law authorities. It is also noteworthy in this context that nothing would prevent the assured to rely on excuses available under different subsections of s 49.[55]

(b) Excuses for alteration of the risk and not for breach of warranty

10.30 The breach of s 48 results in the discharge of insurers from liability which was identical to the consequence of a breach of warranty under the Marine Insurance Act 1906 prior to the entry into force of the Insurance Act 2015.[56] This however did not in any way connote that the breach of s 48 was a breach of warranty. As part of their consultation which resulted in the Insurance Act 2015, the Law Commission of England and Wales and the Scottish Law Commission enumerated s 48 and other voyage conditions in their joint Consultation Paper[57] under the title 'implied warranties' yet described them as 'conditions which operate in the same way as warranties, in that the risk may never attach or the insurer may be discharged from liability'.[58] The Commissions did not make any proposals about ss 48 and 49 given that they were voyage conditions and not warranties and that accordingly their proposals on warranties did not affect them.[59] The Commissions merely asked the consultees whether these sections should in their view be retained[60] and a majority of the consultees expressed that they were in favour of their retention.[61]

10.31 The Australian Law Reform Commission however, considered the provisions about delay[62] in their Review of the Marine Insurance Act 1909 Report No 91[63] and proposed that the equivalent of ss 48 and 49 of MIA 1906 should be treated in the same way as the reforms proposed in respect of warranties, i.e. that

---

54 Delay was necessary for the safe accomplishment of the journey of the cargo and was therefore justified. There was a liberty clause in the policy giving rise to a liberty to deviate.

55 An analogy may be drawn from *Rickards v Forestal Land Timber & Railways Co Ltd (The Minden)* (1941) 70 Ll L Rep 173, where deviation was excused under both s 49(1)(b) or 49(1)(d).

56 The Insurance Act 2015 has drastically changed this rule in s 10.

57 The Law Commission Consultation Paper No 204 and The Scottish Law Commission Discussion Paper No 155, *Insurance Contract Law, The Business Insured's Duty of Disclosure and the Law of Warranties*, published on 26 June 2012.

58 At para 12–16.

59 At para 16–24.

60 At 18.33.

61 See The Law Commission of England and Wales and the Scottish Law Commission's joint paper *Insurance Contract Law: Summary of Responses to Third Consultation Paper, The Business Insured's Duty of Disclosure and the Law of Warranties*, Chapter 2: The Law of Warranties, paras 8.20–8.24 for the views expressed by the consultees. The Law Commissions' decision to retain the conditions is found at para 8.19.

62 Both s 48 of MIA 1909 and s 54 of MIA 1909 (which is equivalent to s 48 of MIA 1906).

63 The Australian Law Commission, *Review of the Marine Insurance Act 1909 Report No 91* (hereinafter referred to as 'ALRC 91').

they should be repealed and be dealt with as an express term of the contract.[64] The insurers' remedies would also be limited to discharge from liability for loss proximately caused by the breach.[65] If for a moment, the ALRC's proposal as to repealing the relevant sections could be adopted in the United Kingdom, one of the questions that could be raised would be whether the standard wordings currently used in the market cover this aspect. The Institute Cargo Clauses 2009 for instance provide that the insurance remains in force during delay beyond the control of the assured, and that the assured shall act with reasonable despatch in all circumstances within their control.[66] Whether these clauses are reflections of s 48 in the standard form cargo policies is a matter that would accordingly have to be determined and will be discussed in the following paragraphs of this chapter.

10.32 One of the reasons why the breach of the requirement that the assured should prosecute the voyage with reasonable despatch could not have been considered as a breach of warranty under the Marine Insurance Act 1906 prior to the entry into force of the Insurance Act 2015 is as follows: no cause however good or necessary would excuse a non-compliance with a warranty and merely two exceptions to this rule appeared under s 34 of the MIA 1906; these were 1) the warranty would cease to be applicable to the circumstances of the contract by reason of a change of circumstances; 2) the compliance with the warranty would become unlawful by any subsequent law. Section 49 excuses are fairly distinct from those exceptions and are based on the principle that delays with a cause mentioned in s 49 or another justifiable cause arising from common law would excuse the assured. Section 49 excuses may therefore not be considered as excuses for a breach of warranty, but for alteration of the risk insured.

(c) Excuses other than the ones enumerated in s 49

10.33 There is no clear authority as to whether justifications which are not enumerated in the MIA yet which had been the subject of the pre-MIA decisions could excuse unreasonable delays subsequent to the entry into force of the MIA. As pointed out before, in the assumption that the s 49 excuses are not exhaustive, excuses arising from common law could justify unreasonable delays along with s 49 excuses. One type of these excuses is where delay occurs in the usage of trade which will be elaborated below.

(I) DELAY OCCURRING IN USAGE

10.34 Usage of trade may affect both the length of delay and the assessment of whether delay is necessary/justifiable in the field of trade in which the assured

---

64 ALRC 91, 9.213–9.214. This view was also advanced by some consultees in The Law Commission of England and Wales and the Scottish Law Commission's joint paper *Insurance Contract Law: Summary of Responses to Third Consultation Paper, The Business Insured's Duty of Disclosure and the Law of Warranties*, Chapter 2: The Law of Warranties; see para 8.22.

65 9.214.

66 See ICC 2009 cll 8.3 and 18 respectively.

operates.[67] It was stated in *Pearson v Commercial Union*[68] where the policy was on time basis that doing what is usual though not necessary is excused if it is done for the purpose of the voyage insured (i.e. in this case to go into dry dock).[69] Therefore, so as to be justifiable, delay had to be incurred for the purpose of going back to the Docks, and not in re-fitting the paddles in the river which was not on the usual course of transit from the dry dock to the Docks.[70]

10.35 In *Phillips v Irving*[71] it was held that whether delay is unreasonable should be determined not by any positive or arbitrary rule but according to the state of things existing at the time at the port where the ship happens to be. This was a judgment where it was held that delay was for the purpose of the voyage insured given the circumstances at the port and was not unreasonable. However what establishes usage and its relevance to justification and length of delay need to be ascertained. The length of time usually spent in waiting to sell or to obtain a cargo at a particular port may assist an assured in proving that the actual delay incurred at the port was not unnecessary, yet may not establish a fixed period of time that could be considered as usage.[72] Usage of trade may also well affect whether delay is unreasonable where the usage of trade limits the right to take in cargo to a particular period, and not to a certain amount of time.[73]

Ordinary course of transit and interruption of the voyage

Delay which is not in the 'ordinary course of transit' discharges the insurers

10.36 An interruption on the voyage has significance in respect of the transit clause under the Institute Cargo Clauses 2009, particularly cl 8.1 which states that the assured is covered during the ordinary course of transit and cl 8.1.2 which

---

67 In *Columbian Insurance v Catlett* (1827) 25 U.S. 383 Story J noted that the parties entering into a contract of insurance were governed by the ordinary length of voyage and the course of trade. A delay however unreasonable, if necessary to accomplish the objects of the voyage and if bona fide made, could not discharge the insurers. What type of delay could end the adventure insured would depend on the nature of the voyage and the usage of trade.

68 (1876) 1 App Cas 498 per Lord Penzance at 508.

69 The other two judges Lord Cairns and Lord O'Hagan noted that the usage did not facilitate the transit of the ship to the docks and that it did not have to be known to the insurers as it was collateral to the voyage insured. *Arnould* (9th edn), vol I, s 414 expressed the view that the result might have been different in a voyage policy.

70 For instance while going back to the Docks, if the ship had waited for a certain tide in the river and had been delayed because of that, the delay which was usual but not necessary would have been within the limits of the policy cover.

71 *Phillips v Irving* (1844) 7 Man & G 325.

72 This was raised in *Oliver v Maryland Insurance Company* (1813) 11 U.S (7 Cranch 487) by Lord Chief Justice who also stated: 'The vessel might certainly remain as long as was necessary to complete her cargo, but it is scarcely to be supposed this was regulated by usage and custom. The usages and customs of a port, or of a trade, are peculiar to a port or trade. But the necessity of waiting where a cargo is to be taken on board until it can be obtained is common to all ports and all trades'.

73 *Columbian Insurance v Catlett* (1827) 25 U.S. 383.

DELAY IN VOYAGE

provides that storage other than in the ordinary course of transit terminates the insurance. The case law on this point has mostly been developed by the courts in Australia, South Africa and Hong Kong and will be analysed in detail hereunder.

10.37 Not any interruption during the transit but '. . . a delay or interruption which, objectively viewed, is not part of the usual and ordinary means of effecting transit, and which is occasioned by some collateral purpose, will disturb the ordinary course of transit'.[74] Whereas cl 8.1.2 imports a subjective element into the election-making of the assured for storage,[75] it also requires an objective test as to whether or not delay or interruption is part of the usual and ordinary means of transit.

(a) Interruption of transit brought about by the requirements
     of transport

10.38 Ordinary course of transit was taken to be when the goods are in transit for the reasonable furtherance of their carriage to their ultimate destination.[76] More generally, ordinary course of a voyage or transit would involve the ordinary length of the voyage which can be determined according to the course of trade in question and any interruption of the voyage brought about by requirements of transport.[77] This may be the reason why premiums are paid to insurers for the ordinary length of the voyage in that particular trade and not for an unnecessary interruption of the voyage.[78] Such an ordinary interruption is diametrically oppo-site to the interruption of transit by the voluntary decision of the assured whereby the cover ceases. It was enunciated in *Wiggins Teape Australia Pty Ltd v Baltica Insurance Co Ltd*[79] that:

> 'the purpose of a warehouse-to-warehouse clause is to insure during a limited land movement. . . it has never been suggested it is intended to cover indefinite storage at some place not brought about by the requirements of transport, but determined by the voluntary decision of the consignee'.[80]

10.39 Breach of cl 8.1.1 of the Institute Cargo Clauses (All Risks) 1982 was considered in *ELAZ* in respect of the interruption of transit.[81] In this case, for a

---

74 *Fedsure General Insurance Limited v Carefree Investments (Proprietrary) Limited* (477/99) [2001] ZASCA 88 per Howie JA at para 12.

75 ibid, at para 14.

76 *Verna Trading Pty Ltd v New India Assurance Co Ltd* [1991] 1 VR 129 by reference to Ackner J in *SCA. (Freight) Ltd v Gibson* [1974] 2 Lloyd's Rep 533, at p 535. The *Gibson* case involved a land transit policy (the Lloyd's Goods in Transit (CMR) Policy), containing a term whereby cover would be provided in the 'normal course of transit'. Ackner J had further noted that it was a question of degree, as to what is or is not a reasonable furtherance of the carriage of the goods.

77 As was stated in *Verna Trading Pty Ltd v New India Assurance Co Ltd* [1991] 1 VR 129 with reference to *Leaders Shoes (Aust.) Pty Ltd v Liverpool and London and Globe Insurance Co Ltd* [1968] 1 NSWR 279, unduly protracted steps in the cargo's transportation are not within, and may terminate, the 'ordinary course of transit'.

78 See the speech of Story J in *Columbian Insurance Co v Catlett* (1827) 12 Wheat. 383, 388.

79 [1970] 2 NSWR 77, 80 per Macfarlan J.

80 ibid, 80 per Macfarlan J.

81 *ELAZ International Co v Hong Kong & Shanghai Insurance Co Ltd* [2006] HKEC 825.

voyage from China to Mexico via Texas, the goods (garments) had been loaded in a trailer-container at Texas for the remaining part of the transit. They remained at Texas for 31 days and then were stolen. The insurer alleged that the loss occurred while the goods were not in the ordinary course of transit according to cll 8.1.1 and 8.1.2.1. The Court approached the interruption merely from the point of the purpose thereof and given that the purpose of delay was on-shipment of goods for their carriage to their ultimate destination, the interruption was within the ordinary course of transit and did not discharge the insurers. It was also noted that the burden was on the assured who must prove on the balance of probabilities that the loss occurred whilst the goods were in the ordinary course of transit,[82] it followed that the onus was on the assured to prove that the interruption occurred due to a justified purpose. The length of the delay and whether it was unreasonably long even if it was incurred for a justified purpose was not canvassed.

(I) THE MOMENT COVER CEASES

10.40 Under the transit clause, the moment the cover ceases is of importance when there is an interruption due to storage other than in the ordinary course of transit.[83] Clause 8.1.4 provides a general limit of sixty days at the expiration of which the cover ceases automatically; however the situation of an interruption in the course of the voyage prior to the expiration of the 60 days is a curiosity. The motive behind the 60 day limit after the discharge overside of the goods is to safeguard the insurer against unduly protracted land carriage after the sea transit.[84] It would follow that unless the purpose of the storage is something else than conveying the goods to their destination as soon as is practicable, the cover ceases at the expiration of sixty days. This is a maximum period goods can be covered by the policy if the goods are being stored for delivery to their destination and is subject to the avoidance of delay clause.[85] Assuming that the cover may cease before the expiry of sixty days when the goods are stored other than in the ordinary course of transit, the question that could follow is whether it would cease when the decision is made to store them other than in the ordinary course of transit or when the goods are actually stored.[86]

---

82 *ELAZ International Co v Hong Kong & Shanghai Insurance Co Ltd* [2006] HKEC 825, at para 101.

83 See cl 8.1.2.

84 This was stated in *Wiggins Teape Australia Pty Ltd v Baltica Insurance Co Ltd* [1970] 2 NSWR 77 with reference to Chorley and Giles, *Shipping Law* (5th edn 1963), p 441.

85 The avoidance of delay clause (Institute Cargo Clauses A-B-C 2009 cl 18) or reasonable despatch clause (Institute Cargo Clauses A-B-C cl 18) shall be analysed at paras 10.59–10.77.

86 In *Verna Trading Pty Ltd v New India Assurance Co Ltd* [1991] 1 VR 129, the insurer alleged that the insurance terminates when the assured decides to leave the goods until a certain date (the decision was made to leave them for a month in the customs house). Beach J (in the first instance) confirmed this view, and commented that this was in line with *Wiggins Teape Australia Pty Ltd v Baltica Insurance Co Ltd* [1970] 2 NSWR 77. It shall be noted that the policy in *Wiggins* case did not contain any clause referring to 'ordinary course of transit' and this point was raised by Ormiston J in *Verna*.

DELAY IN VOYAGE

10.41 Albeit under the common law, delay in voyage ceases cover when the delay becomes unreasonable, i.e. when the purpose was unjustifiable and the length of delay excessive for the specific voyage insured, in situations involving modern standard market terms on cargo cover was held to have ceased when the goods were unloaded for storage in the warehouse which caused the interruption not brought about by the requirements of transport.[87] Insurers would accordingly not be liable for a loss occurring after the moment of unloading. It would follow that the goods do not have to stay in the warehouse for an excessive amount of time for the transit to terminate. In *Nec Australia Pty Ltd v Gamif*,[88] where the insurance policy did not contain a warehouse-to-warehouse clause and was not a marine insurance policy the length of delay for the stolen goods was not made the subject of thorough discussion, however it was stated that part of the stolen goods could wait in the warehouse for a considerable amount of time pending their sale and then delivered to the customers. If there was no theft, part of the goods would have been sold over varying periods of time.

10.42 It was enunciated in *Commercial Union Assurance Co v The Niger Co Ltd*[89] in terms of the warehouse-to-warehouse clause that 'in transit' does not necessarily require the goods to be in constant motion or subject to a brief interruption in motion. According to the circumstances then existing, the length of suspended movement would be determinative in finding out whether the transit comes to an end. It would follow that, by way of analogy to pre-MIA cases which elaborated on the purpose and length of delay, where the purpose of delay/interruption is not brought about by the requirements of transport or does not arise from the course of trade, the cover ceases there when the decision to interrupt the transit is exercised, i.e. when the goods are unloaded from the carrying vehicle to be stored in the warehouse. However, where the purpose of interruption is in line with the purpose of the transit,[90] any delay great in length is determinative as to whether the transit comes to an end. This latter situation would seldom arise in practice given that in most of the circumstances delay may not become excessive before the expiry of 60 days, yet it would be more determinative in a policy where there is no such time limit for the expiry of transit.

10.43 An example of a non-marine policy, not having a time limit for the expiry of transit was found in *Tension Overhead Electric (Pty) Ltd v National Employers General Insurance Co Ltd*.[91] The policy was a contract works policy where the

---

87 This was the case in *Nec Australia Pty Ltd v Gamif Pty Ltd; Neway Transport Industries Pty Ltd; Australian Eagle Insurance Co Ltd; Colonial Mutual General Insurance Company Ltd and Webden Pty Ltd* [1993] FCA 252, see para 40.

88 *Nec Australia Pty Ltd v Gamif Pty Ltd; Neway Transport Industries Pty Ltd; Australian Eagle Insurance Co Ltd; Colonial Mutual General Insurance Company Ltd and Webden Pty Ltd* [1993] FCA 252.

89 *Commercial Union Assurance Co v The Niger Co Ltd* (1922) 13 Ll L Rep 75 per Lord Sumner at pp 81–2, the pages were referred to in *Nec Australia Pty Ltd v Gamif* [1993] FCA 252, para 28.

90 As in *Commercial Union Assurance v The Niger Co Ltd* (1922) 13 Ll L Rep 75.

91 *Tension Overhead Electric (Pty) Ltd v National Employers General Insurance Co Ltd* 1990 4 SA 190.

subject-matter insured was 'materials in transit for incorporation in the works, other than on the contract site'. The goods arrived at the premises of the consignee and were stored in a premise adjacent to the consignee's factory for five days, before they were forwarded to their destination. The consignee had intended to send the goods off the day after the goods were stolen from the store yet the court decided that the intention of the assured could not change the objective meaning of 'in transit'. The question was whether the goods were in transit when they were stolen. The explanation of the assured in storing the goods for so long was that he did not wish to expose the goods to additional risks at the building site.

The Court decided that the fact that the assured has a perfectly valid explanation for the delay does not mean the goods are still in transit.[92] The interruption of transport could be of such duration that whatever the purpose of the interruption was, the transit must be said to have come to an end.[93] Whether a delay terminates the insurance had to be assessed according to the nature, duration and the circumstances giving rise to delay, and that in each case the overriding consideration should be whether delay had occurred as 'part of the usual and ordinary means ... of ... effecting ... the transit'.[94] In this case as well, delay not in the ordinary course of transit operated as a warranty discharging the insurers. As this case shows, where the purpose of the delay is excused, the moment when the transit is deemed to have terminated is when the delay becomes unreasonably long for the voyage. This is in line with some pre-MIA authorities on s 48, with the sole difference that in modern cargo clauses and non-marine policies, reasonable despatch applies also to land transits and not only to sea transit.[95]

(b) Storing pending payment for goods: whether storage in the
      ordinary course of transit

10.44 Some types of commercial sales inevitably involve a certain amount of time before the goods are paid for and the goods may therefore have to be stored in a warehouse pending payment. In particular, sales made on documents against payment terms or sales through letter of credit whereby payment is made upon receipt of documents by the buyer's bank and their check pursuant to the conditions of the letter of credit, could involve a certain amount of interruption to transit. In *Miruvor Ltd v National Insurance Co Ltd*,[96] the assured was the consignor of eight shipments from Hong Kong to Paraguay. As Paraguay was landlocked, the goods had to be transported via Brazil where they were discharged and stored in a warehouse. The consignee, through forged bills of lading produced to the carrier's agents, managed to obtain the goods without paying for them. The assured brought

---

92 At 195.

93 At 195. In this respect, the judgment is in line with *Hyderabad v Willoughby* [1899] 2 QB 530.

94 At 196, the Court also referred to the speech of Lord Cairns in *Pearson v Commercial Union* (1876) 1 App Cas 498.

95 *Verna Trading Pty Ltd v New India Assurance Co Ltd* [1991] 1 VR 129.

96 *Miruvor Ltd v National Insurance Co Ltd* [2003] HKEC 237.

a claim against the insurers whereby the issue was whether the goods had been stored other than in the ordinary course of transit at the assured's election.[97]

10.45 The case involved a sale on 'documents against payment' terms according to which the assured had to store the goods pending payment by the buyer of the goods. Albeit insurers were protected by the duration clause whereby the transit terminates at the expiry of sixty days after the discharge of the goods over the vessel,[98] the rather complex question was whether they can be discharged before the expiry of such period. The answer would lie in whether such delay is within the control of the assured or whether storage is in the ordinary course of transit. Where storage is due to events such as in *Miruvor*, i.e. where the assured is not the consignee and has to await payment under its sale contract in order to release the goods and documents, storing the goods in a warehouse is for the furtherance of the transit as it aims at delivery upon receipt of payment. Considering that insurers would also not be on risk indefinitely as per the time limit of sixty days after the discharge of goods, any temporary storage for eventual delivery should not take insurers off risk prior to the expiry of such period as it would relate to the requirements of transport and not to a voluntary decision of the assured.

10.46 In the same line, in *First Art Investments Ltd v Guardian Insurance Ltd*[99] where the contract between the consignor (assured) and consignee was on terms 'D/P 30 days',[100] the goods were retained by the carrier's agents on behalf of the carrier and were released to the consignee within 30 days after their unloading from the aircraft, although no documents were presented to the agents. The Court held that the transit comes to an end if the relevant documents are presented within 60 days,[101] otherwise any delay in presenting the documents within those sixty days would not terminate the transit.[102] Albeit the consignee's financial arrangements might have involved possible delay in the presentation of documents, such delay was usual between the arrival of the goods at their destination and the presentation of documents for their collection which are known facts to carriers and insurers.[103]

---

97 The insurers relied upon cl 8.1.2 of the ICC A there at issue.

98 This point was raised in *First Art Investments Ltd v Guardian Insurance Ltd* (2002), unreported decision of Judge Hallgarten QC in the Central London County Court dated 14 February 2002, cited in *Miruvor Ltd v National Insurance Co Ltd* [2003] HKEC 237. Hallgarten J noted that insurers are well aware of the complexities in such sales, and insofar as the delay increases insurers' risk, the problem is solved by the duration provision of 60 days, whereby insurers are protected by the time limit.

99 *First Art Investments Ltd v Guardian Insurance Ltd*, (2002) Unreported decision of Judge Hallgarten QC in the Central London County Court dated 14 February 2002, cited in *Miruvor Ltd v National Insurance Co Ltd* [2003] HKEC 237.

100 The abbreviation stands for 'documents against payment 30 days', which according to the Court, either meant that the documents would be taken by the consignee by presentation of bills of exchange payable at 30 days or that the consignee had 30 days to pay against the documents.

101 This was the general time limit for the duration of transit after the goods were discharged.

102 per Hallgarten J, at para 24.

103 per Hallgarten J, at para 21.

10.47 It is submitted however that not all the contractual arrangements between the consignee and consignor may be known to insurers, and if the interruption of voyage is not usual in the course of trade, the term 'transit' shall not be interpreted by reference to the circumstances and facts agreed by the consignee and consignor. It is doubtful whether ordinary transit should comprise the storage period until the goods are released against payment (if that period ends before the expiry of 60 days), even where payment is delayed. Storage pending payment would rather be of interest under the contract between the consignee and consignor, and in the absence of clear evidence that insurers knew about the possibility that the goods could be stored against the risk of not having been paid on time, that storage should be taken to be not in the ordinary course of transit. It may be ordinary in the course of business and under a sale contract, however this shall not mean that it is ordinary as per the 'transit' under an insurance policy.[104]

10.48 In *Industrial Waxes v Brown*[105] the policy was a marine insurance policy under a Lloyd's open cover incorporating the Institute Cargo Clauses (W.A.) for five shipments from New Orleans to Valparaiso in Chile for inland shipment. The policy contained a warehouse-to-warehouse clause whereby the cover would cease 30 days after the arrival of the vessel at Valparaiso; however the open cover contained a warehouse extension clause which stated that thereafter the assured could be held covered against payment of additional premium. This was subject to notification by the assured of an event giving rise to the held covered clause. The insurance certificates included a storage declaration clause which read: 'Including, *if so declared hereon*, risk whilst in store after arrival at port of discharge. . .for 30 days thereafter held covered at an additional premium'.[106] The goods stayed in the customs warehouse for five months and then were destroyed due to a fire.

10.49 The issue was whether the assured could benefit from further coverage provided under the policy which was subject to notification and payment of additional premium after the expiry of thirty days following discharge at the final destination. It was held that provided that the assured declared that it sought coverage for 30 days after the goods were warehoused, it could do so with no cost according to the storage clause; however for the period which follows the assured had to pay additional premium. Given that the assured had neither made any declaration nor had paid any additional premium, the cover ceased when the goods were stored in the warehouse. Albeit this case involved specific clauses upon which the central matter turned, its relevance to the standard market terms currently in use can be elaborated as below.

In this case, the five-month delay was for the purpose of awaiting the procurement by the purchaser to make the payment to meet the sight documents. It was

---

104 It is submitted that support for this view can be found in *Nec Australia Pty Ltd v Gamif Pty Ltd; Neway Transport Industries Pty Ltd; Australian Eagle Insurance Co Ltd; Colonial Mutual General Insurance Company Ltd and Webden Pty Ltd* [1993] FCA 252, para 31.

105 *Industrial Waxes Inc v Brown* (1958) 258 F.2d 800 (United States Court of Appeals Second Circuit).

106 Emphasis added.

not disputed whether a delay of five months in the warehouse was unusual or unexpected and such delay was found in the first instance as a matter of common knowledge to exporters to the West Coast of South America.[107] It could be argued therefore that such delay was in the ordinary course of transit and storing for that purpose could not be outside of it. It would follow that the transit would not terminate upon unloading of the goods for such storage, but at a later stage, at the expiry of sixty days after such completion. Accordingly any loss occurring until then should be covered by the policy if caused by a covered peril.

10.50 As to whether there is a higher risk that any decision to store the goods for an amount of time could be held to disturb the ordinary course of transit where the assured is the consignee of the goods, see *Groban v American Casualty Company.*[108]

(c) Commercial convenience of the assured versus requirements of transport

10.51 In several standard market terms on cargo, delay during transit which is beyond the control of the assured does not terminate the cover.[109] Conversely, causing interruption of transit due to a decision of the assured based on commercial convenience and not requirements of transport takes the goods off risk. This decision may be expressed by the assured by electing to store the goods.[110] The election, when made where delay and storage is inevitable until the sale documents are received[111] may not be considered as purely for commercial convenience of the assured; yet when the circumstance causing delay is known to the assured when the contract is made and the assured knowingly leaves the goods in the warehouse awaiting the circumstance to cease, this would rather be considered as an instance of delay for the commercial convenience of the assured.[112]

---

107 At 801.

108 (1972) 331 F.Supp. 883.

109 Institute Cargo Clauses 1982 cl 8.3, Institute Cargo Clauses 2009 cl 8.3. Certain earlier cargo clauses in the US used the same wording that the '. . . insurance shall remain in force during deviation, delay beyond the control of the Assured. . .', as in the Extended Cover Clauses cl 2(i) in Corn Trade F.P.A. Clauses 1961 (North Atlantic Shipment) and Corn Trade F.P.A Clauses (1961).

American Institute of Marine Underwriters All Risks Cargo Clauses 1/1/2004 suggest a more complex regime in this respect compared to ICC 2009. The provisions as to the termination of transit after the expiration of 60 days following the completion of discharge (see cll 8.1.4 in ICC 2009 and 6(A)(1)(c) in AIMU 2004) and as to continuance of cover for delay beyond the control of the assured (see cl 8.3. of ICC and cl 6(A)(2)(a) of AIMU) are essentially similar in both documents. However AIMU provides in cl 6(A)(1)(c) that in the event of delay in excess of 60 days after completion of discharge which is beyond the control of the assured the insurance is held covered against a premium for an additional 30 days provided that the assured gives notice as promptly as possible, or in any event before the expiry of 60 days after completion of discharge.

110 Within the meaning of cl 8.1.2 of the Institute Cargo Clauses 1982 and 2009.

111 As was the case in *Miruvor Ltd v National Insurance Co Ltd* [2002] HKEC 1033, pending payment for goods.

112 *Safadi v Western Ass Co* (1933) 46 Ll L Rep 140, see also *Fedsure General Insurance Limited v Carefree Investments (Proprietrary) Limited* (477/99) [2001] ZASCA 88.

This view was also found in *Nec Australia Pty Ltd v Gamif Pty Ltd and others*[113] where it was held that the transit may be interrupted to permit efficient and economical loading, unloading or storage, however the interruption cannot be merely for the commercial convenience of the assured.[114] A temporary storage[115] must be for the furtherance of the carriage of goods to their final destination[116] and the transit may be interrupted by circumstances associated with the requirements of their transportation.[117]

'Delay beyond the control of the assured' and the transit clause

10.52 The term has been in use in the transit clause of the Institute Cargo Clauses A-B-C 2009 which provides:

> 'This insurance shall remain in force (subject to termination as provided for in Clauses 8.1.1 to 8.1.4 above and to the provisions of Clause 9 below) *during delay beyond the control of the Assured*, any deviation, forced discharge, reshipment or transhipment and during any variation of the adventure arising from the exercise of a liberty granted to carriers under the contract of carriage.'[118]

Whether or not delay was within the control of the assured may not be a very intricate issue if for instance the assured deliberately avoids shipping,[119] or where the interruption is caused due to a mistake on the part of the assured. An example for the latter can be found in *Groban v American Casualty Company*[120] where the policy stated that the goods were covered during delay beyond the control of the assured. The policy also contained a marine extension clause whereby the assured had the right to declare the goods for warehouse-to-warehouse coverage from the point of origin to the point of destination. The assured was held covered in case of omission or error in the description of the voyage or of the vessel. The assured misstated that the voyage was from Freetown to New York which was due to a mistaken information on his part whereas the voyage was actually from Marampa Mines to New York through Freetown. The goods when arrived at Freetown had been discharged and remained on the Freetown pier awaiting loading aboard the

---

113 For the full citation, *Nec Australia Pty Ltd v Gamif Pty Ltd; Neway Transport Industries Pty Ltd; Australian Eagle Insurance Co Ltd; Colonial Mutual General Insurance Company Ltd and Webden Pty Ltd* [1993] FCA 252.

114 At para 27.

115 The term 'in transit' was defined in the policy as involving temporary housing.

116 As was the case in *ELAZ International Co v Hong Kong & Shanghai Insurance Co Ltd* [2006] HKEC 825 in the context of interruption of the transit for on-shipment, which eventually aimed at delivering the goods to their final destination.

117 *Nec Australia Pty Ltd v Gamif Pty Ltd; Neway Transport Industries Pty Ltd; Australian Eagle Insurance Co Ltd; Colonial Mutual General Insurance Company Ltd and Webden Pty Ltd* [1993] FCA 252, para 28.

118 cl 8.3, emphasis added. An almost identical clause is found in the Institute Cargo Clauses A-B-C 1982 cl 8.3.

119 This argument was mentioned in *Commercial Union Assurance v The Niger Co* [1922] 12 Ll L Rep 235, at 236.

120 (1972) 331 F.Supp. 883.

vessel for the next stage of the transit. It was held that the assured was protected by the marine extension clause and that the considerable interruption of the transit at Freetown was beyond its control and therefore the transit had not terminated.

10.53 In *Safadi v Western Assurance Company*[121] the insurance cover would not be terminated during 'transhipment, if any, otherwise than as above, and/ or *delay arising from circumstances beyond the control of the assured*'.[122] The assured decided to store the goods for a long time in the Beirut Customs House due to an insurrection at the destination, fearing they would be lost if they were forwarded. The issue was whether the insurrection at the time of the transit and which had been going on for more than two years at the time when the assured decided to store the goods for longer than usual, rendered the delay as one that is beyond the control of the assured because the insurrection itself was a circumstance beyond its control.

It was noted that 'cause or circumstances and matters beyond the control of the assured' could not excuse the assured where those circumstances are in existence or are known to be in existence by the assured at the time when the contract of insurance is made; at the time goods are sent on by the assured (in case of a cargo policy); and at the time, if available, the documents representing the goods are forwarded.[123] The evidence found showed that the assured could have perfectly paid the customs duties and sent the goods on to their destination, as the insurrection was an ongoing event for two years and was known to the assured at the time the insurance contract was made. The delay was therefore within the control of the assured.

10.54 Another issue arising in respect of delay beyond the control of the assured is whether it can excuse a prolonged detention of goods after the expiry of the time limit for their transit. This argument was raised by the assured in *Safadi v Western Assurance Company*[124] and was argued on the ground of excuses available under s 49 of the MIA 1906. The Court did not have to deal with those issues as on the facts of the case it was clear that the delay was not beyond the control of the assured. The counter-argument of the insurers was that the cover ended by the expiration of the time limit mentioned in the transit clause[125] and the clause with respect to delay beyond the control of the assured could by no means extend the period of cover itself; it merely operated during the course of the transit. The Court approached the insurer's argument favourably yet this point was *obiter*. Therefore albeit *Safadi* may not be authority for the suggestion that delay beyond the control of the assured could only excuse the assured during transit, i.e. until the time limit expressed as to the period of cover ceases, it is controversial whether an authority is at all needed given that in ICC 2009 and 1982, sub-cl 8.3 is made subject to cll

---

121 (1933) 46 Ll L Rep 140.
122 Emphasis added.
123 At 143.
124 (1933) 46 Ll L Rep 140.
125 In this case it was 30 days.

8.1.1 to 8.1.4 enumerating the circumstances terminating the transit. It is noteworthy that in *Wiggins*[126] it was held and then repeated in *Verna*[127] that delay beyond the control of the assured is not capable of extending the sixty days period, neither can it render the exclusion of delay losses in s 55(2)(b) inapplicable.[128]

10.55 In *Northern Feather International Inc v Those Certain London Underwriters Subscribing to Policy No JWP108 Through Wigham Poland Ltd*[129] the goods were rolls of dyed cotton ticking which had been refused entry by the customs authorities in the United States on the ground that they had not entered the country under the correct visa number as a result of which the goods had been stored in a warehouse pending resolution of the dispute. They were insured under an open cargo policy against 'against all risks of physical loss or damage from any external cause' which also contained a warehouse clause providing 'Held covered at a premium to be arranged in the event of transshipment, if any, other than as above *and/or in the event of delay in excess of the above time limits arising from circumstances beyond the control of the Assured.*'[130] Under the policy, the assured had to give prompt notice when they became aware of an event for which they would be held covered. The policy further contained a marine extension clause which provided that the insurance specifically covered the goods during deviation, delay, forced discharge, reshipment and transhipment and that it was a condition of the insurance that there shall be no interruption or suspension of transit unless due to circumstances beyond control of the assured.

10.56 A fire occurred while the goods were kept in the warehouse upon which the assured claimed against the insurers who resisted the claim, *inter alia*, on the ground that the interruptions of transit of shipments were not due to circumstances beyond the assured's control and that therefore the assured was not covered under the policy's marine extension clause; and additionally that the cover had ceased under the warehouse clause by the time of the fire. With respect to whether the delay in the customs was a delay within the control of the assured within the

---

126 *Wiggins Teape Australia Pty Ltd v Baltica Insurance Co Ltd* [1970] 2 NSWR 77.
127 *Verna Trading Pty Ltd v New India Assurance Co Ltd* [1991] 1 VR 129 per Ormiston J.
128 *Lam Seng Hang Co Pte Ltd v The Insurance Corporation of Singapore Ltd* [2001] SGHC 31.
129 714 F.Supp. 1352 (United States District Court, D. New Jersey).
130 Emphasis added. The full warehouse-to-warehouse clause read as follows: 'This insurance attaches from the time the goods leave the warehouse and/or store at the place named in the policy for the commencement of the transit and continues during the ordinary course of transit, including customary transshipments, if any, until the goods are discharged overside from the overseas vessel at the final port. *Thereafter the insurance continues whilst the goods are in transit and/or awaiting transit until delivered to final warehouse at the destination named in the policy or until the expiry of 15 days (or 30 days if the destination to which the goods are insured is outside the limits of the port) whichever shall first occur.* The time limits referred to above to be reckoned from midnight of the day on which the discharge overside of the goods hereby insured from the overseas vessel is completed. *Held covered at a premium to be arranged in the event of transshipment, if any, other than as above and/or in the event of delay in excess of the above time limits arising from circumstances beyond the control of the Assured.*'

meaning of the warehouse clause, the Court stated that the inquiry must lie in whether the assured had control over the categorisation of its shipments under the incorrect visa number. The Court pronounced that without knowing this, it was not possible for the Court to determine as a matter of law whether the delay in the transportation of the shipments was beyond the assured's control. In respect of the warehouse clause however the assured had not given any notice to the insurers as required by the clause and he was therefore not entitled to rely thereon. The same inquiry as to whether the assured had control over the interruption of transit had to be raised in respect of the marine extension clause, and the Court, having found a genuine issue of material fact in this regard, could not find as a matter of law that the condition precedent to coverage to the marine extension clause had or had not been met.

'Delay beyond the control of the assured' and justification for delay

10.57 A delay may at the same be a delay within the control of the assured and be excusable in nature if it is incurred, for instance, because of the circumstances enumerated in s 49. Section 49(1)(a) provides that delay in prosecuting the voyage contemplated by the policy will be excused where such delay is authorised by a term in the policy. Clause 8.3 which reads that delay beyond the control of the assured does not terminate the cover is indeed such a term; a more intricate issue would however be whether a delay within the control of the assured would discharge the insurers from liability where such delay is reasonably necessary for the safety of cargo[131] or is incurred for the purpose of saving human life.[132] The decision of the assured to delay a voyage shall not necessarily and on its own render a delay within the control of the assured if the circumstances which give rise to the decision are beyond its control.

10.58 In *Hyderabad (Deccan) Co v Willoughby*[133] the delay although not expressly stated to be a 'delay within the control of the assured' was discussed as such upon the facts. It was incurred for the purpose of the furtherance of the voyage[134] and therefore was justifiable. However the assured was merely slow in arranging the forwarding of goods, and delay was accordingly held to be unreasonable. If this judgment is considered in light of ICC 1982 and 2009, the question would be whether a delay within the control of the assured would be sufficient to take the goods off risk if delay is not unreasonable in terms of its length and is justifiable in terms of its purpose.

---

131 As per s 49(1)(d).
132 As per s 49(1)(e).
133 *Hyderabad (Deccan) Co v Willoughby* [1899] 2 QB 530.
134 The delay was both in the interest of the assured and insurer and was to secure the safe accomplishment of the journey of the cargo.

Duty of the assured to act with reasonable despatch (avoidance of delay clause)

10.59 Clause 18 of the Institute Cargo Clauses 2009 the title of which is 'avoidance of delay' provides as follows:

> 'It is a condition of this insurance that the Assured shall act with reasonable despatch in all circumstances within their control.'

The earlier version of the clause[135] was identically worded although it was entitled 'reasonable despatch clause'.[136] Given that the clause refers to 'reasonable despatch', the question arises as to whether it is a clause that is similar in function to s 48 of the MIA, i.e. whether it requires the assured to prosecute the sea voyage or both the sea voyage and the land transit in a timely manner.[137] The clause does not expressly stipulate that the delay has to be unreasonable as required by s 48 so as to discharge the insurers, therefore it is not clear whether any interruption during the course of transit under the Institute Cargo Clauses which is within the control of the assured would trigger the clause.

10.60 The alternative view as to the function of the clause is that it encompasses a different duty for the assured such as the duty to sue and labour given the expression 'in all circumstances within their control' which arguably is not confined to prosecuting the sea voyage or the land transit with reasonable despatch.[138] This expression could also denote a general reasonable despatch requirement which all other clauses are subject to.[139] There is currently no binding authority in the United Kingdom on the scope of application of the clause however few cases in other common law jurisdictions shed light on this matter[140] which will be further considered below.

Scope of the clause

10.61 The use of the phrase 'in all circumstances' may give rise to the question of whether the clause applies during the ordinary transit as well as after a loss occurs and in pursuit of a claim.[141] Before proceeding with whether the clause has such a wide scope of application, the link between the transit clause[142] and avoidance of delay clause would need to be analysed.

---

135 Institute Cargo Clauses 1982 cl 18.

136 ibid.

137 For the view that 'in all circumstances' refer to land transit and that accordingly the clause has a wider scope than s 48, please see Hodges, 66.

138 In Gilman and Merkin, *Arnould's Law of Marine Insurance and Average* (18th edn at para 19–37) it is stated that the clause applied both to delay in transit and delay in responding to a casualty.

139 This shall be considered below at para 10.65.

140 For the illustrations under the Australian law see *Wiggins Teape Australia Pty Ltd v Baltica Insurance Co Ltd* [1970] 2 NSWR 77; *Verna Trading Pty Ltd v New India Assurance Co Ltd* [1991] 1 VR 129.

141 *Arnould* (18th edn), 19–37. This view had also been expressed in the 17th edition.

142 In particular, cl 8.3. of ICC 2009.

(a) The transit clause and the avoidance of delay clause

(I) 'DELAY BEYOND THE CONTROL OF THE ASSURED' AND AVOIDANCE OF DELAY

10.62 Whether the avoidance of delay clause is a clause strengthening the position of the insurer in respect of the transit clause in that it imposes on the assured a duty to act with reasonable despatch for the circumstances within their control is fairly controversial and unclear under the Institute Cargo Clauses 2009. The American Institute Cargo Clauses All Risks 2004 contains a clearer wording which reads:

> 'It is a condition of this insurance that there shall be no interruption or suspension of transit unless due to circumstances beyond the control of the Assured, Assignee, Consignee or Claimant and the Assured, Assignee, Consignee or Claimant shall act with reasonable dispatch in all circumstances within their control.'[143]

Under these Clauses the assured is accordingly under a duty to act with reasonable despatch both during the transit *and* in all circumstances within their control whereby the operation of the clause is not confined to a duty to act with reasonable despatch during the ordinary course of transit.

10.63 Institute Cargo Clauses (Wartime Extension) 1/5/1941 used during World War II provided unlimited cover during delay and the 'reasonable despatch clause' excluded cover for delay which the assured could control.[144] The wording continued in the Institute Cargo Clauses (Extended Cover) introduced in 1952 however delay in the transit clause was limited to 'delay beyond the control of the assured'.[145] The avoidance of delay clause was retained in the following sets of clauses[146] along with the transit clause whereby the transit terminated in case of delay within the control of the assured.

Against this background, it can be submitted that prior to the introduction of 'delay beyond the control of the assured' term into the transit clause, the avoidance of delay clause which provided that the assured should act with reasonable despatch in all circumstances 'within their control' was retained so as to qualify the unlimited cover for delay in the transit clause and may arguably be considered to have been confined solely to that purpose. Following the introduction of the expression 'delay beyond the control of the assured' into the transit clause, the avoidance of delay clause should now comprise a wider or a different scope and not be a mere repetition.[147]

---

143 cl 6(A)(5).

144 O'May, *O'May on Marine Insurance*, 491. No reasonable despatch clause was contained in the Institute Cargo Clauses (F.P.A) 11/2/1946 although cover was provided during 'delay beyond the control of the assured'; the same could be said of the Institute Cargo Clauses (W.A) 11/2/1946 and the Institute Cargo Clauses (All Risks) 1/1/1951. See also Dunt, *Marine Cargo Insurance* (2nd edn), para 11–34.

145 O'May, 491.

146 The reasonable despatch clause appeared in many sets of clauses: Coal Clauses (Great Britain-Coastwise Voyages) 1/1/1953 cl 15; Institute Cargo Clauses (Extended Cover) 1/2/1956 cl 6; Institute War Clauses 1/10/1955 cl 7; Institute Strikes Clauses (Extended Cover) 1/2/56 cl 6.

147 For the views which considered the clause in terms of the transit clause only, please see J.K. Goodacre, *Marine Insurance Claims* (3rd edn, London: Witherby 1996), 313.

10.64 The connection between the transit clause and the avoidance of delay clause has been the subject of *Wiggins Teape v Baltica*[148] which sheds light on the scope of application of these clauses and their overlaps. The policy in this case incorporated the Institute Cargo Clauses 1958 which contained a warehouse-to-warehouse clause providing that the period of cover after the completion of discharge overside the goods from the oversea vessel at the final port of discharge should not extend beyond 60 days. The policy further stipulated that the insurance was to remain in force during delay beyond the control of the assured and contained an avoidance of delay clause.

10.65 The goods in this case could not be taken to the final destination because of the insufficiency of storage space and instead were stored by the assured at the port of discharge which was commercially convenient in the circumstances. The goods were lost in the warehouse following a fire before the expiration of the sixty days. It was held by the Supreme Court of New South Wales that the goods were protected by the policy provided that the goods reached the final warehouse within sixty days from the discharge of the goods and that the assured acted with reasonable despatch in all circumstances within its control. According to Macfarlan J, the avoidance of delay clause was a condition governing all other clauses[149] and pointed to a policy concerned with transit.[150] The warehouse clause granting cover for delay beyond the control of the assured meant that the transit should be prosecuted with 'reasonable despatch', i.e. a despatch which is related to the movement of goods.[151] Accordingly, the avoidance of delay clause would become obsolete if the assured could discharge the goods at the discharge port and leave them there for sixty days for a reason not connected with the requirements of transport. This reasoning was criticised by the assured in *Verna*, on the ground that the sixty days was a fixed period of time and was irreconcilable with reasonable despatch and that it would require an express term within the transit clause if the intention of the insurer was to extend the reasonable despatch clause to the transit provisions.[152]

---

148 *Wiggins Teape Australia Pty Ltd v Baltica Insurance Co Ltd* [1970] 2 NSWR 77.

149 At 80. This approach was mentioned in *Verna Trading Pty Ltd v New India Assurance Co Ltd* [1991] 1 VR 129 per Kaye J who noted that the construction to be given to the avoidance of delay clause depends 'upon its terms when read in conjunction with all the provisions of the Institute Clauses', at 146. He further noted that the movement of the goods after having been discharged was a matter essentially within the control of the assured. The purpose of the policy would be reached by requiring the assured to deliver the goods to the final destination with reasonable despatch, at 146.

150 The phrase 'in transit' was considered as equivalent to 'in movement' in *Parkinson v Mathews and Drysdale* 1930 WLD 58, at 62 by Feetham J. This shall not however mean that storing goods for a short period without abandoning the aim to deliver them could be taken to take the goods off risk. Albeit the policy in *Wiggins* did not contain any such clause as cl 8.1. in the Institute Cargo Clauses 2009, the phrase 'the transit continues during the ordinary course of transit' would also strengthen the position of insurers as any delay which is not in the ordinary course of transit would terminate the policy, notwithstanding the occurrence of the circumstances mentioned in 8.1.1 to 8.1.4.

151 *Wiggins Teape Australia Pty Ltd v Baltica Insurance Co Ltd* [1970] 2 NSWR 77, 81.

152 Mentioned in Kaye J's speech in *Verna Trading Pty Ltd v New India Assurance Co Ltd* [1991] 1 VR 129.

The decision in *Wiggins* reiterates the view that goods in transit are goods in movement to their final destination, i.e. the final warehouse, and the act of storing the goods for an indefinite period in a place commercially convenient for the assured is not part of transit.

(II) 'ORDINARY COURSE OF TRANSIT' AND AVOIDANCE OF DELAY

10.66 The Institute Cargo Clauses 2009 cl 8.1 provides that the insurance continues during the 'ordinary course of transit',[153] a phrase which was not found in some of the earlier versions of the Clauses.[154] In *John Martin of London Ltd v Russell*[155] the policy was on the Institute Cargo Clauses (Extended Cover) 1952 terms which contained both an avoidance of delay clause and a transit clause; the latter however did not provide that the insurance would continue during the 'ordinary course of transit'. The goods were discharged and left in a transit shed awaiting delivery to ultimate consignees. One of the defences of the insurer was that the insurance ceased upon the discharge of the goods because the consignees had not intended to send the goods to the final warehouse. The avoidance of delay clause was not specifically invoked by the insurers in support of this contention, and did not form any part of their defence.

10.67 Pearson J in deciding whether the insurance policy came to an end on the ground that the goods were discharged in the transit shed that could be taken to be the 'final warehouse' noted that the transit and avoidance of delay clauses together 'afford clues to assist the search' where the goods do not go to the final warehouse.[156] Holding that the transit shed was not the 'final warehouse' and that there was no condition that goods were only covered so long as they were intended to go to a final warehouse, Pearson J decided that there was still insurance cover at the time of loss. As a result of this decision, new transit wording containing the words 'during the ordinary course of transit' was re-introduced to 'overcome the lack of indication of transit in the Institute Cargo Clauses' and to 'strengthen Clause [18], the Avoidance of Delay Clause'.[157]

10.68 Where an act of the assured triggers both the transit clause whereby transit continues during ordinary course of transit and the avoidance of delay clause, the moment cover ceases would be highly important in determining for what losses would the insurers not be liable. In *Verna*,[158] Beach J in the first instance enunciated that the insurance terminated when the assured made the decision to leave the goods in the customs house for more than a month; he was also in breach of the avoidance of delay clause insofar as delivery of the goods to their final destination was concerned. In the appeal, Ormiston J was of the view that Beach

---

153 The 1982 version of the clauses have the same wording, see cl 8.1.

154 e.g. Institute Cargo Clauses (Extended Cover) 1952.

155 *John Martin of London Ltd v Russell* [1960] 1 Lloyd's List Law Reports 554.

156 At 563.

157 Historic Records Report HR5, at p 103, as cited in Dunt and Melbourne, *Insuring Cargoes in the New Millenium: The Institute Cargo Clauses 2009*, para 6.80.

158 *Verna Trading Pty Ltd v New India Assurance Co Ltd* [1991] 1 VR 129.

J had primarily rested his conclusion on the reasonable despatch clause, however it was preferable to start by looking at the transit clause on the ground that, if the transit had terminated according to that clause, that finding would be conclusive.

(b) Post-casualty situations and the avoidance of delay clause

10.69 It was submitted that the clause applied both to delay during the transit and to the actions taken by the assured after the occurrence of a casualty.[159] One of the examples to be given in this respect can be the giving of notice of the loss suffered by the assured to the insurer and not delaying the claim for an indemnity. The Institute Cargo Clauses contain a separate 'duty of assured' clause which requires the assured, their employees and agents to take all reasonable measures for the purpose of averting or minimising losses incurred following a casualty and to ensure all rights against all third parties are preserved.[160] There may be a degree of overlap between the two clauses in terms of scope of application, yet their distinction lies in the persons who are within the scope of the clauses.

Under the Institute Cargo Clauses 2009, the only person who has to act with reasonable despatch under the avoidance of delay clause is the assured. Whether this would also include the assured's agents or servants has yet to be judicially construed; however in case of ambiguity, the clause should be construed against the insurer and the term 'assured' should be construed narrowly.[161] This being the case, the Duty of Assured clause provides that the duty is not only of the Assured yet also of their employees and agents. It may accordingly be submitted that in terms of the overlapping scope of the two clauses, the point of distinction would be the consequence of the breach of the provision and the person who commits the breach. By way of example, if a customs agent of the assured delays notifying the assured of a loss, the insurers can argue that the duty of assured clause has been breached, although an avoidance of delay clause may arguably not be invoked.

10.70 Not acting with reasonable despatch following a casualty could encompass the failure to notify a loss in time as well as an event for which the assured is held covered under the policy, such as change of voyage or termination of the contract of carriage due to circumstances beyond the control of the assured. This suggestion may however present several caveats. The Institute Cargo Clauses

---

159 *Arnould* (18th edn), 19–37; (17th edn), 19–35. It was submitted in Sir Michael Mustill and Jonathan Gilman, *Arnould's Law of Marine Insurance and Average* (16th edn), vol II, para 704 that the scope of the clause was with respect to post-casualty actions of the assured. The suggestion that the avoidance of delay clause governs all other clauses in the Institute Clauses as was stated in *Wiggins Teape Australia Pty Ltd v Baltica Insurance Co Ltd* [1970] 2 NSWR 77, 80 per Macfarlan J; *Verna Trading Pty Ltd v New India Assurance Co Ltd* [1991] 1 VR 129 per Kaye J seems in part to support this view.

160 Institute Cargo Clauses 2009 cl 16.

161 The American Institute Cargo Clauses All Risks 2004, cl 6(A)(5) provides '. . . and the Assured, Assignee, Consignee or Claimant shall act with reasonable dispatch in all circumstances within their control.' and relatively widens the scope of the clause in respect of persons having the duty to act with reasonable despatch.

1982 and 2009 contain a special 'Note' recorded at the foot of the policy[162] which requires the assured to give prompt notice of such an event when they become aware thereof. The operation of the note lies in that the right to be held covered is dependent upon prompt notice; otherwise the insurance terminates. 'Prompt notice' was taken to denote 'notice in reasonable time' in *Liberian Insurance Agency Inc v Moussa*[163] per Donaldson J.[164] Therefore, should the suggestion that the avoidance of delay clause governs all the other clauses in the Institute Cargo Clauses be tenable, one view can be that it strengthens the position of insurers when it is read in conjunction with the Note to discharge them from liability where the assured fails to notify the change of voyage or termination of the voyage promptly. A contrary view was expressed by Kaye J in *Verna*[165] according to whom if avoidance of delay clause was confined to after casualty situations where the assured fails to give notice of the loss suffered or change of voyage, the note recorded at the foot of the policy would be 'tautological'.[166]

10.71 The Institute Cargo Clauses 2009 cl 8.3 which states that the insurance is still in force during delay beyond the control of the assured is not a held covered clause within the meaning of the Note and the assured is not required to give prompt notice to insurers if it seeks to be held covered thereunder. Delay beyond the control of the assured may however cause termination of the contract of carriage where the delay is of a nature that would frustrate the object of the adventure and it may be contended that for this reason has to be notified to the insurers as per cl 9 for the assured to be covered despite the termination of the contract of carriage.[167]

Operation of the clause

(a) Section 48 and the avoidance of delay clause

10.72 The avoidance of delay clause has many similarities with s 48 and determining the scope of s 48 could therefore be of help in construing the avoidance

---

162 The wordings of the note in 1982 and 2009 Clauses are fairly similar. The one found in the 2009 Clauses provides as follows:

> 'NOTE: Where a continuation of cover is requested under Clause 9, or a change of destination is notified under Clause 10, there is an obligation to give prompt notice to the Insurers and the right to such cover is dependent upon compliance with this obligation.'

163 [1977] 2 Lloyd's Rep 560.

164 At 566–567. Donaldson J expressed some doubt as to whether the note was contractual, nevertheless expressed the view that he was satisfied it accurately stated the law.

165 *Verna Trading Pty Ltd v New India Assurance Co Ltd* [1991] 1 VR 129, 146.

166 The note contained in the policy in *Verna* read as follows:

> 'NOTE: It is necessary fort he assured when they become aware of an event which is 'held covered' under this insurance to give prompt notice to the underwriters and the right to such cover is dependent upon compliance with this obligation.'

167 It is to be noted that this would seldom occur in practice, given that cl 8.3 is also subject to the usual circumstances terminating the transit (cl 8.1.1 to 8.1.4) whereby the policy may already have come to an end during the frustrating delay.

of delay clause. The 'adventure insured' in terms of s 48 is a 'marine adventure' whereby the subject-matter is exposed to maritime perils;[168] moreover an insurance policy may, by its terms, be extended to cover the assured for land risks.[169] Accordingly, 'in so far as applicable', the provisions of the Marine Insurance Act would apply to the policy where there is an adventure analogous to the marine adventure.[170] The wording 'in so far as applicable' would raise the question of whether s 48 would be implied into a marine insurance contract for both land and sea legs if the Marine Insurance Act applies to sea and land risks. If affirmative, the avoidance of delay clause can be considered, *inter alia*, as an instance of s 48 in the Institute Cargo Clauses; otherwise, where it is to be taken that s 48 only applies in the sea leg of the adventure insured, the question is whether the avoidance of delay clause would merely apply with respect to the land transit as s 48 would already be implied.

It was submitted in *Verna*[171] that the purpose which is reached by the reasonable despatch requirement with respect to sea risks was achieved in relation to land risks by the avoidance of delay clause.[172] However before the MIA 1906 was enacted, it was enunciated in *Mount v Larkins*[173] that all elements of the adventure, i.e. both land and sea voyage elements must be prosecuted with 'proper and ordinary diligence'.[174] A view supporting this approach was expressed in *Verna* by Ormiston J.[175]

10.73 In addition to whether s 48 and the avoidance of delay clause overlap in terms of their period of application, another question would arise as to whether the delay has to be unreasonable for the clause to apply in the absence of express stipulation to that effect. The clause merely mentions that the assured shall act with reasonable despatch in all circumstances within their control, without referring to whether any delay within the control of the assured has to be unreasonable to trigger the clause. Ormiston J in *Verna* was of the view that there was no such requirement in the avoidance of delay clause and that any delay within the control of the assured would render the clause applicable.[176]

---

168 As per s 3 of the Marine Insurance Act 1906, 'maritime perils' include 'perils, of the like kind or which may be designated by the policy'.

169 s 2(1).

170 s 2(2).

171 *Verna Trading Pty Ltd v New India Assurance Co Ltd* [1991] 1 VR 129.

172 At 146 per Kaye J. This view was expressed in respect of s 54 of the Australian Marine Insurance Act 1909 which is identical to s 48 of the Marine Insurance Act 1906.

173 *Mount v Larkins* (1831) 8 Bing 108.

174 ibid, 122 per Tindal CJ.

175 At 165. It was stated that the land transit element of a policy was covered by the Marine Insurance Act including the provisions which relate to 'voyages' (of which both s 42 and 48 are parts) on the basis of the textbook of Sir M.D. Chalmers and E.R.H. Ivamy, *Marine Insurance Act 1906* (7th edn, Butterworth-Heinemann 1971), 4–5 and of *Leon v Casey* [1932] 2 KB 576, 585–587 per Scrutton LJ and 590 per Greer LJ.

176 *Verna Trading Pty Ltd v New India Assurance Co Ltd* [1991] 1 VR 129, 174 per Ormiston J.

DELAY IN VOYAGE

(b) Whether the clause operates as a warranty and burden of proof

10.74 There is currently no binding authority under English law as to whether the avoidance of delay clause operates as a warranty however it was enunciated in *Ostra Insurance Public Company Ltd v Kintex Shareholding Company (M/V Szechuen)*[177] that 'There are plainly strong arguments in favour of treating this as a breach of warranty'.[178] Various views were expressed as to the meaning of the phrase 'It is a condition of this insurance' found in the avoidance of delay clause. One of the views was that this wording could not be equated to 'duty' as in the duty of the assured clause which merely gives rise to a claim for damages in the event of breach.[179] It was further stated that insofar as the clause related to delay during the adventure within the meaning of s 48,[180] it would not bring an alternative ground of defence to insurers which can in any case be discharged as per s 48.[181] As for the application of the clause to actions of the assured following a casualty or in pursuit of a claim as well as delays in transit, it was contended that the clause should be construed as an innominate term.[182] If the avoidance of delay clause can indeed apply to circumstances after the occurrence of a casualty in terms of the assured's actions, delay in notifying the casualty may result in loss of evidence and accordingly difficulties in challenging third party claims for insurers.[183] This breach can be so serious for the insurers as to treat the contract as terminated.[184]

10.75 In the leading cases decided in Australia, the avoidance of delay clause was held to operate as a promissory warranty whereby the insurer is discharged from liability when the assured does not act with reasonable despatch.[185] It is controversial whether this approach is in line with s 48[186] in construing the avoidance of delay clause. This is due to the fact that s 48 may not strictly be taken to be a promissory warranty, given its background as a branch of the law relating to

---

177 [2004] EWHC 357 (Comm).

178 per Cooke J, at para 52.

179 O'May, 491.

180 Which is equivalent to s 48, except that it is subject to whether it encompasses a wider scope of application, and not only in sea transit. This shall be discussed below.

181 Arnould (18th edn), para 19–37.

182 Arnould (18th edn), para 19–37. In the 17th edition, para 19–35, reference was made in this respect to *McAlpine Plc v BAI (Run Off) Ltd* [1998] 2 Lloyd's Rep 694 (Colman J); [2000] 1 Lloyd's Rep 437 CA; *Friends Provident Life & Pensions Ltd v Sirius Intl Insurance* [2005] 2 Lloyd's Rep 517. According to the editors of the 17th edition, the word 'condition' was to be taken to mean a 'term', at para 19–35.

183 As were mentioned in *McAlpine Plc v BAI (Run Off) Ltd* [1998] 2 Lloyd's Rep 694. See *Moussi H. Issa NV v Grand Union Insurance Co Ltd* [1984] HKLR 137, *obiter* that the reasonable despatch clause would not elevate the breach of the Bailee Clause in the Institute Cargo Clauses into a breach of condition so that any failure to preserve rights against third parties would operate automatically as a defence.

184 As to the fact that the consequence of a breach is such as substantially depriving the innocent party of the whole benefit of the contract, see *Hongkong Fir Shipping Co Ltd v Kawasaki Kisen Kaisha Ltd (The Hongkong Fir)* [1961] 2 Lloyd's Rep 478; [1962] 2 QB 26.

185 *Wiggins Teape Australia Pty Ltd v Baltica Insurance Co Ltd* [1970] 2 NSWR 77, 80–81 per Macfarlan J. Also see *Verna Trading Pty Ltd v New India Assurance Co Ltd* [1991] 1 VR 129 per Kaye and McGarvie JJ.

186 Or to the equivalent of this clause in the MIA 1909, i.e. s 54.

201

deviation. Instead s 48 takes part in the voyage conditions of the Marine Insurance Act 1906 and is, by nature, an alteration of risk provision. Albeit this classification may not make an obvious difference in terms of the consequence of the breach of the term that is discharge from liability,[187] it may nevertheless be of importance in respect of the burden of proof. Construing the avoidance of delay clause as a warranty would place the onus on the insurer to prove that the loss occurred after the breach of warranty whereas under s 48 the assured has to prove that he suffered a loss at a time and place when covered by the policy.[188]

10.76 The Insurance Act 2015 which entered into force in August 2016 abolished the long-established rule that a breach of the warranty would automatically discharge the insurers from liability as from the time of the breach.[189] Given that the avoidance of delay clause has not yet been litigated in the United Kingdom, the courts are yet to decide whether it is a warranty in which case s 10 of the Insurance Act 2015 will apply. It has been suggested that in light of the recent decisions on warranties it is unlikely that the courts will construe the avoidance of delay clause as a warranty on the ground that the wording of the clause is not sufficiently clear.[190] The question remains however whether the scope of s 11 would encompass situations caught by the avoidance of delay clause.

Section 11 applies both to any risk-related term, express or implied, and to warranties set out under s 10, in the latter case in addition to s 10. Two questions must be answered before determining whether s 11 can apply to the avoidance of delay clause: the preliminary question would be whether the avoidance of delay clause defines the risk as a whole because s 11 would not be applicable in this circumstance.[191] It is submitted that the way the avoidance of delay clause is drafted does not necessarily result in the finding that the policy will not apply where the assured does not act with reasonable despatch within their control and in that sense cannot be considered as a term defining the risk as a whole. The second question is whether the compliance with the term would tend to reduce the risk of loss of a particular kind and loss at a particular location or time.[192] A failure by the assured to notify the insurer with reasonable despatch of any loss that has occurred can result in at least two types of losses; the first is the loss of the right of the insurer to claim against third parties, and the second is any aggravation of the loss already suffered resulting from such failure. The latter being a loss suffered by the assured can be caught by s 11 according to which the insurer can exclude or discharge its liability unless the

---

187 In both cases of breach of warranty and change of risk undertaken by the insurer, the consequence would be discharge from liability for insurers.

188 It is necessary to remember that in most of the pre-MIA cases, the assured had the onus of proving that the loss occurred during the period of cover, see as example *Hyderabad (Deccan) Co v Willoughby* [1899] 2 QB 530; *Smith v Surridge* (1801) 4 Esp 25; *Grant v King* (1802) 4 Esp 175; *Schroder v Thompson* (1817) 7 Taunt 462.

189 See s 10(1).

190 See *Arnould* (18th edn), para 19–38. This view has found support by Dunt in *Marine Cargo Insurance* (2nd edn) at para 11.39.

191 s 11(1).

192 s 11(1).

assured shows that the non-compliance with the avoidance of delay clause could not have increased the risk of the loss actually occurred.[193] The relation between the non-compliance with the term and the loss which actually occurred is most likely to be based on causation although the Law Commissions in the Explanatory Notes of the Insurance Bill stated that 'the insurer should not be able to rely on that non-compliance to escape liability unless the non-compliance could potentially have had some bearing on the risk of the loss which actually occurred'[194] which arguably suggests a lesser degree of connection between the non-compliance and the risk of loss than causation.

The above observations on the applicability of s 11 of the Insurance Act 2015 in the context of the avoidance of delay clause shall also be relevant for s 48. The Law Commissions had enunciated before the entry into force of the Insurance Act 2015 that their proposals on warranties would not affect the voyage conditions as they were expressed as conditions precedent to the attachment of risk.[195] Section 48 is clearly not a provision expressed as such and could well be caught by s 11.

(a) Section 49 excuses and the avoidance of delay clause

10.77 The clause can be seen as an example of s 49(1)(a) which provides that delay in prosecuting the voyage is excused where authorised by a special term in the policy on the ground that the assured is not required to act with reasonable despatch in circumstances beyond its control. This line of thought would give rise to the query of whether the circumstances that are not within the control of the assured are those enumerated in s 49 for which the assured will be excused. It is to be noted however that the excuses in s 49 are of a nature to operate only at sea[196] and s 49(2) provides that the 'ship' must resume her course and prosecute 'her voyage' with reasonable despatch after the delay ceases to operate. Given that s 49 provides excuses for delay under s 48, the wording of s 49 arguably suggests that s 48 is also confined to sea transit whereas the avoidance of delay clause would apply to both land and sea transit risks.

It is also noteworthy that what can be excused under s 49 may be caught by the avoidance of delay clause. s 49 excuses are not all beyond the control of the assured in the sense that delaying the voyage for instance for saving human life at sea may perfectly be voluntary and within the control of the assured and would be considered as a breach of the avoidance of delay clause, however such delay would be justifiable under s 49. The question arises therefore whether the phrase 'in all circumstances within their control' refers at the same time to an unjustifiable delay. Should the clause ever be litigated in the United Kingdom, the issue whether the clause would operate where delay is both caused by circumstances within the control of the assured and is unjustifiable will have to be assessed.

---

193 As per s 11(3).

194 Rob Merkin and Özlem Gürses, 'The Insurance Act 2015: Rebalancing the interests of Insurer and Assured', *Modern Law Review* (2015) 78(6) MLR 1004–1027, at 1022.

195 The Law Commission Consultation Paper 204, the Scottish Law Commission Discussion Paper 155, 16.24.

196 e.g. 49(1)(e), (f), (g).

INDEX

abandonment: voyage 9.40; unreasonable delay 9.40

abnormal delay 1.15; proximate causes 2.17, 2.25

advance loss of profits insurance *see* delay in start-up (DSU) insurance

'all risks' policies 1.17; loss of market value, and 3.30

alteration of risk 9.31–9.49; consequences 9.41–9.45; justifiable delays 9.46–9.47; limits to 9.46–9.47; reasonableness 9.36–9.37; relation of justifiable and unreasonable delays 9.48–9.49; types 9.34; unreasonable delay 9.35–9.39; unreasonable delay amounting to abandonment 9.40

assured: control of, beyond the *see* 'delay beyond the control of the assured'; control of, within the 1.18–1.19, 9.13–9.14; delay in making repairs 8.21; duties of, subsequent to delayed delivery of goods 3.19; duty to act with reasonable despatch 10.59–10.77; excessive delay and knowledge 10.24; knowledge 1.21; mitigation of losses and loss of time 8.19–8.22

avoidance of delay clause 10.59–10.77; burden of proof 10.74–10.76; 'delay beyond the control of the assured' 10.62–10.65; operation of clause 10.72–10.76; ordinary course of transit 10.66–10.68; post-casualty situations 10.69–10.71; scope 10.61–10.70; section 48, and 10.72–10.73; section 49 excuses, and 10.77; warranty, whether clause operates as 10.74–10.76

capture, seizure, arrest, restraint or detainment 2.21, 3.25

cargo policies: absence of physical loss of or damage to goods 3.20–3.22; common law 1.2; loss of market and market value as consequential loss in 3.32–3.34; interest of 2.1; peace time 2.21; project *see* delay in start-up (DSU) insurance; tangible objects 3.8; time of delivery 3.3

causation: breaking chain of 2.24; loss, of 1.6; philosophical meaning 2.23

civil unrest 2.22

common law: exclusions 1.2, 2.2; fortuity 1.7, 1.11; hull and machinery insurance 7.1; loss of time clause 6.10–6.11; mere delay not resulting in loss of marine adventure 3.6–3.7; unreasonable delay 10.17; wages and maintenance expenses arising during repairs at port of refuge 7.10–7.13

concealment 9.8–9.10

concurrent causation 2.27–2.33; independent cause of loss, delay 2.31–2.33; limits to rule in *Wayne Tank* 2.30

contract of carriage: delay in delivery 3.2–3.4

delay, meaning 1.4; delivery *see* delivery, delay in; exclusion of 1.10, 1.17; factors of 1.1–1.2; ordinary and extraordinary losses 1.8; use of term 1.3

'delay beyond the control of the assured': avoidance of delay, and 10.62–10.65; justification for delay, and 10.57–10.58; prolonged detention of goods 10.54; third parties, and 10.56; transit clause, and 10.52–10.56

delay in start-up (DSU) insurance 5.1–5.22; contractors 5.5; duration of risks 5.9–5.10; duty of insured clause 5.14–5.22; duty to act with reasonable dispatch 5.19–5.22; exclusions 5.12–5.13; indemnifiable claim 5.9; 'insured' 5.3–5.6; lenders 5.8; measure of indemnity 5.11; mitigation of loss 5.15–5.18; purpose 5.1; recoverability of mitigation expenses 5.15–5.18; scope of cover 5.9; site owners 5.4

delivery, delay in 3.1–3.36; calculating loss 3.4; cargo policies and absence of physical loss of or damage to goods 3.20–3.22; contract of carriage, and 3.3; due arrival of insurable property 3.13–3.14; duties of the assured subsequent to the delayed delivery of goods 3.19; loss of adventure and the MIA 1906 3.8–3.11; loss of market and market value as consequential loss in cargo policies 3.32–3.34; loss of profit, market and adventure by delay 3.15; loss of use of cargo and resulting loss of sale contracts 3.35–3.36; Marine Insurance Act 1906, and 3.5; meaning 3.2–3.5; mere delay not resulting in loss of marine adventure and common law authorities 3.6–3.7; scope of loss of market and market value caused by 3.23–3.31; temporarily missing goods and delay 3.16–3.18; time of 3.3

deprivation perils: delay, and 2.19–2.22; frustration 6.14; loss of market value, and 3.28; irretrievable 3.7; partial loss 2.19

deterioration, loss by and delay 2.2–2.35; aggravating loss 2.25; agreements altering proximate cause rule and delay 2.34–2.35; delay and concurrent causation 2.27–2.33; delay as contributing factor other than proximate cause 2.23–2.26; delay as proximate cause 2.8–2.22 see also proximate causation; last cause in time rule 2.7; *Leyland* 2.9–2.11; pre-MIA authorities 2.3–2.6

deviation and delay 10.3–10.9; liberty clauses on, and impact on delay 10.6–10.9

expenses 4.2–4.17; forwarding and storage charges 4.13–4.17; general average 4.2–4.9; loss of hire 8.8–8.16; loss of market caused by delay and general average 4.7–4.9; ransom negotiations 4.3–4.5; recoverability 4.1; repairs *see* repairs; sue and labour expenses 4.10–4.12; time-sensitive goods 4.11–4.12

fortuity: assessing 1.20; existing policy language 1.9; general considerations 1.6; marine peril and risk 1.4–1.5; naturally occurring losses, and 1.11–1.17; negligence 1.7; obscure 1.2

freight insurance: actual and apprehended loss of time and the loss of time clause 6.19–6.21; consequent on loss of time' and causation 6.22–6.23; early authorities 6.4–6.9; frustration, and 6.14–6.18; loss of hire *see* loss of hire; loss of marine adventure and delay 6.12–6.13; loss of time clause when delay not cause of the loss of adventure 6.14–6.18; time and voyage basis, on 6.1–6.36; time charters and loss of time clause 6.24–6.36 *see also* loss of time clause

Hamburg Rules 3.2

hull and machinery insurance 7.1–7.21: 3/4th collision liability clause 7.21; common law origin 7.1; damage to 7.3–7.5; deterioration of the hull by lengthy delays 7.4–7.5; loss of possession and use of the vessel, delay and constructive total loss 7.18–7.20; ordinary wear and tear 7.4–7.5; repairs *see* repairs

implied conditions: acquiescence 9.21; circumstances known to insurer 9.24–9.26; location of vessel 9.25; negating 9.20–9.26; precedent to the attachment of risk 9.5–9.27; pre-contractual non-disclosure of circumstances which may result in delay 9.7–9.11; reasonable time 9.1, 9.34; representation to qualify or rebut 9.24; usage of trade, and 9.27; waiver by insurer 9.21–9.23

implied warranties 9.42–9.43

inherent vice: delay, and, 2.17–2.18; rationale 1.2

Institute Cargo Clauses 1.9; delay before risk attached 9.15–9.17; deprivation perils 2.21–2.22; general delay exclusion 1.18; "physical loss" 3.21

justifiable delays 10.26–10.35; excuses for alteration of the risk and not for breach of warranty 10.30–10.32; excuses other than under s. 49 10.33; excuses under s. 49 10.26–10.29; lawful excuse 10.27; unreasonable delay, and 9.48–9.49; usage of trade 10.34–10.35

INDEX

last cause in time rule 2.7
liberty clauses 10.6–10.9
loss, meaning 1.1: cause of 1.5; certainty 1.21; likelihood 1.6; naturally occurring 1.11–1.17
loss of use of cargo 3.35–3.36
loss of hire 8.1–8.22; aggregation of losses and delay 8.17–8.18; delay is not a direct consequence of general average act 8.13–8.16; events triggering cover under ABS forms 8.3–8.5; expenses arising from delay 8.7–8.16; foreseeability 8.14; general average repairs, during 8.8–8.16; indirect losses 8.14; occurrences, determining 8.18; loss of time in removing cargo and consequent loss of hire 8.6; loss of time proportionate to interests of the parties 8.12; mitigation of losses by assured and loss of time 8.19–8.22; resulting from loss or damage to hull 8.4
loss of market and market value: consequential loss in cargo policies 3.32–3.34; damaged goods 3.27–3.31; delay in delivery, caused by 3.23–3.31: exclusion of 3.25; general average act, and 4.7–4.9; general contract law and carriage of goods by sea 3.32–3.33; goods arriving late and undamaged 3.24–3.26
loss of time clause 6.3; early cases on loss of hire and off-hire clause 6.30–6.31; full/partial loss, and 6.24–6.29; introduction to 6.10–6.11; loss of time a cause of loss or merely a measure of loss, whether 6.33–6.36; meaning of 'loss of time' 6.32; off-hire clauses and the loss of time clause 6.30–6.36; origins 6.24–6.29; time charter parties 6.32; time charters, and 6.24–6.36

marine adventure 3.6–3.7; delay or mere suspension of voyage 3.10; due arrival of insurable property 3.12–3.15; excluding claim of loss 3.11; freight insurance 6.12–6.13; frustrating delay 3.10; loss of and MIA 1906 3.8–3.11; loss of profit, market and adventure by delay 3.15

ordinary course of transit 10.36–10.51: avoidance of delay clause, and 10.66–10.68; commercial convenience of the assured versus requirements of

transport 10.51; delay not in, which discharges insurers 10.36–10.50; interruption of transit brought about by the requirements of transport 10.38–10.43; moment cover ceases 10.40–10.43; storage 10.44–10.50; unknown contractual arrangements 10.47
ordinary delay 1.13–1.17; distinguishing from extraordinary 1.8; frustration 1.15; proximate causes 2.5; rationale for exclusion 1.13

perils of the sea: concurrent causation 2.31; damage caused by 7.3, 7.9; delay, and 2.16; loss of market 4.9; loss of profit 3.36; loss of time clause 6.14; proximate clause 6.27
perishable cargo 2.15; importance of delay 2.3, 2.12; natural loss, as 1.12; storage 1.14, 3.20
physical loss: absence of 3.20–3.22; subject-matter insured, to 2.1–2.35
see also deterioration, loss by and delay
pirates: capture by 2.19; ransom 4.4–4.5
port of refuge: wages and maintenance expenses during repairs at 7.10–7.14
post-attachment of risk delay 9.28–9.30; breach of condition subsequent or innominate term 9.45; breach of warranty and Insurance Act 2015, whether 9.44; consequences 9.41–9.45; effect on insurer 9.30; insured voyage 9.28; remedy 9.42
pre-attachment of risk delay 9.2–9.27: 'at and from' policy 9.3; avoidance of delay clause and s.42 9.18; circumstances which may result in delay 9.7–9.12; control of the assured, within and beyond 9.13–9.14; implied condition precedent to the attachment of 9.5–9.27 see also implied conditions; Institute Cargo Clauses and s.42 9.15–9.17; particular voyage 9.2; pre-contractual non-disclosure of representations as to the time of sailing 9.13; standard market terms and s.42 9.19
pre-contractual non-disclosure: cases on delay and concealment 9.8–9.10; circumstances which may result in delay 9.7–9.12; representations as to the time of sailing 9.11
prosecuting voyage, delay in 10.1–10.77: beyond control of the assured 10.52–10.56

207

see also 'delay beyond the control of the assured'; duty of the assured to act with reasonable despatch 10.59–10.77 see also avoidance of delay clause; common law authorities 10.17–10.23; delay and deviation 10.3–10.9; excessive delay and knowledge of assured 10.24; interruption of voyage 10.36–10.51; length of delay 10.17–10.23; meaning of unreasonable delay 10.16–10.35; ordinary course of transit 10.36–10.51 see also ordinary course of transit purpose of delay 10.23; time policies, mixed policies and s. 48 10.10–10.15; unreasonable delay under s.48 and the delay exclusion 10.25
proximate causation 2.8–2.21; altering rule 2.34–2.35; applying *Leyland* to delay cases 2.11; 'arising from delay' 2.34; capture, seizure, arrest, restraint or detainment 2.21; 'caused by delay' 2.35; civil unrest 2.22; deprivation perils and delay 2.19; general overview 2.8; following *Leyland* 2.9–2.10; inherent vice and delay 2.17–2.18; *Lansana Fruit* 2.12–2.16; *Norwich Union* 2.12–2.16; perils of the sea and delay 2.16; terrorism 2.22

reasonable despatch clause *see* avoidance of delay clause
reasonable time: implied condition, as 9.1, 9.34
repairs: delay in carrying out and increased cost of 7.6–7.8; expenses incurred during 7.9–7.17; fuel and stores and port charges occurring in general average 7.16; fuel and stores and port charges occurring other than in general average 7.17; losses proximately caused by delay 7.9; wage and maintenance expenses arising during repairs at port of refuge 7.10–7.14; wage and maintenance expenses arising during repairs other than in general average 7.15; wage and maintenance expenses under common law 7.10–7.13; wage and maintenance expenses under York-Antwerp Rules 7.14, 8.15
risk: alteration of at commencement of voyage 9.31–9.49 see also alteration of risk; delay after risk has attached, before voyage commences 9.28–9.30

see also post-attachment of risk delay; delay before risk attaches 9.2–9.27 see also pre-attachment of risk delay; implied condition as to commencement of 9.1–9.49 see also implied conditions; peril, and 1.4; pre-contractual non-disclosure of circumstances which may result in delay 9.7–9.12 see also pre-contractual non-disclosure
Rotterdam Rules 3.2

sale contracts: loss of 3.35–3.36
salvage: delayed delivery, and 3.19
slaves and slavery 2.3–2.4, 2.17, 10.17
standard form policies: exclusion from, delay 1.10, 2.2; loss of time and hire 8.2; project cargo and marine delay 5.1–5.2

temporarily missing goods and delay 3.16–3.18; reasonable time 3.16; time limits 3.16–3.18
terrorism 2.22
transit: delay, in 3.1, 3.25, 4.1, 4.13; expiry of 10.40–10.43; interruption 10.38–10.39; normal/ordinary course of 1.13, 5.21 see also ordinary course of transit; termination of, covered by peril 4.15

unreasonable delay: common law authorities 10.17–10.23; delay exclusion 10.25; delay must be 9.35–9.39; justifiable delays, and 9.48–9.49 see also justifiable delays; justification for 9.40; length of delay 10.17–10.23; prosecution, in 10.16–10.35; purpose of delay 10.23; reasonableness 9.35; reasonable time commencement 9.39; remedy of avoidance 9.37; under s.48 10.25

voyage charterparty: freight loss 6.35; frustration by excessive delay 6.32; loss of time clause 6.11

wilful conduct of the assured 1.11, 1.18–1.19; non-fortuitous event 1.20

York-Antwerp Rules: loss of market caused by delay and general average 4.7–4.9; wages and maintenance expenses arising during repairs at port of refuge 7.14, 8.15